The Complete

SLOW COOKER

COOKBOOK

FOR BEGINNERS AND ADVANCED USERS

Alexa Jacob

Thank you for reading my book, I hope you enjoyed it as much as I enjoyed writing it. Won't you please consider leaving a review? Even just a few works would help others decide if the book is right for them.

Size: 8.5×11

CONTENTS

BREAKFAST RECIPES 23

LUNCH RECIPES 42

SIDE DISHES RECIPES 52

MAIN DISHES RECIPES   83

SNACKS AND APPETIZERS   101

FISH AND SEAFOOD RECIPES   119

POULTRY RECIPES 138

MEAT RECIPES   156

VEGETABLE RECIPES   175

DESSERTS RECIPES   195

INTRODUCTION

Cooking time can sometimes be stressful for all of us. Busy schedules, cranky kids, and other challenges can test our patience when it comes to putting a good Recipes on the table. Well, I'm here to help you. I develop delicious recipes for homemade, family-friendly slow cooker Recipes, and in this book, I share my recipes with you.

In 2012, I was a stay-at-home mom with two small children. I'll never forget trying to make dinner with a kid (or two) hanging off my leg. I thought, "There has to be a better way!" Fortunately, I discovered the slow cooker and fell in love with it.

The slow cooker allowed me to get Recipes started in the middle of the morning while my kids were napping. In fact, I loved the freedom the slow cooker gave me so much that I decided to use it to cook dinner for 365 days straight and to write a blog to share the recipes with my readers. Writing the blog provided accountability, which helped me fulfill my goal, and I learned how to cook along the way! Now, many years later, my kids are involved in sports and other activities and they still keep me busy. They aren't hanging off my leg at five o'clock anymore, but they need me to drive them here and there or help with homework. Lucky for me, I still use the slow cooker, and I love the support it provides to busy people. I truly appreciate how my family can eat when we're ready because the slow cooker is waiting for us on warm until we get home.

I've created over a thousand slow cooker recipes over the past eight years. I have also discovered all sorts of handy tips and tricks for the slow cooker that I will share with you in this book. For example, I've learned what cuts of meat to use, why you can't add dairy to a recipe at the beginning, why you shouldn't lift the lid of the slow cooker for the first 2 hours, and how to intensify flavors. I've also learned from my blog readers that they mostly want super simple and fast recipes they can get going in the morning.

I want to help you make delicious, highly nutritious food in the least amount of preparation time possible. I've kept my recipes short and sweet by limiting the primary ingredients to 5 items in each. Whether you are a working professional who is tired when you get home, a busy parent with a very hungry family, a college student who needs to study instead of cook, or an empty-nester working on your golf game, this book can help you. So let's get cooking!

SLOW & EASY

Whether you're a working professional, a stay-at-home parent, a student, or a retiree, weeknight dinners just seem to be a challenge to get on the table, don't they? We're all busy rushing around at work or at home getting errands done, homework accomplished, household duties looked after, and appointments kept. And the hour that we should be preparing dinner from 5 to 6 p.m. seems to be the busiest! Some moms of young toddlers call it the witching hour because their young children seem to turn into crazy monsters then. That's why I'm a huge fan of the slow cooker.

The slow cooker can help you get a home-cooked meal on the table without any stress. My favorite recipes for the slow cooker have very few ingredients and minimal preparation time. You just put the ingredients in the slow cooker in the morning and let this incredible appliance slowly cook your meal all day long. Then when you're ready to eat, your dinner will be waiting for you! In this opening chapter, I will discuss the benefits of using the slow cooker and I'll give you some of my best slow cooker tips and tricks. I'll also preview what's ahead in the recipes and tell you how to stock your pantry so you'll be ready to start cooking. And I'll share some ideas on how to round out a meal.

THE ALMIGHTY SLOW COOKER

I just love how easy slow cookers are to use. Usually they have only a few temperature settings, and there are no burners to be afraid of if you are a first-time cook. The slow cooker is an appliance that should be in every household. Here are some essential things to know about the slow cooker

The slow cooker uses an indirect heat source and doesn't scorch. You don't need to stir the food as you would if it were on a stove-top burner. The slow cooker uses moist heat to cook food, so don't lift the lid every time you do, you are

releasing the steam that is surrounding and cooking the food.

Make sure to taste your food before serving. Because moisture does not evaporate in the slow cooker, flavors and spices can mellow and dissipate as time goes by. I often add seasonings right before serving slow-cooked food.

Slow cookers typically have just three settings warm, low, and high, so they are easy to work with. All slow cookers cook differently. I have ten different slow cookers, and some cook faster than others. So you will want to get to know your slow cooker.

There are several different sizes of slow cookers. In this book all recipes were written using a 6-quart oval slow cooker, which seems to be the most popular size.

If you are often away from home for several hours at a time, I suggest that you invest in a slow cooker with a timer on it. When you set the timer for the cooking time in the recipe, the slow cooker will switch to warm when the food is done, and will stay on warm (safely for up to 4 hours) until you can get home.

Don't reheat slow cooker leftovers in the slow cooker, because bacteria can grow in the time it takes for the food to reach a safe temperature.

I've learned the hard way not to place a hot slow cooker insert on a cold countertop or in a cold sink. The ceramic insert can crack if it is exposed to abrupt temperature shifts.

To remove stains in your slow cooker insert, simply fill it with water, add 1 cup of white vinegar, cover, and cook on high for 2 hours.

PLAN-AHEAD TIME-SAVERS

- The recipes in this book are easy to make and require very little preparation time. There are a few steps you can take to make them even easier
- Read the entire recipe and collect all the ingredients (and any equipment needed) before you begin cooking. This will save you

from the frustration of finding out you don't actually have potatoes in your pantry as you thought.

- Put frozen foods in the refrigerator to thaw the day before you want to cook them. I make a menu plan for the week, which helps me remember when to defrost frozen meats or other foods. Onions add lots of flavor to savory dishes. Dehydrated onions (also called onion flakes or dried minced onion) save a lot of time at the cutting board. About ¼ cup dried onion is equal to 1 cup chopped fresh onion.
- If you're constantly in a rush in the morning, prepare some or all parts of the recipe the night before. Store the food in an airtight container in the refrigerator, and then pop it into the slow cooker in the morning, set the timer, and off you go.
- Many soups and stews start off with a flavor base of aromatic vegetables, namely carrots, celery, and onion, called mirepoix. To avoid peeling and chopping, I often use a package of frozen "mirepoix-style blend," which you can find in the frozen vegetable aisle of many supermarkets.

SLOW COOKER OR CROCK-POT?

The term slow cooker is the generic name for an appliance that uses heating elements all around the insert, which bring food up to safe temperatures. Crock-Pot is the Rival corporation's registered trademark for its slow cookers. All Crock-Pots are slow cookers, but not all slow cookers are Crock-Pots. Other popular slow cooker brands include All-Clad, Cuisinart, and Hamilton Beach.

When you're shopping for a slow cooker, please keep in mind that there are appliances on the market referred to as slow cookers that have their heating element only on the bottom. Don't buy one of these to use for the recipes in this book. Appliances with heating elements only on the bottom heat food more slowly than those with heating elements all around the insert. Experts do not recommend cooking large cuts of meat in this type of slow cooker (although it works for soups and stews). So when purchasing your slow cooker, please make sure it is a true one with heating elements all around the insert.

EASY, ESSENTIAL PREP

- There are two kinds of slow cooker prep essential, like peeling and chopping, and optional, like sautéing, roasting, and browning. This book is designed to help home cooks get their dinners together as fast as possible, so the recipes do not include any optional kinds of prep. However, if you have a little extra time and want to develop more depth of flavor, here are some guidelines Sautéing certain ingredients will give the dish a more balanced, mellow aroma and a slightly sweeter, smoother flavor. When aromatics are heated in fat like butter or oil at the beginning of a recipe, the heated fat helps these ingredients release aromas and impart deep flavors into the dish as it is being cooked. Aromatics include onions, garlic, carrots, celery, and ginger.
- Roasting involves cooking food in the oven in an uncovered pan. Dry, hot air surrounds the food, cooking it evenly on all sides. I like to prepare a side dish of roasted vegetables to go with a meat dish that has been slow cooked; three of my favorite roasted veggies are beets, potatoes, and butternut squash.
- There are no rules about browning meat before placing it in the slow cooker. For recipes that contain many spicy aromatic ingredients, you may achieve a tasty dish without browning. But if you do have the time, I suggest browning the following meats for enhanced flavor ground turkey, ground beef, ground sausage, pork loin, and eye of round roast.

EASY 5-INGREDIENT RECIPE MANIFESTO

Here's what to expect from the recipes you'll find in this cookbook

5 INGREDIENTS As you flip through this book and peruse some of the recipes, you will probably notice that some of the recipes have more than 5 ingredients listed. That's because each recipe contains only 5 primary ingredients, plus some pantry staples and simple spices. These pantry staples and spices are listed in the sections that follow.

ONE-POT MEALS The recipes in this book are intended to be complete meals. Sometimes you may want to serve a side dish (like a salad or a steamed vegetable), but usually the dish is enough for a meal on its own. These recipes will help you get a meal on the table effortlessly.

DELICIOUSNESS I've tested all these recipes on my family and friends, and they all ate them happily. I'm sure you'll find many recipes in the book that will become family favorites.

15 MINUTES OF PREP The recipes found in this book will require no more than 15 minutes of prep time and no mandatory precooking requirements. If you want, you'll be able to throw everything into the slow cooker in the morning, leave, and come home later to a nutritious, delicious cooked meal.

THE RECIPES COOK FOR 8+ HOURS I know that many of you are hardworking professionals who simply want dinner "done" by the time you get home from work. So at least half of the recipes I developed for the book require 8 hours of cooking time. Some recipes require less time; you may want to make these on the weekends or consider investing in a slow cooker with a timer and automatic warming function.

ZERO PROCESSED FOODS The recipes in this book don't contain ingredients like canned soup, dry soup mix, packaged seasoning mixes, or other highly processed, artificially flavored ingredients. I love recipes that use ingredients such as dried beans cooked from scratch and fresh vegetables. Some recipes in the book use real-food convenience products such as canned beans, canned tomatoes, tomato sauce, tomato paste, canned broth, frozen vegetables, salsa, dried spices, and other similar items. If you want to eat more healthfully, when a recipe calls for any of these ingredients, you can always choose an organic and/or low-sodium version of the item.

MIX OF RECIPES I've tried to include a wide variety of recipes in this book that incorporate plenty of your favorite comfort foods but also include a range of international dishes.

SLOW COOKER TEMPERATURES

Slow cookers typically have three settings low, high, and warm. Most slow cookers set on low reach temperatures ranging from 185° to 200°F, depending on the individual slow cooker. On high, they reach temperatures between 250° and 300°F. I own several different slow cookers and they all cook differently. So when you are getting to know your slow cooker, regard the recipe cooking times as guidelines but not hard truths. I used a 6-quart oval slow cooker to test the recipes in this book. If you're finding that all your recipes are getting overdone, then you may want to reduce the recommended cooking times given here.

RECIPE TIPS AND LABELS

Every recipe in this book includes a tip or label to address common questions and concerns

SUPER EASY this tip will help you make the recipe even easier and faster. For example, you could use frozen diced onions instead of dicing the onions yourself.

TASTY TIP i'll Share With You An Optional Step To Enhance The Flavor Of The Dish, If You Wish

To Try It. For Example, I May Suggest Sautéing The Onions Before Adding Them To The Stew.

INGREDIENT TIP If there's a hint I know about prepping a particular ingredient, I'll share it with you for example, how to clean leeks or how to remove the skin from chicken thighs.

BIG 8 ALLERGEN FREE This label indicates that a recipe is free of any of the Big 8 Allergens dairy, eggs, fish, crustacean shellfish, peanuts, tree nuts, wheat, or soybeans.

ALLERGY TIP If a recipe includes one of the Big 8 Allergens, I'll recommend an ingredient substitution if possible. (But if the recipe is, say, an egg casserole, where the main ingredient is eggs, which can't be substituted in a satisfactory way, you'll need to forgo making that recipe.)

SET AND FORGET This label indicates a recipe that requires 8 or more hours of cooking time and no prep at the end.

THE SUPER SIMPLE PANTRY

The basic staple ingredients you should have in your refrigerator or pantry to make the recipes in this book are listed below. These staples are not part of the 5 primary ingredients, because they are considered general kitchen supplies.

BROTH Most of the recipes that call for broth use chicken broth. But a few recipes call for beef broth or vegetable broth. Broth adds a deep flavor that can't be duplicated by simply adding water.

BUTTER There's no substitute for butter! Sometimes a couple of tablespoons of butter can make all the difference in a recipe. I use unsalted butter, so I can control the amount of salt going into my recipes.

CORNSTARCH Slow cooker recipes can end up runny because no evaporation occurs over the long cooking time. A little cornstarch can thicken up a sauce in just minutes.

FLOUR Just as cornstarch is used to thicken several of the recipes, so is flour. I use all-purpose flour, but you can use whole-wheat flour if you prefer.

MILK I use milk in several recipes to add a touch of creaminess. You can use 1 percent, 2 percent, or whole milk, whichever you prefer.

SUGAR Not many of my recipes call for sugar or brown sugar, but sometimes just a tablespoon of brown sugar can make a barbecue recipe go from meh to memorable.

OIL Several of the recipes in this book call for olive oil or canola oil. Keep your oil in a glass or glazed ceramic container in a cool, dark cupboard. I also use nonstick cooking spray.

THE SUPER SIMPLE SPICE RACK

I'll always remember my husband's uncle saying, "Spices are 1 percent of the volume of ingredients in a recipe but account for how it turns out 99 percent of the time." Food always turns out better when it's properly seasoned.

Something as simple as salt and freshly ground black pepper can turn a bland, tasteless dish into a fantastic one. I'll never forget going to a local restaurant and ordering a curry soup. It tasted very mediocre. When I took the leftovers home and added a touch of salt and freshly ground black pepper, the soup was outstanding.

The following dried herbs and spices should be kept in a dark cupboard, ready for use. Herbs and spices listed in recipes don't count toward the 5 primary ingredients in my recipes.

DRIED BASIL If a kitchen has only a few herbs in the cupboard, basil will likely be one of them. Its

fragrant essence combines well with rosemary and thyme in dishes containing meat, fish, vegetables, cheese, and eggs.

DRIED OREGANO Whether fresh or dried, oregano is one of the foundations of Greek and Italian cuisine because of its ability to draw out the best of any ingredient it's blended with, particularly in tomato-based dishes.

DRIED THYME Fresh or dried thyme leaves and flowers lend a sprightly essence to casseroles, soups, stews, and sautéed vegetables.

BAY LEAF Bay leaves are unlike the other herbs in the spice cabinet. While we eat most herbs, these aromatic leaves are best used whole and then removed from the pot before serving. The leaf itself doesn't taste like much, but when steeped in a warm broth or sauce, the dish becomes infused with fragrant flavor.

GROUND CAYENNE PEPPER Used in both savory and sweet recipes, just a pinch of this powerful red powder is all you need to punch up the heat.

CHILI POWDER Chili powder is a blend of the herbs and spices most commonly found in Latin American cooking. The base ingredients are usually ground ancho chile, paprika, ground cumin, and dried Mexican oregano.

GROUND CUMIN Cumin (whole or ground) is one of those spices that's essential for any spice cupboard. Just 1 teaspoon adds a hint of smokiness. Use more and your dish will be infused with sweet, earthy flavors.

GROUND CINNAMON You are probably familiar with cinnamon, which is used in treats like apple pie and cinnamon rolls. But cinnamon is a versatile spice that is sometimes used in savory dishes as well.

GROUND GINGER Ground ginger has a warm, spicy bite, is a little bit sweet, and is not as strongly flavored as fresh ginger.

GARLIC POWDER Garlic powder is ground dehydrated garlic.

ONION POWDER Onion powder is ground dehydrated onion.

SMOKED PAPRIKA Smoked paprika is made from smoked red peppers. It can be used to add authentic smoky flavor to dishes.

GET WITH THE PROGRAM

If you don't own a programmable slow cooker, you may want to buy a socket timer. A socket timer allows the slow cooker to automatically turn off at a certain time. Simply plug the timer into an outlet and then plug the slow cooker into the timer. Then you can set the timer according to the recipe directions. For example, if you want the food to cook for only 7 hours but you'll be away for 8 hours, set the timer to shut off the slow cooker 1 hour before you return. But keep in mind that you don't want any meal containing meat to sit in the slow cooker for more than 2 hours, because this can cause bacteria to grow and cause foodborne illness. But if you're cooking something like steel-cut oatmeal, you can set the socket timer to start the slow cooker hours after you leave (or go to bed) for a delayed start time.

ROUNDING OUT SLOW COOKER MEALS

The slow cooker dinner recipes in this book are one-pot meals. With some of them, though, you may want to add a side dish. Here are a few suggestions for rounding out your dinner

BREAD OR ROLLS A good-quality whole-grain bread is a perfect dipper for soup or stew. You can easily pick up a loaf of fresh French bread or quickly thaw previously purchased bread stored in your freezer.

BROCCOLI One of my standard side dishes is broccoli. I either steam a package of frozen broccoli in the microwave, or roast fresh broccoli for 15 minutes in the oven with a bit of olive oil, lemon, and grated Parmesan cheese.

BROWN RICE Several of the recipes in this book are meats with sauces of some sort. Brown rice is perfect to provide a whole grain with the meat and to soak up the sauce. Brown rice takes a long time to cook on the stove (about an hour), so I make a big batch all at one time and freeze 1-cup portions in resealable plastic bags in the freezer. Then when I need some rice, all I have to do is reheat it in the microwave.

CORN BREAD There's nothing like a hunk of cornbread to go with your chili or stew. You can get fancy and search for a jalapeño corn bread recipe or sour cream corn bread recipe or just use the recipe on the cornmeal package.

GREEN SALAD I always keep a big bag or tub of mixed greens, such as washed and dried spinach, chard, and kale, in our refrigerator. These greens are ready for making an easy salad with some of our favorite salad dressings, like balsamic vinaigrette or Italian dressing. I also keep grape or cherry tomatoes handy to slice up and serve on the salad.

RAW VEGGIES Once a week I cut up fresh vegetables, like celery, carrots, bell peppers, and cucumbers, and keep them in an airtight container in my refrigerator. Then I prepare an easy Greek yogurt dip by mixing plain yogurt with dried herbs, garlic powder, salt, and pepper. These veggies and dip are a perfect side dish for a meaty meal.

FREEZING SLOW-COOKED FOOD

Depending on how many people you are serving, some of the recipes in this book may provide you with leftovers. Freezing leftovers is a great option for upcoming busy nights or an easy way to bring lunch to work next week. I like to freeze my leftovers in resealable plastic freezer bags and lay them flat in my freezer so they'll stack nicely. Some meals freeze better than others. Here are some tips

- Don't freeze recipes that are cream-based. They will separate, and the texture will be off when reheated.
- Don't freeze potatoes unless they're hash browns. Potatoes take on a grainy texture if frozen and then reheated.
- Don't freeze cooked pasta. The flavor will be diminished and the texture will be mushy. Make sure the food you are

freezing has had a chance to cool down before you freeze it. Cover it tightly with foil in a casserole dish or place it in a resealable plastic freezer bag.
- Defrost and serve frozen leftovers within 3 months.

THE DIRTY DOZEN AND THE CLEAN FIFTEEN

A nonprofit and environmental watchdog organization called Environmental Working Group (EWG) looks at data supplied by the US Department of Agriculture (USDA) and the Food and Drug Administration (FDA) about pesticide residues and compiles a list each year of the best and worst pesticide loads found in commercial crops. You can refer to the Dirty Dozen list to know which fruits and vegetables you should always buy organic. The Clean Fifteen list lets you know which produce is considered safe enough when grown conventionally to allow you to skip the organics.

This does not mean that the Clean Fifteen produce is pesticide-free, though, so wash these fruits and vegetables thoroughly.

These lists change every year, so make sure you look up the most recent before you fill your shopping cart. You'll find the most recent lists as well as a guide to pesticides in produce at

2017 Dirty Dozen

- Apples
- Celery
- Cherry tomatoes
- Cucumbers
- Grapes
- Nectarines
- Peaches
- Potatoes
- Snap peas
- Spinach
- Strawberries
- Sweet bell peppers

- In addition to the Dirty Dozen, the EWG added two foods contaminated with highly toxic **organophosphate insecticides**
- Hot peppers
- Kale/Collard greens

2017 Clean Fifteen

- Asparagus
- Avocados s
- Cabbage
- Cantaloupe
- Cauliflower
- Eggplant
- Grapefruit
- Kiwis
- Mangoes
- Onions
- Papayas
- Pineapples
- Sweet corn
- Sweet peas (frozen)
- Sweet potatoes

The Slow Cooker prepares food slowly at the low temperatures between 170F/77C (LOW) and 280F/138C (HIGH). Some of the online sources refer to the upper temperature limits of 190-200F/88-93C, so it is better to read the instructions attached to a specific device. In some Slow Cookers there are only two temperature modes LOW and HIGH, in others there are MEDIUM and WARMING.

The combination of heating over the entire area of the pan, prolonged cooking and circulation of hot steam under the lid makes it possible to destroy all potentially harmful bacteria and make the food healthier. However, in LOW mode the Slow Cooker will need a few hours to reach the temperature that will kill the bacteria. Therefore, you should always remember to clean your Slow Cooker before cooking, especially clean the ceramic dish. Such products as meat, fish, and poultry should be frozen and stored in the refrigerator before laying in the Slow Cooker. When adapting traditional recipes that involve pre-heat treatment with high temperatures before conventional quenching, the same is ready before cooking in the Slow Cooker. However, this is not the rule. For example, low temperatures make it possible to cook low-grade or lean meat soft and without weight loss due to fluid loss. In these cases, it is better to use these advantages of the Slow Cooker and to cook without a preliminary roasting. A very good rule of thumb is to prepare the first hour of dishes that include meat in HIGH mode, and then switch to LOW. (1 hour of cooking in HIGH mode is equal to 3 hours of cooking in LOW mode.)

Do not fill the Slow Cooker with ingredients for less than a half and more than two thirds of its volume. If the filling is less than half, then the food will be cooked too quickly, if more than two-thirds – then the dish will not warm up evenly. To get more benefits from cooking in the Slow Cooker, refrain curiosity about what is going on under the lid. Most often, do not touch the lid cannot be touched at all until the cook messenger tells you the meal is ready. Look under the lid only in cases when you need to mix or check the readiness. For example, in the LOW mode, every peeking under the lid extends cooking for 20-30 minutes.

Once the dish is ready, you can turn off the Slow Cooker and leave food in it before serving. The saucepan liner keeps the heat very well. However, in cases where the cooked is supposed to be stored in the refrigerator, it is safer to cool it faster by transferring it to a container. Also, do not try to use The Slow Cooker for warming the dishes that already are prepared – because the warming

will be too slow and it is not worth your time.

Remember that the vegetables need more time to be cooked than meat or poultry, so it is recommended to start simmering them earlier than the other ingredients and to place them on the bottom of the cooking dish.

In most cases, meat requires 8 hours of cooking on LOW mode. The Slow Cooker is perfect for cooking fresh meat and poultry. Sometimes it is recommended to fry minced meat before adding it to the Slow Cooker, but this is not necessary and you can do it only if you like.

The Seafood should be added to the Slow Cooker dish only at the last hour of cooking, otherwise they will be prepared too fast and overcooked.

Some gentle ingredients like tomatoes, zucchini, and mushrooms should be placed in the Slow Cooker at the last 45 minutes of cooking.

If the prescription involves adding cream or milk, they should be added in the last 30 minutes (if only it is not some specific recipe).

Also, remember that the cayenne pepper and the pepper sauces become sharper after a long heat treatment, so for the Slow Cooker is recommended to use a smaller amount of this ingredient and add it just in the end. In general, remember the rule to add the spices during the last hour of cooking. Almost all spices lose their flavor during long cooking too.

While using the Slow Cooker remember, that the liquids are not evaporate here, so if the recipe requires evaporation - it needs to be adapted. For example, the amount of liquids should be is reduced by one-third or half (except for the cases of preparing soups or other liquid meals).

It is noteworthy that a removable pot from the Slow Cooker can be used in a microwave oven (since it is ceramic). The technical characteristics of the Slow Cooker are simply impressive. The power of this kitchen equipment is 350 watts. The transparent cover is made of impact-resistant glass. The case of the Slow Cooker is made of stainless steel, and the bottom is equipped with rubberized legs that protect the table surface from heating. The pot handles do not heat up.

Virtually all Slow Cooker models have an electronic control panel. A display is built in into the case – that makes it very easy to control the cooking process by selecting the desired program just in one touch.

When you choose your first Slow Cooker take into account the mentioned features and your taste preferences. Nowadays the first type of Slow Cookers is the most popular. The two main modes for cooking and the time – everything you need to start cooking delicious dishes.

While you choose the Slow Cooker, pay attention to the dish size and the maximum cooking time of the model.

There are some Slow Cookers with removable and stationary dishes. Ones with the removable dish are more preferred (they are easier to clean).

Glazed ceramic pans with thick walls are preferable too – so they can keep the heat more stable. Know about the temperatures that are behind each of the cooking modes. Sometimes that happens that the lower temperatures are too high and the difference between LOW and HIGH is not big. In some Slow Cookers, there are "WARMING" solutions, lower than LOW. In addition, there can be an intermediate MEDIUM between the lowest and highest temperatures. The presence of them is not important, but if there is an opportunity to buy them for the same price, then why not.

Some of Slow Cookers may have a built-in timer, where you can set the time and mode to cook and choose when to turn the Slow Cooker off. The timer is helpful for situations where you have no time to switch the temperature after an hour from starting the cooking from HIGH to LOW.

It is preferable to choose the Slow Cooker with the heating element that completely covers the ceramic pan.

You can compare the characteristics of the popular manufacturers and make a choice in favor of which is better for you.

The Slow Cooker is a wonderful and necessary device for your kitchen. It helps to make the each one's dream of tasty and healthy food truth. Meanwhile, the cooking process will not take much time and will not be very complicated or expensive.

This book is created for those who thinks about getting the new kitchen device or already have the Slow Cooker. You can find here a wide range of the cooking receipts for any occasion – from breakfast and dinner dishes to snacks and desserts. Don't be afraid to try something new and amuse your friends and relatives! Remember, even the traditional and usual dish can be tastier and healthier, when you cook it in the Slow Cooker!

BREAKFAST RECIPES

Spiced pears in chocolate sauce

You will definitely love cooking and tasting the delicious and ripe fruit in chocolate sauce

Prep time: 10 minutes Cooking time: 50 minutes Servings: 4

INGREDIENTS:

Two cups brown sugar

One vanilla pod

One cinnamon stick

Anise star

Lemon (for strips)

4 cloves

Fresh root ginger

4 peers

One dark chocolate bar

Cup of milk

Vanilla ice cream (optionally) to serve

DIRECTIONS:

1. Firstly, prepare the INGREDIENT Speel the pears, cut 2-3 strips of the lemon zest (you can use a potato peeler), peel and slice the ginger.
2. Preheat your Slow Cooker.
3. Put all the ingredients (except lemon zest and the ice cream) in a pan and fill it with water. Simmer in Slow Cooker on HIGH for 10 minutes to infuse.
4. Drop the pears, put the pan back into Slow Cooker and stew for 30 minutes until soft.
5. For the chocolate sauce, put the chocolate into a medium bowl, add milk and cinnamon, and stir until melted.
6. To serve, take out the pears, dip them in sauce to cover with the chocolate. Serve each fruit with scoop of ice cream and a stripe of lemon zest.

Nutrition: Calories: 500 Fat: 35g Carbohydrates: 45g Protein: 6g

Apple crumble cake

Tasty apple pie will be a perfect start for your perfect day! Taste it with your favorite juice or tea, you surelyl will like it!

Prep time: 15 minutes Cooking time: 30 minutes Servings: 6

INGREDIENTS:

6 big sweet apples

4-5 tbsp apricot or apple jam

One orange juice

One cup oats (porridge)

Half cup flour

1 tsp cinnamon

1 tbsp butter

Half cup muscovado sugar

1 tbsp honey

DIRECTIONS:

1. Preheat Slow Cooker to 185 degrees.
2. Peel and core the apples, slice them into small half-moons.
3. Mix the apple slices with the apricot or apple jam and orange juice. Butter the Slow Cooker dish and spread the apples over its bottom.
4. Mix the oat porridge, cinnamon and flour in another bowl. Add the small butter chunks, stir gently, mix in the sugar and the honey, mix until clumps.
5. Cover the apple pieces with the crumbles, leave in the Slow Cooker for 30 minutes. To serve cool the dish for 10 minutes, add ice cream or custard.

Nutrition: Calories: 400 Fat: 10g Carbohydrates: 30g Protein: 6g

Banana French Toast with Milk

Delicious breakfast with ingredients you probably will find in your refrigerator. Simple and easy!

Prep time: 10 minutes Cooking time: 2 hours Servings: 4

INGREDIENTS:

1stale French baguette (or a day old bread)

4 ripe bananas

Half cup cream cheese

3 chicken eggs

2tbsp brown sugar

Half cup chopped pecans or walnuts

5 tbsp skim milk

2 great tbsp honey

Cinnamon, nutmeg, vanilla extract

2 tbsp butter

DIRECTIONS:

1. Cut the baguette or bread into small slices; cover it with cheese on both sides. Arrange the bread slices in one row on the bottom of your Slow Cooker dish.
2. Slice bananas into rounds and layer them over the bread, cover with small butter slices. Mix sugar and nuts, sprinkle the bananas with it.
3. In another bowl, beat and slightly mix the eggs with a whisk. Add milk, nutmeg, cinnamon, honey and vanilla extract. Stir until fully combined. Pour this mixture over the bananas.
4. Preheat Slow Cooker to 200 degrees and cook the dessert on HIGH for 2 hours. Serve warm, with honey and milk.

Nutrition: Calories: 180 Fat: 3g Carbohydrates: 30g Protein: 6g

Cheese Grits in Slow Cooker

Nourishing but light cheese grits will be a source of your energy from the beginning of the day!

Prep time: 5 minutes Cooking time: 5-7 hours Servings: 8

INGREDIENTS:

Half cup stone ground grits

5-6 cups water

2 tsp salt

Half cup Cheddar cheese (shredded)

6 tbsp butter

Black pepper (optionally)

DIRECTIONS:

1. Preheat Slow Cooker, spray the dish with cooking spray or cover with butter. In a wide bowl, mix together grits and water, add salt.
2. Cook on LOW temperatures for 5-7 hours (you can leave it overnight)
3. Remove the dish from Slow Cooker, cover butter on top. Stir with the whisk to an even consistency and fully melted butter.
4. To serve, sprinkle more cheese on top and black pepper to your taste. You can also add some chopped parsley or basil.
5. Serve warm.

Nutrition: Calories: 173 Fat: 7g Carbohydrates: 4g Protein: 6g

Pineapple Cake with Pecans

Delicious pineapple cake is perfect both for breakfast and as a dessert! You will love cooking and eating this!

Prep time: 20 minutes Cooking time: 3-4 hours Servings: 10

INGREDIENTS:

Two cups sugar

Two cups plain flour

2 eggs

4 tbsp vegetable oil

Can pineapple with juice (crushed)

1 tsp baking soda

1 tsp vanilla extract

Salt

For icing:
1 cup sugar

Hal cup butter

6 tbsp evaporated milk

3tbsp shredded coconut

Half cup chopped pecans (toasted)

DIRECTIONS:

1. Preheat your Slow Cooker to 180-200 degrees.
2. Take a medium bowl and combine all cake ingredients.
3. Mix a dough until evenly combined and then pour into Slow Cooker dish. Bake for 3 hours on HIGH; check if it is ready with a wooden toothpick.
4. When the cake is ready, make the icing: in a medium saucepan, combine sugar, evaporated milk, butter, and salt. Bring to boil, and then simmer with a lower heat for 10 minutes.
5. Add the coconut (to the icing).
6. Pour the icing over hot cake and sprinkle with nuts.
7. To serve, let cake cool, then cut it and serve with your favorite drinks.

Nutrition: Calories: 291 Fat: 7g Carbohydrates: 6g Protein: 5g

Potato Casserole for Breakfast

Perfect gluten-free breakfast to feed a really big family! Tasty and healthy!

Prep time: 5 minutes Cooking time: 4 hours Servings: 10

INGREDIENTS:

4big potatoes

5-6 sausages

Half cup cheddar cheese (shredded)

Half cup mozzarella cheese

5-6 green onions

10 chicken eggs

Half cup milk

Salt

Black pepper

DIRECTIONS:

1. Preheat Slow Cooker; spray its dish with non-stick cooking spray. Rub the potatoes into small pieces and put them into the dish.

2. Cover the potatoes with rubbed sausages. Add both cheeses and the green onions.

3. Continue the layers until all space in the dish is full.

4. In a medium bowl, mix together wet ingredients (milk, eggs). Pour it into the main dish. Add salt and pepper.

5. Leave to cook on LOW during 5 hours (or until the eggs are set). Serve with guacamole or green onions.

Nutrition: Calories: 190 Fat: 10g Carbohydrates: 5g Protein: 10g

Delicious cinnamon rolls

Easy to make, great flavor, perfect for fast breakfast! You will definitely enjoy it!

Prep time: 30 minutes Cooking time: 2 hours Servings: 10

INGREDIENTS:

Two cups warm water

1 tbsp active yeast (dry)

2 tbsp wild honey

3cups plain flour

1 tsp salt

4tbsp butter

4 tbsp brown sugar

1 tsp cinnamon

DIRECTIONS:

1. In a bowl, mix up water, yeast and honey. Stir with a mixer and after the dough is homogenous, let it rest for several minutes (mixture will rise).

2. Sift flour and add salt. Mix on low to let the ingredients come together, then increase the mixing speed to medium.

3. Remove dough and allow to rise on a floured table.

4. Roll dough into medium rectangles. You can use a pizza cutter to make the sides even. Spread butter over the dough. Sprinkle it with sugar and cinnamon.

5. Roll the dough rectangles into long log, and then cut it into 10-12 pieces.

6. Cover the bottom of your Slow Cooker with foil, place the rolls over it and cook on HIGH for 2-3 hours.

7. To serve use fresh berries or mint leaves.

Nutrition: Calories: 190 Fat: 5g Carbohydrates: 7g Protein: 8g

Quinoa Pie in Slow Cooker

Healthy and juicy homemade pie. Incredible way to amaze your guests with delicious breakfast!

Prep time: 10 minutes Cooking time: 4 hours Servings: 8

INGREDIENTS:

2 tbsp almond butter

2 tbsp maple syrup

Cup vanilla almond milk

1 tsp salt

Half cup quinoa

2 chicken eggs

Cinnamon

Half cup raisins

5 tbsp roasted almonds (chopped)

Half cup dried apples

DIRECTIONS:

1. Spray the Slow Cooker dish with no-stick spray or cover it with foil (or parchment paper).

2. In another bowl, mix the almond butter and maple syrup. Melt in in a microwave until creamy (about a minute).

3. Add almond milk, salt and cinnamon. Whisk the mass until it is completely even. Add the eggs and remaining products, Mix well.

4. Preheat your Slow Cooker to 100-110 degrees.

5. Pour the dough into the dish and place it into Slow Cooker. Cook for 3-4 hours on HIGH mode. To serve, remove the pie out of the dish with a knife. Cool in the refrigerator.

Nutrition: Calories: 174 Fat: 8g Carbohydrates: 20g Protein: 6g

Quinoa Muffins with Peanut Butter

The perfect breakfast for summertime!

Prep time: 10 minutes Cooking time: 4 hours Servings: 8

INGREDIENTS:

One cup strawberries

Half up almond vanilla milk

1 tsp salt

5-6 tbsp raw quinoa

2 tbsp peanut butter (better natural)

3 tbsp honey

4 egg whites

2 tbsp peanuts (roasted)

DIRECTIONS:

1. Preheat your Slow Cooker to 190 degrees.

2. Line the cooking dish bottom with parchment paper; additionally spray it with cooking spray. Dice the strawberries and place them over the dish.

3. Sprinkle with honey and place the dish into the Slow Cooker for 10-15 minutes (for releasing juices).

4. In another pot, mix up the almond milk and salt. Boil with quinoa until ready.

5. In a separate bowl, combine egg whites and almond butter. Join with the quinoa and wait until milk is absorbed.

6. Fill the muffin forms with quinoa mixture; place the strawberries on the top. Bake in Slow Cooker on LOW until quinoa is set (about 4 hours).

7. To serve, cool the muffins and decorate them with whole strawberries.

Nutrition: Calories: 190 Fat: 6g Carbohydrates: 8g Protein: 6g

Veggie Omelette in Slow Cooker

Tasty and healthy vegetable omelette. Super easy to make!

Prep time: 5 minutes Cooking time: 2 hours Servings: 4

INGREDIENTS:

6 chicken eggs

Half cup milk

Salt

Garlic powder

White pepper

Red pepper

Small onion

Garlic clove

Parsley

5 small tomatoes

DIRECTIONS:

1. Grease the Slow Cooker dish with butter or special cooking spray.

2. In separated bowl, mix up eggs and milk. Add pepper and garlic. Whisk the mixture well and salt. Add to the mixture broccoli florets, onions, pepper and garlic. Stir in the eggs.

3. Place the mixture into the Slow Cooker dish. Cook on HIGH temperatures (180-200 degrees) for 2 hours.

4. Cover with cheese and let it melt.

5. To serve, cut the omelette into 8 pieces and garnish the plates with parsley and tomatoes.

Nutrition: Calories: 210 Fat: 7g Carbohydrates: 5g Protein: 8g

Apple pie with oatmeal

Healthy and beneficial breakfast for you and your home mates! You will find the source of happiness and energy while tasting this!

Prep time: 10 minutes Cooking time: 4-6 hours Servings: 4

INGREDIENTS:

1cup oats

2large apples

2 cups almond milk

2 cups warm water

2 tsp cinnamon

Pinch nutmeg

Salt

2 tbsp coconut oil

1 tsp vanilla extract

2 tbsp flaxseeds

2 tbsp maple syrup

Raisins

DIRECTIONS:

1. Grease your Slow Cooker. Rub a couple spoons of coconut (or olive) oil. Peel the apples. Core and chop them into medium size pieces.

2. Starting with the apples, add all the ingredients into Slow Cooker. Stir (not too intensively) and leave to bake for 6 hours on LOW. When ready, stir the oatmeal well.

3. Serve the oatmeal into small cups. You can also garnish it with any berries or toppings you like.

Nutrition: Calories: 159 Fat: 12g Carbohydrates: 9g Protein: 28g

Vanilla French Toast

You will be pleased with this receipt and the excellent taste!

Prep time: 15 minutes Cooking time: 8 hours (overnight)

Servings: 6

INGREDIENTS:

One loaf bread (better day-old)

2 cups cream

2 cups milk (whole)

8 chicken eggs

Almond extract

One vanilla bean

5 tsp sugar

Cinnamon

Salt

DIRECTIONS:

1. Coat the Slow Cooker dish with the cooking spray.
2. Slice bread into small pieces (1-2 inches). Place them into the dish overlapping each other. In another dish, combine the remaining ingredients until perfectly blended.
3. Pour the wet mixture over the bread to cover it completely.
4. Place the dish into Slow Cooker and cook on very LOW temperatures (100-120 degrees) for 7-8 hours. You can leave it overnight so the next morning it will be ready).
5. To serve, slightly cool and cut the French Toast.

Nutrition: Calories: 200 Fat: 6g Carbohydrates: 4g Protein: 8g

Pumpkin Spiced Oatmeal

Low in sugar and fats, this will be a perfect choice for your daily start.

Prep time: 5 minutes Cooking time: 3 minutes Servings: 4

INGREDIENTS:

One cup dry oats

Four cups water

Half cup milk (fat free)

Half pumpkin

2 tbsp light brown sugar

Salt

Cinnamon

Gloves

Ginger

Nutmeg

DIRECTIONS:

1. Spray the inside of the Slow Cooker dish with cooking spray or coat it with oil. Preheat your Slow Cooker to 120 degrees.
2. Mix-up oats with milk and water. Wait until soft. Peel the pumpkin and cut it into small pieces.
3. Combine the pumpkin with oats in the dish and place it into the Slow Cooker for an hour.
4. Take it off and smash the pumpkins. Place the dish back to Slow Cooker and leave for 8 hours (overnight) on LOW.
5. In the morning, serve the oatmeal into small bowls.

Nutrition: Calories: 190 Fat: 8g Carbohydrates: 4g Protein: 6g

Greek Eggs Casserole

Easy to cook and healthy to eat. This receipt will amaze your home mates and guests!

Prep time: 15 minutes Cooking time: 6 hours Servings: 8

INGREDIENTS:

10 chicken eggs

Half cup milk

Salt

1tsp black pepper

1 tbsp red onion

Half cup dried tomatoes

1 cup champignons

2cups spinach

Half cup feta

DIRECTIONS:

1. Set the temperature of your Slow Cooker to 120-150 degrees.
2. In a separate wide bowl combine and whisk the eggs. Add salt and pepper. Mix in garlic and red onion. Whisk again.
3. Wash and dice the mushrooms. Put them into wet mixture. At last, and add dried tomatoes.
4. Pour the mixture into the Slow Cooker crockpot.
5. Top the meal with the feta cheese and cook on LOW into the Slow Cooker for 5-6 hours. Serve with milk or vegetables.

Nutrition: Calories: 180 Fat: 8g Carbohydrates: 4g Protein: 8g

French Toast with Chocolate Chip

Love chocolate but want to stay healthy? So this receipt is for you!

Prep time: 5 minutes Cooking time: 3 minutes Servings: 3

INGREDIENTS:

One loaf French bread

4 chicken eggs

2 cups milk

brown sugar

vanilla extract

1 tsp cinnamon

4 tbsp chocolate chips

DIRECTIONS:

1. Cut the bread into small cubes.
2. Coat the bottom and side of the Slow Cook crockpot with special cooking spray or olive oil. Place the bread cubes into the dish.
3. Take another medium bowl and mix the eggs, sugar, and milk. Whisk with cinnamon and vanilla until all the ingredients well mixed. Pour the mixture over the bread cubes. Toss slightly to coat.
4. Cover the dish and place it in your refrigerator overnight. Cover with the chocolate chips, and cook on LOW for 4 hours.

Nutrition: Calories: 200 Fat: 8g Carbohydrates: 2g Protein: 7g

Crock Pot Egg Bake

Unusual taste with simple products! You'll be happy with this receipt!

Prep time: 15 minutes Cooking time: 8 hours Servings: 8

INGREDIENTS:

One pack tater tots

Diced Canadian bacon

2 small onions

Cheddar cheese

12 chicken eggs

Parmesan

1 cup milk

4 tbsp simple flour

1 tsp salt

Pepper

DIRECTIONS:

1. Cover the bottom of the crockpot with cooking spray or just oil. Preheat Slow Cooker to 120-130 degrees.

2. Divide all the dry ingredients into three parts. Place the tots, sliced bacon, onion and cheeses. Repeat all the layers for three times.
3. In a separate mixing bowl, combine the eggs, milk, pepper and salt. Pour the egg mixture over the other ingredients.
4. Place the dish into your Slow Cooker for nine hours on LOW mode.

Nutrition: Calories: 164 Fat: 9g Carbohydrates: 9g Protein: 19g

Delicious Banana Bread

So healthy and light! This banana bread will fill you with energy and good mood!

Prep time: 15 minutes Cooking time: 4 hours Servings: 3

INGREDIENTS:

Two chicken eggs

Half cup softened butter

One cup sugar

Two cups plain flour

Half teaspoon baking soda

Salt

Three medium bananas

DIRECTIONS:

1. First, cover with cooking spray and preheat your Slow Cooker. Combine eggs with sugar and butter. Stir well.
2. Mix in baking soda and baking powder.
3. Peel and mash bananas, mix them with flour and combine with eggs. Pour the dough into cooking dish and place it into Slow Cooker.
4. Cook on LOW temperature regimes for 3-4 hours.
5. When ready, remove the bread with a knife and enjoy your breakfast! To serve use fresh bananas, apples or berries to your taste.

Nutrition: Calories: 130 Fat: 8g Carbohydrates: 5g Protein: 7g

Drinkable Vanilla Yogurt

Yes, this is long enough to cook, but it is cheaper and healthier than store-bought! Moreover, it is totally worth it!

Prep time: 5 minutes Cooking time: 18 hours Servings: 8

INGREDIENTS:

Half gallon organic milk

Half cup organic yogurt (NOTE: with live cultures)

Maple syrup

Pure vanilla extract

Bananas or berries (optional)

DIRECTIONS:

1. Pour the milk into your Slow Cooker and leave to cook for three hours on LOW setting.

2. When the mixture reaches 150-170 degrees, take it out and allow to rest for three hours (until it is 110 degrees).

3. Ladle milk from the Slow Cooker to another mixing bowl and add in the yogurt. Place it back to Slow Cooker and stir well.

4. Do not turn it on, just cover with a large blanket and leave for 10-12 hours.

5. You can remove a little part of yogurt and save it as a starter for your next batch. Add the vanilla extract or maple syrup.

6. Serve with your favorite fruits or berries.

Nutrition: Calories: 150 Fat: 7g Carbohydrates: 3g Protein: 8g

Chocolate Banana Bread

Healthy and delicious – all in one!

Prep time: 15 minutes Cooking time: 5 hours Servings: 8

INGREDIENTS:

Four medium bananas

One cup brown sugar

Two chicken eggs

Melted butter

Half cup Greek yogurt

Vanilla extract

Two cup plain flour

One tsp. baking powder

Salt

Cinnamon

One chocolate chunk

DIRECTIONS:

1. Preheat Slow Cooker to 180 degrees. Peel and mash bananas well.

2. Add in sugar, yogurt, butter, eggs and vanilla.

3. Mix up flour with baking powder, soda, salt and cinnamon. Sift flour mix into banana mixture. Stir gently.

4. Fold in the chocolate.

5. Coat the Slow Cooker dish with olive oil and pour the dough in.

6. Cook for 4-5 hours on LOW temperature mode, until the bread is ruddy.

Nutrition: Calories: 210 Fat: 4g Carbohydrates: 5g Protein: 8g

Banana Bread with Granola

Easy and fast enough to make! You will like this delicious banana bread!

Prep time: 15 minutes Cooking time: 3 hours Servings: 5

INGREDIENTS:

Three cup granola

One cup banana chips

One cup salted peanuts

Half cup quinoa (uncooked)

Brown sugar

Cinnamon

Salt

6 tbsp. butter

Half cup peanut butter

2 tbsp. honey

One ripe banana

2 tbsp. vanilla extract

DIRECTIONS:

1. Preheat the Slow Cooker to 200 degrees. Cover the Slow Cooker dish with baking sheets.

2. In a big bowl, combine banana oats, granola, peanuts, quinoa, sugar and salt. In a pan, heat butter and peanut butter, add honey. Melt for 4 minutes.

3. After butter and honey melted, stir in vanilla and banana.

4. Pour the granola mixture in the baking dish and place it into the Slow Cooker. Cook for 4-5 hours on HIGH mode.

Nutrition: Calories: 180 Fat: 4g Carbohydrates: 5g Protein: 6g

Treacle Sponge with Honey

Taste the perfect duo and it could be your favorite receipt!

Prep time: 30 minutes Cooking time: 3 hours Servings: 4

INGREDIENTS:

One cup unsalted butter

3 tbsp. honey

1 tbsp. white breadcrumbs (fresh)

One cup sugar

One lemon zest

3 large chicken eggs

Two cup flour

2 tbsp. milk

Clotted cream (to serve)

Little brandy splash (optional)

DIRECTIONS:

1. Grease your Slow Cooker dish heavily and preheat it. In a medium bowl, mix the breadcrumbs with the honey.
2. Melt butter and beat it with lemon zest and sugar, until fluffy and light. Sift in the flour slowly.
3. Add the milk and stir well.
4. Spoon the mixture into the Slow Cooker dish. Cook for several hours on LOW mode. Serve with honey or clotted cream.

Nutrition: Calories: 200 Fat: 10g Carbohydrates: 20g Protein: 10g

Sticky Pecan Buns with Maple

Easy and tasty to make!

Prep time: 15 minutes Cooking time: 5 hours Servings: 12

INGREDIENTS:

6 tbsp. milk (nonfat)

4 tbsp. maple syrup

Half tbsp. melted butter

1 tsp. vanilla extract

Salt

2 tbsp. yeast

Two cup flour (whole wheat)

Chopped pecans

Ground cinnamon

DIRECTIONS:

1. Lightly coat the inside of your Slow Cooker with non-stick cooking spray. For dough, combine milk, vanilla butter and maple syrup. Mix well.
2. Microwave the mixture until warm and add the yeast. Let sit for 15 minutes. Sift in the flour and mix in until the dough is no more sticky.
3. For filling, mix together the maple syrup and cinnamon.
4. Roll out the dough and brush it with the maple filling. Roll up into a log and slice into 10-12 parts. Place the small rolls into the Slow Cooker.

5. Prepare the caramel sauce: combine milk, butter and syrup. Pour the sauce into the Slow Cooker. Bake for 2 hours on HIGH mode.

Nutrition: Calories: 230 Fat: 5g Carbohydrates: 29g Protein: 42g

Village Pie

Homemade pie tastes like in childhood and brings health and happiness!

Prep time: 30 minutes Cooking time: 2 hours Servings: 10

INGREDIENTS:

Three tbsp. olive oil

Beef mince

Two small onions

Three carrots

Three celery sticks

Two garlic gloves

Three tbsp. flour

Thyme

Five big potatoes

One tbsp. butter

Cheddar

Nutmeg

DIRECTIONS:

1. In a large saucepan, fry the beef mince until browned.
2. Finely chop all the vegetables and add to the mince. Cook on a gentle temperature until soft. Add the garlic, tomatoes and flour. Cook for several minutes.
3. For the mash, boil potatoes until tender and mash with the milk and three quarters of the cheese. Prepare the Slow Cooker6 spray the inside with the cooking spray.
4. Place the meat into the dish and cover with the mash.
5. Sprinkle over the remaining cheese and cook on HIGH for 2-3 hours.

Nutrition: Calories: 500 Fat: 25g Carbohydrates: 29g Protein: 19g

Egg and Ham Casserole for Slow Cooker

Tired of eggs with bacon? Try this one and fall in love with the receipt.

Prep time: 10 minutes Cooking time: 2 hours Servings: 6

INGREDIENTS:

6 chicken eggs

Half teaspoon salt

Black pepper

Half cup milk

Half cup Greek yogurt

Thyme

Half teaspoon onion powder

Half teaspoon garlic powder

Champignons

Spinach

Cup pepper jack cheese

Cup hum (diced)

DIRECTIONS:

1. In a wide bowl, whisk the eggs with pepper, salt, milk and yogurt. Add garlic powder and onion powder.

2. When smooth, dice and stir in the champignons, cheese, spinach and ham. Spray your Slow Cooker with a cooking spray.

3. Pour your egg-and-mushroom mixture into the Slow Cooker. Cook on HIGH temperature for 2 hours.

Nutrition: Calories: 250 Fat: 4g Carbohydrates: 9g Protein: 10g

Vegetarian Pot Pie

Even vegetarians can taste this one!

Prep time: 15 minutes Cooking time: 5 hours Servings: 6

INGREDIENTS:

6 cups chopped vegetables (peas, potatoes, tomatoes, carrots, brussels sprouts)

1-2 cups diced mushrooms

Two onions

Half cup flour

4 gloves garlic

2 tbsp. garlic

Thyme (fresh)

Cornstarch

2 cups chicken broth

DIRECTIONS:

1. Wash and chop vegetables (or by frozen packed). Toss with flour to cover vegetables well.

2. Mix with the broth slowly, when well combined with flour. Preheat the Slow Cooker and place the vegetables into it.

3. Cook on LOW temperatures for 8-9 hours, or on HIGH – for 6-7 hours. Mix up cornstarch with the water and pour into the vegetable mix.

4. Place it back to the Slow Cooker for 15 minutes. Serve hot with fresh vegetables.

Nutrition: Calories: 267 Fat: 7g Carbohydrates: 29g Protein: 7g

Baked Beans for Slow Cooker

Healthy and delicious beans for your energy breakfast!

Prep time: 10 minutes Cooking time: 8 hours Servings: 8

INGREDIENTS:

1 cup dried beans

1 medium onion

Half cup brown sugar

Molasses

Tomato sauce or plain ketchup

1 tbsp. Worcestershire sauce

1 tbsp. balsamic vinegar

Salt

Pepper

DIRECTIONS:

1. Start with preheating your Slow Cooker.

2. Rinse dried beans and place them in Slow Cooker overnight. Cover beans with the water. Drain the beans in the morning and place them back into Slow Cooker.

3. Dice all the other vegetables and add them in Slow Cooler too. Pour two cups of water and molasses.

4. Add salt and pepper.

5. Cook on LOW temperature for 8-9 hours (or 4 hours on HIGH). Serve warm with preferred vegetables.

Nutrition: Calories: 210 Fat: 4g Carbohydrates: 5g Protein: 8g

Blueberry Porridge

Perfect for berry-lovers – healthy and tasty!

Prep time: 5 minutes Cooking time: 5-6 hours Servings: 4

INGREDIENTS:

One cup jumbo oats

Four cups milk

Half cup dried fruits

Brown sugar or honey

Cinnamon

Blueberries

DIRECTIONS:

1. Heat the Slow Cooker before the start.
2. Put the oats into The Slow Cooker dish, add some salt/
3. Pour over the milk (or the mixture of milk and water for less creamy).
4. Place the dish into the Slow Cooker and cook on LOW temperature for 7-8 hours (overnight). Stir the porridge in the morning.
5. To serve, ladle into the serving bowls and decorate with your favorite yogurt or syrup. Add blueberries (or any other berries or fruits you like).

Nutrition: Calories: 210 Fat: 4g Carbohydrates: 5g Protein: 8g

Eggplant Parmesan in Slow Cooker

Perfect receipt for the spring season – try and you will love this!

Prep time: 20 minutes Cooking time: 8 hours Servings: 12

INGREDIENTS:

Three eggplants

Salt

3 large chicken eggs

Half cup milk

One cup breadcrumbs (gluten-free)

Parmesan cheese

Four cups marinara sauce

Mozzarella cheese

DIRECTIONS:

1. Prepare the eggplant, peel and cut into thin rounds. Rinse the eggplant rounds, add salt and pat dry.
2. Preheat Slow Cooker before using.
3. Pour the marinara sauce in the bottom of Slow Cooker. In a shallow bowl, whisk together milk and the eggs.
4. In another bowl, stir together the breadcrumbs and Parmesan cheese.
5. Dip the eggplant rounds firstly in the egg mixture and secondly in the breadcrumbs. Layer the eggplant slices in the Slow Cooker.
6. Pour with the sauce and cook on LOW temperature for 8 hours.

Nutrition: Calories: 158 Fat: 10g Carbohydrates: 20g Protein: 26g

Golden Veggie Pie

Another vegetarian pie – and another healthy receipt for your daily start!

Prep time: 15 minutes Cooking time: 5 hours Servings: 8

INGREDIENTS:

Butter

Two onions

Four carrots

Celery (1 head)

Four garlic gloves

Chestnut mushrooms

Thyme

Dried green lentil

Half cup milk

Cheddar cheese

Cup red wine (optional)

3 tbsp. tomato puree

DIRECTIONS:

1. Clean and dice the vegetables.
2. For the sauce: melt the butter on a pan and fry carrots, onions, celery and garlic until mild. Add the mushrooms and cook for another 5 minutes.
3. Add herbs and lentils.
4. Pour over the wine and simmer for around 50 minutes. Take off heat and mix in the tomato puree.
5. Preheat your Slow Cooker and add the diced potatoes. Cover with water and cook for one hour. Remove water and combine the potatoes with the pan mix.
6. Place back to the Slow Cooker and cook for 2-3 hours on HIGH temperatures.

Nutrition: Calories: 168 Fat: 4g Carbohydrates: 6g Protein: 8g

Muscovado Cheesecake for Slow Cooker

Unusual cheesecake with muscavado will amuse you with its perfect taste!

Prep time: 30 minutes Cooking time: 2 hours Servings: 10

INGREDIENTS:

Melted butter

3-4 oat biscuits

6 tbsp. hazelnuts (blanched)

One cup muscovado sugar

4 tbsp milk (full-fat)

Cream cheese

2tbsp flour (plain)

1 tsp vanilla extract

3large chicken eggs

1tbsp Frangelico (optional)

2 tsp corn flour

2tbsp golden sugar

One cup blackberries

DIRECTIONS:

1. Prepare the Slow Cooker: grease the inside with a foil or parchment.

2. Roll the foil in circle and place it on the bottom of the dish (as a trivet for the future cheesecake). Put the biscuits into a food processor and make fine crumbs.

3. Add the butter and blend well. Tip the mix into the tin and chill for 10-20 minutes. In a pan, combine the muscovado and milk, then leave to cool.

4. In another bowl, beat the cream cheese, vanilla, eggs and flour and stir until smooth. Pour everything into the tin and place it inti Slow Cooker.

5. Cook for 2 hours on HIGH. Cool before serving.

Nutrition: Calories: 613 Fat: 29g Carbohydrates: 47g Protein: 10g

Veggie Breakfast Casserole

Simple casserole for breakfast – and one of the favorite Slow Cooker meals.

Prep time: 15 minutes Cooking time: 5 hours Servings: 8

INGREDIENTS:

6 big potatoes

Bacon

1 small onion (diced)

Cheddar Cheese (Shredded)

Red Bell pepper (diced)

10-12 chicken eggs

One cup milk

DIRECTIONS:

1. Start preheating the Slow Cooker.

2. Spray the bottom of the Slow Cooker with special cooking spray to avoid sticking.

3. Cut bacon into small stripes and cook (or buy already dried bacon to fasten the process). Place three potatoes on the bottom of the Slow Cooker.

4. Layer your bacon and the other INGREDIENTSpeppers, cheese, onions, and remaining potatoes. In another medium bowl, mix eggs with mil. Pour this mixture over the layered ingredients.

5. Salt and pepper.

6. Cook on LOW temperature for 4 hours.

Nutrition: Calories: 198 Fat: 5g Carbohydrates: 8g Protein: 12g

Nutella French Toast

Nutella and bananas – what a perfect duo for your daily start!

Prep time: 15 minutes Cooking time: 2 hours Servings: 8

INGREDIENTS:

One loaf bread

6 large eggs

Two cups vanilla almond milk

Cinnamon

Vanilla extract

2 tbsp. Nutella

Salt

1 tbsp butter

Four bananas

1tbsp brown sugar

DIRECTIONS:

1. Cover the bottom of Slow Cooker with olive oil or baking spray. Cut the bread into cubes and place it into the Slow Cooker.

2. Combine the eggs with milk.

3. Add vanilla extract, cinnamon, salt and Nutella. Pour the mixture over the bread and mix well. Cook on HIGH temperature for 2 hours.

4. When it is almost ready, slice the bananas and add to a bowl.

Nutrition: Calories: 124 Fat: 6g Carbohydrates: 8g Protein: 9g

Soufflé with Scallions and Dill

Light and healthy breakfast!

Prep time: 15 minutes Cooking time: 4 hours Servings: 6

INGREDIENTS:

One red bell pepper

Half cup milk

Six table spoons flour

Three tablespoons crumbs

Five tablespoons butter

Salt

Five egg yolks

Seven egg whites

Two large scallions

Two tablespoons dill (chopped)

Half tablespoon pepper (freshly ground)

DIRECTIONS:

1. Roast the pepper directly over an open flame. Turn it until blistered on all sides. Preheat your Slow Cooker to 100-130 degrees.

2. Put the peppers into the Slow Cooker dish and leave for 20-30 minutes to steam. When ready, remove skin, stem and seeds. Chop the pepper.

3. Coat your Slow Cooker dish with a cooking spray and whisk milk and butter with flour. In another medium bowl mix the egg yolks and add them to flour mixture.

4. Then, mix the egg whites just a little and mix with other products. Bake for 2-3 hours on LOW and garnish with dill.

Nutrition: Calories: 210 Fat: 4g Carbohydrates: 5g Protein: 8g

Cranberry Apple Oatmeal

Cranberries and apple – the real way to make the oatmeal very delicious!

Prep time: 15 minutes Cooking time: 5 hours Servings: 8

INGREDIENTS:

Four cups water

2 cups oats

Half cup dried cranberries

Two big apples

Half cup brown sugar

Fresh cranberries

2tbsp butter

Cinnamon

Salt

DIRECTIONS:

1. Grease your Slow Cooker with a cooking spray. Preheat. Peel and core the apples. Dice into small cubes.

2. Add the apples in the Slow Cooker and cover with the water. Add other ingredients into the dish.

3. Cook on HIGH temperature for 8 hours (or on LOW for 3). Serve with milk and fresh cranberries.

Nutrition: Calories: 190 Fat: 4g Carbohydrates: 9g Protein: 9g

Chicken Casserole

Chicken casserole will give you energy to star your day!

Prep time: 10 minutes Cooking time: 4-7 hours Servings: 4

INGREDIENTS:

Butter

Half tbsp olive oil

One large onion

Two chicken thigh fillets

Three garlic gloves

Six baby potatoes

Two carrots

Mushrooms (any)

Chicken broth

2 tsp Dijon mustard

DIRECTIONS:

1. In a frying pan, combine butter and olive oil. Heat.

2. Dice onions and add to pan for 10 minutes to caramelize. Toss the chicken in the mix of flour, salt and pepper.

3. Add the chicken and garlic to pen and fry for 5 minutes.

4. Transfer the pan mixture to the Slow Cooker and add the remaining ingredients. Stir well and cook on LOW temperature for 7 hours.

5. Serve with Dijon mustard.

Nutrition: Calories: 382 Fat: 9g Carbohydrates: 30g Protein: 4g

Blueberry and Corn Muffins

Blueberry muffins – perfect for tea with your family!

Prep time: 15 minutes Cooking time: 5 hours Servings: 12

INGREDIENTS:

One cup cornmeal

One cup flour

2tsp baking powder

Granulated sugar

One chicken egg

One cup buttermilk

6 tbsp butter

One cup blueberries

One cup corn kernels (fresh)

DIRECTIONS:

1. Preheat your Slow Cooker to approximately 200 degrees. Grease the muffin forms with olive oil.
2. Mix flour, cornmeal, sugar, salt and baking powder.
3. In another large bowl mix egg, butter, buttermilk, and stir until combined well. Fold in corn and blueberries.
4. Combine egg-mixture with flour mixture.
5. Pour the dough into muffin forms and cook on HIGH for 5 hours.

Nutrition: Calories: 315 Fat: 5g Carbohydrates: 12g Protein: 8g

Crunchy Toast with Cinnamon

Cinnamon toast – great choice for cold mornings and hot tea!

Prep time: 15 minutes Cooking time: 5 hours Servings: 8

INGREDIENTS:

3chicken eggs

Half cup milk

2 tsp cinnamon

Nutmeg

Salt

2 cups cornflakes

Sliced almonds

2 tbsp butter

8 bread slices

DIRECTIONS:

1. Cover your cooking form with olive oil. Preheat your Slow Cooker to 200 degrees.
2. In a large bowl, whisk together the eggs, milk, nutmeg, cinnamon, salt. Set aside. Melt the butter in a small bowl.
3. Dip each bread slice into butter and egg mixture.
4. Layer the bread slices in the Slow Cooker and cook for 2-3 hours on LOW temperatures.

Nutrition: Calories: 345 Fat: 3g Carbohydrates: 7g Protein: 9g

Pumpkin Creamy Muffins

Pumpkin is favorite for every meal – check it out in your breakfast!

Prep time: 15 minutes Cooking time: 6 hours Servings: 24

INGREDIENTS:

Cream cheese

Three chicken eggs

Two cups sugar

Two cups flour

2tbsp pecans

3tbsp butter

Cinnamon

Salt

2tsp baking powder

1 small pumpkin

3tbsp vegetable oil

Vanilla extract

DIRECTIONS:

1. Prepare for cooking: heat your slow cooker and coat muffin forms with olive oil or melted butter. In a separate bowl, mix one egg, cream cheese, three tablespoons sugar, half cup flour, butter, cinnamon and pecans. Set this bowl aside.
2. Take another large bowl and combine the remaining sugar, salt, flour, soda, baking powder in a large bowl.
3. Beat the remaining eggs with eggs, vanilla and oil.
4. Combine both mixtures together and divide the batter on two parts.
5. Divide the first part of the batter between forms evenly, place the cream in the center of each one, then fill with a second part of the batter.
6. Place into the Slow Cooker and cook for 6 hours on LOW temperatures.

Nutrition: Calories: 380 Fat: 4g Carbohydrates: 14g Protein: 12g

Egg Souffle with Cheese

Make your morning a little bit French with this amazing meal!

Prep time: 15 minutes Cooking time: 4 hours Servings: 10

INGREDIENTS:

Six chicken eggs

1 tsp dry mustard

Salt

Half tsp ground pepper

Four cups milk

12 slice sandwich bread

One large red bell pepper

Cheddar cheese

DIRECTIONS:

1. Beat eggs and mix them with mustard, pepper, salt and milk.
2. Cover the Slow Cooker dish with anti-sticking cooking spray and preheat to 180 degrees. Cut red pepper into small pieces.
3. Stir the pepper with bread mixture and add cheese.
4. Pour the bread mixture into the Slow Cooker and cook on HIGH temperatures for 4 hours. Before cutting and serving leave to cool for 10 minutes.

Nutrition: Calories: 234 Fat: 4g Carbohydrates: 5g Protein: 8g

Onion Tart

Unusual, but very tasty and healthy start to your morning!

Prep time: 15 minutes Cooking time: 4 hours Servings: 8

INGREDIENTS:

Green onions

2 tbsp lemon juice

Half cup red wine

Salt

Black pepper (fresh-ground)

2 tbsp olive oil

1tsp thyme (fresh leaves)

Manchego cheese

2clove garlic

Lemon zest to taste

DIRECTIONS:

1. Heat your Slow Cooker to 200 degrees.
2. Pour the water into the Slow Cooker dish, add one tablespoon to boil. Take green onions and add them to the water, boil for 2-3 minutes.
3. Remove the onions from the Slow Cooker and cut.
4. In a large pan, combine the onions, lemon juice, olive oil, pepper and red wine. Cook until caramelized.
5. Combine the Manchego cheese, garlic and lemon zest. Spread on the bottom of the Slow Cooker. Add the onions as a top and cook on LOW temperatures for 4 hours.

Nutrition: Calories: 330 Fat: 5g Carbohydrates: 22g Protein: 9g

Crunchy Cake with Coffee

Try this one with a cup of hot coffee and wake up for a new day!

Prep time: 15 minutes Cooking time: 5 hours Servings: 8

INGREDIENTS:

Two cup plain flour

Half cup milk (whole)

One teaspoon baking powder

Salt

Half cup unsalted butter

Salt

Sugar

Two chicken eggs

Half teaspoon vanilla extract

Half teaspoon lemon extract

DIRECTIONS:

1. Heat the Slow Cooker to 200 degrees. Coat the Slow Cooker dish with butter and dust with flour. In a large baking bowl, mix the sifted cake flour, salt, baking powder and cinnamon.
2. Bat in utter, the sugar and the eggs.
3. Add vanilla, lemon extract, and beat with milk on medium speed until it is very blended. Pour the batter into prepared Slow Cooker and bake for 5 hours on MEDIUM temperatures.

Nutrition: Calories: 380 Fat: 4g Carbohydrates: 12g Protein: 8g

Twisted Roll with Caramel and Pecan

Caramel and pecan will give you strengths to start your working day!

Prep time: 15 minutes Cooking time: 4 hours Servings: 8

INGREDIENTS:

Two tbsp. softened butter

Half cup brown sugar (dark)

Softened Cream Cheese

Toasted pecans

Ground cinnamon

Prepared pizza dough

DIRECTIONS:

1. Butter the bottom and sides of your Slow Cooker. Sprinkle the bottom with 2-3 tablespoons sugar. In a separate bowl mix together butter and cream cheese until smooth.

2. In another bowl, stir pecans, salt, remaining sugar and cinnamon.

3. Roll the dough, spread it with the cream cheese and sprinkle with sugar.

4. Cut the dough into 5-6 even strips. Twist each strip into a spiral. The ends of each strip pinch together. Complete making big twisted roll.

5. Place the roll into the Slow Cooker and cook on LOW for 4 hours.

6. Before serving, cover with caramel glaze. Mix up the brown sugar (three tablespoons), butter and three tablespoons cream and boil in a small pan.

Nutrition: Calories: 349 Fat: 7g Carbohydrates: 32g Protein: 9g

Ginger and Pineapple Oatmeal

A little spicy, but very energetic meal for your morning tea!

Prep time: 15 minutes Cooking time: 4-5 hours Servings: 4

INGREDIENTS:

Two cups rolled oats

Two cups chopped pineapple (or one half)

Ginger

One cup chopped walnuts

Salt

Two cups milk (whole)

Maple syrup (to taste)

2 chicken eggs

2 tsp vanilla extract

DIRECTIONS:

1. Preheat the Slow Cooker to 200 degrees.

2. Meanwhile, stir pineapple, oats, ginger, walnuts, and salt in a large bowl. Divide the oat mixture among four ramekins.

3. In another bowl, whisk all another ingredients.

4. Pour the milk and syrup mixture among the ramekins.

5. Place the ramekins into the Slow Cooker and bake on HIGH temperatures for 4-5 hours. To serve, add the extra maple syrup on the side.

Nutrition: Calories: 440 Fat: 4g Carbohydrates: 13g Protein: 10g

Country French Toast with Ham

Toast with ham and maple syrup – unusual taste for an unusual morning!

Prep time: 15 minutes Cooking time: 5 hours Servings: 6-8

INGREDIENTS:

4 large chicken eggs

2 tsp vanilla extract (pure)

Half teaspoon nutmeg (ground)

Pure maple syrup

Salt

Butter (for griddle)

One cup milk

One cup cream

8 slices ham

8 slices toast bread

DIRECTIONS:

1. Start with preheating your Slow Cooker over medium temperatures.. Mix up milk, eggs, cream, and maple syrup.

2. Stir until combined well. Add nutmeg and vanilla to the eggs mixture, and some salt to taste.

3. Cover the Slow Cooker bottom with some butter or special baking spray. Place the ham slices on the bottom and cover with the bread.

4. Cook for 2 hours on LOW temperatures.

5. To serve slice the French toast into medium portions and add maple syrup alongside.

Nutrition: Calories: 500 Fat: 7g Carbohydrates: 5g Protein: 22g

Candid Orange Granola

The delicious granola with oranges will wake you up!

Prep time: 15 minutes Cooking time: 2 hours Servings: 4

INGREDIENTS:

Four big oranges

Three cup sugar

Two cups granola

Yogurt (plain)

Dark chopped chocolate

DIRECTIONS:

1. Take off the peel from the oranges and cut half of it into small strips.

2. Preheat your Slow Cooker and fill with water. Simmer the orange strips for 30 minutes. Add sugar and boil until it dissolved. Then take the orange strips off.

3. Chop remaining orange strips and mix them with almond granola. Boil for 2-3 hours on HIGH temperatures until ready.

4. Serve with finely chopped chocolate and plain yogurt. You can also add clementine segments, if you like.

Nutrition: Calories: 223 Fat: 4g Carbohydrates: 9g Protein: 7g

Chocolate Rolls with Cherries

Chocolate with cherries – yes, you can eat this on your breakfast!

Prep time: 15 minutes Cooking time: 5 hours Servings: 12

INGREDIENTS:

Butter (room temperature)

Active dry yeast

Half cup granulated sugar

3 chicken eggs

4 cups plain flour

Cinnamon

Two cup fresh cherries

5 tbsp. cherry preserves

One bar bittersweet chocolate

DIRECTIONS:

1. Butter your Slow Cooker and start preheating it.

2. In another bowl, stir together granulated sugar with milk. Add the yeast to your milk mixture and wait until foamy.

3. Sift one cop flour into your milk and combine with electric mixer or kitchen combiner. Add egg, salt, butter and remaining flour and beat until combined.

4. Place the dough in a warm place and wait until begins to rise. In a separate bowl, mix together cinnamon and brown sugar.

5. Cut the dough into 12 pieces, form of each one a strip and roll it.

6. Cover with cinnamon mixture and bake in Slow Cooker for 5-6 hours on LOW.

Nutrition: Calories: 335 Fat: 8g Carbohydrates: 12g Protein: 12g

Tunisian Flavored Eggs

Egg with Tunisian flavors – add to your breakfast another spice taste!

Prep time: 15 minutes Cooking time: 5 hours Servings: 4

INGREDIENTS:

2 tbsp butter

1 tsp harissa

Half cup Merguez sausage (chopped)

8 chicken eggs

Salt

8 tbsp milk yogurt (whole)

Fresh mint leaves

Black pepper (ground)

DIRECTIONS:

1. Brush four cooking forms with butter or spray with cooking spray. Heat the sausage in a pan for 3-4 minutes to cook thoroughly.

2. In a small bowl, whisk half teaspoon water, four teaspoons olive oil and harissa. Add 2 eggs into each bowl, spice with salt and pepper.

3. Combine both mixtures together.

4. Preheat your Slow Cooker and place the jars in it. Cook for 3 hours on LOW temperatures or 5 hours on HIGH.

Nutrition: Calories: 450 Fat: 5g Carbohydrates: 22g Protein: 7g

Charlotte with Herbs

You can taste this with some herbal tea as well!

Prep time: 15 minutes Cooking time: 5 hours Servings: 8-10

INGREDIENTS:

White bread

Salt

6 tbsp butter

One cup onion (chopped)

2 clove garlic

1 cup artichoke hearts (chopped)

1 cup fontina cheese

8 chicken eggs

Milk cream

5 tbsp. ricotta cheese

Half cup chopped parsley

Fresh parsley

Ground black pepper

3 tbsp. grated cheese

DIRECTIONS:

1. Heat Slow Cooker to 200 degrees. Brush the cooking dish with butter.

2. Place the bread slices over the bottom. Slightly overlap each slice.

3. In a pan, heat the remaining butter; add the chopped onions and salt. Fry until lighty golden (around 10 minutes).

4. Add the garlic for one more minute.

5. Add Fontina and remove the pan from heat.

6. In large bowl, whisk milk cream, ricotta eggs, herbs, salt and pepper. Pour this mixture over the bread.

7. Place the cooking dish into Slow Cooker and cook for 4-6 hour on HIGH.

Nutrition: Calories: 313 Fat: 6g Carbohydrates: 19g Protein:12

Tortilla with Cheese and Green olives

Love olives! This receipt is created for you!

Prep time: 15 minutes Cooking time: 5 hours Servings: 8

INGREDIENTS:

Olive oil

One yellow onion

Salt

6-7 red potatoes

Half teaspoon ground pepper

8 chicken eggs

Half cup green olives (chopped)

Manchego cheese

DIRECTIONS:

1. Preheat your Slow Cooker to 200 degrees.

2. In a pan, heat 2 tablespoons oil, add chopped onion and salt. Cook until translucent and set aside. Into the same pan, add 2 tablespoons oil and half of potatoes. Cook for 10 minutes or until potatoes begins to soften.

3. When ready, mix with onions, eggs and olives.

4. Pour the mixture into the baking dish and top with cheese.

5. Transfer the baking dish to Slow Cooker and bake on LOW until eggs are set.

Nutrition: Calories: 423 Fat: 4g Carbohydrates: 23g Protein: 33g

Currant and Raspberry Pudding

Summer season is for berry puddings. This one – a must have to try!

Prep time: 15 minutes Cooking time: 5 hours Servings: 12

INGREDIENTS:

One loaf bread

Unsalted butter

Red currants (fresh)

Raspberries (fresh)

3 chicken egg

2 egg yolks

Half cup sugar

Salt

1 tsp vanilla extract

One cup milk (whole)

DIRECTIONS:

1. Preheat your Slow Cooker well.

2. Cut the bread into slices and brush each one with butter.

3. Place the bread slices in a baking dish. Overlap each slice slightly. Cover the bread with half of raspberries and currants.

4. In another bowl, whisk the eggs, egg yolks, salt, vanilla, sugar and milk. Pour this mixture over the bread.

5. Place the dish into Slow Cooker and bake for 2 hours on HIGH temperatures or 4-5 hours on LOW.

Nutrition: Calories: 334 Fat: 6g Carbohydrates: 34g Protein: 9g

Broccoli Strata with Tomatoes and Cheddar

Love eggs with cheese? Add some broccoli for a delicious taste!

Prep time: 15 minutes Cooking time: 5 hours Servings: 8

INGREDIENTS:

Butter

Four cups bread cubes

1-2 cups shredded Cheddar cheese

1 cup tomatoes

8 chicken eggs

1 cup broccoli florets (frozen)

1 tbsp parsley (fresh and chopped)

3 cups milk

Salt

Ground pepper

Ricotta cheese

1 tsp herbs de Provence

DIRECTIONS:

1. Butter your baking dish and place the bread in it.

2. Cover the bread with one cup Cheddar, diced tomatoes, broccoli and parsley. In a separate bowl, mix together milk, eggs, pepper and salt.

3. Pour the egg mixture over the bread cubes, press gently.

4. Cover with Ricotta cheese, remaining Cheddar and herbs de Provence sprinkles. Preheat Slow Cooker to 200 degrees.

5. Place the cooking dish with bread inside and bake on LOW for 5-6 hours. Serve warm with fresh vegetables.

Nutrition: Calories: 311 Fat: 4g Carbohydrates: 18g Protein: 14g

Slow Cooker Cake with Honey

Honey and vanilla – delicious and healthy way to start your day!

Prep time: 15 minutes Cooking time: 4 hours Servings: 10

INGREDIENTS:

One cup butter

One cup sugar

Honey

5 large chicken eggs

2 tsp vanilla extract

One cup flour

1tsp baking powder

DIRECTIONS:

1. Preheat the Slow Cooker to 200 degrees.

2. Spray the baking dish with cooking spray or cover with butter.

3. In a large bowl, beat the butter, honey and sugar with a mixer until fluffy and light. Beat in the eggs and vanilla extract.

4. Sift the flour, add baking powder, and salt. Stir until smooth.

5. Transfer the dough into the baking dish and prepare on HIGH temperatures for 4 hours. Cool for 15 minutes before serving.

Nutrition: Calories: 311 Fat: 4g Carbohydrates: 19g Protein: 43g

Slow Cooker Quiche

Creamy, delicious and tasty.

Prep time: 15 minutes Cooking time: 3-5 hours Servings: 10

INGREDIENTS:

2roll-out pie crusts

9 large chicken eggs

One cup heavy milk cream

Mozzarella cheese (shredded and smoked)

One cup smoked ham (shredded)half teaspoon ground mustard

Half cup onion (diced)

One garlic clove

Broccoli florets

DIRECTIONS:

1. Chop all the vegetables and ham.

2. Place bell peppers, onions, and garlic into a skillet for 5 minutes to soften.

3. Place out the pie crusts on the parchment. Overlap in the center, and you will get one piece of crust.

4. Gently place your crust in the Slow Cooker, pressing the bottom and sides.

5. In a separate bowl, whisk the eggs, ground mustard, cream and salt until frothy.

6. Add the vegetables, cheese and ham to the eggs and pour this mixture over the crust. Cook on HIGH for 4 hours

7. Cool for 10 minutes before cutting and serving.

Nutrition: Calories: 346 Fat: 13g Carbohydrates: 33g Protein: 45g

Mashed Potatoes with Ricotta

Tasty and milky, full of energy for your daily start!

Prep time: 15 minutes Cooking time: 5 hours Servings: 8

INGREDIENTS:

6-7 large yellow potatoes

2 tsp salt

Half cup milk (whole)

Ground black pepper

One cup Ricotta (fresh)

DIRECTIONS:

1. Preheat the Slow Cooker.

2. Peel the potatoes and cut them into one-inch cubes.

3. Place the potatoes into the baking dish, add salt and cover with water.

4. Transfer the cooking dish to Slow Cooker and cook on LOW for 4-5 hours until softened. When ready, mash the potatoes and stir in milk, ricotta, butter and pepper.

5. Blend until all the ingredients are fully combined. Serve only hot.

Nutrition: Calories: 455 Fat: 6g Carbohydrates: 23g Protein: 9g

Ricotta Cheesecake with Lemon

Cheesecake with lemon – sweet and unforgettable breakfast!

Prep time: 15 minutes Cooking time: 3-4 hours Servings: 10

INGREDIENTS:

One cup cracker crumbs

4 tbsp butter

4 lemons

One cup sugar

4 tbsp cornstarch

Reduced-fat cream cheese

4 chicken eggs

Ricotta cheese (part-skim)

2 cups light cream

2 tsp vanilla extract

DIRECTIONS:

1. Preheat your Slow Cooker to 150 degrees.
2. In a baking form, combine cracker crumbs and butter. Firmly press to the bottom and bake for 1 hour on HIGH temperatures.
3. Meanwhile, grate the peel from lemons and squeeze the juice. In a separate bowl, blend cornstarch and sugar.
4. In a large bowl beat ricotta with cream cheese until smooth (use a kitchen mixer). Beat in the sugar mixture, eggs, light cream, vanilla and lemon juice and peel.
5. Pour dough onto crust and bake for 2 more hours.
6. To serve, use the center slices of lemon as a garnish.

Nutrition: Calories: 290 Fat: 4g Carbohydrates: 17g Protein: 9g

Fritata with Goat Cheese and Ham

Cheese and ham – a perfect couple for your breakfast idea!

Prep time: 15 minutes Cooking time: 5 hours Servings: 8

INGREDIENTS:

8 large chicken eggs

Half cup heavy cream

Chopped ham

Salt

Black pepper (freshly ground)

Asparagus (cut into two-inch pieces)

1 garlic clove

6 radishes

Goat cheese (crumbled)

DIRECTIONS:

1. Preheat your Slow Cooker to 200 degrees.
2. In a separate bowl, whisk the eggs, cream, ham with pepper and salt.
3. In a skillet, melt butter and add asparagus. Simmer for 4 minutes (until crisp-tender) Add scallions, radishes, garlic and cook for another 4 minutes.
4. Transfer the pan mixture into buttered baking dish and cover with eff mixture. Cover with goat cheese and cook in the Slow Cooker for 3-4 hours on HIGH. Serve as soon as ready.

Nutrition: Calories: 400 Fat: 18g Carbohydrates: 22g Protein: 33g

Crumbled Gooseberry Flapjack

Another summer receipt for your good mood and healthy body!

Prep time: 20 minutes Cooking time: 5 hours Servings: 8

INGREDIENTS:

5 large apples

Zest 1 lemon

Juice 1 lemon

Half cup golden caster sugar

1 cup gooseberry

2 tsp cornflour

Vanilla ice-cream or custard (to serve)

DIRECTIONS:

1. Preheat the Slow Cooker to 140 degrees. In separate pan, melt the butter and syrup.
2. Mix the dry ingredients and stir theminto the butter mixture. Peel, core and dice apple to small cubes.
3. Place the apples into a pan and add lemon juice. Stir in corn flour with the sugar. Stir in the gooseberries and lemon zest.
4. Heat the Slow Cooker again and butter it.
5. Place the dough in it and cook for 5 on LOW temperatures.

Nutrition: Calories: 500 Fat: 17g Carbohydrates: 40g Protein: 8g

Cheesy Tater Tot

Try this delicious one – and it will be your favorite!

Prep time: 15 minutes Cooking time: 5 hours Servings: 8

INGREDIENTS:

4 slices bacon (cooked)

5 breakfast sausages

2cups cheddar cheese

2 cups milk (whole)

3large chicken eggs

Half teaspoon onion powder

Half teaspoon black pepper

Pinch of salt

Pack tater tots (frozen)

Parsley (for garnish)

DIRECTIONS:

1. In a large skillet, cook sausage over medium heat.
2. Drain the sausages and layer them onto the buttered bottom of Slow Cooker dish. Cover the sausages with two cups of the cheese.
3. In separate bowl, hand-whisk eggs with milk, onion powder, salt and pepper. Then pour gently over the cheese.
4. Cover the upper layer with the frozen tater tots.
5. Set your Slow Cooker to 200 degrees and bake on LOW for 4-5 hours.

Nutrition: Calories: 435 Fat: 19g Carbohydrates: 33g Protein: 35g

Egg Casserole in Slow Cooker

Casserole for morning tea – energetic start for your day!

Prep time: 15 minutes Cooking time: 5 hours Servings: 8

INGREDIENTS:

Butter

2 tbsp olive oil (extra virgin)

One cup cremini mushrooms (sliced)

12 croissants (mini)

Baby spinach

Half cup Gruyere cheese (grated)

8 large chicken eggs

Salt

Pepper

2cups whole milk

DIRECTIONS:

1. Butter your baking dish.
2. Cook the mushrooms on a buttered pan, until golden brown.
3. Stuff the croissants with spinach and half-cup cheese. Transfer the croissants to the baking dish. Place the mushrooms into the baking dish among the croissants.
4. In separate bowl, combine egg with milk and add pepper and salt. Pour this mixture over the croissants.
5. Sprinkle with the remaining cheese and bake for 2 hours at LOW temperatures.

Nutrition: Calories: 551 Fat: 33g Carbohydrates: 40g Protein: 7g

Corn Pudding with Cheese

Light pudding is perfect for any season and good for your health!

Prep time: 15 minutes Cooking time: 5 hours Servings: 8

INGREDIENTS:

One cup milk (whole)

Pepper (freshly ground)

4 tbsp grits

Cheddar

3large chicken eggs

Half can creamed

corn Salt

DIRECTIONS:

1. Preheat Slow Cooker to 200 degrees.
2. Bring milk to a simmer in a small saucepan. Add grits and salt. Cook for 5-30 minutes until grits thicken.
3. Meanwhile, using the food processor, combine the corn to puree. Mix the corn, 2 egg yolks, Cheddar into grits, add salt and pepper.
4. In a separate bowl beat egg whites to stiff peaks with a mixer. Gently fold into egg mixture. Divide the dough among 8 ramekins and bake on HIGH in the Slow Cooker for 2-3 hours.

Nutrition: Calories: 500 Fat: 19g Carbohydrates: 45g Protein: 40g

LUNCH RECIPES

Spicy chicken with fennel stew

The long time infuses the chicken flavor and makes your lunch delicious and spicy!

Prep time: 15 minutes Cooking time: 5 hours Servings: 4

INGREDIENTS:

Olive oil

Two fennel bulbs

Two chicken thighs

Two tablespoons flour (plain)

Four anchovies (chopped finely)

Three garlic cloves

One red chili (chopped)

Can diced tomatoes

Half cup white wine

Italian bread (to serve)

Fennel fronds (to garnish)

DIRECTIONS:

1. Heat a skillet over medium temperature and add one tablespoon of olive oil. Add fennel and cook stirring until golden (for 6-8 minutes)
2. Transfer kennel to the Slow Cooker and heat the remaining olive oil in the same skillet.
3. Cut the chicken and toss in flour, so it will coat evenly. Fry for 6-7 minutes (until browned well). Add anchovy, garlic and chili to chicken and cook for another 2-3 minutes.
4. Add wine, wait until boil and then simmer for a couple minutes. Add tomatoes and transfer chicken to Slow Cooker.
5. Cover and cook on LOW for 5 hours.
6. To serve, cut the bread and garnish with fennels.

Nutrition: Calories: 1536 Fat: 25g Carbohydrates: 18g Protein: 48g

French Farmhouse Chicken Soup

Perfect for a winter or fall day, when you need to warm with a bowl of hot soup.

Prep time: 10 minutes Cooking time: 6 hours Servings: 4

INGREDIENTS:

2 tsp olive oil (extra virgin)

6 chicken eggs

2 carrots (diced)

2 celery stalks (trimmed and sliced)

One leek (thinly sliced)

1 fennel bulb (diced)

Chicken stock (salt-reduced)

3 thyme sprigs (fresh)

Half cup frozen peas

Four slices crusty bread (to serve)

DIRECTIONS:

1. Heat the olive oil in a non-stick skillet over medium heat.
2. Add chicken and fry for 5-7 minutes until browned from all sides. Transfer to the Slow Cooker. Cover the chicken with carrot, celery, fennel, leek, thyme and stock. Add salt and pepper to taste. Cover the lid of the Slow Cooker and cook for around 5 hours on LOW temperature.
3. When cooking time is almost over, add the peas (in the last 10-15 minutes).
4. Take the chicken off the soup and remove all the bones. Shred roughly and place back to soup. Sprinkle with fennel fronds and serve the soup with crusty bread.

Nutrition: Calories: 850 Fat: 12g Carbohydrates: 64g Protein: 50g

Bean soup served with toasts

Warm and satisfying soup with beans and toasts to maintain your day!

Prep time: 12 minutes Cooking time: 7 hours Servings: 4

INGREDIENTS:

One cup borlotti beans (dried)

One large brown onion (finely chopped)

1 tsp olive oil (extra virgin)

4 celery sticks

1large carrot

Finely chopped pancetta

3 garlic cloves

2tsp fresh rosemary (chopped)

1 red chili

2 cups chicken stock

2 cups water

Tuscan cabbage

4 slices grilled bread

1 tbsp. fresh basil

DIRECTIONS:

1. Place the beans in a large bowl and cover with cold water. Leave overnight to soak then drain. Put the beans in a

saucepan and cover with cold water. Set the medium heat and wait until boil. Cook for around 10 minutes.

2. Preheat the olive oil in a non-stick skillet over medium heat.

3. Chop the onion, carrot, celery and pancetta and cook until soft (for 4-5 minutes). Add the garlic, chili and rosemary. Cook until aromatic.

4. Preheat the Slow Cooker and place in the onion mixture, stock, beans and water. Cover and boil on LOW for 6-7 hours.

5. Serve in small bowls with toast.

Nutrition: Calories: 540 Fat: 9g Carbohydrates: 35g Protein: 20g

Chicken ragout with red wine

Just try and taste this! Perfect meal to get warm on a cold winter day!

Prep time: 25 minutes Cooking time: 7 hours Servings: 6

INGREDIENTS:

1 tbsp olive oil (extra virgin)

1 chicken fillet

1red onion

2celery stalks

2 garlic cloves

1 carrot

Finely chopped pancetta

One cup red wine

One cup chicken stock

Barilla Fettuccine

Half cup pecorino

3 sprigs rosemary (fresh)

Steamed green beans

Chopped parsley (to serve)

DIRECTIONS:

1. Dice all the vegetables finely.

2. Heat a frying pan with olive oil, set over medium heat.

3. Cook chicken for 5 minutes until it is browned. You can work in batches.

4. Add celery, onion, pancetta and carrot. Stir and cook for 8-9 minutes until the vegetables start to soften.

5. Add garlic and simmer for a minute to fragrant. Add wine, wait until boil and cook for 1-2 minutes.

6. Transfer the pan mixture to Slow Cooker and combine with rosemary, stock and tomato paste. Cook for 6 hours on LOW.

7. Shred chicken in Slow Cooker with two forks and cook for another 30 minutes. Add pasta to the chicken and combine well.

8. To serve sprinkle with pecorino, add parsley and beans.

Nutrition: Calories: 745 Fat: 15g Carbohydrates: 43g Protein: 334g

Egg noodles with Red Beef

Fast, healthy and delicious lunch for you and your family!

Prep time: 15 minutes Cooking time: 4-5 hours Servings: 4

INGREDIENTS:

2 tbsp. plain flour

Beef steak

1-2 tbsp. peanut oil

One cup chicken stock

Half cup dry sherry

4 tbsp. soy sauce

6 crushed cardamom pods

Sliced ginger (fresh)

1cinnamon stick

Half teaspoon fennel seeds

Egg noodles (to serve)

Coriander sprigs, to serve)

DIRECTIONS:

1. In a large bowl, toss the beef with the flour to fully coat.

2. Take a large non-stick skillet and heat 2 teaspoons olive oil (over medium heat).

3. Separate the beef into three parts and cook in batches each one for 3-4 minutes. After ready, transfer the beef to slow cooker.

4. Cover the beef with sherry, stock, cardamom, ginger, anise star and fennel seeds. Sprinkle with soy sauce.

5. Cook on HIGH temperatures until tender beef (for 4-5 hours). Before serving top with coriander.

Nutrition: Calories: 930 Fat: 19g Carbohydrates: 7g Protein: 45g

Autumn Pumpkin Soup

Get warm and eat a tasty autumn soup!

Prep time: 30 minutes Cooking time: 4 hours Servings: 4-6

INGREDIENTS:

Half medium-sized butternut pumpkin

2-3 medium potatoes

Salt

Black pepper (cracked)

1-2 tsp mild curry powder

1 onion

One cup cream (full)

Chili powder to taste (optional)

2 cups vegetable stock

DIRECTIONS:

1. Cut and peel the pumpkin, remove skin and seeds. Chop the potatoes and fine dice the onion.

2. Place the vegetables in the Slow Cooker. Add salt and pepper.

3. Cook for 4-6 hours on LOW temperatures until the pumpkin and potatoes are tender. When ready, wait until cool and stir with a food processor until smooth consistence. Stir in the chili powder and cream.

4. To serve, warm again a little bit.

Nutrition: Calories: 355 Fat: 9g Carbohydrates: 5g Protein: 21g

Bone Broth in Slow Cooker

The perfect choice for a cold winter day!

Prep time: 15 minutes Cooking time: 24 hours Servings: 6

INGREDIENTS:

Beef bones (you can gather a mix of knuckle, marrow and meat bones)

6 sprigs thyme

2tbsp apple cider vinegar

1 browned onion (halved)

2 quartered carrots

4 garlic cloves

One bay leaf

2 chopped stalks celery

DIRECTIONS:

1. Preheat your oven 200 degrees (or 180, if your oven is fan-forced). Place your bone mix on a roasting tray and cook for 30-40 minutes. Place all the bones and fat in Slow Cooker.

2. Add the quartered carrots, garlic, halved onion and chopped celery. Pour the water to cover the ingredients.

3. Close the lid and simmer for 24 hours on LOW (you can add more water if some vaporize during the cooking time).

4. Take off and strain into a separate large bowl. Chill before serving.

Nutrition: Calories: 293 Fat: 1g Carbohydrates: 5g Protein: 13g

Creamy vegetable curry with chickpea

Try to cook this during summer season!

Prep time: 20 minutes Cooking time: 4 hours Servings: 6

INGREDIENTS:

2 tsp vegetable oil

2 tbsp. Madras curry paste

One can light coconut cream

1 red capsicum

1 small cauliflower (cut into florets)

One medium pumpkin (cut into small cubes)

3 chopped tomatoes

One cup green beans

Two cups chickpeas

1Lebanese cucumber

One cup plain Greek yogurt

4 bread slices

DIRECTIONS:

1. Cut the capsicum, pumpkin and cucumber into small cubes, Chop the tomatoes, halve the beans, drain and rinse chickpeas.

2. Heat olive oil in a large saucepan over medium heat.

3. Add curry paste and stock. Wait until simmer and transfer to Slow Cooker. Add the pumpkin, capsicum and coconut cream to the Slow Cooker.

4. Cook on LOW temperature for 3 hours.

5. Add tomato and cauliflower. Cook for another 15 minutes. Cover with chickpeas and beans, prepare for 30 minutes.

6. To serve, combine coriander, cucumber and yogurt in a separate bowl. Serve with the bread and yogurt.

Nutrition: Calories: 773 Fat: 20g Carbohydrates: 51g Protein: 20g

Lamb Chunks with Honey

Make your lunch warm and sweet!

Prep time: 20 minutes Cooking time: 4 hours Servings: 4

INGREDIENTS:

Half cup soy sauce

3 tbsp honey

2garlic cloves

Black pepper

1 star anise

Fresh ginger

1 brown inion

1 tbsp vegetable oil

1 sliced orange

4 lamb shanks

1 red chili

1 tsp sesame oil

1 green onion

4 cups rice (steamed)

Halved baby pak choy

DIRECTIONS:

1. In separate bowl, combine honey, soy sauce, garlic, ginger, black pepper and star anise. Put diced brown onion and carrots in Slow Cooker.

2. Add the sliced orange over the onion and carrot.

3. In a large frying pan heat the vegetable oil and cook lamb for 4-5 minutes on medium heat (or until browned all sides). Place to Slow Cooker.

4. Cover with the lid and prepare on HIGH temperatures for 4 hours).

5. Transfer lamb to a baking tray and cook in the oven for 14 minutes on 180 degrees. Meanwhile, add sesame oil, star anise to Slow Cooker. Cook for 15 minutes.

6. Serve lamb with pac choy and rice.

Nutrition: Calories: 549 Fat: 10g Carbohydrates: 37g Protein: 30g

Chickpea curry with vegetables

So delicious and spicy – your lunch will bring you new powers for your day!

Prep time: 15 minutes Cooking time: 4 hours Servings: 4

INGREDIENTS:

1 tbsp vegetable oil

One brown onion (large)

2 garlic cloves

3 tsp ground cumin

2 tbsp curry powder

Half juiced lemon

One can diced tomatoes

One cup chickpeas

One large carrot

1 red capsicum

One cup cauliflower

Half cup mushrooms

4 small yellow squash

1,5 cup broccoli florets

To serve, jasmine rice, salt, natural yogurt

DIRECTIONS:

1. Preheat vegetable oil in a large skillet (over medium heat). Add chopped onion, stir and cook for 3 minutes until soft. Add garlic, cumin and curry powder and cook until aromatic. Stir in mashed potatoes and simmer for 3-5 minutes.

2. Pour half-cup water, vegetables, chickpeas and 2 tablespoons lemon juice. Bring to boil. Spoon to the Slow Cooker and prepare on HIGH for 4-6 hours.

3. Serve with the rice and yogurt.

Nutrition: Calories: 938 Fat: 7g Carbohydrates: 19g Protein: 15g

Soup with lentils and goat cheese

Set the work on pause for a bowl of hot soup!

Prep time: 25 minutes Cooking time: 3 hours Servings: 4

INGREDIENTS:

One brown onion

2 celery sticks

1 swede

1 carrot

1 garlic clove

Half cup red lentils

One can diced tomatoes

2 cups vegetable stock

2 tbsp fresh chives

1baguette (sliced diagonally)

3 teaspoons ground cumin

Half cup goat cheese

DIRECTIONS:

1. Finely chop the onion, carrot, celery, swede, fresh chimes. Crush the garlic clove.

2. Place the vegetables along with lentils, stock, tomatoes and cumin in your Slow Cooker. Cover with the lid and cook until thick soup and tender vegetables (for 3 hours on HIGH temperature).

3. Preheat your grill and place the bread on the baking tray. Cook until golden for 2-3 minutes each side.

4. In a small bowl, combine the cheese with chimes and spread over the toasted bread. Serve the soup in a bowls with toast and cheese.

Nutrition: Calories: 957 Fat: 9g Carbohydrates: 16g Protein: 27g

Ragout with Beef and Carrot

Healthy and satisfying dish for any occasion!

Prep time: 15 minutes Cooking time: 4 hours Servings: 4

INGREDIENTS:

2tbsp plain flour

Gravy beef

3tbsp olive oil

2large onions (brown)

Half cup tomato paste

2 crushed garlic cloves

Half cup red wine

3large carrots

1cup Massel beef stock

DIRECTIONS:

1. Cut beef into small cubes and place it into a wide dish with flour, salt and pepper. Coat the beef with flour mixture and remove the excess.
2. Heat one tablespoon olive oil in a large skillet and fry the beef cubes over medium heat. Place the beef into Slow Cooker.
3. Add onion to skillet, stir and cook for 4-6 minutes until soft. Add tomato paste and garlic. Simmer for one more minute.
4. Pour in wine and bring to boil slowly. Simmer until wine reduced or for 5 minutes. Pour sauce over beef and combine softly.
5. Cook on HIGH for 4 hours. Serve with the pasta.

Nutrition: Calories: 731 Fat: 22g Carbohydrates: 10g Protein: 33g

Ham and pea soup foe Slow Cooker

Easy to make and very tasty – you should try this!

Prep time: 15 minutes Cooking time: 7 hours Servings: 4

INGREDIENTS:

One tablespoon olive oil

One brown onion (small)

2 sticks celery

2garlic cloves

One cup ham hock

5 large potatoes

One cup green peas (split)

3cups chicken stock-salt-reduced

Fresh parsley (to serve)

DIRECTIONS:

1. Chop small brown onion, rush garlic cloves and dice celery.
2. In large frying pan, heat the oil over medium-high temperature. Add onion and prepare, stirring, around three minutes.
3. Wait until the onion is soft, add celery, garlic, and diced potatoes. Stir and cook for three minutes, then transfer to Slow Cooker.
4. Add ham hock, stock and peas. Pour with 4-5 cups cold water. Cover the lid and cook on LOW mode for six hours.
5. Shred ham and return the dish in Slow Cooker for an hour. To serve, sprinkle with chopped parsley.

Nutrition: Calories: 458 Fat: 16g Carbohydrates: 50g Protein: 32g

Summer Curry in Slow Cooker

Hot and spicy – just like the summer!

Prep time: 10 minutes Cooking time: 8-9 hours Servings: 4

INGREDIENTS:

1 tbsp peanut oil

Beef steak

4 tbsp massamam curry paste

6 cardamom pods

1 medium brown onion (halved)

2 garlic cloves

1cinnamon stick

2large carrots

Steamed rice

1-2 cup coconut milk

6 large potatoes

2 tbsp. fish sauce

1 tbsp. palm sugar

1 tbsp. lime juice

Coriander leaves and peanuts (to serve)

DIRECTIONS:

1. Trim the beef steak, chop into small cubes.

2. Place the beef cubes into the preheated large skillet with peanut oil. Cook until browned (for 5-6 minutes).

3. Transfer the meat to buttered Slow Cooker.

4. Heat the same pan again and add onion. Fry until softened, then add curry paste and garlic. Prepare until aromatic, and then transfer to Slow Cooker.

5. Cover with cinnamon, cardamom, potatoes, carrots, sugar and wish sauce. Pour in the coconut milk.

6. Cover the lid and leave to cook for 8 hours on LOW mode. Serve with rice and sprinkled peanuts.

Nutrition: Calories: 534 Fat: 33g Carbohydrates: 45g Protein: 52g

Slow Cooker meatballs with rigatoni

Delicious and healthy lunch for busy people!

Prep time: 20 minutes Cooking time: 7 hours Servings: 4

INGREDIENTS:

Pork and veal mince

1 tbsp. olive oil

Pecorino cheese (finely grated)

3 garlic gloves

1medium onion (brown)

2tbsp. parsley (fresh leaves)

2 celery stalks

One jar tomato paste

2 tbsp. sherry (dry)

2 tsp sugar

Rigatoni pasta

Pecorino cheese and baby rocket to serve

DIRECTIONS:

1. Take a large bowl and combine cheese, parsley, mince, breadcrumbs and garlic in it. Using a tablespoon, roll small parts of the mixture and form into balls.

2. Heat the olive oil in a large skillet and add chopped onion and celery. Stir and cook for 3-5 minutes until softened.

3. Add sherry and cook for another 2 minutes (until reduced by half). Add tomato paste and sugar. Cover with six cups of cold water.

4. Place the meatballs into the Slow Cooker and pour in tomato mixture. Cook on LOW mode for 6 hours, and then add pasta. Stir well to combine. Cook for 45 minutes and season with pepper and salt.

5. Serve warm with rocket and cheese.

Nutrition: Calories: 495 Fat: 19g Carbohydrates: 64g Protein: 51g

Pumpkin couscous with lamb

Perfect for autumn!

Prep time: 10 minutes Cooking time: 2-3 hours Servings: 6

INGREDIENTS:

2 tbsp. olive oil

Two red onions (halved and sliced)

2 cinnamon sticks

6 lamb shanks

3 garlic cloves

3tsp cumin (ground)

2 tsp paprika

4cups Massel beef stock

Cherry tomatoes (canned)

Half cup chopped coriander (fresh)

2 tbsp. brown sugar

Butternut pumpkin

2 cups couscous

Half cup fresh mint (chopped)

DIRECTIONS:

1. Heat your Slow Cooker to 180 degrees.

2. Cover the frying skillet with 1-tablespoon olive oil and cook the lamb for 5-7 minutes (until brown). Transfer to the Slow Cooker dish.

3. Using the remaining oil, fry the onion until soft. Add cumin, crushed garlic, cinnamon, paprika and coriander. Leave for a minute until aromatic.

4. Add sugar, tomato, half the mint and half the fresh coriander. Stir in the beef stock. Pour the mixture into Slow Cooker.

5. Cook for 3-4 hours on HIGH temperature mode.

6. To serve, divide among bowls and garnish with remaining mint and coriander.

Nutrition: Calories: 480 Fat: 14g Carbohydrates: 31g Protein: 32g

Pappardelle ragout with duck

Hot ragout for lunch – what else do you need for a beautiful day?

Prep time: 30 minutes Cooking time: 4-5 hours Servings: 6

INGREDIENTS:

One small onion (brown and chopped)

Frozen duck

Half cup pancetta

One celery stick

Two garlic cloves

One carrot (small)

2 bay leaves (dried)

Three rosemary sprigs

One cup chicken stock

One cup pinot noir

Half cup green olives

Pappardelle pasta (to serve)

Parmesan (finely grated, to serve)

Chopped parsley (to serve)

DIRECTIONS:

1. Prepare the duck: discard backbone and take off all exec fat. Quarter the duck and cover with salt. Cook the duck in a deep buttered skillet over high heat until it gets brown (for 5-6 minutes).

2. Preheat your Slow Cooker to 110 degrees. Cover the dish with reserved chicken fat.

3. In a separate pan, cook the onion, pancetta, carrot, celery, bay leaves and garlic. Stir time after time.

4. Place duck and vegetable mixture into Slow Cooker. Cover with wine, tomato and stock. Add rosemary.

5. Cover the lid and cook on high mode for 4 hours. Serve with parmesan, pasta and parsley.

Nutrition: Calories: 504 Fat: 23g Carbohydrates: 7g Protein: 51g

Oxtail and Chorizo Stew

This is easier than you think! Just let it try and cook this!

Prep time: 25 minutes Cooking time: 4 hours Servings: 4

INGREDIENTS:

Oxtail pieces

4 tbsp olive oil (extra virgin)

1 garlic cloves

1 onion (chopped)

1 tsp paprika

1 primo chorizo

1carrot (chopped)

Half orange zest

2rosemary sprigs

2 cans tomatoes (whole peeled)

2 cups red wine

14-16 cherry tomatoes

Flat-leaf parsley (to garnish)

3 cups beef stock

DIRECTIONS:

1. Preheat your Slow Cooker to 170 degrees and butter the dish.

2. Place oxtail to a large saucepan and cover with cold water. Slowly bring to the boil and prepare for 15-20 minutes. Rinse and set aside.

3. Preheat olive oil in a large saucepan. Add onion, carrot, chorizo and garlic. Stir and cook for 4 minutes.

4. Add paprika, 1 rosemary sprig and orange zest. Salt and pepper.

5. Place oxtails in the Slow Cooker dish, cover with vegetables and tomato. Pour in wine and stock. Cook for 3-4 hours on high.

6. Serve with mash potatoes or any other side dish you like.

Nutrition: Calories: 544 Fat: 39g Carbohydrates: 49g Protein: 33g

Slow Cooker Soup with Ham

Delicious and healthy soup for your middle day!

Prep time: 23 minutes Cooking time: 8 hours Servings: 8

INGREDIENTS:

2 cups navy beans

2 large carrots

6 large potatoes

2 medium shallots

2 large celery stalks

1 ham bone

Salt

8 cups water

Thyme leaves

Minced sage

1 loaf crusty bread

DIRECTIONS:

1. In a large plate, stir the potatoes, celery, beans, carrots, shallots sage and thyme. You can do it right in Slow Cooker, but then do not forget to butter it.

2. Place the vegetable mix into Slow Cooker and nestle the ham bone in the middle. Pour in the water to cover evenly all the ingredients.

3. Cover with the lid and cook on LOW regime for 8 hours.

4. Remove ham bone, cool and shred it, then combine again with the soup. Serve hot with crusty baguette.

Nutrition: Calories: 467 Fat: 28g Carbohydrates: 43g Protein: 52g

Slow Cooker Soup with Celery and Bacon

Try to cook it overnight – and you will get a perfect dish the next day!

Prep time: 27 minutes Cooking time: 7 hours Servings: 4-6

INGREDIENTS:

One yellow onion (large)

10-12 small white potatoes

One bunch celery

3garlic cloves

4cups chicken broth

6-4 slices bacon (thick-cut)

Salt

Half teaspoon white pepper

4 tbsp heavy cream or milk

DIRECTIONS:

1. Preheat your Slow Cooker for 100-110 degrees and butter the cooking dish.

2. Chop the celery, potatoes and onion into medium and equally sized cubes. Mince the garlic. Place the prepared vegetables in your Slow Cooker and cover with chicken broth.

3. Season with pepper and salt to taste. Cook on LOW mode for 5-7 hours.

4. Before serving, puree the soup with a stick blender (can do iy right in Slow Cooker) and serve in small bowls with bacon over top.

Nutrition: Calories: 577 Fat: 43g Carbohydrates: 46g Protein: 33g

French Onion Soup for Slow Cooker

Perfect choice for French cuisine fans!

Prep time: 30 minutes Cooking time: 12 hours Servings: 6

INGREDIENTS:

3 yellow onions

2 tbsp. olive oil

2 tbsp. melted butter (unsalted)

Black pepper (freshly ground)

Pinch salt

10 cups beef broth

2 tbsp. balsamic vinegar

3 tbsp. brandy (optional)

6 baguette slices (to serve)

2 cups Gruyere cheese (to serve)

Chopped shallot or onion

DIRECTIONS:

1. Chop the onion and place it into large Slow Cooker. Mix in the butter, salt, olive oil and black pepper. Cook on low overnight.

2. In the morning, add to onion the broth and balsamic vinegar.

3. Cover with the lid and cook for another 6-8 hours on LOW (the longer you cook, the more intensively flavors you will get).

4. Pour the soup into small bowls and place them into preheated oven. Top each bowl with the toast and cheese and bake for 30 minutes.

5. To serve, place the chopped onions on a side of each bowl.

Nutrition: Calories: 455 Fat: 33g Carbohydrates: 61g Protein: 54g

Maple Bacon and White Bean Soup

Try this soup with bacon – and it will be your favorite!

Prep time: 25 minutes Cooking time: 12 hours Servings: 8

INGREDIENTS:

Two cups white beans (dried)

One red pepper

1 ham bone

8 cups chicken broth

5 slices maple bacon

2 carrots

1 red pepper

1 onion

Half cup diced ham

2 celery stalks

Thyme

4 cloves garlic

Zest and juice of half lemon

Salt and pepper to taste

Chopped parsley (fresh)

DIRECTIONS:

1. In a deep bowl, cover the beans with cold water and leave to soak overnight.

2. In the morning drain the beans and place them into Slow Cooker, cover with broth and add ham. Cook on high for 3-4 hours.

3. In a small frying pan, cook the bacon slices until crispy. Add the red pepper, onion, celery, garlic and carrots. Add salt and cook for ten minutes

4. Add the aromatic mixture into Slow Cooker and stir well with beans.

5. Let cook on HIGH for an hour or two. In the end, add the chopped parsley and lemon zest. You can serve it hot or cold – it is tasty both ways.

Nutrition: Calories: 443 Fat: 32g Carbohydrates: 65g Protein: 33g

Chicken Minestrone in Slow Cooker

Easy to make and very delicious!

Prep time: 5 minutes Cooking time: 3 hours Servings: 3

INGREDIENTS:

2 chicken thighs

1 bay leaf

One medium leek

1 can tomatoes

Three cloves garlic

3 medium carrots

One teaspoon salt

2 celery stalks

4 cups chicken broth

2 cups water

4 cups shredded cabbage

1 can beans

One medium zucchini

DIRECTIONS:

1. To make the broth, preheat Slow Cooker and place in it the chicken, leek, tomatoes with juice, celery, bay leaf, carrots, garlic. Add some pepper and salt to taste.

2. Cover with water and chicken broth and cook for 6 hours on low mode. Cut the chard leaves into one-inch pieces and place in separate bowl.

3. Add the sliced cabbage, halved zucchini and refrigerate until the broth is prepared.

4. When the broth is ready, add in the vegetable and combine well. Turn the Slow Cooker on HIGH and leave for 30 minutes.

5. To serve, add the pasta into your soup.

Nutrition: Calories: 551 Fat: 37g Carbohydrates: 42g Protein: 53g

Tomato Soup with Rigatoni

You should try this Italian receipt!

Prep time: 25 minutes Cooking time: 3 hours Servings: 8

INGREDIENTS:

6 cups tomato sauce

2 tbsp. olive oil

Salt

Half tsp sugar

One package rigatoni

4 cloves garlic

2cups whole-milk

Half cup Parmesan Cheese

Red pepper to taste

DIRECTIONS:

1. Coat the inside dish of your Slow Cooker with a cooking spray Rinse the rigatoni in cold water and drain carefully.

2. Right in the bowl of your Slow Cooker mix the noodles, cottage cheese, tomato sauce, one cup shredded mozzarella, olive oil, spinach, garlic, sugar, red pepper and salt. Stir well.

3. Turn on the Slow Cooker and set the LOW temperature mode. Prepare the rigatoni for 3-4 hours. In ten minutes before ready cover with Parmesan and cook until the cheese is melted.

Nutrition: Calories: 469 Fat: 43g Carbohydrates: 55g Protein: 63g

Chicken and Burrito Bowls

Small bowl and plenty of energy!

Prep time: 5 minutes Cooking time: 3 hours Servings: 3

INGREDIENTS:

One or two chicken breasts (boneless)

2 tsp chili powder

One cup brown rice

2 tsp salt

One cup chicken stock

One can diced tomatoes

One teaspoon cumin

One cup frozen corn

One can black beans

DIRECTIONS:

1. Cover the chicken breasts with diced tomatoes, mix well and add half-cup chicken stock, cumin, chili powder and salt.

2. Place in a wide Slow Cooker dish. Ingredients should cover chicken evenly. Cover the lid and leave the chicken to cook on HIGH for 3-4 hours.

3. When it is time, add the rice, frozen corn, black beans and chicken corn. Continue to cook under the lid for another 4 hours.

4. When the rice is ready, use two forks and shred the chicken into small pieces (bite-size). Serve the burrito in small bowls garnished with cheese or diced green onions.

Nutrition: Calories: 551 Fat: 30g Carbohydrates: 146g Protein: 51g

Mac and Cheese pasta in Slow Cooker

Amazing pasta for your healthy lunch!

Prep time: 26 minutes Cooking time: 2-3 hours Servings: 8

INGREDIENTS:

3 cups shredded Cheddar

Half teaspoon salt

Two cups whole milk

One cap elbow macaroni

Half teaspoon dry mustard

Two cups whole milk

DIRECTIONS:

1. Combine the ingredients (except cheese) in Slow Cooker. Stir well to combine everything evenly. Cover with the lid and cook on HIGH from 2 to 4 hours.

2. In 2 hours after you started the cooking process, check if the pasta is soft and there is no liquid. When it is 10 minutes remaining to finish, sprinkle the cheese over the pasta and cook until the cheese is melted.

3. Serve this pasta straight from the cooking dish.

Nutrition: Calories: 566 Fat: 36g Carbohydrates: 48g Protein: 61g

Lamb Shank in Slow Cooker

Try this lamb – and you will not forget it!

Prep time: 15 minutes Cooking time: 3 hours Servings: 6

INGREDIENTS:

2 tbsp. plain flour

2 tbsp. olive oil

Six lamb shanks

One brown onion

Half cup red wine

2 cups tomato pasta

2 garlic cloves

2 cups chicken broth or stock

3 sprigs rosemary (fresh)

5 small potatoes

One peeled turnip

chopped fresh parsley

DIRECTIONS:

1. Mix the flour with salt and pepper. Place the lamb shanks into the mixture and toss to cover well. Cover a large frying pan with olive oil and fry lamb shanks until browned from both sides.

2. Add the garlic and chopped onion to the pan and cook until lightly softened.

3. Place the lamb into Slow Cooker; add wine, stock, rosemary, pasta and bay leaves. Add carrots and peas to the dish.

4. Cover the dish and cook for 3-4 hours on HIGH temperature.

5. Before the serving stir in minced parsley and season with salt and pepper.

Nutrition: Calories: 602 Fat: 9g Carbohydrates: 21g Protein: 60g

SIDE DISHES RECIPES

Sweet Potato Lentils in Slow Cooker

Sweet, fast and healthy potatoes!

Prep time: 23 minutes Cooking time: 3 hours Servings: 6-8

INGREDIENTS:

Three sweet potatoes

One minced onion

Three cups vegetable broth

One cup water

Four cloves garlic

Half teaspoon salt

One can coconut milk

Chili powder

Coriander

Garam masala

1-2 cups red lentils (uncooked)

DIRECTIONS:

1. Peel and dice the potatoes, mince the onion.
2. Preheat the Slow Cooker and fill it with sweet potatoes, minced onion, vegetable broth, garlic and spices.
3. Cover with vegetable broth and cook on high mode for 2-3 hours (or until the vegetables are soft). Add the lentils and cook on HIGH for one more 1-2 hours until ready.
4. Pour in the coconut milk and water (as you need to get the right consistency) Serve with fresh bread or toasts.

Nutrition: Calories: 326 Fat: 11g Carbohydrates: 44g Protein: 13g

Butternut Squash with Chili

Delicious squash can be healthy – try it!

Prep time: 10 minutes Cooking time: 6 hours Servings: 8

INGREDIENTS:

One small onion

2 carrots

2 stalks celery

1 medium butternut squash

2 medium apples

4 cloves garlic

2 tsp chili powder

2 cups vegetable broth

One can black beans

1 can coconut oil (low-fat)

1 can chickpeas (medium)

2 tsp oregano (dried)

1tbsp ground cumin

Basmati rice (optional)

Pepper/salt to taste

2tbsp tomato paste Fresh parsley

Shredded coconut (to garnish)

DIRECTIONS:

1. Place all the ingredients (except the garnish and rice) into Slow Cooker.
2. Cook on HIGH temperature mode for 3 to 6 hours. If you want, you can leave it overnight for 8 hours (then cook on low mode).
3. On the last hour of cooking taste and add some salt and pepper.
4. If you like it spicy, you can also add some chili powder or a pinch of cayenne pepper. In the last 30-40 minutes remove the lid and let the chili to thicken.
5. To serve, pour the chili over basmati rice and garnish shredded coconut and parsley.

Nutrition: Calories: 544 Fat: 28g Carbohydrates: 65g Protein: 50g

Tikka Masala with Chicken in Slow Cooker

Try this delicious chicken soup as your lunch!

Prep time: 5 minutes Cooking time: 4-8 hours Servings: 8

INGREDIENTS:

2-3chicken thighs (without bones)

2 cloves garlic

2 tbsp tomato paste

2 tsp paprika

2 tbsp garam masala

1 can diced tomatoes

Small ginger

1 large onion

Salt

Fresh cilantro

3 tbsp coconut milk

2 cups cooked rice

DIRECTIONS:

1. Cut the chicken into bite-sized pieces. Place the chicken into Slow Cooker.

2. Dice the onion and place it over the chicken, add minced ginger and garlic, garam masala, salt, paprika. Cover with tomato paste and stir everything well to fully cover the chicken.

3. Cover the Slow Cooker and set HIGH temperature for 4 hours or LOW for 8 hours.

4. 15 minutes before the end of cooking time mix in the cream and add more species if needed. Serve with the rice and fresh cilantro.

Nutrition: Calories: 477 Fat: 34g Carbohydrates: 61g Protein: 55g

Enchilada Soup with Chicken

Unusual, but healthy and amazing receipt!

Prep time: 27 minutes Cooking time: 6-7 hours Servings: 6

INGREDIENTS:

Cooking oil

1 tbsp sugar

2 tbsp chili powder

1 medium onion

2 garlic cloves

One can tomato sauce

Two medium tomatoes

2 cups chicken stock or broth

1 tbsp ground cumin

1 large jalapeno

1 can yellow corn

1can black beans

2-3 chicken thighs

Salt and black pepper to taste

DIRECTIONS:

1. Heat two tablespoons of oil in a large frying pan (medium heat).

2. Place the jalapeno and diced onions and cook until soft (5-7 minutes).

3. Add chili powder, garlic, sugar, cumin, and cook until fragrant. Add the tomatoes, the stock and tomato sauce. After a little boil transfer to Slow Cooker.

4. Add the chicken, beans, corn, and cook covered for 6-7 hours on LOW temperature mode. Before serving shred the chicken with two forks and stir in the heavy cream (optional).

5. Serve with a bit of Cheddar cheese, cilantro or tortilla chips as a garnish.

Nutrition: Calories: 501 Fat: 41g Carbohydrates: 55g Protein: 61g

Pea Soup with Cheese Croutons

One soup is good, but with cheese croutons, it is so much better!

Prep time: 12-20 minutes Cooking time: 5-6 hours Servings: 4

INGREDIENTS:

Green split peas (dried)

Two bay leaves

One small onion

Two celery stalks

Two tbsp. olive oil

One tsp salt

Two carrots (medium)

Black pepper (freshly ground)

For croutons: 4 slices bread and smoked cheese

DIRECTIONS:

1. Cover the bottom of your Slow Cooker with split peas (place them in an even layer). Chop well and add the onion, celery, bay leaves, carrot, salt and pepper.

2. Pour in the water (do not stir) and cook for 5 to 6 hours on HIGH temperature mode. In the end of cooking time check the peas – they should be soft.

3. After ready, stir the soup to integrate the broth with the peas.

4. To make the croutons, cut bread into small cubes and place on the baking sheet. Sprinkle with the cheese and fry until golden brown.

5. Serve only hot.

Nutrition: Calories: 478 Fat: 43g Carbohydrates: 52g Protein: 29g

Greek lamb shanks with lemon and cheese

Overnight, but so delicious meal for your lunch!

Prep time: 15 minutes Cooking time: 8 hours Servings: 6

INGREDIENTS:

2tbsp. olive oil (extra virgin)

6 lamb shanks

One cup beef stock

Half cup tomato passata

One brown onion (chopped)

Three sprigs thyme

2 tbsp. lemon juice

3 garlic cloves

1tbsp. dried oregano

5-6 large potatoes

DIRECTIONS:

1. Heat the olive oil in a large frying pan. Add chopped onion and fry, stirring, for five minutes just to get soft. Then, transfer to Slow Cooker.

2. Increase the heat under the pan and cook lamb for 3-4 minutes until browned from all sides. Place to Slow Cooker.

3. Cover the lamb with lemon juice, passata, minced garlic, stock, thyme, oregano and sugar. Set the Slow Cooker on HIGH mode and cook for 4-5 hours (for LOW mode cook for 8 hours).

4. In a large saucepan, bring to boil the potatoes and cook for 8 minutes (untill tender). Drain.

5. To serve cut potatoes and sprinkle the shanks with cheese. Garnish with the olives.

Nutrition: Calories: 532 Fat: 15g Carbohydrates: 38g Protein: 41g

Coconut soup with red lentil and spinach

The unusual combination of the ingredients will amuse you!

Prep time: 5 minutes Cooking time: 3 hours Servings: 4-6

INGREDIENTS:

One tbsp. olive oil

2tbsp. minced garlic

1 tsp coriander seed (ground)

1 tsp ground cumin

1 large onion

Half tsp Garam Masala

1 tsp ground turmeric

1 tsp cinnamon

One cup red lentils

4 cups vegetable stock

4 cups chopped spinach

1 can coconut milk

Salt and black pepper to taste

DIRECTIONS:

1. Heat the oil in your favorite frying pan and cook chopped onion until brown (for 6-8 minutes).

2. Add ground cumin, minced garlic, ground turmeric, coriander, cinnamon and Garam Masala. Cook for 1-2 minutes and transfer this spiced mixture right to your Slow Cooker.

3. Pick over and rinse the lentils, combine with vegetable stock and transfer to Slow Cooker. Cook on HIGH for 2-3 hours (LOW for 4-5).

4. In the end add to Slow Cooker the coconut milk and chopped spinach. Serve with sliced lime or plain Greek yogurt.

Nutrition: Calories: 601 Fat: 54g Carbohydrates: 77g Protein: 57g

Barbecue Sandwich with Lentils

So simple and satisfying!

Prep time: 5 minutes Cooking time: 1-2 hours Servings: 3

INGREDIENTS:

Canned tomatoes

Half cup blackstrap molasses

2 tbsp. white vinegar

3 garlic cloves

Canned tomato paste

Half teaspoon salt

Cayenne pepper

Red pepper flakes

2 tbsp. apple cider vinegar

1 medium sweet onion

1 tsp. coconut sugar

1teaspoon dry mustard

DIRECTIONS:

1. Preheat your Slow Cooker and cover with olive oil.

2. Place all the ingredients (except lentils) in a food processor or mix them with usual kitchen blender.

3. Place the sauce mixture in the Slow Cooker and boil for 1-2 hour on LOW temperature mode. In separate saucepan, bring to boil the lentils and set aside.

4. When the sauce is ready, mix in the lentils.

5. To serve, cut the bread into slices and cover them with butter.

Nutrition: Calories: 472 Fat: 44g Carbohydrates: 62g Protein: 71g

Pumpkin Oats with Vanilla

Another autumn and healthy lunch!

Prep time: 5 minutes Cooking time: 6-8 hours Servings: 3-4

INGREDIENTS:

One cup steel cut oats

2tbsp. pumpkin pie spice

4 cups water

2 tsps. vanilla extract (pure)

One cup canned pumpkin puree

1 cup brown sugar

DIRECTIONS:

1. Preheat your Slow Cooker for 150-170 degrees.
2. In a large bowl, combine one-cup oats, pumpkin puree one-cup brown sugar.
3. Cover with four cups of water and spice with the pumpkin pie spice and vanilla extract.
4. Place all ingredients in your Slow Cooker and prepare for 6 (for LOW temperature mode) or 8 (for HIGH mode) hours. Stir the mixture time after time, if possible.
5. Before serving. Season to taste with salt or add (if needed) more brown sugar.

Nutrition: Calories: 688 Fat: 48g Carbohydrates: 60g Protein: 78g

Indian Spiced Lentils

Indian cuisine is perfect for your lunchtime!

Prep time: 10-15 minutes Cooking time: 3 hours Servings: 3-5

INGREDIENTS:

Two cup cooked lentils

1 medium onion (finely diced)

1 yellow pepper

1 large sweet potato

Half tsp ground ginger

1 can tomato sauce

3 cloves diced garlic

2 tsp cumin

Cayenne pepper

2 tsp paprika

1tsp turmeric (ground)

1 tsp coriander

Half cup vegetable broth

Juice of 1 lemon

Pepper and salt to taste

DIRECTIONS:

1. Chop all the vegetables to small cubes. To make the process a way faster, use a food processor or kitchen blender.
2. Place all your vegetables in the Slow Cooker and cover with species. Pour over the organic vegetable broth.
3. Cook on HIGH temperature mode for 3 hours (until the potatoes are soft). To serve, prepare the brown rice or just cut the naan bread.

Nutrition: Calories: 576 Fat: 44g Carbohydrates: 76g Protein: 51g

Quinoa Risotto with Asparagus

Make your lunch tastier with asparagus!

Prep time: 15 minutes Cooking time: 4 hours Servings: 6

INGREDIENTS:

One cup rinsed quinoa

Chicken breasts

Salt

2cups chicken broth

One bunch asparagus

Black pepper (freshly ground)

2 cup peas (canned or frozen)

Three large carrots

2 cloves garlic

DIRECTIONS:

1. Spray your slow cooker with a special cooking spray.
2. Right in a cooking dish, combine chicken, one cup chicken broth, rinsed quinoa, carrots and garlic. Season with pepper and salt as you like.
3. Cover with the lid and cook on HIGH for 3-4 hours (until the chicken is easy to shred). Shred the chicken, add the peas and asparagus and cook for 30-40 minutes more.
4. Add the remaining cup of chicken broth and continue stirring until creamy.

Nutrition: Calories: 668 Fat: 54g Carbohydrates: 83g Protein: 67g

Rice noodles with Coconut Beef

This will satisfy you until the dinner!

Prep time: 15 minutes Cooking time: 7 hours Servings: 4

INGREDIENTS:

2 tbsp. red curry paste

5 tbsp. light coconut milk

2 clove garlic

Salt

2 tsp ginger (grated)

Rice noodles

Half red onion

Snap peas

2 tbsp. fresh lime juice

Beef stew meat

Half cup basil leaves (fresh)

Chopped peanuts (optional)

DIRECTIONS:

1. Right in your Slow Cooker whisk the coconut milk with minced garlic, curry paste, salt and ginger. Cut the beef and add it inti coconut milk mixture. Toss well to cover the meat fully.

2. Turn on your Slow Cooker and cook under the lid for 6-7 hours on LOW mode or 4-5 hours on HIGH (check when the meat easily falls apart).

3. Cook the rice noodles according to directions on the package.

4. 15 minutes before the end of cooking time fold in the peas, lime juice and onion. Cook for 3 more minutes.

5. Serve with sprinkled peanuts.

Nutrition: Calories: 767 Fat: 43g Carbohydrates: 68g Protein: 54g

Chicken with rice and sesame

Asian dish for a lunch? Give it a chance!

Prep time: 15 minutes Cooking time: 5-6 hours Servings: 6

INGREDIENTS:

3 tbsp soy sauce

3-4 tbsp rice wine

1 tbsp brown sugar

8 clove garlic

3 tbsp toasted sesame oil

2 boneless chicken breasts without skin

1 fresh ginger

Half cup broccoli florets

4 cup white rice (can use frozen cooked)

2 green onions (sliced)

DIRECTIONS:

7. Take a small bowl and whisk the rice wine, toasted sesame oil, soy sauce and brown sugar in it. Spray the Slow Cooker with anti-sticking spray.

8. Place the chicken into the cooking dish, cover with soy mixture, fresh chopped ginger and garlic. Cover the cooking dish and turn the Slow Cooker on LOW mode. Cook for 5-6 hours.

9. Shred the chicken when ready.

10. Serve with warmed rice and broccoli florets. Garnish the meal with sliced green onions.

Nutrition: Calories: 812 Fat: 54g Carbohydrates: 78g Protein: 69g

Steak with Onions and Pepper

Meat and vegetables – a perfect lunchtime couple!

Prep time: 11 minutes Cooking time: 8 hours Servings: 4-5

INGREDIENTS:

One red pepper (diced)

One onion

Salt/pepper to taste

One tsp chili powder

One flank steak

Half mango

Cinnamon

One cup rice (long-grain)

3 tbsp fresh cilantro

DIRECTIONS:

1. Cover the bottom and sides of your Slow Cooker with cooking spray or butter.

2. Dice the onion and bell pepper, mix in tomatoes, cinnamon. Chili powder, add salt and pepper to taste.

3. Place the beef parts among the vegetable mixture.

4. Cover with the cooking dish lid and prepare for 4-5 hours (on HIGH temperature) or 6-7 (on LOW). In the end, check if the meat is tender and easy falls apart.

5. 25-30 minutes before serving cook the rice (follow the package directions). To serve, shred the meat with two forks and garnish the mango pieces.

Nutrition:

Calories: 677 Fat: 43g Carbohydrates: 66g Protein: 32g

Caesar sandwiches with Chicken

Don't have much time? Try this one!

Prep time: 20 minutes Cooking time: 3-4 hours Servings: 4-7

INGREDIENTS:

4 chicken breasts (skinless and boneless)

Half cup shredded parmesan

Half cup Caesar dressing

1 tbsp parsley

Romaine leaves

2 tsp pepper

Hamburger buns

DIRECTIONS:

1. Place the chicken breasts into the Slow Cooker dish ansd pour in half cup water.
2. Turn on the Slow Cooker and prepare the chicken for 3-4 hours on LOW temperature mode. Take out the chicken and shred the meat with the forks.
3. Return the meat back to Slow Cooker and stir well.
4. Add the Caesar dressing, parmesan, pepper, parsley and combine well. Cook on low mode for another 30 minutes, the remove.
5. Serve as sandwiches on the buns with romaine leaves.

Nutrition: Calories: 674 Fat: 39g Carbohydrates: 78g Protein: 98g

Thai Chicken in Slow Cooker

Another amazing Asian dish!

Prep time: 17 minutes Cooking time: 4 hours Servings: 6

INGREDIENTS:

Half coconut milk (light)

1 tbsp red curry paste

2 tbsp natural peanut butter (fat0reduced)

1 tsp grated ginger

1 large onion

1cup frozen peas

2 red bell pepper

Fresh cilantro leaves

2 chicken thighs (boneless)

Lime wedges (to serve)

1 cup rice noodles

DIRECTIONS:

1. In the Slow Cooker dish mix together the coconut milk, curry paste, peanut butter and ginger. Mix in the diced onion, peppers and whole chicken.
2. Cover with the dish lid and cook on LOW (for 5-6 hours) or HIGH (3-4 hours) temperatures. 12-15 minutes before serving cook the noodles (follow the package directions).
3. Add the peas into the chicken mixture, cook for another 3 minutes. Serve together, garnishing with lime wedges.

Nutrition: Calories: 469 Fat: 39g Carbohydrates: 65g Protein: 57g

Pork Tacos with Cabbage

Small and delicious tacos for the fast lunch!

Prep time: 15-17 minutes Cooking time: 5 hours Servings: 4

INGREDIENTS:

One large orange

Two clove garlic

1 medium carrot

Salt

1 pork shoulder

Pepper

Pinch red pepper flakes

2 tbsp soy sauce

3 tbsp brown sugar

2 tbsp olive oil

8 small flour tortillas

1 tbsp grated fresh ginger

Half red cabbage

DIRECTIONS:

1. Cut for strips of zest from orange (you can use a vegetable peeler).
2. Right in the Slow Cooker dish, mix the vinegar, soy sauce, sugar, red pepper, ginger, orange zest and garlic.
3. Add pork and toss well to cover.
4. Turn the Slow Cooker on and cook until tender – 7-8 hours on LOW or 3-5 hours on HIGH modes. Prepare the slaw: take a large bowl and squeeze the orange juice into it. Add the oil, pepper and salt. Add the carrot and other vegetables.
5. Warm the tortillas and fill them with the slaw and shredded pork.

Nutrition: Calories: 601 Fat: 42g Carbohydrates: 53g Protein: 78g

Simple Salsa Chicken

Easy to make and very satisfying!

Prep time: 5-11 minutes Cooking time: 6-8 hours Servings: 6

INGREDIENTS:

4 chicken breasts (skinless and boneless)

Salt

2 cups salsa (take your favorite)

Pepper

Fresh lime wedges (optional for serving)

DIRECTIONS:

1. Cover the bottom of your Slow Cooker with butter or anti-sticking spray. Place whole chicken breasts into the cooking dish and cover with salsa.

2. Cover the lid, turn on the Slow Cooker and prepare for 4 hours on HIGH or up to 6-8 hours on LOW.

3. When the chicken is soft, shred with two forks, toss well with salsa.

4. You can serve in with bread or any dish immediately or refrigerate up to 5-6 days.

Nutrition: Calories: 433 Fat: 55g Carbohydrates: 65g Protein: 38g

Summer Risotto with mushrooms and peas

So delicious risotto will make your day brighter!

Prep time: 20 minutes Cooking time: 3-4 hours Servings: 8

INGREDIENTS:

3 tbsp olive oil

4 cups vegetable broth

Half cut dry white wine

Half cup sliced shallots

Parmesan cheese (grated)

Half teaspoon black pepper

1 cup uncooked rice

1 cloves garlic

3 cups mushrooms (sliced)

DIRECTIONS:

1. Warm olive oil in a large skillet (over medium heat).

2. Add the shallots, garlic and mushrooms. Stirring, sauté for several minutes (5-7), until lightly browned. The mushrooms are ready when all the liquid is evaporated.

3. Stir the rice into the mushroom mixture and cook for another 1-2 minutes. Place the saucepan mixture into the Slow Cooker.

4. Add the wine, broth, and pepper.

5. Cover the lid and leave cooking for 2-3 hours on HIGH. In the end stir in peas and cover with cheese.

6. Serve while hot.

Nutrition: Calories: 552 Fat: 64g Carbohydrates: 78g Protein: 87g

Spring Minestrone in Slow Cooker

Perfect for springtime and fresh vegetables!

Prep time: 15 minutes Cooking time: 4-6 hours Servings: 4-7

INGREDIENTS:

One sweet onion

Three cups water

3 cups vegetable stock

3 carrots

3 garlic cloves

One can diced tomatoes

2 cans beans

Fresh spinach

Uncooked pasta

12 asparagus spears

One cup frozen peas (sweet)

Half cup cheese (freshly grated)

DIRECTIONS:

1. Start with dicing the vegetables, cut the onions, carrots, mince garlic. Add the can of diced tomatoes and beans.

2. Place these ingredients into Slow Cooker and pour over with the stock. Leave cooking on LOW temperature modes for 4-6 hours.

3. When it is 15-17 minutes left before serving, add asparagus. If you want, season with salt and any pepper you like.

4. Serve hot and covered with some cheese.

Nutrition: Calories: 752 Fat: 45g Carbohydrates: 63g Protein: 76g

Frittata with Red Pepper and Feta

So heathy and delicious, you will not forget it!

Prep time: 5 minutes Cooking time: 2-3 hours Servings: 3-5

INGREDIENTS:

1-2 tsp olive oil

3 tbsp sliced green onion

Half cup crumbled Feta

Baby kale

Roasted red pepper

8 chicken eggs

Fresh ground black pepper

DIRECTIONS:

1. Tale a large saucepan. Cover the bottom with olive oil and add kale. sauté the kale for 3-5 minutes until it is softened.

2. Spray the bottom of your Slow Cooker with anti-sticking spray and place the kale inside of it. Turn the Slow Cooker and set on LOW mode.

3. Chop the red peppers into small pieces. Crumble the peppers with feta, sliced onions, and add to the kale in Slow Cooker.

4. Pour in the beaten egg and stir well until fully combined. Continue cooking on LOW temperature for another 2-3 hours. Serve hot.

Nutrition: Calories: 577 Fat: 43g Carbohydrates: 69g Protein: 44g

Chicken Taquitos in Slow Cooker

Small and fast - just try and prepare it!

Prep time: 5 minutes Cooking time: 10 hours Servings: 3-6

INGREDIENTS:

2 chicken breasts

Half cup sour cream

Half cup chicken broth

1 tsp chipotle chili powder

Cream cheese

2 diced chipotles

1 tsp cumin

Ground black pepper

1 tsp onion powder

1 tsp garlic powder

Half teaspoon salt

8-12 tortilla rounds

1 cup cheddar cheese

Avocado, sour cream, red onion (for topping)

DIRECTIONS:

1. Place the chicken breasts in your Slow Cooker, cover with chicken broth, sour cream, chipotles, cream cheese, chipotle chili powder garlic, cumin, salt, onion and black pepper.

2. Turn the Slow Cooker on and prepare for 4-6 hours (using LOW temperature mode) or up to 10 hours (on HIGH mode).

3. Preheat your oven to 180-200 degrees and spray the baking tray with cooking spray.

4. Place the couple of tablespoons of shredded chicken into each tortilla and cover with cheese. Roll in and bake in oven for 10-13 minutes.

5. Serve hot with your favorite topping.

Nutrition: Calories: 533 Fat: 23g Carbohydrates: 29g Protein: 61g

Korean Beef Tacos in Slow Cooker

A little spicy Korean dish for your lunch!

Prep time: 5 minutes Cooking time: 9-10 hours Servings: 4

INGREDIENTS:

One beef steak

3 tbsp soy sauce

1\4 white wine (dry)

One red onion

4 tbsp brown sugar

4 garlic cloves

Half tsp freshly ground pepper

2 limes

1 cup cilantro

Salt

Halg cup seedless cucumbers

3 chopped scallions

5 medium tomatoes

8 corn tortillas

DIRECTIONS:

1. Right in the cooking dish of Slow Cooker mix soy sauce, brown sugar, white wine, smashed garlic cloves and black pepper.

2. Place the steak into the spice mixture and add halved onion. Cook on LOW for 9 hours. On a sheet pan, broil the peeled and halved tomatoes (until brown on both sides).

3. With a food processor, mix the tomatoes, cilantro, garlic, half red onion, juice of two limes, salt and scallions.

4. To serve, shred the beef and place it in part along with other ingredients over corn tortillas. Roll in and enjoy!

Nutrition: Calories: 376 Fat: 42g Carbohydrates: 21g Protein: 34g

Quinoa Chicken in Slow Cooker

Fast and easy! Just try this healthy one!

Prep time: 10-13 minutes Cooking time: 3-4 hours Servings: 8

INGREDIENTS:

One and half cups quinoa

1-2 chicken breasts (boneless and skinless)

4-7 cloves garlic

4-7 cups chicken broth

Salt and other spices (to your taste)

1 tbsp olive oil

Oe lemon juice

1 bunch asparagus

2 cups peas (frozen)

Parmesan (for topping)

DIRECTIONS:

1. Wash and rinse the quinoa.
2. Cut the chicken into small pieces (it will be ready much faster).
3. Place the chicken, quinoa, garlic, seasonings in your Slow Cooker, Cover with chicken broth. Cover with the lid and leave to cook on LOW temperature for 3-4 hours.
4. When ready, add the lemon juice, pesto and peas, stir well.
5. Meanwhile heat the pan and sauté asparagus until tender-crisp. Add to Slow Cooker. Top each tortilla with shredded cheese and fresh herbs.

Nutrition: Calories: 235 Fat: 31g Carbohydrates: 23g Protein: 43g

Slow Cooker ham and pea soup

Easy-to-make soup! Perfect for springtime!

Prep time: 10 minutes Cooking time: 8 hours Servings: 9

INGREDIENTS:

5 medium carrots

Chopped ham

4 stalks celery

4 cups chicken broth

1 chopped onion

2 cups water

1 bag split peas

Smoked paprika (optional)

Fresh chopped parsley

DIRECTIONS:

1. Peel and cut all the vegetables into small pieces.
2. Combine the onion, carrots, ham, celery, peas with broth and water. You can do it right in your Slow Cooker.
3. Turn the Slow Cooker and on set to LOW mode. Cook for 7-10 hours. The peas should be broken. Add one more cup of water if needed.
4. Serve into small bowl. Use chopped parsley as a garnish.

Nutrition: Calories: 538 Fat: 29g Carbohydrates: 52g Protein: 33g

Baked beans in Slow Cooker

It takes a lot of cooking time, but it totally worth it!

Prep time: 5 minutes Cooking time: 12-16 hours Servings: 6

INGREDIENTS:

1 cup bourbon

Dried navy beans

1 cup barbecue sauce

3 tbsp. olive oil

1 cup water

1 cup maple syrup

2 tbsp. Worcestershire sauce

1 cup brown sugar

Mustard molasses

2 tbsp. apple vinegar

DIRECTIONS:

1. Sort dry beans and rinse them over sink.
2. In a large pot, cover the beans with some water and leave to soak overnight.
3. Place the beans with 6 cups of water into separate bowl pot and simmer for 45 minutes. Meanwhile, combine all the remaining ingredients in the Slow Cooker and mix well.
4. Add the beans in your Slow Cooker and cook on LOW mode for 12 hours (but start to check the readiness at about 7-8 hours).
5. Serve while hot.

Nutrition: Calories: 612 Fat: 34g Carbohydrates: 29g Protein: 45g

White Chicken Chili in Slow Cooker

Chicken with beans – a perfect lunchtime match!

Prep time: 5 minutes Cooking time: 4 hours Servings: 6-8

INGREDIENTS:

One yellow onion (large)

3 cloves garlic

Two boneless chicken thighs

1 bay leaf

Half tsp dried oregano

1 cup frozen corn

2 stalks celery

2 tsp cumin

1 can chili pepper (green)

Salt

4cups chicken stock

1 can navy beans

Monterey jack cheese to serve

DIRECTIONS:

1. Prepare you Slow Cooker and place into it the chicken, celery, garlic, onions, green chili peppers, salt, coriander, cumin, bay leaf and oregano. Stir to cover the meat with spices.

2. Pour in the chicken broth to cover the ingredients.

3. Place the Slow Cooker lid and prepare for 6 hours on HIGH modes (or 4 on low). In 30 minutes before the end, add the beans and corn.

4. Shred the chicken well and stir with another ingredients.

5. Serve with lime wedges, shredded cheese or chopped cilantro.

Nutrition: Calories: 434 Fat: 34g Carbohydrates: 46g Protein: 28g

Thai Red Curry in Slow Cooker

A little spicy, but healthy and delicious!

Prep time: 30 minutes Cooking time: 8-9 hours Servings: 4

INGREDIENTS:

Salt

Half cup brown sugar

1 cup coconut milk

Black pepper

Pork shoulder

2 tbsp curry paste

1 quartered onion

Ginger

16 corn tortillas

4 crushed garlic cloves

Vegetable oil

Chopped jalapenos

2 tbsp radishes (chopped)

2 tbsp green onions (chopped)

DIRECTIONS:

1. Right in Slow Cooker, toss pork pieces with salt and pepper.

2. In separate bowl, combine coconut milk, curry paste and brown sugar. Pour the mixture to the Slow Cooker dish.

3. Add ginger, garlic, chicken broth and onion, mix and cook on LOW temperature mode for 8-9 hours.

4. Drain and finely shred the pork.

5. Warm corn tortillas on nonstick skillet. Fill them with the shredded pork. To serve, sprinkle with sour cream or add radishes or green onions.

Nutrition: Calories: 563 Fat: 54g Carbohydrates: 32g Protein: 28g

Slow cooker peas with asparagus

Another dish with asparagus – overnight and healthy!

Prep time: 15 minutes Cooking time: 9 hours Servings: 4

INGREDIENTS:

2 tbsp olive oil

Salt

Boneless beef

2 cup red wine (dry)

2 bay leaves

Black pepper (freshly ground)

1 tbsp tomato paste

2 large onions

Frozen peas

Trimmed asparagus

1 cup chicken broth

2 cloves garlic

DIRECTIONS:

1. Take a large skillet and heat it with olive oil. Place the meat and fry well from all sides.

2. In the Slow Cooker bowl, mix salt, bay leaves, tomato paste, pepper, garlic and crushed tomatoes. Pour over with the broth, stir well and cook on LOW temperature mode for 6-9 hours.

3. In a large skilled, half-filled with water, bring to boil asparagus. Then cook for 4-5 minutes. Add frozen peas and leave cooking for another 2 minutes.

4. Slice the meat into small pieces.

5. Serve with veggies and topped with braising liquid.

Nutrition: Calories: 672 Fat: 62g Carbohydrates: 27g Protein: 34g

Tacos and Sriracha Mayo

Fast answer to your lunchtime question!

Prep time: 10 minutes Cooking time: 8 hours Servings: 4

INGREDIENTS:

Half cup whole milk

One halved orange

One small onion

Olive oil

Half cup mayonnaise

5 garlic cloves

2 limes

1 tbsp sriracha

1 tsp oregano

Red onion

Cilantro

Radishes

Salt

Pork shoulder

DIRECTIONS:

1. In the Slow Cooker bowl, mix the orange juice, 1-cup water, oil, milk, orange rinds, oregano, onion, pork shoulder and garlic.

2. Mix well and cook on LOW temperature modes for 8 hours.

3. In another small bowl, combine Sriracha, mayonnaise, lime juice and salt.

4. Take out the pork and reserve the excess fat and liquid. Cut meat into small slices. Warm tortillas in nonstick frying pan.

5. Serve the pork wrapped in tortillas.

Nutrition: Calories: 439 Fat: 35g Carbohydrates: 65g Protein: 43g

Apple Cider Chicken in Slow Cooker

Fast and healthy dish for a family dinner!

Prep time: 5 minutes Cooking time: 3 hours Servings: 10-12

INGREDIENTS:

1-2 tablespoon olive oil

2 bay leaves

2 tsp chopped thyme

4 celery stalks

1 tbsp chopped fresh sage

Two small chickens

4 garlic cloves

1 medium yellow onion

3 cups chicken stock

1 tbsp cornstarch

Cayenne, paprika, black pepper

Salt

One tsp chili powder

Sliced apples for garnish

DIRECTIONS:

1. Preheat a large saucepan with olive oil. Add celery, bay leaves, garlic, and onion. Cook for 3-6 minutes until soften.

2. Add thyme, sage and cornstarch and cook, stirring, for one more minute. Add beans and chicken; pour over with the chicken stock.

3. Season with cayenne, salt, chili powder, paprika and cider.

4. Transfer the saucepan ingredients to preheated Slow Cooker and leave for 12 hours on LOW mode.

5. To serve, garnish with apple slices.

Nutrition: Calories: 349 Fat: 6g Carbohydrates: 45g Protein: 54g

Sweet Potatoes with Apples

Sweety apple recipe tastes awesome with meat or vegetables.

Prep time: 5 minutes Cooking time: 6-7 hours Servings: 10

INGREDIENTS:

6-7 not big sweet potatoes

One cup whipping cream

1-2 tsp pumpkin spice

2 medium red apples

Half cup cranberries (dried)

DIRECTIONS:

1. Peel and cut the potatoes into small pieces (approximately one-inch cubes) Core and cut the apples into thin wedges

2. Spray your Slow Cooker with a cooking spray or cover with butter. Right in a cooking bowl combine the apples, potatoes and dried berries.

3. In a separate bowl, join the cream, pumpkin spice and apple butter. Pour the mixture over the apples.

4. Cover with the lid and cook for 6-7 hours on LOW-heat regimes or 3 hours on HIGH.

Nutrition: Calories: 351 Fat: 9g Carbohydrates: 65g Protein: 2g

Spinach Lasagna in Slow Cooker

Love Italian? Cook this easy-to-make lasagna!

Prep time: 30 minutes Cooking time: 3 hours Servings: 8

INGREDIENTS:

Frozen spinach

Half cup water

1 tsp dried parsley

One chicken egg

1 tbsp Italian seasoning

4 cups shredded mozzarella

3 tbsp tomato paste

12 lasagna noodles (uncooked)

Pinch red pepper

Half teaspoon garlic powder

2 jars tomato paste

1 cup grated parmesan

DIRECTIONS:

1. Take a large bowl and combine the ricotta, spinach, parmesan cheese, parsley and one egg.
2. In another bowl, whisk together water, pasta sauce, seasoning, garlic powder, and tomato paste and garlic powder.
3. Butter your Slow Cooker and spread the tomato paste over the bottom.
4. Place the lasagna noodles and ricotta mixture over the bottom. Cover with one cup Mozzarella. Repeat in 2-3 layers.
5. Cover the lid of Slow Cooker and prepare on LOW modes for 4-3 hours. To serve, leave lasagna for 30 minutes to cool.

Nutrition: Calories: 570 Fat: 31g Carbohydrates: 41g Protein: 33g

Broccoli and Cauliflower with Cheese topping

Amazing vegetable receipt for you and your family!

Prep time: 25 minutes Cooking time: 7 hours Servings: 10

INGREDIENTS:

1 large onion

Ground black pepper (to taste)

Four cups cauliflower florets

Four cups broccoli florets

Half cup almonds

1-2 cups Swiss cheese

One jar pasta sauce

Dried thyme

Crushed basil

DIRECTIONS:

1. Butter the bottom of your Slow Cooker or cover it with the anti-sticking cooking spray.
2. In a separate jar, combine chopped onion, broccoli, pasta sauce, cauliflower, Swiss cheese, thyme and pepper to taste.
3. Transfer the mixture into the Slow Cooker dish.
4. Cover with the lid and leave to cook for 6-7 hours (on LOW temperature modes) or for around 3 hours (on HIGH).
5. Serve while hot, sprinkled with almonds.

Nutrition: Calories: 177 Fat: 12g Carbohydrates: 10g Protein: 8g

Summer Vegetables with Chickpeas

Healthy and delicious choice for the summer!

Prep time: 25 minutes Cooking time: 8 Servings: 6

INGREDIENTS:

One can Garbanzo beans

2 tbsp olive oil

2 tbsp rosemary (fresh)

4 cups baby spinach

2 cups grape tomatoes

2 cloves garlic

Half teaspoon black pepper (ground)

10 baby carrots

2 fresh sweet corn

7-8 small potatoes

2 cups chopped chicken

1 medium onion

2 cups chicken broth

Zucchini

DIRECTIONS:

1. Combine garbanzo beans, oil, garlic, rosemary and pepper. You can do it in a plastic bowl with a lid or in a resalable plastic bag.

2. Place the bowl into the refrigerator and leave for 12-48 hours. Put the marinated (undrained) chickpeas into Slow Cooker.
3. Add corn, carrots, onion, tomatoes and potatoes.
4. Pour in the broth and cook on LOW-heat for 8-10 hours.
5. To serve, add zucchini, spinach and chicken (if desired). Stir until spinach wilts and serve immediately.

Nutrition: Calories: 273 Fat: 8g Carbohydrates: 42g Protein: 12g

Sweet Potatoes with Bacon

Try this one with bacon for your lunch or dinner!

Prep time: 17 minutes Cooking time: 5-6 hours Servings: 10

INGREDIENTS:

Half spoon dried thyme

8 large sweet potatoes

4 bacon slices

2 tbsp butter

Half tsp sage (dried)

Half cup orange juice

1 tsp salt

3 tbsp brown sugar

DIRECTIONS:

1. Peel and cut the potatoes into two-inch pieces.
2. To avoid sticking, cover the bottom of your Slow Cooker with some butter or special cooking spray.
3. Place the potatoes into Slow Cooker.
4. In a separate cooking bowl, combine the INGREDIENTS: juice, thyme, brown sugar, sage and salt. Add some butter.
5. Cover your Slow Cooker with the lid and cook on LOW heat temperature for 5-6 hours (or HIGH for 2-3 hours).
6. When serving, sprinkle slightly over with crumbled bacon.

Nutrition: Calories: 189 Fat: 4g Carbohydrates: 36g Protein: 4g

Mashed Potatoes with Garlic

Simple and healthy dish for your healthy lifestyle!

Prep time: 27 minutes Cooking time: 6-8 hours Servings: 12

INGREDIENTS:

5-6 large potatoes

1 leaf of bay

6 garlic cloves

One cup whole milk

3 tbsp butter

Black pepper (freshly ground)

1 tsp salt

2-3 cups chicken broth

DIRECTIONS:

1. Peel and cut potatoes into thin one-inch slices.
2. Place the potatoes into your Slow Cooker dish along with bay leaf and garlic. Mix in the chicken broth.
3. Cook covered on LOW temperature mode for 6-8 hours, or on HIGH temperature – for 3-4 hours. When ready, drain the potato using a colander (save the liquid) and remove the bay leaf.
4. Place the potatoes back to Slow Cooker and then mash with a potato masher.
5. In a small sauce pan, heat the milk with butter and add stir the mixture into the mash. Serve sprinkled with freshly ground pepper.

Nutrition: Calories: 135 Fat: 5g Carbohydrates: 21g Protein: 3g

Sweet and Spice beetroots

Sweet and unusual part of your diet!

Prep time: 15 minutes Cooking time: 6-7 hours Servings: 8

INGREDIENTS:

Half cup pomegranate juice

3 tbsp sugar

Salt to taste

1 tbsp cornstarch

2 tsp fresh ginger (grated)

5-6 golden or red beets

12 small carrots

DIRECTIONS:

1. Peel the carrots and beetroots with a vegetable peeler and cut into small three-inch pieces. Take a medium saucepan and mix in it pomegranate juice with salt and cornstarch. Stir in sugar and whisk until cornstarch is dissolved.
2. Stir in grated ginger and mix until smooth.
3. Right in a Slow Cooker dish, combine the pomegranate juice with the carrots and beetroots. Cover the Slow Cooker lid and prepare for 6 to 7 hours on HIGH heat –temperature setting (or 4-5 on LOW).

4. You can serve this meal warm (as a side dish) or cold (as a salad).

Nutrition: Calories: 126 Fat: 1g Carbohydrates: 29g Protein: 3g

Macaroni with American Cheese

Perfect for big cheese fans!

Prep time: 15 minutes Cooking time: 2 hours Servings: 8

INGREDIENTS:

One cup cayenne pepper sauce

2-3 medium carrots

Milk (optional)

Celery

Multigrain rotini pasta (can be packaged)

Dry salad dressing mix

American cheese

DIRECTIONS:

1. Peel and shred the carrots and thinly slice the celery. Torn the American cheese into bite-size pieces.
2. Cover the inside of your Slow Cooker with the butter. Add multigrain rotini pasta, carrots, celery and one cup cayenne pepper sauce.
3. Cover with four cups of water and stir well to combine completely.
4. Cover your Slow Cooker with the lid and cook on HIGH for a couple hours (until the pasta absorbs all the liquid).
5. Five minutes before the end add cheese and do not stir. To serve, add some milk for creamy taste.

Nutrition: Calories: 307 Fat: 11g Carbohydrates: 39g Protein: 14g

Squash Summer Gratin

Easy, healthy and delicious meal for any summer night!

Prep time: 13 minutes Cooking time: 7 hours Servings: 6

INGREDIENTS:

Three cloves garlic

Small butternut squash (or half big one)

Ground black pepper

One medium onion

Half cup water

Salt

One package frozen spinach

2 cups vegetarian broth

One cup plain barley

Half cup Parmesan

DIRECTIONS:

1. Pell, seed and cut butternut squash into small cubes (about 5-6 full cups). Cut the onion into small wedges.
2. In a Slow Cooker, mix the squash cubes, onion, barley, spinach, salt, garlic and pepper. Cover with the broth.
3. Turn on the Slow Cooker and cover with the lid. Cook for 6-7 hours at LOW temperature (or for 3 at HIGH).
4. Turn off the cooker and sprinkle with Parmesan. Let stand for 10 minutes and then serve.

Nutrition: Calories: 196 Fat: 3g Carbohydrates: 36g Protein: 9g

Squash in Cranberry Sauce

Try this one with cranberry sauce! So tasty and healthy, you will not regret!

Prep time: 19 minutes Cooking time: 7 hours Servings: 4

INGREDIENTS:

3-4 tbsp raisins

One can cranberry sauce (jellied)

4 tbsp orange marmalade

4 acorn squash

Ground cinnamon

Black pepper and salt

DIRECTIONS:

1. Wash each squash and cut in length; remove seeds and dice into one-inch wedges. Butter the bottom and sides of your Slow Cooker.
2. Place the squash wedges into Slow Cooker.
3. Heat the small saucepan with marmalade, cranberry sauce, cinnamon and raisins. Pour into the Slow Cooker and stir all the ingredients until smooth.
4. Set your Slow Cooker to LOW-temperature mode and leave the squash cooking for 6-7 hours (you can use HIGH temp as well and cook for 3 hours).
5. Before serving, add some salt and pepper to taste.

Nutrition: Calories: 328 Fat: 5g Carbohydrates: 71g Protein: 2g

Brussels sprouts and Maple Syrup

Unusual syrup will make the dish more delicious! Try this with your friends!

Prep time: 23 minutes Cooking time: 4 hours Servings: 12

INGREDIENTS:

Red onion (one cup)

Maple syrup

Half tsp salt

3 tbsp butter

Brussels sprouts

1 tbsp fresh thyme (snipped)

2-3 tbsp apple cider

Black pepper

DIRECTIONS:

1. Halve the Brussels sprouts; chop red onion and fresh thyme.
2. Combine the sprouts with onion right in your Slow Cooker dish, season a little with salt/pepper. Pour in the apple cider to cover slightly the vegetables.
3. Cover the lid and set the Slow Cooker on LOW-heat temperature regime for 3 hours (if want faster, cook on HIGH for 1-2 hours).
4. Meanwhile, mix together maple syrup, thyme and melted butter. Stir with the sprouts. To serve, garnish with fresh thyme leaves.

Nutrition: Calories: 90 Fat: 4g Carbohydrates: 13g Protein: 3g

Wild Rice with Cherries

Taste this combination of rice and berries!

Prep time: 20 minutes Cooking time: 5-6 hours Servings: 15

INGREDIENTS:

2-3 cups wild rice

2 cups chicken broth

2 tsps marjoram (dried and crushed)

2 tbsp melted butter

2 medium carrots

Half cup dried cherries

2 green onions

Salt to taste

Half cup chopped pecans

One cup sliced and drained mushrooms

DIRECTIONS:

1. Peel and coarsely shred the carrots and green onions.

2. Butter your Slow Cooker and fill it with uncooked wild rice, mushrooms, carrot, marjoram, salt, melted butter and pepper.
3. Pour in the broth to cover all the ingredients. Stir slightly.
4. Cover the Slow Cooker lid and prepare on LOW-temperature mode for 5 or 6 hours. Then turn off Slow Cooker.
5. Add dried cherries, pecans, green onions, and stir to combine the ingredients. To serve, use chopped green onions.

Nutrition: Calories: 169 Fat: 5g Carbohydrates: 27g Protein: 5g

Vegetable Curry with Garbanzo

Try to cook this vegetable dish with basil and beans!

Prep time: 25 minutes Cooking time: 5 or 6 hours Servings: 4

INGREDIENTS:

Three cups cauliflower florets

2-3 medium carrots

One cup green bean (frozen)

One can vegetable broth

One can coconut milk

2 tbsp fresh basil (shredded)

One can garbanzo beans

3-4 tsp curry powder

DIRECTIONS:

1. Cut the carrots and onions into small pieces.
2. In a separate bowl, gather cauliflower, green and garbanzo beans, onion and carrots. Season with curry powder.
3. Transfer the vegetable mix into the buttered Slow Cooker and pour in the broth.
4. Cover with the Slow Cooker lid and do not open until ready. Cook on LOW temperature for 5 or 6 hours or on HIGH – for 2 or 3.
5. In the end of cooking time add some basil and coconut milk and stir well to combine all the ingredients.

Nutrition: Calories: 219 Fat: 7g Carbohydrates: 32g Protein: 8g

Kale and Eggplant Panzanella

Healthy and spicy, it may become your favorite!

Prep time: 24 minutes Cooking time: 2 or 4 hours Servings: 6

INGREDIENTS:

Two medium eggplants

One medium pepper (sweet and yellow)

One can roasted tomatoes

3 tbsp red wine vinegar

2 tbsp olive oil

Half cup shredded Parmesan

One clove garlic

1 tsp Dijon mustard

Half cup basil (fresh leaves)

4 cups cubed French bread

One red onion

4 cups chopped kale leaves

DIRECTIONS:

1. Butter the inside of your Slow Cooker and put into it chopped eggplant, wedged onion and red pepper.

2. Cover Slow Cooker and set low temperature for 4 hours or HIGH temperature for 2 hours. In 2-3 hours stir in kale and cook for another 15 minutes.

3. Prepare the dressing: in a separate bowl, combine oil, mustard, vinegar, garlic and black pepper. Whisk all together well.

4. Serve the vegetables in a large bowl, sprinkled with the cheese and basil leaves.

Nutrition: Calories: 243 Fat: 9g Carbohydrates: 34g Protein: 9g

Thai Vegetable Hash

Easy and fast to make!

Prep time: 20 minutes Cooking time: 3 hours Servings: 8

INGREDIENTS:

Yellow summer squash

2 cloves garlic

Zucchini

2 tbsp. curry paste (Thai red)

2 tbsp broth (chicken or vegetable)

4-5 tbsp coconut milk (unsweetened)

3 tbsp torn basil leaves

2 cups fresh cremini mushrooms

2 medium sliced leeks

1 red sweet pepper

1 tbsp fresh ginger

DIRECTIONS:

1. Halve zucchini lengthwise and then cut into small slices. Quarter the mushrooms. Seed and cut red sweet pepper.

2. Spray your Slow Cooker with cooking spray.

3. Gather yellow squash, mushrooms, zucchini, leeks, sweet pepper and garlic in the Slow Cooker dish.

4. In a separate small bowl, whisk the broth with curry paste. Add this mixture to the vegetables. Cook covered on LOW temperature mode for 3 hours. In the end, stir in the coconut milk and add ginger.

5. Serve sprinkled with basil.

Nutrition: Calories: 60 Fat: 2g Carbohydrates: 9g Protein: 2g

The Potatoes with Three Cheeses

The best cheese mix for your potato meal!

Prep time: 20 minutes Cooking time: 6-8 hours Servings: 8

INGREDIENTS:

Half cup chicken broth

Sour cream

6-7 large Yukon potatoes

One can condensed potato soup

One onion

Salt to taste

Half cup shredded Parmesan

Black pepper

One cup Gouda cheese

Half cup blue cheese (crumbled)

DIRECTIONS:

1. Cover the inside of your Slow Cooker with a nonstick cooking spray. Slice ½ potatoes and ½ onion into small slices and cover the bottom.

2. In a separate dish, mix together Gouda cheese, parmesan cheese, blue cheese, sour cream and soup.

3. Add the species to taste and cover with the chicken broth.

4. Pour a half of the liquid mixture over the potatoes in Slow Cooker. Then, repeat the layer one more time.

5. Cook covered on LOW mode for 6-8 hours, or on HIGH – for 3-4. Let to cool for 10-15 mins before serving.

6. Serve sprinkled with parsley.

Nutrition: Calories: 306 Fat: 14g Carbohydrates: 33g Protein: 12g

Carrots and Parsnips in Orange Glaze

This glaze will amuse your guests!

Prep time: 26 minutes Cooking time: 10 hours Servings: 10

INGREDIENTS:

3-4 large carrots

One cup orange juice

2 parsnips

Half cup orange marmalade

Orange peel (shredded)

3 tsp butter

4 tbsp dry white wine

Vegetable broth

1 tbsp quick cooking tapioca

Fresh parsley

DIRECTIONS:

1. Peel and cut the parsnips and carrots into small two-inch chunks.

2. Spray your Slow Cooker with cooking spray and place the carrots with parsnips into it.

3. In a separate bowl mix together vegetable broth, orange juice, wine, salt, marmalade, tapioca and pepper.

4. Pour the orange mixture over the veggies in the Slow Cooker. Toss a little to combine everything well.

5. Cook on HIGH temperature for 4-5 hour, or, better, on LOW temperature for 8-10 hours (till the vegetables get tender).

6. When it is about 30 minutes left, stir in shredded orange peel and some butter. To serve, sprinkle with snipped parsley.

Nutrition: Calories: 159 Fat: 4g Carbohydrates: 31g Protein: 2g

Summer Casserole with Vegetables

Healthy dish is perfect for summertime and easy to make!

Prep time: 20 minutes Cooking time: 4-6 hours Servings: 8

INGREDIENTS:

One can cannellini beans

4 cloves garlic

One can fava or garbanzo beans

One cup torn radicchio

One large tomato

1 tsp Italian seasoning

2 cups fresh spinach

4-5 tbsp basil pesto

2 cups Italian cheese blend

2 cups plain polenta (cooked)

DIRECTIONS:

1. Prepare the vegetables, cut finely the onion, mince the garlic and thinly slice the tomato. Rinse well the beans and leave to drain.

2. Take a large bowl and combine the beans, garlic, two tablespoons of pesto, onion, Italian seasoning.

3. Butter your Slow Cooker and place in it the bean mixture with cheese and polenta. Cook covered for 5 hours on LOW mode or for 2 on HIGH.

4. By the end of cooking time, add spinach, tomato and radicchio. Combine 1 tablespoon of water with remaining pesto.

5. Let cool for just 5 minutes, and then serve.

Nutrition: Calories: 360 Fat: 12g Carbohydrates: 46g Protein: 21g

Multigrain and Veggie Pilaf

Easy and delicious, try this with fresh berries!

Prep time: 20 minutes Cooking time: 6-8 hours Servings: 12

INGREDIENTS:

Half cup ordinary barley

One medium sweet pepper

3-4 tbsp. wheat berries

2 cans chicken or vegetable broth

Half cup wild rice

Dried sage

Salt

1 tbsp. margarine or butter

Black pepper

2 cups sweet soybeans (frozen)

One medium onion

4 cloves garlic

DIRECTIONS:

1. Rinse wheat berries with some cold water and drain them well. Also, rinse the rice and barley. Spray the inside parts of your Slow Cooker and combine uncooked barley, wheat berries and wild rice with soybeans.

2. Add diced fresh sweet pepper, butter and diced onions. Season as well with black pepper, sage, garlic and salt.

3. Pour in the chicken or vegetable broth to cover all the ingredients evenly.

4. Cover the Slow Cooker with the lid and prepare on LOW-heat temperature regimes for 6-8 hours. If you want to cook a bit faster, use HIGH-heat settings for 3-4 hours.

5. To serve, stir finely one more time.

Nutrition: Calories: 542 Fat: 8g Carbohydrates: 31g Protein: 52g

Spinach Salad with Beans and Carrots

Perfect side dish for any fish or meat!

Prep time: 30 minutes Cooking time: 7-8 hours Servings: 6

INGREDIENTS:

1-2 cups Great Northern beans (use dry)

2 cloves garlic

5-6 medium carrots

Salt to taste

Crumbled feta cheese (fat-reduced)

Half tsp dried oregano

One medium onion

One medium avocado

2 tsp shredded lemon peel

Lemon juice (3 tbsp.)

4 cups chicken stock

Fresh baby spinach

3 tbsp. pistachio nuts

DIRECTIONS:

1. Rinse and drain the beans. Place the beans into a medium saucepan and, covered with some water, bring to boil. Simmer on low heat for 10 minutes, then let stand and cool for one hour.
2. Spray your Slow Cooker with anti-stick spray and fill it with carrots, soaked beans, garlic, oregano, onion. Season with some pepper and salt to taste.
3. Pour the stock mixture into Slow Cooker.
4. Turn on the Slow Cooker and set for 7-8 hours of LOW temperature mode (or 3-4 hours on HIGH mode).
5. Remove the mixture and stir in lemon peel, spinach, and lemon juice. Serve with avocado, pistachios and cheese.

Nutrition: Calories: 319 Fat: 9g Carbohydrates: 43g Protein: 19g

Potatoes with Cheese in Slow Cooker

Potatoes and cheese – classics for every kitchen!

Prep time: 12 minutes Cooking time: 4 hours Servings: 8

INGREDIENTS:

2 cans Cheddar cheese soup (condensed)

One can French fried onions

One can evaporated milk

Hash brown potatoes

DIRECTIONS:

1. Grease your Cooker with olive oil or cooking spray.
2. In a bowl, combine the hash brown potatoes, half of the French fried onions. Add milk and cheese soup.
3. Place the mixture into your Slow Cooker and leave to prepare on HIGH temperature mode for four hours, or on LOW temperature – for eight.
4. Serve while hot, garnishing with the remaining onions on top.

Nutrition: Calories: 308 Fat: 14g Carbohydrates: 37g Protein: 9g

Western Omelet in Slow Cooker

A little bit long, but tasty and easy!

Prep time: 22 minutes Cooking time: 12 hours Servings: 12

INGREDIENTS:

12 chicken eggs

Salt/pepper

Medium onion

Hash brown potatoes

Cup milk

One cup shredded Cheddar

Ham (diced and cooked)

One green bell pepper

DIRECTIONS:

1. Grease the bottom and side parts of your Slow Cooker.
2. Shred hash brown potatoes and place 1/3 of it in an even layer over the bottom of your slow cooker.
3. Cover with 1/3 of the diced onion and pepper, Cheddar cheese and ham. Repeat all the layers for 2-3 times.
4. In a separate bowl whisk together milk with eggs. Add salt and pepper just to taste. Pour in the Slow Cooker.
5. Cover and cook for 10-12 hours on LOW temperatures.

Nutrition: Calories: 310 Fat: 22g Carbohydrates: 16g Protein: 20g

Baked Beans in Texas Style

Hot beans can be both side and main dish!

Prep time: 17 minutes Cooking time: 2 hours Servings: 12

INGREDIENTS:

Half cup brown sugar

One cup barbeque sauce

One pound ground beef

One can chili peppers (green)

Garlic powder

Hot pepper sauce

Small Vidalia onion

4 cans baked beans

DIRECTIONS:

1. Peel and chop the onion. Cut the beef into small bite-sized pieces.

2. Preheat a small skillet over medium heat and prepare the beef until it is no longer pink. Cover your Slow Cooker with some butter or special cooking spray.

3. Fill the ceramic bowl of your slow Cooker with the ground beef, green chili peppers, baked beans, barbeque sauce and diced onion.

4. Season with spices: add chili powder, garlic powder, hot pepper sauce and some sugar. Cook on HIGH temperature for 2 hours or on LOW for 4 or 5 hours.

Nutrition: Calories: 360 Fat: 12g Carbohydrates: 50g Protein: 14g

Squash with Apple in Slow Cooker

Sweet and healthy, the squash is awesome with any kind of meat!

Prep time: 15 minutes Cooking time: 4 hours Servings: 10

INGREDIENTS:

4 large apples

One tsp ground cinnamon

Half cup dried cranberries

Half white onion

1-2 tsp nutmeg (ground)

One butternut squash

DIRECTIONS:

1. Peel and seed the squash, remove the skin and core from apples. Chop both into small cubes. Also, dice the onion.

2. In separate bowl, combine your INGREDIENTS: onion, a teaspoon of each nutmeg and cinnamon, apples, cranberries and squash,

3. Butter your Slow Cooker (or, cover the inside of it with anti-stick cooking spray) on start preheating.

4. Transfer all the ingredients into Slow Cooker and cover with the lid. Prepare on HIGH temperature mode for 4-5 hours. Stir time after time.

5. Serve, when the squash is tender and fully cooked

Nutrition: Calories: 123 Fat: 1g Carbohydrates: 32g Protein: 2g

Lasagna with Turkey and Spices

The perfect choice for a busy working day!

Prep time: 20 minutes Cooking time: 3 hours Servings: 8

INGREDIENTS:

Ground turkey (uncooked)

Half cup water

Crushed red pepper

1 tsp dried oregano

Light ricotta cheese

12 lasagna noodles (no-boil)

1-1 ,2 cups shredded Mozzarella (no-fat)

1 package frozen spinach

1-2 cups Italian five-cheese blend

3 cups chunky pasta sauce (with green pepper and mushrooms)

Fresh basil (optional)

DIRECTIONS:

1. Cover a large nonstick frying pan with some oil and cook the turkey pieces until they are no longer pink. Add red pepper and oregano.

2. In a separated cooking bowl, combine the cheeses and spinach. Cover the bottom of your Slow Cooker with the pasta sauce.

3. Add lasagna noodles, half of turkey mixture, half of the water and one-cup pasta sauce. Repeat all the layers with remaining ingredients.

4. Set your Slow Cooker on LOW-temperature mode and prepare for 3-4 hours. In the end, top with some Mozzarella and let stand for ten more minutes.

5. To serve, cut lasagna into eight portions and sprinkle with basil.

Nutrition: Calories: 391 Fat: 15g Carbohydrates: 34g Protein: 26g

Wild Rice with Herbs

Hot and aromatic side dish for any occasion!

Prep time: 25 minutes Cooking time: 6-7 hours Servings: 12-14

INGREDIENTS:

4 cloves garlic

1 tsp minced garlic

1-2 medium carrots

Half tsp dried thyme

Black pepper

1 cup uncooked wild rice

1 tsp dried basil

1 cup brown rice (also uncooked)

1 tbsp butter

Rosemary

2-3 small onions

2 cups chicken broth (or vegetable)

DIRECTIONS:

1. Mince the garlic, dice the carrots and onions. Rinse and leave to drain wild and brown rises.
2. In a large dish (you can use the Slow Cooker cooking dish, as well), combine brown and wild rice, carrots, mushrooms, onion.
3. Season with some basil, rosemary, thyme, and garlic. Add some butter and salt/pepper to taste. Cook covered with the lid, using LOW-heat temperature modes for 6-7 hours (or HIGH for 3-4 hours).
4. To serve, stir well and enjoy!

Nutrition: Calories: 315 Fat: 5g Carbohydrates: 71g Protein: 22g

Slow Cooker Salad with Taco

Easy and healthy salad for your Slow Cooker!

Prep time: 25 minutes Cooking time: 5-6 hours Servings: 15

INGREDIENTS:

One jar green salsa

Ground beef or ground turkey (to choose)

One medium sweet pepper

One large onion (sweet)

One can Northern beans

DIRECTIONS:

1. Cut the onion into thin wedges. Coarsely chop medium sweet pepper.

2. Take a large frying pan to cook the meat. Prepare it over medium fire until it is browned. Then drain off all the fat.
3. Cover the bottom of your Slow Cooker with some butter or olive oil, to avoid sticking. Place the fried meat into your Slow Cooker and cover it with remaining ingredients.
4. Cover the lid and prepare for 5-6 hours on LOW temperature mode, if you have the time. If not – use HIGH temp mode and cook for 2-3 hours.
5. You can save the half of the meat mixture to use it next time.

Nutrition: Calories: 298 Fat: 18g Carbohydrates: 21g Protein: 15g

French Casserole with onion and Green Beans

Hot bean casserole – easy and tasty!

Prep time: 20 minutes Cooking time: 5-6 hours Servings: 12

INGREDIENTS:

1-2 cups shredded Cheddar cheese

4 tbsp milk

1 tbsp Worcestershire sauce

Half cup French-fried onions

Fresh mushrooms

One can cream of chicken soup (condensed)

1 can French-fried onions

3 cups fresh green beans

DIRECTIONS:

1. Trim and cut the beans into one-inch pieces, shred finely the white Cheddar cheese.
2. In a separate cooking bowl, combine the green beans, soup, cheese, half-cup French-fried onions and mushrooms.
3. Add to the mixture Worcestershire sauce and milk, stir everything well.
4. Cover the Slow Cooker with lid and leave to cook for 5-6 hours (if using LOW-temperature cooking mode) or for 2-3 hours (if using HIGH-temperature regime).
5. To serve, sprinkle the dish with French-fried onions.

Nutrition: Calories: 298 Fat: 6g Carbohydrates: 39g Protein: 27g

Mashed potatoes with Cheddar

Quick and delicious recipe!

Prep time: 20 minutes Cooking time: 3-4 hours Servings: 10

INGREDIENTS:

Half cup buttermilk

3 tbsp. butter

1 cup chicken or vegetable broth

6-7 red potatoes

Salt

1 cup crumbled bacon

Cheddar cheese

2 cups cauliflower florets

Half teaspoon pepper

DIRECTIONS:

1. Peel the potatoes and cut it finely to get one-inch thin pieces. Spray your Slow Cooker with a cooking spray.

2. Cover the bottom of your Slow Cooker with sliced potatoes. Pour in the vegetable or chicken broth.

3. Cover the lid and cook on LOW temperatures for 8 hours or on HIGH for 4 hours. When it is around 30 minutes left, add cauliflower and stir well.

4. At the end, stir in butter, buttermilk and pepper with salt. Mash everything until smooth.

5. Serve while hot, with the bacon slices.

Nutrition: Calories: 211 Fat: 2g Carbohydrates: 131g Protein: 18g

New Potatoes in Slow Cooker

Easy to make, but try it – and it will be your favorite side dish!

Prep time: 20 minutes Cooking time: 3-4 hours Servings: 12

INGREDIENTS:

2 tbsp olive oil

10-15 small new potatoes

1 tsp salt

8 cloves garlic

Half tsp black pepper (coarse ground)

1 tbsp fresh or dried rosemary

DIRECTIONS:

1. Peel and cut into halves the tiny new potatoes. Peel the garlic. Take a large bowl and combine the garlic with potatoes.

2. Add rosemary, pepper and salt. Slightly drizzle with some oil.

3. Toss well to combine all the ingredients and transfer them into greased Slow Cooker.

4. Cover the potato mixture with the lid and cook using HIGH-temperature settings for 3-4 hours. You can also check the readiness of potatoes with the knife.

Nutrition: Calories: 103 Fat: 2g Carbohydrates: 19g Protein: 2g

Refried Beans in Slow Cooker

Easy, but healthy and delicious meal!

Prep time: 13 minutes Cooking time: 8 hours Servings: 8-10

INGREDIENTS:

One medium onion

5 tsp salt

Minced garlic

9 cups water

Small jalapeno pepper

Dry pinto beans

Ground black pepper

Ground cumin (optional)

DIRECTIONS:

1. Cut the onion, peel and seed jalapeno pepper.

2. Prepare your Slow Cooker and fill it with onion, rinsed beans, garlic, jalapeno pepper, pepper, cumin and salt.

3. Pour in the water, slightly stir (just to combine) and turn on the Slow Cooker.

4. Cook during 8 hours on HIGH temperature. You can also add some water in the process, if needed.

5. When the beans are ready, strain them. Save the liquid.

6. Mash the beans (you can use a potato masher) and add reserved water, until the meal gets the needed consistency.

Nutrition: Calories: 155 Fat: 5g Carbohydrates: 23g Protein: 1g

Creamed Corn and Onions in Slow Cooker

The perfect hot side dish for summertime!

Prep time: 20 minutes Cooking time: 2 hours Servings: 6-8

INGREDIENTS:

4 cups whole kernel corn

Half teaspoon salt

4 slices bacon

Half cup plain cream or half-and-half

One teaspoon sugar

Half cup red bell pepper

Ground red pepper

3 tbsp unsalted butter

One cup chive and onion cheese

DIRECTIONS:

1. Fry the bacon in a large skillet for 8-10 minutes. Turn the heat off as soon as the bacon gets evenly browned. Drain with paper towels.
2. Coat the bottom and sides of your Slow Cooker with cooking spray.
3. Right in Slow Cooker, mix the INGREDIENTS: red bell pepper, corn, half-and-half, salt, sugar, black pepper and half the bacon.
4. Cook on HIGH temperature mode for 1-2 hours.
5. In the end, stir in the cream cheese and wait until it melts. Top with remaining bacon to serve.

Nutrition: Calories: 511 Fat: 7g Carbohydrates: 23g Protein: 6g

Mashed Seasoned Potatoes in Slow Cooker

Not just healthy, but simple and delicious dish for any time of year!

Prep time: 30 minutes Cooking time: 3 hours Servings: 8

INGREDIENTS:

One package cream cheese

1-2 cups chicken broth

One container sour cream

8-10 medium red potatoes

Half cup butter

Salt to taste

1 tsp garlic powder

DIRECTIONS:

1. Cup the potatoes into chunks and cover with salt water in large pot. Bring to boil and simmer for 20 minutes on low heat, then drain.
2. In a large bowl, mash the potatoes with adding sour cream and cream cheese. Pour in the chicken broth, add salt and garlic powder. Combine.
3. Beat the potatoes with kitchen blender for 2-3 minutes.
4. Place the mixture in buttered Slow Cooker and leave on LOW temperature modes for 3 hours. To serve, stir in the melted butter and sprinkle with minced parsley.

Nutrition: Calories: 342 Fat: 6g Carbohydrates: 6g Protein: 9g

Creamy Corn in Slow Cooker

You can try it with fresh corn in summer or use frozen!

Prep time: 10 minutes Cooking time: 4 hours Servings: 6-8

INGREDIENTS:

One package corn kernels (frozen)

Half cup milk

Half cup butter

1 tbsp white sugar

Cream cheese

Pepper and salt

DIRECTIONS:

1. Grease your Slow Cooker with some olive oil.
2. In a separate bowl, combine cream cheese, sugar, corn, milk and butter. Season the mixture with salt and butter easily, just to taste.
3. Transfer the mixture into slightly preheated Slow Cooker and set on HIGH temperature for 2-4 hours or on LOW for 4-6 hours.
4. Serve hot, sprinkled with minced parsley or shredded cheese.

Nutrition: Calories: 192 Fat: 15g Carbohydrates: 13g Protein: 3g

Spicy Black Eyed Peas in Slow Cooker

Spicy beans will perfectly fit with meat!

Prep time: 30 minutes Cooking time: 6 hours Servings: 6-8

INGREDIENTS:

One medium onion

6 cups water

2 cloves garlic

One cube bouillon

One red bell pepper

4 slices bacon

Diced ham

One jalapeno chili

1 tsp cumin

Ground black pepper and salt to taste

DIRECTIONS:

1. Start preheating your Slow Cooker.
2. Pour in the water and add one cube of chicken bouillon, stir slowly to dissolve.
3. In a separate bowl, combine the INGREDIENTS: chopped onion, bell pepper, black-eyed-peas, jalapeno pepper, garlic, ham and bacon.

4. Season the mixture with cayenne pepper, salt, cumin and black pepper, Stir everything well. Transfer the mixture to your Slow Cooker and cook under the lid for 6-8 hours (using LOW temperature mode).

5. Serve until the beans are ready and tender.

Nutrition: Calories: 199 Fat: 3g Carbohydrates: 30g Protein: 14g

Tender Taters in Slow Cooker

Easy to make and very tasty to eat!

Prep time: 19 minutes Cooking time: 4 hours Servings: 6

INGREDIENTS:

Half cup butter

Water

One pinch black pepper (freshly ground)

6-8 large Yukon potatoes

One can skim milk (evaporated)

1 package gravy mix

DIRECTIONS:

1. Peel the potatoes and dice them into 2-inch slices.

2. Spray your Slow Cooker with cooking spray (to avoid sticking).

3. Place the potato pieces in your Cooker and sprinkle just a little with a freshly grounded black pepper.

4. In another bowl, whisk together water and the country gravy mix. Stir until ingredients are well blended. Pour into Slow Cooker.

5. Add the evaporated milk and cook, covered, for 4 hours on LOW temperature level. To serve. Drain all excess liquid and mash with butter.

Nutrition: Calories: 367 Fat: 16g Carbohydrates: 48g Protein: 9g

Parmesan Rice with Chicken

Soft chicken meat tastes amazing with melted Parmesan!

Prep time: 32 minutes Cooking time: 4 hours Servings: 6

INGREDIENTS:

1-2 cups white rise (take long0grain)

1/3 cup water

Half cup green peas (frozen)

Half tsp basil (can use dry)

2 cans chicken broth

2 cloves garlic

2 medium onions

Grated Parmesan

2 tbsp pine nuts

Italian seasoning

DIRECTIONS:

1. Dice the onion and mince the garlic before the start.

2. Butter your Slow Cooker and fill it with rinsed rise, garlic and onion.

3. Take a medium saucepan and bring the water and chicken broth to boil (use high heat). Pour the liquid into rice. Add the basil and Italian seasoning. Stir finely.

4. Cook under the lid for 2-3 hours on LOW temperature settings (check the readiness when all liquid is absorbed).

5. Add peas and cook for another hour.

6. To serve, stir in Parmesan and cover with pine nuts.

Nutrition: Calories: 271 Fat: 4g Carbohydrates: 46g Protein: 9g

Collard Greens in Slow Cooker

Fast and easy dish – cook it when you are busy or do not have much time!

Prep time: 25 minutes Cooking time: 3-4 hours Servings: 8

INGREDIENTS:

Two cans beef stock

1 tsp white sugar

1 bay leaf

2-3 small onions

2 tsp red wine vinegar

Half tsp red pepper flakes

2 bunches collard greens

Salt

2 bunches mustard greens

1 tsp garlic powder

2 bunches turnip greens

1 can diced tomatoes

DIRECTIONS:

1. Chop the onions; thinly slice collard and mustard greens. Prepare your Slow Cooker and cover it thinly with melted butter.

2. Right in the Slow Cooker dish, combine green chilies, diced tomatoes and chopped onions. Add beef stock, vinegar, sugar, ham, salt, garlic powder, red pepper flakes and one bay leaf.

3. Stir in the collard greens, mustard greens and turnip greens into Slow Cooker (follow this order). Cover and cook on LOW temperature regime until the greens are tender enough.

Nutrition: Calories: 131 Fat: 4g Carbohydrates: 16g Protein: 9g

Mexican Pinto Beans with Cactus

Spicy beans with an unusual accent!

Prep time: 10 minutes Cooking time: 4 hours Servings: 10

INGREDIENTS:

Two cups pinto beans

3 slices bacon

One small onion

2 cactus leaves (no pales and large)

One jalapeno pepper

2 tbsp salt

DIRECTIONS:

1. Rinse the beans and place it into your Slow Cooker. Pour in the hot water to fill the dish to the top. Add the onion, seeded and chopped jalapeno pepper and the bacon.
2. Season with salt to taste and cook on HIGH regime for 3-4 hours.
3. After removing all the thorns from the cactus leaves, slice them into small pieces.
4. In a saucepan filled with water, bring cactus to boil and wait 15 minutes. Drain and rinse with cold water.
5. Add the cactus to the beans and leave cooking for another 15-20 minutes.

Nutrition: Calories: 153 Fat: 1g Carbohydrates: 25g Protein: 9g

Pizza Potatoes in Slow Cooker

Love pizza and potatoes? Just combine them in one meal!

Prep time: 25 minutes Cooking time: 6 hours Servings: 6

INGREDIENTS:

1 tbsp olive oil

A can pizza sauce

Mozzarella cheese (grated)

1 large onion

6 medium potatoes

Pepperoni (sliced)

DIRECTIONS:

1. Start with greasing and preheating your Slow Cooker.

2. Take a large skillet and heat the oil over medium high heat.
3. Thinly slice the onion and place it into skillet. Add potatoes and fry until the onion is mild and translucent (about 7-10 minutes).
4. Drain the potatoes and place into Slow Cooker.
5. Add pepperoni and Mozzarella cheese. Pour with pizza sauce. Cook under the lid on LOW temperatures about 6-9 hours.

Nutrition: Calories: 248 Fat: 7g Carbohydrates: 36g Protein: 9g

Carrots with Chinese species

Healthy vegetables with spicy seasoning!

Prep time: 10 minutes Cooking time: 8-9 hours Servings: 6

INGREDIENTS:

10-15 baby carrots

4 tbsp tamari sauce

Half cup orange juice (better use concentrate)

2 cloves garlic

1 tsp orange zest (grated)

1 tbsp honey

1 tbsp Asian sesame oil

1 tsp fresh ginger (minced)

DIRECTIONS:

1. Peel and cut baby carrots, mince ginger and garlic.
2. In Slow Cooker dish, mix the baby carrots, tamari juice concentrate, orange zest, toasted sesame oil on honey. Add minced garlic and ginger.
3. Pour in the orange juice concentrate and mix everything well.
4. Place the dish into Slow Cooker and turn on the LOW temperature mode.
5. Cook for 8 hours, then turn your Slow Cooker to high temperature and continue cooking for another 30 minutes.

Nutrition: Calories: 140 Fat: 2g Carbohydrates: 27g Protein: 3g

Baked Beans in Slow Cooker

Try these unusual beans for your dinner!

Prep time: 11 minutes Cooking time: 9 hours Servings: 8

INGREDIENTS:

Four cups water

Brown sugar

1 pack navy beans (dried)

1 tsp salt

Half cup molasses

One medium onion

Dry mustard to taste

4-5 slices salt pork

Ground pepper

DIRECTIONS:

1. Cover the beans with cold water and let stand overnight. Drain and transfer to pot.

2. Cover with water again and bring to boil. Then simmer about 1 hour to make the beans tender. In a separate bowl, mix 4 cup water, mustard, salt, molasses, pepper and brown sugar.

3. Place all the ingredients into Slow Cooker and mix everything well until smooth.

4. If needed, add more water and cook covered for 8 to 10 hours on LOW temperature regime.

Nutrition: Calories: 374 Fat: 12g Carbohydrates: 54g Protein: 13g

Sweet Sauerkraut In Slow Cooker

Sweet and unusual dish!

Prep time: 20 minutes Cooking time: 8 hours Servings: 8

INGREDIENTS:

1-2 cups water

2 cups sauerkraut

One medium apple

3 tbsp brown sugar

One medium carrot

Half sweet onion

1 tsp caraway seeds

Kielbasa (fully cooked)

Ground black pepper and salt to taste

DIRECTIONS:

1. Drain and rinse well the sauerkraut. Core and dice apple, mince carrot and onion.

2. Butter your Slow Cooker and fill it with sauerkraut, apple, carrot, brown sugar, caraway seeds, sweet onion and salt/pepper.

3. Turn on the Slow Cooker and set the low temperature mode. Cook for 7 hours on LOW mode, stirring occasionally.

4. In the end of the process add kielbasa and stir one more time. Cook for another hour.

Nutrition: Calories: 264 Fat: 15g Carbohydrates: 23g Protein: 8g

Collard Greens in Slow Cooker

Fits for any family gathering!

Prep time: 30 minutes Cooking time: 7-8 hours Servings: 4

INGREDIENTS:

Three slices bacon

One bunch collard greens

2 cups chicken stock

Salt to taste

2 tbsp jalapeno pepper slices

Ground black pepper

DIRECTIONS:

1. Cover the collard greens with salted water and bring to boil. Then, reduce the heat and simmer for 10-15 minutes.

2. Transfer the drained collard greens to your Slow Cooker.

3. Fry the bacon pieces in a deep skillet over medium heat. Turn occasionally until it is evenly browned.

4. Combine all the ingredients in Slow Cooker, add the jalapeno slices and cover with chicken stock. Add some seasoning with black pepper and salt.

5. Cook covered on LOW temperatures for 8 hours (tip: you can leave it cooking overnight).

Nutrition: Calories: 124 Fat: 10g Carbohydrates: 5g Protein: 4g

Creamed Corn in Slow Cooker

Creamy and healthy corn for summertime!

Prep time: 15 minutes Cooking time: 4 hours Servings: 8

INGREDIENTS:

One cup heavy whipping cream

Half tsp salt

5 cups sweet corn (can be frozen)

2 tbsp white sugar

1 pack cream cheese (softened)

Half tsp black pepper (freshly ground)

3 tbsp unsalted butter

DIRECTIONS:

1. Prepare your Slow Cooker: grease it with some butter or olive oil.

77

2. In a separate bowl, stir together cream cheese, whipping cream, salt, sugar and pepper. Transfer the cream mixture into Slow Cooker.

3. Cook covered with the lid for 10 minutes. Then add the corn. Continue cooking on LOW temperatures regimes for 4-5 hours.

Nutrition: Calories: 354 Fat: 27g Carbohydrates: 26g Protein: 9g

Casserole with Spinach Noodles

Unusual Spinach noodles for any meat or fish!

Prep time: 19 minutes Cooking time: 3-4 hours Servings: 8

INGREDIENTS:

Dry spinach noodles

Cps cottage cheese

1-2 cups sour cream

Vegetable oil

Green onion

Garlic salt

Worcestershire sauce

All-purpose flour

Hot pepper sauce

DIRECTIONS:

1. In a large pot, cook the noodles in salted water. Drain well and combine, tossing, with vegetable oil.

2. Meanwhile, take a large bowl and combine flour and sour cream.

3. Add cottage cheese, Worcestershire sauce, garlic salt, green onions, and hot pepper sauce. Stir everything well.

4. Combine the cheese mixture with the noodles.

5. Grease your Slow Cooker and place the noodle mixture into it. Cook, covered, on HIGH temperature mode for 1-2 hours.

Nutrition: Calories: 226 Fat: 14g Carbohydrates: 14g Protein: 8g

Slow Cooker Squash

An amazing autumn meal with summer squash!

Prep time: 10 minutes Cooking time: 1 hour Servings: 6

INGREDIENTS:

Large summer squash

4 tbsp butter

One small onion

Half cup cubed cheese

DIRECTIONS:

1. Peel and slice the yellow summer squash. Chop one small onion. Place the vegetables into a small pot and cover with cold water.

2. Bring the squash to boil, and then just simmer for 10 minutes to get the squash tender. Drain the onion with squash with colander (do not stir!)

3. Gentle place the vegetables with all other ingredients into Slow Cooker. Turn it on and set on LOW mode. Cook for one hour.

Nutrition: Calories: 183 Fat: 13g Carbohydrates: 12g Protein: 7g

Hot Beans with Pork

Pork notes can make this more than just a side dish!

Prep time: 20 minutes Cooking time: 7 hours Servings: 8

INGREDIENTS:

Dried pinto beans

5 tbsp chopped pork (better salted)

4 tbsp chopped celery

2-3 tbsp bacon grease

Half cup green bell pepper

1-2 cups yellow onion

Half tsp black pepper

Chipotle chile powder

3 bay leaves

Smoked sausage

2 tbsp fresh parsley (chopped)

Fresh thyme

Water (as needed)

3 tbsp chopped garlic

DIRECTIONS:

1. Soak beans for 15-20 minutes. Rinse and drain.

2. Place a large pot over medium high heat and heat the bacon grease.

3. Add celery, chopped onion, black pepper, chipotle powder, black pepper to the pot. Cook for about 4-5 minutes.

4. Add smoked sausage, garlic, parsley, thyme and bay leaves. Prepare to get the sausage browned.

5. Transfer the bean and sausage mixture into Slow Cooker and cook on high for about an hour. Then, reduce to LOW and

leave for 6 hours (you can add water during the process, if needed). To serve, remove the bay leaves and mash slightly.

Nutrition: Calories: 460 Fat: 20g Carbohydrates: 41g

Protein: 19g

Beans with Bacon and Cranberry Sauce

Hot cranberry sauce makes this one sweet and spicy!

Prep time: 5 minutes Cooking time:

Servings:

INGREDIENTS:

One poblano pepper

One onion

One shallot

Dried cranberry beans

1 tsp salt

1 tbsp. barbeque sauce

5 cups chicken stock

5 cloves garlic

Diced bacon

Half tsp hot sauce (chipotle flavored)

DIRECTIONS:

1. Cut poblano, remove the seeds and place it all over buttered baking sheet.
2. Cook until the skin of pepper a little blackened and blistered (about 5-8 minutes). Leave to cool, remove the skin.
3. Dice the poblano pepper and combine it with bacon, beans, shallot, salt, onion, beans, garlic and black pepper.
4. Mix the ingredients and transfer to greased Slow Cooker. Pour in the chicken stock over the vegetables.
5. Cook on HIGH mode for about three hours (until the beans are softened). In the end, stir in hot sauce and barbeque sauce.

Nutrition: Calories: 271 Fat: 5g Carbohydrates: 40g Protein: 17g

Stuffing with Cranberries and Apple

Amazing duo or berries and apples!

Prep time: 20 minutes Cooking time: 3 hours Servings: 10-15

INGREDIENTS:

2 cups celery (chopped)

3 tbsp butter

1 cup dried cranberries

1 tsp garlic salt

Parsley

Rubbed sage

2 cups chicken stock

1 cup chopped onion

Black pepper

8 cups cubed bread

2 cups chopped celery

2 medium apples

DIRECTIONS:

1. In a wide skillet, melt the butter over medium heat.
2. Add chopped onion and celery. Cook, stirring, for 5 minutes (just to get soft). Stir in the mixture cranberries and cubed apples.
3. Cover the inside of your Slow Cooker with some cooking spray.
4. Add stock and seasonings, place in the vegetable mixture and bread cubes. Cover and cook for three hours on LOW temperature mode.

Nutrition: Calories: 122 Fat: 3g Carbohydrates: 20g Protein: 2g

Barbeque Beans in Slow Cooker

Just bbq sauce and beans – and you can prepare an amazing meal!

Prep time: 30 minutes Cooking time: 8-10 hours Servings: 12-14

INGREDIENTS:

One package dry beans

Ground beef

1 bay leaf

2 tbsp maple syrup

2/3 bourbon whiskey

1 green bell pepper

One chopped onion

Sliced kielbasa sausage

2 tbsp honey

2 cans chicken broth

3 tbsp coarse-grain mustard

1 red bell pepper

Bacon

1-2 Worcestershire sauce

DIRECTIONS:

1. Place the rinsed beans in a large and wide pot. Cover with water and add bay leaf. Bring to boil, and then simmer until the liquid is absorbed. Take off the bay leaf.
2. Cook the bacon in a large skillet until evenly browned (around 5 minutes). Drain with paper towels. Mix all the ingredients in the Slow Cooker and stir well to get a smooth mixture.
3. Turn on the cooking device and choose the LOW mode. Cook for 8-10 hours.

Nutrition: Calories: 466 Fat: 19g Carbohydrates: 44g Protein: 21g

Ratatouille in Slow Cooker

Now you can do your favorite meal in Slow Cooker!

Prep time: 25 minutes Cooking time: 5 hours Servings: 8

INGREDIENTS:

1 medium onion

1 red bell pepper (medium)

1 diced zucchini

1 tsp dried basil

Olive oil

2 garlic cloves

1 medium green bell pepper

1 medium eggplant

1 yellow squash

Half tsp dried thyme

2 tbsp. chopped parsley

Black pepper and salt (to taste)

1 can crushed tomatoes

1 can tomato paste

DIRECTIONS:

1. Preheat the large skillet with a drizzle of olive oil.
2. Add chopped onions and garlic and then cook for around two minutes.0 Stir with tomato paste and transfer to buttered Slow Cooker.
3. Heat the skillet again and prepare green and red bell peppers, eggplant, summer squash and zucchini. Cook till tender for 10-15 minute, then place to Slow Cooker.
4. Add crushed tomatoes and season with thyme and basil.
5. Cook about 5 hours on LOW mode and serve sprinkled with chopped parsley.

Nutrition: Calories: 164 Fat: 7g Carbohydrates: 21g Protein: 4g

Hot German Salad with Potatoes

Hot salad in Slow Cooker – just try this one!

Prep time: 25 minutes Cooking time: 5 hours Servings: 4

INGREDIENTS:

8-10 small red potatoes

Half tsp celery seed

1 tsp salt

Half cup water

1 small onion

2 tbsp flour

2 tbsp sugar

5-6 tbsp apple cider vinegar

4 slices bacon

Chives (to serve)

DIRECTIONS:

1. Scrub the potatoes and slice into thin pieces. Layer the potatoes and halved onions into the buttered Slow Cooker.
2. Add water and cook on LOW temperature regime for 5-6 hours.
3. Slice the bacon and slightly fry it until brown. Drain with a paper towel.
4. In a separate bowl combine sugar, vinegar, flour, salt and celery seed. Mix to avoid any lumps. Add to Slow Cooker with fried bacon. Cook for additional 30 minutes.
5. To serve, garnish with chives.

Nutrition: Calories: 155 Fat: 8g Carbohydrates: 1g Protein: 7g

Chicken and Cole Slaw

Chicken with slaw – perfect both for lunch and dinner!

Prep time: 30 minutes Cooking time: 6-8 hours Servings: 6-8

INGREDIENTS:

1 medium onion

One cup barbeque sauce

1 chicken breast

2 tbsp vinegar

2 tbsp olive oil

Half head cabbage

Avocado

3 medium carrots

1 tbsp pickle juice

2 tbsp mayonnaise

3 tbsp Greek yogurt

DIRECTIONS:

1. Butter your Slow Cooker and layer its bottom with a part of diced onions.

2. Place the salted and peppered chicken on the onions. Pour with bbq sauce and leave to cook for 6-8 hours on LOW mode.

3. Shred the carrots and remaining onions with a food processor. Transfer the vegetables to a wide bowl. Add thinly sliced cabbage.

4. In a separate bowl, combine the ingredients for dressing: Greek yogurt, avocado, pickle juice, mayonnaise, vinegar, sauce and pepper with salt.

5. When the chicken is ready, drain it and toss with two forks. Combine with the cabbage mix and top with the dressing.

Nutrition: Calories: 344 Fat: 5g Carbohydrates: 42g Protein: 7g

Slow Cooker Carrots with Herbs

Try this one and you will cook it very often!

Prep time: 15 minutes Cooking time: 4-6 hours Servings: 4

INGREDIENTS:

6-7 long carrots

1 tsp dried dill

Salt to taste

3 tbsp butter

1 tbsp honey

DIRECTIONS:

1. Wash and peel the carrots, cut them into one-inch size coins.

2. In a separate saucepan, melt the butter and stir it with salt, honey and dill. You can also take a separate bowl and mix the species with already melted butter.

3. Grease the bottom of your Slow Cooker and cover it with carrot coins. Pour the honey and butter mixture over the slices.

4. Cook, covered with the lid, for 2-3 hours (if you use HIGH temperature mode), or for 4-6 hours (for LOW temp mode).

5. To serve, transfer the carrots to a wide dish. Serve while hot.

Nutrition: Calories: 171 Fat: 4g Carbohydrates: 31g Protein: 21g

Tricolor potatoes with Garlic and Rosemary

Spiced potatoes for any occasion!

Prep time: 13 minutes Cooking time: 4 hours Servings: 5-6

INGREDIENTS:

One bag tricolor potatoes

1 tsp salt

4 cloves garlic

Black pepper

1 tsp oregano

2 tbsp. Parmesan (grated)

2-3 sprigs thyme (fresh)

4-5 tbsp. olive oil

DIRECTIONS:

1. Wash and dry the potatoes with a towel. Do not peel – just cut in quarters or halves (depending on the size of each potato).

2. Cover the bottom of your cooking dish with a cooking spray or, even better, line it with a foil. Place the potatoes and sprinkle over with olive oil.

3. In a small dish, mix oregano, minced garlic, rosemary and thyme. Sprinkle the potatoes with this mixture. Add some pepper and salt to your taste.

4. Cover the lid and prepare for 2-3 hours (HIGH mode) or 5-6 hours (LOW mode). Serve immediately with the sprinkles of Parmesan.

Nutrition: Calories: 232 Fat: 8g Carbohydrates: 21g Protein: 81g

Spinach and Artichoke in Slow Cooker

Simple and healthy receipt!

Prep time: 25 minutes Cooking time: 2 hours Servings: 8

INGREDIENTS:

2 cans artichoke hearts

Sour cream

5-6 tbsp. milk

1 small onion

Half cup feta cheese (crumbled)

2 cloves garlic

1 pack spinach (frozen)

Half cup parmesan cheese

4 tbsp. mayonnaise

Cubed cream cheese

81

1 tbsp. red wine vinegar

Black pepper (freshly ground)

DIRECTIONS:

1. Chop the artichoke hearts well, dice the onion and crush the garlic. Butter a bottom of your Slow Cooker.

2. Right in the cooking dish, combine artichoke hearts, milk, cheese, sour cream, spinach, mayonnaise, sour cream, onion, garlic, pepper and vinegar.

3. Cover the lid and cook for the next 2 hours on LOW temperature mode.

4. When it is about 15 minutes left, stir the ingredients and let to cook another 15 minutes. Serve hot.

Nutrition: Calories: 355 Fat: 26g Carbohydrates: 19g Protein: 14g

Creamy Corn with Cheese

Creamy and hot meal for everyone!

Prep time: 5 minutes Cooking time: 4-6 Servings: 4-5

INGREDIENTS:

One bag corn kernels (frozen)

2 tbsp butter

Cream cheese

Half tsp sugar (if needed)

DIRECTIONS:

1. Cover the inside of your Slow Cooker with cooking spray or butter.

2. Right in a dish of Slow Cooker, combine the corn with butter and cream cheese.

3. Cover with a special lid and prepare for 4-6 hours (if you prefer the LOW temperature modes) or for 2-3 (for HIGH mode).

4. Taste the meal and add (if needed) the sugar to taste. It depends on the sweetness of the corn). Serve stirred and hot.

Nutrition: Calories: 344 Fat: 24g Carbohydrates: 19g Protein: 61g

Brussels sprouts for Slow Cooker

Perfect for spring and summer seasons!

Prep time: 10 minutes Cooking time: 4 hours Servings: 6

INGREDIENTS:

Half cup balsamic vinegar

Fresh Brussels sprouts

2 tbsp. olive oil

Salt

2 tbsp. brown sugar

4 tbsp. Parmesan cheese (freshly grated)

2 tbsp. unsalted butter

Ground black pepper

DIRECTIONS:

1. To prepare the balsamic reduction, take a small saucepan and preheat balsamic vinegar and brown sugar in it. Bring to boil, and then simmer for 6-8 minutes.

2. Right in the Slow Cooker, combine Brussels sprouts and olive oil. Season with pepper/salt and cover with butter.

3. Cover on LOW temperature mode for 3-4 hours.

4. To serve, drizzle with balsamic reduction and Parmesan

Nutrition: Calories: 193 Fat: 10g Carbohydrates: 21g Protein: 7g

Herbed Fingerling Potatoes in Slow Cooker

Your family definitely will love this!

Prep time: 5 minutes Cooking time: 5-8 hours Servings: 4

INGREDIENTS:

2 tbsp butter (melted)

One bag fingerling potatoes

Crushed rosemary

Pepper

Dried dill

Dried parsley

Dried thyme

1 tsp salt

Half cup cheese (white cheddar or white cheese)

Half cup heavy cream

DIRECTIONS:

1. Wash the potatoes and cut in half. Better, cut lengthwise, if there are big ones – quarter them). Cover the inside of Slow Cooker with butter or cooking spray.

2. Place the potatoes in the Slow Cooker dish and toss them with remaining butter. Add all the herbs, season with salt and pepper.

3. Cover the Slow Cooker with the lid and let to cook for 2-4 hours on HIGH or for 5-8 hours on LOW. In the end, stir in the cheese and cream.

4. Cook for another 16-30 minutes to get the cheese melted and then serve.

Nutrition: Calories: 455 Fat: 8g Carbohydrates: 27g Protein: 18g

Buttered Corn in Slow Cooker

Sweet and tasty for your friends and family!

Prep time: 5 minutes Cooking time: 2-4 hours Servings: 4

INGREDIENTS:

4 fresh corn cobs

Lime juice

Black pepper

Salt

4 tbsp butter (room temperature)

1 tbsp cilantro (fresh and chopped)

DIRECTIONS:

1. Prepare four pieces of aluminum foil. Place each cob on the foil.
2. In a small bowl, combine lime juice, spices and butter. Spread the mixture evenly over each corncob.
3. Wrap each corncob with a foil.
4. Spray the Slow Cooker with a cooking spray and place the corncobs over the bottom. Cook on HIGH for 2 hours or on LOW – for 3-4 hours.
5. To serve, sprinkle the corn with chopped cilantro.

Nutrition: Calories: 349 Fat: 12g Carbohydrates: 73g Protein: 8g

MAIN DISHES RECIPES

Chicken with Lemon Juice and Oregano

Species make this meal just amazing!

Prep time: 34 minutes Cooking time: 3 hours Servings: 6

INGREDIENTS:

Chicken breast halves

1tsp dried oregano

5 tbsp. water

Half tsp salt

2 tbsp. butter

Black pepper

3 tbsp. lemon juice

1 tsp chicken lemon granules

2 cloves minced garlic

parsley

DIRECTIONS:

1. In a separate bowl, combine salt, oregano, pepper. Rub the species into the chicken. Take a medium skillet, then melt the butter. Then brown chicken for about 5 minutes. Grease your Slow Cooker and place the chicken breasts into it.
2. Use the same skillet to mix lemon juice, water, bouillon and minced garlic. Heat until boil and pour over the chicken.
3. Cook, covered, for 3 hours on HIGH or 6 hours on LOW temperature regime. Before the serving, add some chopped parsley.

Nutrition: Calories: 191 Fat: 9g Carbohydrates: 1g Protein: 29g

Lasagna with Beef for Slow Cooker

Try this one in your Slow Cooker!

Prep time: 30 minutes Cooking time: 4,5 hours Servings: 10

INGREDIENTS:

1 tap dried oregano

1 chopped onion

Beef

Minced garlic

One can tomato paste

1 tsp salt

Tomato sauce

Half cup parmesan cheese

Pack lasagna noodles

Shredded mozzarella cheese

DIRECTIONS:

1. In a large skillet over a medium heat, fry some beef with onion and garlic until slightly brown. Add tomato paste and sauce. Cook for 14 minutes, add oregano and some salt.
2. In a separate bowl, combine the cheeses and mix well.
3. Grease your Slow Cooker and place all the ingredients, in even layers, into it. When all the layers are done, top the meal with cheese mix.
4. Cover on LOW temperature mode for 4,5 hours.

Mexican Meat in Slow Cooker

Delicious receipt for flavored meat!

Prep time: 30-40 minutes Cooking time: 8 hours Servings: 12

INGREDIENTS:

One chuck roast

1 tsp ground pepper

chili powder

one onion

Salt to taste

olive oil

Hot pepper sauce

cayenne pepper

garlic powder

DIRECTIONS:

1. Delete all the excess fat from the roast and season meat with pepper and salt. Using a large skillet with olive oil, brown the roast from all the sides.
2. Cover the bottom of cooking dish some butter and place the roast into it. Add chopped onion, pepper sauce, powders and peppers.
3. Pour in the water (slightly cover the roast) and cover the lid.
4. Set your Slow Cooker on HIGH mode (for 6 hours). Then reduce to LOW and carry on cooking for another 2-4 hours (when meat easily fall apart).
5. To serve, shred the roast with two forks and serve in tacos or burritos.

Nutrition: Calories: 260 Fat: 19g Carbohydrates: 3g Protein: 18g

Summer Pot Roast for Slow Cooker

Just a perfect meal for a hot summer!

Prep time: 17 minutes Cooking time: 7,5 hours Servings: 8

INGREDIENTS:

4-5tbsp flour

Pack beef mix

1 sliced onion

One pack ranch dressing mix

Half cup water

1 pack Italian dressing mix

Salt pepper

One beef chuck roast (remove the bones)

5 whole and peeled carrots

DIRECTIONS:

1. Cover the bottom of your cooking dish with butter or a little cooking spray. Place the sliced onion in an even layer onto the Slow Cooker bottom.
2. Sprinkle the beef meat with species and rub into its surface. Roll meat in the flour just to cover from all sides. Place the meat into Slow Cooker.
3. In a large bowl, combine Italian dressing mix, ranch dressing mix and beef gravy mix. Whisk and pour over the meat.
4. Place the carrots around the chuck roast.
5. Set your Slow Cooker on LOW mode and cook for around 8 hours (until tender).

Nutrition: Calories: 385 Fat: 22g Carbohydrates: 20g Protein: 23g

Pork Chops in Sour Cream

Usual pork with amazing dressing!

Prep time: 15 minutes Cooking time: 8 hours Servings: 10

INGREDIENTS:

Six pork chops

Garlic powder (to taste)

Half cup flour

Salt

2 cups water

Black pepper

Container sour cream

chicken bouillon

Large onion

DIRECTIONS:

1. Cover the chops with a spice mixture of pepper, garlic powder and some salt. Lightly brown chops in a large frying pan.
2. Cover the bottom of your cooking dish with some cooking spray and place the chops over it. Cover with onion.
3. Dissolve the cubes of bouillon in boiling water, and then pour the chops with this mixture. Cook, covered, for 7-8 hours using a LOW temperature mode.
4. To serve, mix the sauce out of sour cream and 2 tablespoons flour.

Nutrition: Calories: 257 Fat: 14g Carbohydrates: 14g Protein: 16g

Corned Beef with Cabbage

Try this receipt of the beef with cabbage!

Prep time 17 minutes Cooking time: 9 hours Servings: 8

INGREDIENTS:

Four large carrots

1 onion

Beer

One beef brisket

4 cups water

10 red potatoes

Half head cabbage

DIRECTIONS:

1. Prepare vegetables: peel carrots, cut into matchstick pieces. Quarter the potatoes and slice onion to bite-size pieces. Coarsely chop the cabbage.
2. Grease your cooking dish and place the vegetables over its bottom. Place the beef on top of the vegetables.
3. Pour in beer to cover ingredients and season with spices.
4. Set Slow Cooker to HIGH regime and leave to cook for 8 hours.
5. When the beef is almost ready, add the cabbage and cook for another hour.

Nutrition: Calories: 472 Fat: 19g Carbohydrates: 49g Protein: 23g

Beef Stroganoff in Slow Cooker

Try this with your family – and you will love it forever!

Prep time: 11 minutes Cooking time: 8 hours Servings: 4

INGREDIENTS:

Beef stew meat

Small onion

5 tbsp. water

Worcestershire sauce

Cream cheese

1 can mushroom soup

DIRECTIONS:

1. Grease Slow Cooker with some butter.
2. Cut the beef into cubes, place evenly over bottom of a cooking bowl. Chop the onion, cover the meat with it.
3. Add some mushroom soup and some Worcestershire sauce. Add the water. Cover with the lid. Cook for 5 hours using a

HIGH mode (or for 8 hours on LOW). When the meal is ready, add and stir in cream cheese.

Nutrition: Calories: 377 Fat: 26g Carbohydrates: 11g Protein: 25g

Carnitas in Slow Cooker

Soft pork meat – what else do you need for beautiful dinner?

Prep time: 12 minutes Cooking time: 9-10 hours Servings: 12

INGREDIENTS:

One boneless pork shoulder

Salt

Cumin

Dried oregano

Garlic powder

Ground cinnamon

Bay leaves

Chicken broth

DIRECTIONS:

1. In a small bowl, combine some garlic powder, some salt, dried oregano, cumin, coriander and some cinnamon.
2. Grease your Slow Cooker. Place two bay leaves on the bottom. Place the pork meat to your Slow Cooker. Pour in the broth.
3. Cook under the lid for about 10 hours on LOW, wait until the meat begins to fall off. Shred with forks before serving.

Nutrition: Calories: 223 Fat: 13g Carbohydrates: 1g Protein: 22g

Summer Cabbage Rolls for Slow Cooker

Perfect choice for a summer party!

Prep time: 32 minutes Cooking time: 9 hours Servings: 6

INGREDIENTS:

Cabbage leaves

5 tbsp. milk

Chicken egg

Cup white rice

Worcestershire sauce

Salt

Brown sugar

1 can tomato sauce

lemon juice

Ground beef

Ground pepper

DIRECTIONS:

1. Place the cabbage leaves in a large pot with water. Boil for 2 minutes. Drain.
2. In a separate bowl, mix the cooked rice, beef, minced onion, milk and one chicken egg. Season the rice with salt\pepper.
3. Place the meat mixture in the middle of cabbage leaf. Make a long roll. Repeat this with other products. Transfer into Slow Cooker.
4. In a bowl, get together sugar, tomato and Worcestershire sauce with lemon juice. Add to the rolls. Cook for 9 hours with LOW temperature settings.

Nutrition: Calories: 248 Fat: 9g Carbohydrates: 18g Protein: 19g

Risotto with Bacon and Mushroom

Try this with your family!

Prep time: 23 minutes Cooking time: 2,5 hours Servings: 4

INGREDIENTS:

6 slices bacon

Whipping cream

Broth of chicken

1\2 cup shallots

White wine

Salt

Parmesan

2 cups rice

Mushrooms

DIRECTIONS:

1. Cover the cooking dish with cooking spray.
2. Heat the skillet and cook bacon just for 10 minutes (to get crispy). Transfer to Slow Cooker. Cook the mushrooms with shallots until browned.
3. Add rice and wine. Prepare for 3 minutes. Place to Slow Cooker. Pour in the broth.
4. Prepare on HIGH for 2 hours. Stir occasionally. To serve, stir in Parmesan with sour cream.

Nutrition: Calories: 411 Fat: 8g Carbohydrates: 31g Protein: 9g

Tangy Roast in Slow Cooker

Delicious meat dish for a special occasion!

Prep time: 11 minutes Cooking time: 6,5 hours Servings: 8

INGREDIENTS:

Boneless pork roast

Hot water

Large onion

2 tbsp. soy sauce

Sugar and salt

hot pepper sauce

Half tsp black pepper

Ketchup

Garlic powder

White wine vinegar

DIRECTIONS:

1. Slice the onion into small pieces.
2. Cover the bottom of a cooking dish with some butter. Place the onion over the bottom of your cooking dish. Place the boneless pork roast over the onion.
3. In a separate bowl, combine water, vinegar, ketchup. Add some soy sauce and sugar. Season with black pepper, garlic powder, salt, hot sauce.
4. Pour in the spicy mixture over the meat into Slow Cooker. Cover and leave to cook on LOW temp for 8 hours.

Nutrition: Calories: 210 Fat: 7g Carbohydrates: 9g Protein: 24g

Chicken Stroganoff for Slow Cooker

You will be amazed how tasty chicken could be!

Prep time: 10 minutes Cooking time: 5 hours Servings: 4

INGREDIENTS:

Four chicken breasts

1 tbsp. margarine

One can cream chicken soup

1 pack Italian dressing mix

1 pack cream cheese

DIRECTIONS:

1. Grease your Slow Cooker with olive oil or plain unsalted butter.
2. Remove the skin and bones out of chicken breasts and place them into Slow Cooker dish.
3. In a separate bowl, combine all the dressing mixes. Pour them into Slow Cooker and carefully rub into the breasts.
4. Mix the ingredients one more time and leave to cook for 5 hours on LOW mode. Add the cream of chicken soup and cream cheese to the cooking bowl.

5. Cook for another 30 minutes.

Zesty Chicken Barbeque

A chicken meal with a spicy lemon accent!

Prep time: 11 minutes Cooking time: 4 hours Servings: 6

INGREDIENTS:

Chicken breast halves

Italian salad dressing

2 tbsp. Worcestershire sauce

1 bottle barbeque sauce

Brown sugar

DIRECTIONS:

1. Grease your Slow Cooker with special cooking spray. Remove the bones and skin of chicken.
2. Place the chicken into your Slow Cooker.
3. In a bowl, combine Italian salad dressing, barbeque sauce, Worcestershire sauce, brown sugar. Pour the sauce mix over the chicken.
4. Cover and prepare on HIGH mode for 3-4 hour, or on LOW mode – for 8 hours.

Chicken with Dumplings in Slow Cooker

Just try these dumplings!

Prep time: 13 minutes Cooking time: 6 hours Servings: 9

INGREDIENTS:

chicken breast halves

One onion

2 cans condensed cream of chicken soup

Butter

2 packs biscuit dough

DIRECTIONS:

1. Remove the skin from chicken. Finely dice the onion.
2. Grease your Slow Cooker with some butter.
3. Place the chicken into Slow Cooker. Cover with diced onion, cream of chicken soup, butter. Pour in some water.
4. Prepare during 5 hours on HIGH mode. When it is 30 minutes before serving, place the torned biscuit into the dish.

Beef Roast for Slow Cooker

Try this with fresh vegetables or salad leaves!

Prep time: 19 minutes Cooking time: 6 hours Servings: 9

INGREDIENTS:

Bone-in beef roast

Medium onion

Sliced mushrooms

Vegetable oil

Salt/pepper

Chicken broth

1 tbsp. tomato paste

2 sprigs thyme

3 medium carrots

2 cloves garlic

Simple flour

Celery

1 sprig rosemary (fresh)

1 tbsp. butter

DIRECTIONS:

1. Season the roast from all sides with salt and pepper. Sprinkle a little with flour just to cover. Heat the vegetable oil in a large frying pan and brown the meat evenly.
2. Add butter and mushrooms, cook for 5 minutes. Then, stir in garlic, onion, 1-tablespoon flour and tomato paste.
3. Slowly stir in chicken stock and let to simmer.
4. Cut the carrots and celery. Then place to Slow Cooker along with roast and other vegetables, thyme and rosemary.
5. Pour the mushroom mixture. Cook on LOW for 5-6 hours.

Seasoned Beef with cream

The seasoning of this dish is just incredible!

Prep time: 16 minutes Cooking time: 5 hours Servings: 8

INGREDIENTS:

Lean ground beef

5 tbsp. milk

Half cup water

1 pack dry au jus mix

2 tbsp. vegetable oil

3 tbsp. flour

Half cup Italian seasoned bread crumbs

Dry onion soup mix

2 cans condensed cream of chicken soup

DIRECTIONS:

1. In a separate and large bowl combine the beef, bread crumbs, onion soup mix, milk. Stir with hands.

2. Separate the mixture into 8 parts and form the patties out of them.

3. Heat the vegetable oil in a large frying pan and quickly cook the patties until brown. Transfer the patties into greased Slow Cooker dish.

4. In a separate bowl, combine au jus mix, cream of chicken soup, water. Pour into Slow Cooker. Cook on LOW temperature for 4-5 hours.

Nutrition: Calories: 388 Fat: 24g Carbohydrates: 18g Protein: 23g

Slow Cooker Kalua Pig

Try this tasty receipt!

Prep time: 10 minutes Cooking time: 20 hours Servings: 12

INGREDIENTS:

1 tbsp. liquid smoke flavoring

One pork butt roast

1-2 tbsp. sea salt

DIRECTIONS:

1. Using a carving fork, pierce the pork roast all over.

2. Rub some salt into the meat and sprinkle with liquid smoke. Place the roast into prepared (buttered or oiled) Slow Cooker.

3. Cover the Slow Cooker with lid and leave to cook for around 16-20 hours on LOW mode. When it is half of time passed, torn the pork once.

4. To serve, remove the meat out of Slow Cooker and shred with two forks.

Nutrition: Calories: 243 Fat: 14g Carbohydrates: 1g Protein: 25g

Slow Cooker Spicy Pulled Pork

Easy to make spicy pork with seasoning!

Prep time: 19 minutes Cooking time: 6 hours Servings: 11

INGREDIENTS:

Chili powder

Cayenne pepper

1 tsp cumin

Half cup flour (all-purpose)

1 tsp paprika

Pork loin roast

2 onions

3 tbsp. hot pepper sauce

Brown sugar

2 cloves garlic

3 tbsp. barbeque sauce

Can diced tomatoes

DIRECTIONS:

1. Take a bowl and mix chili powder, plain flour, cumin, cayenne, paprika. Cut the pork into pieces and place them into the spicy mixture.

2. Meanwhile, in a pan melt the butter. Fry the pork until it is browned on all the sides. Transfer to Slow Cooker.

3. Using the same skillet, cook garlic with onion until fragrant. Add barbeque sauce, tomatoes, sugar, hot sauce. Then pour over the pork.

4. Set Slow Cooker on LOW and prepare for 5-6 hours.

Nutrition: Calories: 248 Fat: 8g Carbohydrates: 19g Protein: 22g

Soup with Italian sausage

Try this hot receipt!

Prep time: 23 minutes Cooking time: 6 hours Servings: 8

INGREDIENTS:

Sweet Italian sausage

2 zucchini

Half tsp dried oregano

Beef broth

2 cans peeled tomatoes

2 cloves garlic

Dried basil

3 tbsp. chopped parsley

1 pack spinach pasts

Green bell pepper

Dry red wine

DIRECTIONS:

1. Take a large pot and cook sausage till it is evenly brown. Remove from pan and drain (you can use paper towels).

2. Reserve the fat and cook chopped onion and garlic in it. Add tomatoes, pour in broth and wine, oregano and basil.
3. Transfer the pan mixture into greased Slow Cooker. Add bell pepper, zucchini, parsley and sausage.
4. Cook, covered, for 4-6 hours (use a LOW temperature mode).
5. Meanwhile, cook the pasta until al dente (for 6-7 minutes). Serve along with sausages.

Nutrition: Calories: 436 Fat: 17g Carbohydrates: 43g Protein: 21g

Hot Potatoes with Pork

Tasty and satisfying – what else do you need?

Prep time: 13 minutes Cooking time: 9 hours Servings: 8

INGREDIENTS:

3 carrots

Chuck roast

1 pack dry onion soup mix

Stalk celery

3 large potatoes

Onion

1 cup water

Species to taste

DIRECTIONS:

1. Cube the potatoes. Chop carrots, celery, onion.
2. Rub the roast with pepper and salt. Take a large skillet and brown the meat on other sides. Grease your Slow Cooker with butter or cooking spray, as you like.
3. Place the roast into it and cover with water, soup mix, onion, carrots, celery and potatoes. Cover the lid and leave, cooking, for 8-10 hours with LOW temperature setting.

Nutrition: Calories: 540 Fat: 30g Carbohydrates: 18g Protein: 45g

Pizza for Slow Cooker

Try pizza right from Slow Cooker!

Prep time: 24 minutes Cooking time: 4 hours Servings: 6

INGREDIENTS:

Ground beef

Classic pizza sauce

Shredded mozzarella cheese

1 pack rigatoni pasts

Pepperoni sausage

Cream of tomato soup

DIRECTIONS:

11. Pour cold water into a pot. Add a little salt.
12. Bring liquid to boil and add some pasta. Cook for 10 minutes (try if it is al dente). Place the skillet over medium fire and prepare the beef until it is brown.
13. Grease your Slow Cooker and place the ingredients in layers: noodles, beef, Mozzarella, pepperoni, sauce and soup.
14. Turn Slow Cooker and set on LOW. Prepare for 5 hours.

Nutrition: Calories: 682 Fat: 47g Carbohydrates: 50g Protein: 53g

Autumn Mushroom and Beef Delight

Perfect choice for your autumn dinner!

Prep time: 19 minutes Cooking time: 5-6 hours Servings: 4

INGREDIENTS:

1 can cream of mushroom soup (with garlic)

One yellow onion

2tsp vegetable oil

2 cans cream of mushroom soup

One cup water

1 peck dry onion soup mix

4 beef cube steaks

Half pack egg noodles

DIRECTIONS:

1. Take a deep bowl and whisk water, onion soup and cream of mushroom soup.
2. Place a large skillet over small heat and cook the onion. Rise heat to medium and stir until onion gets brown.
3. Add the cube sticks in the skillet about 7 minutes on every side. Place all the ingredients in Slow Cooker. Pour in mushroom mixture. Turn on the LOW mode and cook until the beef steaks are tender.
4. Meanwhile, cook the noodles following package directions.

Nutrition: Calories: 562 Fat: 21g Carbohydrates: 66g Protein: 26g

Sausages with Sauce

Simple, but delicious!

Prep time: 5 minutes Cooking time: 6 hours Servings: 6

INGREDIENTS:

8 links Italian sausage

6 hoagie rolls

One onion

One green bell pepper

One jar spaghetti sauce

DIRECTIONS:

1. Peel green bell pepper and remove the seeds. Slice, along with onion, into small cuts. Grease your Slow Cooker with some butter or anti-sticking spray.

2. Transfer the Italian sausage links, green pepper, spaghetti sauce and onion into Slow Cooker. Stir well to be sure that everything is covered with sauce.

3. Cover the lid and turn on Slow Cooker on LOW mode. Leave to cook for 6 hours.

Nutrition: Calories: 1024 Fat: 57g Carbohydrates: 88g Protein: 35g

Beef and Broccoli in Slow Cooker

A perfect couple of beef and broccoli

Prep time: 11 minutes Cooking time: 7 hours Servings: 8

INGREDIENTS:

Warm water

Beef bouillon cube

2 cloves garlic

Half cup soy sauce

Sesame oil

Brown sugar

2 tbsp. cornstarch

2 cups cooked jasmine rice

Beef sirloin

1 tbsp. sesame seeds

Broccoli florets

DIRECTIONS:

1. Dissolve bouillon cube in warm water. Add sugar, soy sauce, oil and garlic. Place the beef strips into a cooking dish. Pour the sauce mixture over.

2. Set on Slow Cooker on LOW mode and cook for 7 hours.

3. Take 3 tablespoons out of Slow Cooker mixture and whisk cornstarch into it. Pour it back into Slow Cooker.

4. In a separate saucepan, cook broccoli.

5. To serve, separate broccoli into portions and top with beef.

Nutrition: Calories: 814 Fat: 16g Carbohydrates: 98g Protein: 46g

Chicken with Pineapples in Slow Cooker

Try this one with pineapples or peaches!

Prep time: 17 minutes Cooking time: 4 hours Servings: 4

INGREDIENTS:

1 cup flour

1 cup pineapple chunks

1 clove garlic

Half cup soy sauce

2 tbsp. ketchup

4 tbsp. brown sugar

4 chicken thighs

Half cup pineapple juice

DIRECTIONS:

1. In a shallow bowl, sprinkle the flour and dredge chicken thighs to coat. Tap slightly to remove excess flour.

2. Grease the Slow Cooker with olive oil or cooking spray.

3. Place chicken thighs evenly over the Slow Cooker bottom and top with pineapples. In a small bowl, whisk soy sauce, pineapple juice, ketchup, brown sugar and garlic.

4. Place the lid on the cooking dish and prepare for 4 hours on LOW temperature mode.

Nutrition: Calories: 448 Fat: 11g Carbohydrates: 62g Protein: 23g

Western Omelette in Slow Cooker

Perfect for morning time!

Prep time: 23 minutes Cooking time: 12 hours Servings: 10

INGREDIENTS:

Onion

Diced cooked ham

12 chicken eggs

Salt/pepper to taste

Shredded cheddar cheese

1 cup milk

Green bell pepper

1 pack hash brown potatoes

DIRECTIONS:

1. Grease the inside of your Slow Cooker.

2. Transfer the 1/3 part of hash browns into Slow Cooker and evenly spread them over the bottom. Cover potatoes with 1/3 of onion, ham, bell pepper, Cheddar. Repeat two times.

3. In another bowl, whisk milk with chicken eggs. Whisk in species. Pour into Slow Cooker. Place the lid and set your Slow Cooker on LOW mode for 11 hours.

Nutrition: Calories: 310 Fat: 22g Carbohydrates: 16g Protein: 19g

Western Omelette in Slow Cooker

Perfect for morning time!

Prep time: 23 minutes Cooking time: 12 hours Servings: 10

INGREDIENTS:

Onion

Diced cooked ham

12 chicken eggs

Salt/pepper to taste

Shredded cheddar cheese

1 cup milk

Green bell pepper

1pack hash brown potatoes

DIRECTIONS:

1. Grease the inside of your Slow Cooker.
2. Transfer the 1/3 part of hash browns into Slow Cooker and evenly spread them over the bottom. Cover potatoes with 1/3 of onion, ham, bell pepper, Cheddar. Repeat two times.
3. In another bowl, whisk milk with chicken eggs. Whisk in species. Pour into Slow Cooker. Place the lid and set your Slow Cooker on LOW mode for 11 hours.

Nutrition: Calories: 310 Fat: 22g Carbohydrates: 16g Protein: 19g

Cheesy Macaroni for Slow Cooker

Can easily fit as a supper!

Prep time: 17 minutes Cooking time: 4 hours Servings: 8 servings

INGREDIENTS:

One cup milk

2cups pasta or macaroni

Cubed cream cheese

3tsp butter

Dijon mustard

1can evaporated milk

Whipping cream

Can diced tomatoes

Cubed American cheese

DIRECTIONS:

1. Start with greasing of your Slow Cooker. You can cover the bottom with butter. Place two cups of macaroni pasta into Slow Cooker. Spread evenly over the bottom.
2. One by one, place the other ingredients over the pasta (except tomatoes). Stir everything until combined well.
3. Turn on your Slow Cooker and prepare on LOW temperature mode for about 4 hours. To serve, stir in tomatoes.

Nutrition: Calories: 437 Fat: 29g Carbohydrates: 27g Protein: 16g

Turkey and Summer Vegetables in Slow Cooker

Perfect choice for summer!

Prep time: 5 minutes Cooking time:

Servings:

INGREDIENTS:

Skinless turkey thighs

3 parsnips

2cubes chicken bouillon

4 cups chicken broth

1 yellow squash

1 can garbanzo beans

7-8 baby carrots

1 jar artichoke hearts

1 can diced tomatoes

Salt and black pepper to taste

1 green bell pepper

1 tsp chopped dill

DIRECTIONS:

1. Cut turkey into even cubes and rub in the salt with pepper to your taste. Place the meat into greased Slow Cooker.
2. Pour in the diced tomatoes mixture over turkey. Then, add a layer of artichoke hearts. Place all the other INGREDIENTS: baby carrots, parsnips, green pepper and yellow squash.
3. Pour the chicken broth over the ingredients in Slow Cooker, just to cover them evenly. Add whole bouillon cubes.
4. Cook, covered, on LOW temperature mode for 8-10 hours. To serve, garnish with some fresh chopped dill.

Nutrition: Calories: 339 Fat: 6g Carbohydrates: 34g Protein: 36g

Chicken Spaghetti in Slow Cooker

If you love spaghetti, you should try this!

Prep time: 9 minutes Cooking time: 2 hours Servings: 6

INGREDIENTS:

Can condensed cream of chicken soup

Spaghetti

Processed cheese food

1 can cream of mushroom soup

canned diced tomatoes

Chicken breast halves

DIRECTIONS:

1. Bring cold water to boil and add some salt. Put spaghetti, cook until al dente. Grease your Slow Cooker with some olive oil.

2. Place tomatoes with green peppers, mushroom soup and chicken soup into Slow Cooker. Turn on the MEDIUM temperature heat and cook until the cheese is melted.

3. In the end, stir in spaghetti and prepare for 40-50 minutes.

Nutrition: Calories: 653 Fat: 24g Carbohydrates: 65g Protein: 40g

Slow Cooker Chicken with Carrots

Healthy and satisfying!

Prep time: 29 minutes Cooking time: 8 hours Servings: 8

INGREDIENTS:

Boneless and skinless chicken breasts

5 tbsp. water

Greek style seasoning

4 cubes chicken bouillon

Water

1 head cabbage (medium)

1 tsp poultry seasoning

Cornstarch

3carrots

DIRECTIONS:

1. Grease your Slow Cooker with cooking spray.

2. Place the rinsed chicken breasts into the cooking dish along with one-inch carrot slices. Add enough water to cover the meat.

3. Place the bouillon cubes and season with poultry seasoning and Greek seasoning to taste. Cover the Slow Cooker lid and leave to cook on high temperature on LOW for 8 hours.

Nutrition: Calories: 315 Fat: 3g Carbohydrates: 14g Protein: 54g

Summer Risotto in Slow Cooker

Delicious and satisfying summer meal!

Prep time: 27 minutes Cooking time: 2 hours Servings: 6

INGREDIENTS:

Arborio rice

Parmesan cheese

Salt

Dried onion flakes

4 cloves garlic

Olive oil

Black pepper

4tbsp. white wine

DIRECTIONS:

1. Cover the bottom of your Cooker with olive oil or melted unsalted butter. Right in a cooking pot, mix rice, garlic, salt, oil, onion flakes and black pepper. Add the chicken broth and stir the ingredients until even.

2. Turn on the Slow Cooker and choose HIGH mode. Cook for 1-2 hours.

3. When it is time, stir in shredded parmesan. Cook for 15 minutes, uncovered, until cheese is melted.

Nutrition: Calories: 325 Fat: 12g Carbohydrates: 43g Protein: 7g

Tropical Chicken with Pineapple

Exotic chicken for all family!

Prep time: 24 minutes Cooking time: 6 hours Servings: 6

INGREDIENTS:

2 chicken breasts

1 onion

Dried thyme

1 tbsp. lemon zest

4 sweet potatoes

Jamaican jerk seasoning

Canned pineapple chunks

Dried cumin

1 tsp ginger

Half cup raisins

DIRECTIONS:

1. Cut all the vegetables, grease the Slow Cooker.

2. Place the potatoes, chicken and onion to the cooking dish.

3. In a separate bowl, combine the pineapples (along with juice), jerk seasoning, raisins, Worcestershire sauce, cumin, ginger and lime zest.

4. Pour this mixture over the chicken in your Slow Cooker and sprinkle with dried thyme. Cover the lid and set your Slow Cooker to LOW temp. Cook until tender (for about 6 hours).

Nutrition: Calories: 361 Fat: 2g Carbohydrates: 68g Protein: 19g

Sauerkraut with Sausage in Slow Cooker

Try this one with sauerkraut!

Prep time: 19 minutes Cooking time: 4 hours Servings: 5

INGREDIENTS:

One medium onion

One can sauerkraut

Ground pork sausage

5 tbsp. brown sugar

DIRECTIONS:

1. Grease your Slow Cooker with some melted butter.

2. In a separate bowl of medium size, combine the sugar with sauerkraut and mix well. Place the sauerkraut into Slow Cooker. Then, cover with diced onion and pork sausage.

3. Turn on the Slow Cooker. Top with the lid. Cook for 2-3 hours on HIGH temperature mode. You can also add some water during the process, if needed.

4. Reduce the settings to LOW temperature mode and cook for another 2 hours.

Nutrition: Calories: 640 Fat: 55g Carbohydrates: 18g Protein: 16g

Slow Cooker Vegetarian Mash

Both vegetarian and meat-eater will love this!

Prep time: 7 minutes Cooking time: 5 hours Servings: 6

INGREDIENTS:

1 container vegetable broth

1 cup cremini mushrooms

1 pack cream cheese

1 pack fresh spinach

1pack cheese-filled tortellini (frozen)

DIRECTIONS:

1. Spray your Slow Cooker with anti-stick cooking spray.

2. Right in a cooking pot, stir together cream cheese, tortellini, mushrooms and spinach. Mix until even consistency.

3. Pour in one container of vegetable broth.

4. Stir all the ingredients one more time, place the dish into Slow Cooker and turn it on. Set the LOW temperature mode and prepare for 5 or 6 hours.

Nutrition: Calories: 398 Fat: 20g Carbohydrates: 40g Protein: 15g

Simple Slow Cooker Enchiladas

Perfect dish for busy mornings!

Prep time: 28 minutes Cooking time: 5 hours Servings: 7

INGREDIENTS:

One cup onion

Cheddar

Salt to taste

2cloves garlic

Ground turkey

Ground pepper

Canned black beans

Water

6 corn tortillas

Monterey Jack cheese

Ground cumin

1-2 tsp chili powder

1 can diced tomatoes (with green chili peppers)

1 can kidney beans

Chopped green bell pepper

DIRECTIONS:

1. Place turkey into large frying pan; add bell pepper, garlic and onion. Cook until the meat is completely browned.

2. Stir in kidney beans, water, diced tomatoes, chili powder, salt, black beans, cumin and salt with pepper. Simmer for 10 minutes.

3. Mix Monterey Jack cheese and Cheddar cheese in separate bowl.

4. Divide the pan mixture and cheeses into 3-4 parts and place in layers over the greased Slow Cooker bottom.

5. Set up the LOW cooking mode and leave to cook for 5-7 hours.

Nutrition: Calories: 614 Fat: 31g Carbohydrates: 41g

Protein: 44g

Stuffed Peppers for Slow Cooker

Amazing choice for summertime!

Prep time: 17 minutes Cooking time: 5 hours Servings: 4

INGREDIENTS:

Ground pork

4 green bell peppers

1 cup peas

Water

Cup processed cheese (cubed)

Half cup barbeque sauce

White rice

DIRECTIONS:

1. Peel peppers, remove the seeds and set hollow peppers aside.
2. In a separate bowl, combine rice, peas, meat, half cup water and barbeque sauce. Mix until blended.
3. Fill the pepper shells with the rice mixture.
4. Right in your Slow Cooker cooking pot, combine remaining barbeque sauce and water. Place stuffed peppers into Slow Cooker and cover the lid.
5. Cook on LOW mode for 5-7 hours.

Nutrition: Calories: 383 Fat: 14g Carbohydrates: 42g Protein: 19g

Slow Cooker Chicken with Vegetables

A satisfying meal for great dinner!

Prep time: 17 minutes Cooking time: 3 hours Servings: 8

INGREDIENTS:

4 chicken breasts

Red potatoes

2 carrots

Olive oil

Green bell pepper

Lemon

Garlic

Soy sauce

2 tomatoes

Yellow bell pepper

Red bell pepper

Green peas

Black pepper

DIRECTIONS:

1. Cut the tomatoes and potatoes into cubes, slice the peppers, onion, chop the carrots. Grease your Cooker with some butter.
2. Place cubed chicken breasts, lemon juice, soy sauce, garlic, lemon juice and black pepper into Slow Cooker dish.
3. Add red potatoes, peppers, carrots, peas, onion to Slow Cooker. Set LOW temperature mode and cook for 8 hours.

Nutrition: Calories: 331 Fat: 20g Carbohydrates: 19g Protein: 19g

Baby Carrots Roast in Slow Cooker

Healthy and tasty dish!

Prep time: 17 minutes Cooking time: 6 hours Servings: 11

INGREDIENTS:

Salt to taste

Beef chuck roast (boneless)

Soy sauce

Cream of mushroom soup

Half cup brown sugar

1pack onion soup mix

Ground pepper

White vinegar (distilled)

1 can beef gravy

2tbsp. flour

1 tbsp. Worcestershire sauce

Half cup brown sugar

DIRECTIONS:

1. Grease your Slow Cooker crock and place the boneless beef roast into it.
2. In a separate bowl, mix together beef gravy, vinegar, cream of mushroom soup, soy sauce, salt, Worcestershire sauce and pepper. Stir well.
3. Pour the mixture over the meat into Slow Cooker.
4. Cover the Slow Cooker lid and cook for 6-7 hours on HIGH temperature mode. If you have time – use a LOW mode and cook for 12-14 hours.
5. Ladle the liquid from Slow Cooker to saucepan and bring to boil. Add some flour and stir until thick gravy.
6. Serve the roast with hot gravy.

Nutrition: Calories: 663 Fat: 44g Carbohydrates: 24g Protein: 36g

Slow Cooker Creamy Oatmeal

Just tasty and creamy one!

Prep time: 7 minutes Cooking time: 8 hours Servings: 4

INGREDIENTS:

1 cup half-and-half or any regular cream

3 cups water

1 cup oats

4 tbsp. brown sugar

1pinch salt or to taste

DIRECTIONS:

1. Place the oats into a medium bowl and cover with cold water. Let stand for 1-2 hours. Wash and drain oats and place them into Slow Cooker.
2. Pour in fresh water to cover the beans.
3. Turn on your Slow Cooker, set on LOW temperature mode, and cook for 7-8 hours. As a variant, you can leave it cooking overnight.
4. In the morning, add half-and-half and salt into cooked oats. Serve in small bowls, sprinkled with brown sugar.

Nutrition: Calories: 208 Fat: 8g Carbohydrates: 29g Protein: 4g

Mac in Cheese for Slow Cooker

Try this with your friends!

Prep time: 23 minutes Cooking time: 3 hours Servings: 11

INGREDIENTS:

2cups milk

2 eggs

Half cup butter

1 pack macaroni

1 can evaporated milk

Condensed cheese soup

Paprika

Pepper and salt

DIRECTIONS:

1. Fill a pot with enough water and cook macaroni in salted water, according to package directions. Place to buttered Slow Cooker.
2. Add half cup butter to the pasta. Combine until melted. Season the macaroni with salt, paprika and pepper.
3. Add ½ of Cheddar and stir.

4. In a separate bowl, whisk beaten eggs and evaporated milk to get smooth consistency. Add into Slow Cooker.
5. Top the ingredients with remaining Cheddar cheese and sprinkle with milk and paprika. Mix one more time.
6. Cook on LOW temperature for 3 hours.

Nutrition: Calories: 430 Fat: 21g Carbohydrates: 33g Protein: 17g

Spicy Pasta with Mushrooms and Chicken

Cook this pasta for great dinner!

Prep time: 12 minutes Cooking time: 6 hours Servings: 6

INGREDIENTS:

Boneless chicken breasts

Basil

Small yellow onion

Half green bell pepper

Jar spaghetti sauce

Dried oregano

3 tbsp. minced garlic

Canned tomato sauce

Sliced mushrooms

Red pepper flakes

Black pepper to taste

DIRECTIONS:

1. Cut the chicken breasts into halves. Place to greased Slow Cooker. Add tomato paste and spaghetti sauce.
2. Mince the onion, garlic, peel and seed pepper. Add the veggies into Slow Cooker. Season the chicken with pepper, flakes, basil.
3. Cover and prepare for 6 to 8 hours on LOW temperature mode.

Nutrition: Calories: 364 Fat: 8g Carbohydrates: 42g Protein: 30g

Pepperoni Pizza in Slow Cooker

For pepperoni lovers!

Prep time: 21 minutes Cooking time: 2 hours Servings: 6

INGREDIENTS:

Marinara sauce

1pack klushki noodles

2cans sliced mushrooms

Grong beef

2 cups Cheddar cheese

Canned pizza sauce

2 cups Mozzarella

1 pack sliced pepperoni

DIRECTIONS:

1. Boil water in a large pot, slightly salt. Cook noodles for 5 minutes, then drain.

2. Heat a large frying pan with some oil. Place the beef into frying pan and wait until slightly brown and a little crumbly (around 5-7 minutes). Add marinara and pizza sauce.

3. Grease the bottom of your Slow Cooker with some butter or olive oil and cover with a half of noodles.

4. Add ½ ground beef mixture, ½ mushrooms, ½ cheese and pepperoni. Repeat one more time. Place the lid on Slow Cooker and prepare on LOW mode for 1-2 hours.

Nutrition: Calories: 677 Fat: 31g Carbohydrates: 56g Protein: 40g

Venison Stew in Slow Cooker

Easy-to-make one!

Prep time: 23 minutes Cooking time: 9 hours Servings: 8

INGREDIENTS:

8 medium potatoes

Venison stew meat

3 stalks celery

3 cubes beef bouillon

Pepper/salt to taste

3 medium onions

8 large carrots

3 cans beef broth

2 cups fresh mushrooms

Half cup cornstarch

2 cups green peas

1 cup water

2 tbsp. seasoning and browning sauce

DIRECTIONS:

1. Grease the Slow Cooker pot with some butter or cover with special cooking spray.

2. Place diced potatoes, carrots, celery, seasoning sauce, celery and venison in Slow Cooker. Pour in the broth and bouillon; add some water just to cover ingredients.

3. Turn Slow Cooker on high mode and wait until the liquid starts to boil. Reduce to LOW and leave for 8-10 hours.

4. Add diced mushrooms, pepper, salt and peas.

5. Whisk in some cornstarch and cook on high until the peas are warmed through.

Nutrition: Calories: 407 Fat: 3g Carbohydrates: 61g Protein: 32g

Chile Verde in Slow Cooker

Cook this, if you love spicy food!

Prep time: 17 minutes Cooking time: 8 hours Servings: 8

INGREDIENTS:

1 small onion

Boneless pork shoulder

1 can diced tomatoes

5 cans green salsa

2 cloves garlic

3 tbsp. olive oil

1 can jalapeno peppers (diced)

DIRECTIONS:

1. In a large skillet, preheat the olive oil over medium heat.

2. Add diced onion and minced garlic. Cook, stirring, until fragrant.

3. Cut the pork into cubes and transfer it into skillet. Cook until it is browned on all sides. Place all the skillet ingredients to Slow Cooker.

4. Stir in the jalapeno peppers, green salsa and diced tomatoes.

5. Cook under the lid for 3 hours (on HIGH mode), then reduce to LOW and leave for 4-5 hours.

Nutrition: Calories: 265 Fat: 12g Carbohydrates: 12g Protein: 22g

Slow Cooker Chicken with Pasta and Cream

Great satisfying meal for big company!

Prep time: 11 minutes Cooking time: 6 hours Servings: 4

INGREDIENTS:

One can cream of mushroom soup

1 pack cream cheese (room temperature)

1 tbsp. Italian seasoning

3 tbsp. sour cream

One chicken breast

DIRECTIONS:

1. Remove the skin and bones from chicken breast. Divide it into small cubes.

2. Cover the bottom of your Slow Cooker with some olive oil or melted unsalted butter.

3. Right in the cooking dish, combine cream of mushroom soup, cream cheese, Italian seasoning and sour cream and stir well.

4. Place the chicken cubes into Slow Cooker.

5. Turn on and set your Slow Cooker to LOW temperature. Cook for 6 hours.

Nutrition: Calories: 357 Fat: 27g Carbohydrates: 7g Protein: 19g

Mussaman Potato Curry in Slow Cooker

Amazing and exotic one!

Prep time: 33 minutes Cooking time: 6 hours Servings: 9

INGREDIENTS:

Small onion

2 potatoes

3 tbsp. curry powder

3 cloves garlic

2tbsp. butter

Coconut milk

3tbsp. Thai sauce

Beef broth

3 tbsp. brown sugar

Peanut butter

Half cup peanuts (unsalted)

DIRECTIONS:

1. Dice the potatoes and onions. Place into buttered Cooker.

2. In a skillet, melt the butter and cook beef, along with minced garlic. When the beef is evenly browned, place into Slow Cooker.

3. In the same skillet, heat peanut butter, coconut milk, curry powder. Pour over the beef. Add brown sugar, then fish sauce with beef broth.

4. Turn on the LOW mode and prepare the beef until tender, for 6 hours.

Nutrition: Calories: 545 Fat: 40g Carbohydrates: 29g Protein: 21g

Mexican Roast in Slow Cooker

Mexican and spicy dish for the perfect evening!

Prep time: 32 minutes Cooking time: 10 hours Servings: 7 servings

INGREDIENTS:

Beef broth

Avocado oil

1 tsp ground cumin

2 onions

Beef roast

Some salt

3 bell peppers

Red wine vinegar

Chopped cilantro

1 can tomato paste

2 tbsp. minced garlic

DIRECTIONS:

1. Preheat a large skillet with avocado oil. Cook the beef roast.

2. When it is brown, transfer to Slow Cooker and add tomato paste, bell peppers, beef broth and minced onion.

3. In a bowl, mix vinegar, olive oil, cumin, garlic, tomato paste and salt. Pour over the peppers. Cook on HIGH mode for 1 hour, then reduce to LOW and continue for 8 hours.

4. When almost ready, shred the beef and add cilantro. Leave for another 1 hour.

Nutrition: Calories: 329 Fat: 11g Carbohydrates: 20g Protein: 30g

Chili Chicken with Beans

Amuse your friends with chili meal!

Prep time: 23 minutes Cooking time: 4 hours Servings: 6

INGREDIENTS:

Bay leaf

Green bell pepper

Any chicken meat without bones

Large onion

Chili powder

Tomato paste

Canned kidney beans

Black pepper

Stewed tomatoes

Canned black beans

2 tbsp. rice vinegar

Half cup mango salsa

Salt

Smoked paprika

DIRECTIONS:

1. Peel and seed peppers, cut all the vegetables into small slices. Drain the beans. Grease your Slow Cooker and place bite-sized chicken over its bottom.
2. Add green pepper, black and kidney beans, mango salsa, tomatoes and tomato paste.
3. Mix the beans liquid, rice vinegar, salt, bay leaf, pepper, paprika and chili powder. Pour into Slow Cooker.
4. Set on HIGH temperature mode and leave for 1 hour. Add chili and reduce to LOW. Prepare for 4 hours.

Nutrition: Calories: 213 Fat: 5g Carbohydrates: 26g Protein: 16g

Chicken with Bread Cubes

Just simple and healthy!

Prep time: 13 minutes Cooking time: 8 hours Servings: 6

INGREDIENTS:

3medium onions

Poultry seasoning

Salt

Celery

Half tsp ground pepper

Cup butter

4chicken breast halves

12 cups dry bread cubes

Dried sage

Condensed cream of mushroom soup

Chicken liquid

DIRECTIONS:

1. Finely chop onions and celery.
2. In a pot, boil chicken meat in salted water.
3. Slightly grease your Cooker with some oil, place the boiled chicken breasts over its bottom.
4. In separate bowl, mix butter, onion, poultry seasoning, bread cubes, mushroom soup, reserved cooking liquid with celery,
5. Add pepper, sage, salt and stir everything well. Pour the dressing into Slow Cooker. Turn on Slow Cooker and set the LOW mode. Prepare for 6 hours.

Nutrition: Calories: 158 Fat: 8g Carbohydrates: 1g Protein: 7g

Broccoli Beef in Slow Cooker

A healthy meal for every member of your family!

Prep time: 19 minutes Cooking time: 7 hours Servings: 4

INGREDIENTS:

1cup water

2cloves garlic

Half cup soy sauce

Broccoli florets

Cornstarch

Beef sirloin

2 cups jasmine rice

Sesame oil

Beef bouillon cube

Brown sugar

Sesame seeds (to garnish)

DIRECTIONS:

1. Cut beef into strips and place to Slow Cooker.
2. Into a bowl with warm water, dissolve bouillon cube, sugar, add garlic, sesame oil and soy sauce. Pour over the beef.
3. Turn on LOW mode and cook for 6 hours.
4. Take 3 tablespoons liquid from Slow Cooker and dissolve cornstarch. Place back to the cooking dish and cook for about 30 minutes.
5. In a separate pan cook broccoli and jasmine rice.
6. To serve, place the meat on top of broccoli and rice. Garnish with sesame seeds.

Nutrition: Calories: 814 Fat: 16g Carbohydrates: 91g Protein: 46

Slow Cooker Pizza with Ravioli

Try this one with cold juice!

Prep time: 5 minutes Cooking time: 4 hours Servings: 8

INGREDIENTS:

1 clove garlic

Ground beef

1tsp dried basil

2cups shredded Mozzarella cheese

Half tsp ground black pepper

1 tsp garlic powder

Salt to taste

1 pack frozen ravioli

1 tsp dried oregano

1 tsp Italian seasoning

DIRECTIONS:

1. Cook the beef in a large skillet along with garlic powder, pepper, and garlic, salt. Cook until gets brown and aromatic.
2. Add basil, Italian seasoning, and oregano and pasta sauce. Grease your Slow Cooker with olive oil or plain butter, as you like. Ladle, in several layers, meat, ravioli and tomato mixture.
3. Turn on LOW and cook for 3-5 hours.
4. In the end, sprinkle with Mozzarella and leave until it melts, for another hour,

Nutrition: Calories: 544 Fat: 23g Carbohydrates: 52g Protein: 29g

Stuffed Cabbage with Meat and Tomatoes

Satisfying and delicious one!

Prep time: 31 minutes Cooking time: 2 hours Servings: 8

INGREDIENTS:

One large Savoy

4 garlic cloves

White rice

Olive oil

1 carrot

Yellow onion

Fresh Parmesan cheese

Grated lemon rind

Ground black pepper

Salt to taste1 large chicken egg

Lean ground beef

3 cups tomatoes

DIRECTIONS:

1. Preheat the large pan with one tablespoon olive oil.
2. Mix in onion, carrot, 2 cups chopped cabbage, garlic. Cook for 4-5 minutes, then remove, slightly cool.
3. In a bowl, grate Parmesan cheese.
4. Add rice, lemon rind, chopped dill, salt, beef, pepper, egg. Add cabbage and stir finely. Make the logs out of this mixture and cabbage leaves.
5. Mix tomato paste with remaining oil. Pour one cup mixture over Sow Cooker bottom, place the cabbage logs. Top with remaining tomatoes.
6. Cook on LOW for 6 hours.

Nutrition: Calories: 327 Fat: 16g Carbohydrates: 28g Protein: 19g

Chicken Thighs with Peaches

Just simple, sweet and healthy!

Prep time: 11 minutes Cooking time: 2 hours Servings: 8

INGREDIENTS:

Ground cumin

Olive oil

Chopped basil

Sugar

6 garlic cloves

2 tbsp. red onion

2 tsp lime juice

Chicken thighs on bone

Fresh mint

2 peaches

6 lime wedges (to serve)

Salt to taste

1 jalapeno pepper

Ground pepper

DIRECTIONS:

1. In a bowl, whisk 3 tablespoons oil with minced garlic. Add cumin. Add chicken and toss in the garlic mixture to coat.
2. For salsa, combine fresh mint, basil, chopped onion, lime juice, sugar, jalapeno and diced peaches. Add salt.
3. Grease your Slow Cooker with olive oil. Then, place the chicken into it. Pour a little marinade over it.
4. Cook on LOW for 3 hours.
5. To serve, add salsa and cut the lime into wedges.

Nutrition: Calories: 196 Fat: 11g Carbohydrates: 5g Protein: 20g

Potato Casserole with Cheddar

Classical casserole now in your Slow Cooker!

Prep time: 21 minutes Cooking time: 6 hours Servings: 10

INGREDIENTS:

1 pack hash brown potatoes

1 pack maple-flavored sausage

1 cup milk

12 chicken eggs

1 tbsp. ground mustard

1pack shredded Cheddar

DIRECTIONS:

1. Spray the bottom of your cooking dish with cooking spray.

2. Divide hash browns into halves and spread them over Slow Cooker bottom. In a bowl, whisk milk, mustard, salt, chicken eggs, black pepper.

3. In a skillet, cook sausage until crumbly. Place over hash browns in Slow Cooker. Cover the lid and prepare on LOW for 6 hours.

Nutrition: Calories: 641 Fat: 54g Carbohydrates: 21g Protein: 35g

Baked Potatoes Stuffed with Ham

Baked and stuffed – two in one!

Prep time: 11 minutes Cooking time: 2 hours Servings: 6

INGREDIENTS:

2tbsp. water

5 potatoes

Greek yogurt (fat-free)

Salt to taste

3 small green onions

Black pepper

Bag baby spinach

Lower-sodium ham

Shredded Cheddar cheese

DIRECTIONS:

1. Grease Slow Cooker with unsalted butter.

2. Cut potatoes into halves, place into Slow Cooker. Prepare on LOW for 2 hours. When ready, try with a fork if they are tender.

3. In a skillet, cook spinach with water until wilted. Then, use a paper towel and remove all excess liquid.

4. Take out the potatoes and remove pulp.

5. In a bowl, mix yogurt, potato pulp, pepper, ham, salt, spinach and cheese. Fill the potato shells with this mixture.

6. To serve, sprinkle with diced green onions.

Nutrition: Calories: 273 Fat: 5g Carbohydrates: 46g Protein: 12g

Spaghetti Squash in Slow Cooker

Develop your spaghetti skills!

Prep time: 23 minutes Cooking time: 4 hours Servings: 4

INGREDIENTS:

1 spaghetti squash

Salt

Butter to grease

2 cups water

DIRECTIONS:

1. Grease your Slow Cooker dish with some butter.

2. Take a long knife and prink the whole squash with it for several (up to 10-15) times. Put the squash into a cooking crock and pour in water to cover the squash.

3. Turn on Slow Cooker and set to LOW temperature mode. Cook for 4-6 hours. Take the squash out and drain. Wait to cool.

4. Cut and remove the seeds. To serve, shred with a fork (make strands) and remove the skin.

Nutrition: Calories: 54 Fat: 1g Carbohydrates: 12g Protein: 1g

Hash Brown Casserole with Cheese

Your family will love this one!

Prep time: 27 minutes Cooking time: 9 hours Servings: 9

INGREDIENTS:

Salt to taste

1-2 cups onion

6 chicken eggs

Half cup sour cream

Canada oil

Black pepper

1 pack hash browns

Chopped pancetta

Red bell pepper (chopped)

1 cup milk

Green onions (to garnish)

DIRECTIONS:

1. Mix half cheese, 2 tbsp sour cream, half cup onion, 1 egg in a large bowl. Add salt/pepper to taste. Add hash brown potatoes.

2. Take a skillet and preheat 4 tablespoons into it. Prepare hash browns for 7 minutes. When evenly browned, place to Slow Cooker.

3. In the same skillet, add remaining vegetables and cook for 3 minutes.

4. Whisk half cup cheese, 5 eggs, milk and salt/pepper. Pour into Slow Cooker. Cook on LOW for 4 hours.

Nutrition: Calories: 136 Fat: 9g Carbohydrates: 36g Protein: 12g

100

Chicken Chili Recipe

Hot recipe for those who loves chili!

Prep time: 26 minutes Cooking time: 4 hours Servings: 11

INGREDIENTS:

Large onion

Boneless chicken meat

Green bell pepper

1 bay leaf

Mango salsa

Kidney beans

Canned tomato paste

Black pepper

Rice vinegar

Smoked paprika

Chili powder

Salt to taste

1can stewed tomatoes

Canned black beans

DIRECTIONS:

1. Remove the skin and bones from chicken meat.
2. Place chicken, all beans, green pepper, onion, tomato paste, mango salsa, stewed tomatoes, bay leaf into Slow Cooker.
3. Sprinkle with rice vinegar, season with chili, salt, paprika, black pepper. Turn on the Slow Cooker and set the HIGH.
4. Cook for one hour, then turn to LOW and leave for 3 hours.

Nutrition: Calories: 212 Fat: 5g Carbohydrates: 26g Protein: 16g

Steak with Beans and Crumbs

Just simple and healthy for you and your family!

Prep time: 19 minutes Cooking time: 5 hours Servings: 9

INGREDIENTS:

Vegetable oil

Milk

Lean ground beef

Half cup bread crumbs

6 tbsp. water

Condensed cream of chicken soup

Onion soup mix

Flour

Au jus

DIRECTIONS:

1. Take a bowl, combine onion soup mix with milk and breadcrumbs.
2. Add ground beef. Combine 8 even patties and dredge each one in flour. In a skillet, cook patties real quick.
3. Place into your Slow Cooker, trying to form the pyramid.
4. In a bowl, combine chicken soup, water and au jus. Pour into Slow Cooker. Set LOW and prepare for 5 hours.

Nutrition: Calories: 387 Fat: 24g Carbohydrates: 18g Protein: 23g

SNACKS AND APPETIZERS

Sweet Bacon Pigs

Simple, but very delicious!

Prep time: 17 minutes Cooking time: 5 hours Servings: 10

INGREDIENTS:

Half tsp Chinese spicy powder

1 pack little smokey sausages

Hot pepper sauce (1 dash)

Bacon in slices

1-2 cups brown sugar

Cola-flavored beverage

DIRECTIONS:

1. Wrap each sausage with thin slice of bacon. To secure, pin each one with toothpick. Place all the appetizers over baking sheet and sprinkle with brown sugar.
2. Bake on 165 degrees for 40 minutes (20 minutes for each side).
3. Transfer bacon pigs from baking sheet to Slow Cooker. Sprinkle with sugar and Chinese powder. Drizzle with hot sauce and cola.
4. Set to HIGH mode and cook for 4 hours.

Nutrition: Calories: 291 Fat: 17g Carbohydrates: 24g Protein: 10g

Cheese and Beer Dip

The secret ingredient makes the dish better!

Prep time: 5 minutes Cooking time: 1 hour Servings: 16

INGREDIENTS:

Half cup salsa

Processed cheese food

1 tsp chili powder

Cayenne pepper (optional)

Half teaspoon onion powder

2 tbsp. Worcestershire sauce

1 cup Irish beer

DIRECTIONS:

1. Grease your Slow Cooker with unsalted butter. Place processed cheese food into Slow Cooker.
2. Turn on and set on HIGH temperature mode and cook until melted, for about 20 minutes.
3. In separate bowl, combine salsa, chili powder, Worcestershire sauce, cayenne pepper and onion powder.
4. Stir the spicy mix with cheese and wait for 10 more minutes.

Nutrition: Calories: 224 Fat: 17g Carbohydrates: 2g Protein: 12g

Buffalo Wings for Slow Cooker

The perfect choice for those, who loves wings!

Prep time: 33 minutes Cooking time: 4 hours Servings: 8

INGREDIENTS:

Half cup butter

2tsp garlic powder

1 bottle hot sauce

2 tsp onion powder

2 tsp dried oregano

Chicken wing sections

DIRECTIONS:

1. In a pot, mix together hot pepper sauce, Worcestershire sauce, half-cup butter. Add onion powder, dried oregano, garlic powder. Simmer for about 5 minutes.
2. Put the chicken wings in Slow Cooker and pour the spicy mixture over it.
3. Cook on HIGH mode and prepare for 2 hours. Then reduce to LOW and leave for another 2 hours. Place the wings over buttered baking sheet and bake in oven until browned and crisp.
4. Melt hot sauce with butter and simmer to get thick. Serve the wings with the sauce.

Nutrition: Calories: 385 Fat: 34g Carbohydrates: 3g Protein: 16g

Slow Cooker Sauerkraut Dip

Unusual ingredients for tasty dip!

Prep time: 5 minutes Cooking time: 1-2 hours Servings: 12

INGREDIENTS:

Thousand island dressing

1 jar sauerkraut

2 cups shredded Swiss cheese

1 pack cream cheese

2 cups corned beef (cooked and shredded)

DIRECTIONS:

1. Slightly cover your Slow Cooker with unsalted butter.
2. Right in a cooking dish, mix cream cheese, sauerkraut, Swiss cheese, Thousand Island dressing and corned beef.
3. Cover the lid and cook for 1-2 hours on HIGH temperature mode. Stir occasionally during the cooking process.
4. Serve with crackers or cocktail rye.

Nutrition: Calories: 298 Fat: 22g Carbohydrates: 5g Protein: 17g

Meatballs Appetizer

Funny meatballs are easy and fast to make!

Prep time: 17 minutes Cooking time: 2 hours Servings: 6

INGREDIENTS:

2 tbsp. lemon juice

1 can pineapple chunks in juice

2 tbsp. cornstarch

1 green bell pepper

1bag frozen meatballs

Half cup brown sugar

2 tbsp. soy sauce

DIRECTIONS:

1. Place pineapple chunks (along with the juice) into large saucepan.
2. Add brown sugar, green bell pepper, soy sauce, and cornstarch and lemon juice. Stir to dissolve cornstarch.
3. Bring the cornstarch mixture to boil and wait, stirring, until thick (about 10 minutes). Put the meatball into Slow Cooker and pour in (to cover) the pineapple juice.
4. Cook on MEDIUM temperature regime for 2 hours, stir each 30 minutes.

Nutrition: Calories: 611 Fat: 29g Carbohydrates: 46g Protein: 38g

Barbeque Kielbasa in Slow Cooker

Love barbeque! Try to cook this one!

Prep time: 11 minutes Cooking time: 2 hours Servings: 20

INGREDIENTS:

2bottles barbeque sauce

Polish kielbasa sausage

Butter to grease

1 jar grape jelly

DIRECTIONS:

1. Cover the bottom of your Slow Cooker with a thin layer of butter. Cut the sausage inti small (1-2 inch size) pieces.

2. Place kielbasa slices into Slow Cooker.

3. In separate bowl, whisk together jelly and barbeque sauce. Pour the mixture over the sausage pieces.

4. Turn on Slow Cooker and set on MEDIUM or HIGH temperature mode for 2 hours.

Nutrition: Calories: 262 Fat: 15g Carbohydrates: 23g Protein: 6g

Cheese and Beef Carne

Tasty meat snack for any company!

Prep time: 27 minutes Cooking time: 1 hour Servings: 16

INGREDIENTS:

1 pack taco seasoning

Ground beef

1 loaf processed cheese

4 cans diced tomatoes (with green chili peppers)

Half cup milk

DIRECTIONS:

1. Place the cheese into greased Slow Cooker, sprinkle with milk.

2. Take a large skillet and it over the medium heat. Prepare beef until it is well crumbled and evenly browned.

3. Add taco seasoning and diced tomatoes. Stir everything well and bring to simmer.

4. Transfer the beef and tomato mixture into Slow Cooker and mix in processed cheese with milk. Set Slow Cooker on HIGH mode and cook about 1 hour, or until the cheese is melted.

Nutrition: Calories: 227 Fat: 15g Carbohydrates: 6g Protein: 14g

Superheated Peanuts in Syrup

Simple and fast sweet appetizer!

Prep time: 23 minutes Cooking time: 1 hour Servings: 8

INGREDIENTS:

Half cup salt

1 tbsp. garlic powder

Raw peanuts in shells

Half cup jalapeno peppers

Half cup red pepper flakes

1 pack dry crab boil

Half cup salt

DIRECTIONS:

1. Place crab boil, peanuts, and jalapeno peppers (minced) into your Slow Cooker dish. Season with garlic powder, Cajun seasoning, salt and red pepper flakes.

2. Pour in enough water to cover peanuts and stir well to combine everything.

3. Cover the lid of Slow Cooker and prepare at least for 24 hours om LOW mode, until the peanuts are soft.

4. Stir time after time and add additional water, if needed. Drain to serve.

Nutrition: Calories: 360 Fat: 29g Carbohydrates: 16g Protein: 16g

Spicy Beef Balls

Spicy meatballs for those, who loves hot!

Prep time: 5 minutes Cooking time: 1 hour Servings: 10

INGREDIENTS:

1 small onion

Half cup water

2 cloves garlic

Ground beef

1jigger whiskey

Half cup soy sauce

Half cup seasoned bread crumbs

DIRECTIONS:

1. Into wide bowl, mix ground beef, minced onion and bread crumbs with seasoning. Make small bite-sized balls out of bread and beef mixture.

2. In a large frying pan with oil slightly brown meatballs from every side.

3. In separate bowl, mix soy sauce, whiskey, minced garlic and water. Put the balls into this mixture and place into refrigerator for 1-2 hours.

4. Place the balls into buttered Slow Cooker and sat it on LOW mode. Cook for 30 minutes or, if needed, for 1 hour.

Nutrition: Calories: 185 Fat: 12g Carbohydrates: 5g Protein: 9g

Chicken Dip with Black Beans

Another simple dip!

Prep time: 7 minutes Cooking time: 1-2 hours Servings: 12

INGREDIENTS:

2medium onions

1 can diced tomatoes with green chili peppers

3 tbsp. sour cream

3 jalapeno peppers

1 cup black beans

1-2 tbsp. taco seasoning mix

1 loaf processed cheese

2 chicken breast halves

DIRECTIONS:

1. Mince the onions and jalapeno peppers. Rinse and drain black beans.

2. Grease the Slow Cooker dish and fill it with sour cream, processed cheese, diced tomatoes and chicken meat.

3. Add jalapeno peppers and taco seasoning.

4. Turn on Slow Cooker and set on HIGH. Cook until hot melted cheese (for around 1-2 hours). In the end, stir in black beans and continue cooking for 17 minutes.

Nutrition: Calories: 232 Fat: 13g Carbohydrates: 8g Protein: 19g

Taco Bean for Tortilla or Chips

Tacos with bacon and beans!

Prep time: 5 minutes Cooking time: 1 hour Servings: 12

INGREDIENTS:

Sour cream

Cheddar cheese

3 tbsp. salsa

1pack taco seasoning mix

2cans condensed beans with bacon soup

DIRECTIONS:

1. Shred Cheddar cheese to get half cup or one cup of it.

2. Take a medium bowl and combine the seasoning mix, condensed soup and salsa. Mix well. Transfer the salsa mixture into the greased Slow Cooker.

3. Top with shredded Cheddar cheese and cook on LOW for about 1 hour (or just until the cheese melts).

4. Serve with tacos or any king of cheese.

Nutrition: Calories: 132 Fat: 6g Carbohydrates: 12g Protein: 5g

Little Smokie Sausages

Glazed sausages are small and easy to make!

Prep time: 11 minutes Cooking time: 2 hours Servings: 16

INGREDIENTS:

1 cup brown sugar

1 tbsp. Worcestershire sauce

2 packs little wieners

Half cup ketchup

1bottle barbeque sauce

1 medium onion

DIRECTIONS:

1. Cover the bottom of your Slow Cooker with olive oil or plain unsalted butter.

2. In separate bowl, mix together brown sugar, Worcestershire sauce, barbeque sauce and ketchup. Finely mince the onion and add it to the ketchup mixture.

3. Place little wieners into Slow Cooker dish and pour in over with the ketchup mixture. Turn on Slow Cooker and set on LOW temperature mode. Cook for 1-2 hours.

Nutrition: Calories: 285 Fat: 16g Carbohydrates: 28g Protein: 6g

Mushrooms in Marinade

Love mushrooms? Here is another way to make them delicious!

Prep time: 9 minutes Cooking time: 8 hours Servings: 16

INGREDIENTS:

2cups white sugar

2 cups soy sauce

1 cup butter

2 cups water

4 packs fresh mushrooms

DIRECTIONS:

1. Take a medium saucepan and combine water, butter and soy sauce. Mix until the butter has melted.
2. Add the sugar and continue to stir, until it is dissolved.
3. Grease your Slow Cooker with butter or oil, or spay with a cooking spray.
4. Remove stems and place mushrooms into Slow Cooker dish. Cover with soy sauce mixture. Set up to LOW temperature setting for around 8-10 hours.

Nutrition: Calories: 228 Fat: 11g Carbohydrates: 29g Protein: 3g

Seafood Dip with Cheese

An amazing dish for any case!

Prep time: 5 minutes Cooking time: 1 hour Servings: 10

INGREDIENTS:

1-2 cups sour cream

Half cup cooked lobster

Half cup small shrimp

2 tbsp. cream cheese (reduced fat)

1 tsp Worcestershire sauce

2 tsp seafood seasoning

Half cup crab meat

1 loaf bread

1 pack processed cheese food

DIRECTIONS:

1. Flake crabmeat and lobster, cook half-cup small shrimp.
2. In a medium bowl, combine cream cheese, sour cream, processed cheese food, crabmeat, shrimp and lobster.
3. Grease your Slow Cooker with some melted and unsalted butter.
4. Place the cream and lobster mixture into your Slow Cooker and set the LOW cooking mode. Wait for around 1 hour to get cheese melted.
5. Add Worcestershire sauce and seafood seasoning. To serve, cut French white bread.

Nutrition: Calories: 308 Fat: 14g Carbohydrates: 29g Protein: 15g

Jalapeno Peppers with Chicken

Hot peppers for hot snack!

Prep time: 22 minutes Cooking time: 4 hours Servings: 4

INGREDIENTS:

Cream cheese

1 tsp cumin

4 chicken breasts

1-2 cups shredded cheese

1 tsp salt

Half cup jalapenos

1 tsp garlic powder

16 taco tortillas

DIRECTIONS:

1. Place chicken, jalapenos, cream cheese, salt, garlic powder, cumin and salt into Slow Cooker. Cover the lid and leave to cook for 6-8 hours on LOW mode.
2. Heat the tortillas in microwave and shred chicken meat with forks. Place the chicken onto tortillas and top with cheese.
3. Transfer the tortillas to large baking sheet and cook for 10-13 minutes.

Nutrition: Calories: 321 Fat: 18g Carbohydrates: 61g Protein: 23g

Pumpkin Granola with Nutella

Perfectly fits for autumn!

Prep time: 11 minutes Cooking time: 2-3 hours Servings: 10

INGREDIENTS:

Pumpkin puree

Nutella

Half cup raisins

Honey or maple syrup

Old-fashioned oats

Vegetable oil

Pure vanilla extract

Sunflower or pumpkin seeds

Ground cloves

1cup cereal

Ground ginger and cinnamon

Salt to taste

DIRECTIONS:

1. Grease Slow Cooker to avoid sticking.
2. In a mixing bowl, combine pumpkin puree, maple syrup, Nutella, oil and vanilla. In another bowl, mix rice cereal, oats, cinnamon, seeds, cloves and ginger.
3. Add the wet ingredients into cereal and combine well to coat.
4. Place the mixture into your Slow Cooker and set to HIGH temperature. Cook for 2 hours, stirring every 30 minutes.

Nutrition: Calories: 344 Fat: 17g Carbohydrates: 35g Protein: 2g

Chocolate oatmeal bars

For those, who loves sweet snacks!

Prep time: 11 minutes Cooking time: 8 hours Servings: 8

INGREDIENTS:

Half teaspoon vanilla

2 chicken eggs

Half cup ground flaxseed

1 large banana

2cups rolled oats

Chocolate topping

1 cup milk

1 tsp vanilla stevia

Salt to taste

1 tsp baking powder

Ground cinnamon

DIRECTIONS:

1. In a large bowl, mix eggs, banana, milk, vanilla stevia and vanilla extract.
2. In separate bowl, mix all the other ingredients, except the chocolate topping. Combine the mixtures from both bowls and blend well until fully incorporated.
3. Place the parchment paper over the bottom of Slow Cooker and spread the batter over it. Turn on Slow Cooker and prepare on LOW temperature mode for 7-8 hours.
4. To serve, cut into small portions and cover with chocolate topping.

Nutrition: Calories: 168 Fat: 4g Carbohydrates: 25g Protein: 7g

Chocolate Fudge for Slow Cooker

Just another chocolate appetizer, but so delicious!

Prep time: 7 minutes Cooking time: 2 hours Servings: 10

INGREDIENTS:

1 tsp vanilla extract

Chocolate chips

1 tbsp. salted butter

1can condensed milk (sweetened)

Butter

DIRECTIONS:

1. Spray your Cooker with cooking spray or melted butter.

2. Place all ingredients into Slow Cooker and leave to cook for 2 hours (LOW0 mode) or for 1 hour (for HIGH mode).
3. Stir the mixture in your Slow Cooker every 20 or 30 minutes.
4. When ready, spread the chocolate mixture over the deep baking pan. Place into refrigerator for at least 4 hours, but better overnight.
5. To serve, cut into bite-size cubes.

Nutrition: Calories: 238 Fat: 8g Carbohydrates: 32g Protein: 9g

Balsamic Pork with Honey

Sweet pork for any case!

Prep time: 13 minutes Cooking time: 9 hours Servings: 6

INGREDIENTS:

Half cup chicken broth

Half cup honey

Hoisin sauce

3 cloves garlic

Half cup balsamic vinegar

12 buns

2small onions

1 tbsp. cornstarch

Blackberry notes

Half cup chicken broth

DIRECTIONS:

1. Remove the excess fat from pork and place trimmed meat into greased Slow Cooker.
2. Take a medium bowl and mix balsamic vinegar, chicken broth, jam, honey, garlic, hoisin and onion.
3. Turn on Slow Cooker and set on LOW mode. Cook for 8-9 hours.
4. When ready, shred the pork with two forks (you can do it right in Slow Cooker).
5. Pour the liquid from Slow Cooker into large saucepan and add cornstarch. Simmer until slurry. Serve the pork on buns with slurry sauce.

Nutrition: Calories: 411 Fat: 9g Carbohydrates: 36g Protein: 12g

Jalapeno Peppers stuffed with Sausage

Hot sausages with spicy peppers!

Prep time: 19 minutes Cooking time: 2 hours Servings: 12

INGREDIENTS:

Ground pork sausage

1 bottle Ranch dressing

1 pack cream cheese

Large jalapeno peppers

1 cup Parmesan cheese (shredded)

DIRECTIONS:

1. Grease your Slow Cooker with some butter or olive oil.
2. Take a medium skillet and preheat it with oil. Cook sausage until it is all-sides brown. Drain. Take a large bowl and combine the sausage, Parmesan and cream cheese.
3. Seed and divide jalapeno peppers into halves and stuff each half with sausage mixture. Arrange peppers over the bottom of your Slow Cooker and turn it on. Cook for 2 hours on LOW mode.

Nutrition: Calories: 362 Fat: 34g Carbohydrates: 4g Protein: 9g

Spinach Dip with Artichokes

Healthy dip with spinach!

Prep time: 5 minutes Cooking time: 3 minutes Servings: 3

INGREDIENTS:

Garlic salt

1 package cream cheese

Dried basil

Shredded Mozzarella cheese

Salt/pepper to taste

Grated Romano cheese

1 clove garlic

Half cup chopped spinach

1 can artichoke hearts

3 tbsp. mayonnaise

DIRECTIONS:

1. Lightly grease with olive oil or unsalted butter your cooking dish.
2. In a medium bowl, stir mayonnaise, Romano cheese, cream cheese and Parmesan cheese. Add minced garlic, salt, basil, black pepper and garlic salt.
3. Stir into this mixture chopped spinach and artichoke hearts. Transfer to Slow Cooker and top with shredded Mozzarella. Cook for 3-4 hours on LOW temperature mode.

Nutrition: Calories: 134 Fat: 11g Carbohydrates: 3g Protein: 4g

Stuffed Potato Skins

Simple dish with unusual serving!

Prep time: 29 minutes Cooking time: 1-2 hours Servings: 6

INGREDIENTS:

1 container sour cream

6 large potatoes

Shredded Cheddar cheese

1 cup vegetable oil

Sliced bacon

DIRECTIONS:

1. Grease your Slow Cooker with unsalted and melted butter.
2. Do not peel the potatoes; just pierce them with a fork or knife and place into microwave to get soft for 11-12 minutes.
3. Halve the potatoes and remove the inside part.
4. Put the potato shells into Slow Cooker and set on LOW. Cook for 2 hours. When ready, drain with paper towels.
5. Fill the shells with bacon and place back to Slow Cooker for 30 minutes.

Nutrition: Calories: 519 Fat: 32g Carbohydrates: 40g Protein: 17g

Jalapeno Taquitos in Slow Cooker

Hot taquitos for any kind of party!

Prep time: 32 minutes Cooking time: 3 hours Servings: 4

INGREDIENTS:

16 flour tortillas

8 chicken thighs

Green enchilada sauce

2 cups pepper jack cheese

Salt/pepper to taste

1 can diced jalapenos

2 tbsp. vegetable oil

1 pack cream cheese (softened)

DIRECTIONS:

1. Grease your Slow Cooker and fill in with skinless chicken thighs, green enchilada sauce, cream cheese, salt, jalapenos with juice and black pepper.
2. Set on HIGH and cook, covered, for 3 or 4 hours.
3. Shred chicken with two forks and stir well with Slow Cooker sauce. Heat tortillas in oven or microwave.
4. Fill it with meat mixture, roll and place back to oven and wait, until cheese melts.

Barbeque Bites in Slow Cooker

Small barbeque appetizers for any occasion!

Prep time: 27 minutes Cooking time: 12 hours Servings: 30

INGREDIENTS:

Beef broth

3 cloves garlic

1bison brisket

Sour cream

Chili powder

Cider vinegar

Worcestershire sauce

Fresh cilantro (chopped)

2packs baked phyllo shells

Half cup barbeque sauce

Cayenne pepper

Cheddar cheese

DIRECTIONS:

1. Divide bison brisket into small, bite-sized pieces and transfer to the buttered Slow Cooker.

2. In medium bowl, combine Worcestershire sauce, chili powder, broth, garlic, cayenne pepper and vinegar. Pour the sauce mixture over the meat.

3. Cover the lid and leave cooking on LOW mode for 12 hours.

4. Meanwhile, preheat oven to 200 degrees and place the phyllo dough shells over baking sheet. Fill each shell with shredded bison and cook for 10 minutes.

5. To serve, top with cilantro, cheese or sour cream.

Nutrition: Calories: 119 Fat: 3g Carbohydrates: 6g Protein: 13g

Chicken Bites in Moroccan Style

Just try this exotic recipe!

Prep time: 5 minutes Cooking time: 7 hours Servings: 20

INGREDIENTS:

One large onion

Boneless chicken thighs

Hummus

2 tbsp. cumin

2 tbsp. lemon juice

1 tbsp. paprika

1 tbsp. minced garlic

5-6 slices bread

Minced garlic

Cinnamon

3 tbsp. oil

Salt

Parsley (to garnish)

1-2 cups chicken stock

Green olives

DIRECTIONS:

1. Take a large skillet and cook the minced onion with some oil and peppers. Add ginger and garlic and cook until fragrant, just a minute.

2. Mix in cinnamon and cumin, cook for another 2 minutes.

3. Place the thighs over the bottom of your Slow Cooker and pour in the pepper mixture. Add olives, lemon juice, salt and pepper. Fill with 2 cups chicken stock.

4. Cover and set your Slow Cooker on LOW mode. Cook for 7 hours. To serve, arrange meat with sauce on small bread slices.

Nutrition: Calories: 322 Fat: 8g Carbohydrates: 37g Protein: 22g

Jalapeno Bites with Cheese and Bacon

Hot bacon dips!

Prep time: 9 minutes Cooking time: 2-4 hours Servings: 32

INGREDIENTS:

1 tbsp. bacon bits

1 cup dried bread crumbs

Softened cream cheese

Jalapeno peppers

1 cup flour

Olive oil

1 pack shredded Cheddar

One cup milk

DIRECTIONS:

1. Take a medium bowl and combine bacon bits, Cheddar cheese and cream cheese. Fill the jalapeno peppers halves with this mixture.

2. In two separated bowls, prepare milk and flour. Dip stuffed jalapenos firstly in milk, secondly in flour.

3. Roll jalapenos into breadcrumbs and let dry.

4. Place the parchment onto the bottom of your Slow Cooker and arrange jalapenos over it. Set on HIGH and let cook for 3 hours.

Nutrition: Calories: 149 Fat: 12g Carbohydrates: 6g Protein: 3g

Spicy Cajun Pecans

Just pecans, but so tasty in Slow Cooker!

Prep time: 9 minutes Cooking time: 2 hours Servings: 20

INGREDIENTS:

1 tsp salt

Pecan halves

1 tsp dried thyme

3 tbsp. melted butter

1 tsp dried oregano

Half tsp onion powder

Ground cayenne pepper

Garlic powder

1 tbsp. chili powder

DIRECTIONS:

1. In a separate bowl, combine all the ingredients and stir carefully. Slightly grease your Slow Cooker with cooking spray.
2. Transfer pecan and spices mixture into your Slow Cooker. Cover the lid and prepare for 10-17 minutes on high temperature mode.
3. Turn to LOW and remove the lid. Continue to cook for 2 more hours.
4. Before serve, place the nuts onto baking sheet or plain paper towel and cool.

Nutrition: Calories: 156 Fat: 18g Carbohydrates: 1g Protein: 8g

Seafood Dip Appetizer

Love seafood? This one is for you!

Prep time: 11 minutes Cooking time: 2 hours Servings: 25

INGREDIENTS:

1 cup Cheddar cheese (shredded)

2 cans condensed cream of shrimp

1 cup lobster (cooked and diced)

Dash cayenne pepper

1 cup American cheese

Half cup cooked shrimp

Dash nutmeg

1 cup crabmeat

1 loaf crusty bread

DIRECTIONS:

1. Cover with melted butter the side parts and bottom of your Slow Cooker. Right in Slow Cooker dish, combine all ingredients (except bread).
2. Stir everything well.
3. Cook under the lid for 2 hours on HIGH mode (check if the cheese is melted). Cut the bread into cubes and serve along with seafood dip.

Nutrition: Calories: 178 Fat: 8g Carbohydrates: 22g Protein: 9g

Wrapped Bacon Hot Dogs

Just hot dogs, but in Slow Cooker!

Prep time: 15 minutes Cooking time: 1 hour Servings: 20

INGREDIENTS:

1 pack little smokies or mini cocktail franks

Half cup brown sugar

4 tbsp. maple syrup

1 tsp chili paste

Bacon (about 15 strips)

Ground black pepper

1 tsp Dijon mustard

DIRECTIONS:

1. Wrap each smokie sausage with thin strip of bacon. If needed, pin it with toothpick to avoid falling apart.
2. Preheat the oven to 200 degrees and arrange wrapped smokies over it. Bake around 30 minutes, just until slightly brown.
3. Make a sauce: in saucepan, mix maple syrup, sugar, chili paste, mustard and black pepper. Transfer sausages to Slow Cooker and pour over with sauce. Set on LOW and cook for 1 hour. Serve along with sauce.

Nutrition: Calories: 322 Fat: 12g Carbohydrates: 15g Protein: 9g

Swiss Fondue in Slow Cooker

Amazing fondue that everyone will love!

Prep time: 9 minutes Cooking time: 1 hour Servings: 10

INGREDIENTS:

1 loaf crusty bread

3 tbsp. flour

Ground pepper

Shredded Swiss cheese

2 cups dry white wine

3 tbsp. Kirsch

Paprika

Freshly ground nutmeg

Cheddar cheese

1 clove garlic

DIRECTIONS:

1. Rub the pan with garlic halves. Pour in dry white wine and heat until bubble (use a medium heat). Add lemon juice.

2. In a medium bowl, mix the four with cheeses. Stir the mixture into wine. Cook until the cheese is blended.

3. Cover the inner surface of your Slow Cooker with cooking spray.

4. Pour in the cheese mixture into Slow Cooker and add Kirsch. In addition, sprinkle with pepper, nutmeg and paprika.

5. Cook under cover, firstly on high for 25 minutes, then on LOW for 1-3 hours.

Nutrition: Calories: 212 Fat: 12g Carbohydrates: 7g Protein: 1g

Bean Queso with Cheese

Try this beans with cheese!

Prep time: 15 minutes Cooking time: 2 hours Servings: 16

INGREDIENTS:

1 cup beer

1 cup salsa

Half tsp garlic powder

2 cans cheesy sauce

Ground cumin

1 can green chiles (chopped)

2 cans refried beans

Half cup chopped cilantro

DIRECTIONS:

1. In a large bowl, combine chiles, refried beans. Also, you can do it right in a Slow Cooker dish. Season with oregano, garlic powder, salsa and cumin.

2. Add cheese sauce and one cup of beer.

3. Turn on the LOW temperature mode and cook for 2 hours.

4. At the end, add cilantro and cook well to combine the ingredients. To serve, use bread cubes or tortilla chips.

Nutrition: Calories: 158 Fat: 9g Carbohydrates: 12g Protein: 6g

Spicy Champignons

If you love mushrooms, try this spicy ones!

Prep time: 13 minutes Cooking time: 3 hours Servings: 8

INGREDIENTS:

4 tbsp. water

Half cup hoisin sauce (bottled)

Crushed red pepper

2 tbsp. minced garlic

Cleaned fresh mushrooms

DIRECTIONS:

1. In a small bowl, mix together water, hoisin sauce, crushed red pepper and garlic. Slightly grease your Slow Cooker and pour in the spicy mixture.

2. Place the mushrooms into Slow Cooker and toss to cover with the sauce. Cover the lid and leave to cook for 2-3 hours on LOW temperature mode. Serve with toothpicks and any garnish you like.

Nutrition: Calories: 36 Fat: 1g Carbohydrates: 4g Protein: 1g

Sugared and Spicy Nuts

Unusual taste of your future favorite snack!

Prep time: 5 minutes Cooking time: 3 hours Servings: 12

INGREDIENTS:

Half cup powdered sugar

Pecan or walnuts halves

Ground cloves

Ground ginger

Half cup melted and unsalted butter

Ground cinnamon

DIRECTIONS:

1. Preheat your Slow Cooker before start.

2. When Slow Cooker is hot, stir nuts and melted butter in it. Add the sugar powder and stir until evenly coat.

3. Place the lid and cook for 15 minutes on high. Reduce to LOW and cook without cover for 2-3 hours.

4. Meanwhile, in small bowl combine the spices and stir into nuts. Cool spice nuts to serve.

Nutrition: Calories: 200 Fat: 8g Carbohydrates: 19g Protein: 17g

Small Beef Nachos

Try these homemade nachos!

Prep time: 7 minutes Cooking time: 8 hours Servings: 30

INGREDIENTS:

1 can beef broth

Boneless beef roast

Tortilla chips

Salt/pepper to taste

Chopped tomatoes

1 jar banana pepper rings

1 tbsp. vegetable oil

Shredded Monterey jack cheese

3 garlic cloves

1 can beef broth

Minced onion

1 can black beans

Sour cream, cilantro and avocado to serve

DIRECTIONS:

1. Use salt and pepper to season the beef. Then, brown the meat from all sides in a large frying pan. When ready, transfer beef into your Slow Cooker.
2. Mix in beef broth, garlic and banana pepper rings.
3. Cover the lid and cook for 8 hours using a LOW mode. Shred the beef with two forks, when it is cooked.
4. Top tortillas with shredded meat and place in preheated oven for 10 minutes. To serve, use an avocado, cilantro and sour cream.

Nutrition: Calories: 233 Fat: 15g Carbohydrates: 34g Protein: 7g

Cereal Mix for Slow Cooker

Sweet and perfect for kids!

Prep time: 11 minutes Cooking time: 3 hours Servings: 16

INGREDIENTS:

8 cups cereal

1cup peanuts

2cups pretzels

1 tsp garlic powder

1 cup Cheerios

3 tbsp. Worcestershire sauce

Seasoned salt

DIRECTIONS:

1. Right in the bowl of your Slow Cooker, combine pretzels, cereal, peanuts and cheerios. In another bowl, whisk salt, butter and Worcestershire sauce.
2. Sprinkle this sauce over the cereal mixture and toss to combine ingredients evenly. Cover the Slow cooker with lid and set to LOW.
3. Cook for 3 hours, stirring occasionally.

Nutrition: Calories: 159 Fat: 31g Carbohydrates: 1g Protein: 6g

Baked Tater Tots

Tater tot appetizer – choose this receipt!

Prep time: 11 minutes Cooking time: 3 hours Servings: 30

INGREDIENTS:

1 can Rotel

Browned ground beef

Small onion

Cream of chicken soup

1 pack frozen Tater Tots

Cheddar (shredded)

DIRECTIONS:

1. In a large frying pan, brown the beef with some oil and add Rotel and diced onion. Grease your Slow Cooker and pour beef and onion mix into the cooking dish.
2. Add cream of chicken soup and mix everything well. Across top, place the tater tots.
3. Turn on your Slow Cooker and set to LOW. Cook for 2-3 hours. When it is 30 minutes left, sprinkle with shredded cheese.

Nutrition: Calories: 188 Fat: 8g Carbohydrates: 19g Protein: 27g

Spice Nachos with Chicken

Chicken and nachos – unforgettable taste!

Prep time: 5 minutes Cooking time: 2 hours Servings: 26

INGREDIENTS:

1 container sour cream

3 green onions

Chicken breast strips

1 red bell pepper

1 can black beans

111

3 tsp salsa

1loaf cheese product

DIRECTIONS:

1. Grease your Slow Cooker – use a special cooking spray for it.
2. Right in a cooking dish, combine chicken with salsa, cheese and beans.
3. Set your Slow Cooker on LOW temperature regime and cook for 2 hours, stirring.
4. Add cream, onions and bell pepper. Increase temperature to HIGH and cook for another 45 minutes.
5. To serve, place over tortilla chips.

Nutrition: Calories: 268 Fat: 19g Carbohydrates: 11g Protein: 33g

Fajitas with Chicken and Beef

Cook and try it with your family!

Prep time: 5 minutes Cooking time: 4 hours Servings: 30

INGREDIENTS:

Boneless and skinless chicken breast

Half cup beer

2tbsp tomato paste

Lime juice

2 cloves garlic

2 bell peppers

1 tbsp chili powder

1 yellow onion

1 tsp ground cumin

Avocado

Greek yogurt

DIRECTIONS:

1. Grease your Slow Cooker with oil or simply cover with cooking spray. Place chicken with pepper and onions into greased bowl.
2. In separate bowl, whisk tomato paste, lime juice, beer, cumin and chili powder. Pour over chicken meat.
3. Set Slow Cooker on HIGH and cook for 4 hours.
4. Serve with dressing, made of avocado and Greek yogurt.

Nutrition: Calories: 288 Fat: 22g Carbohydrates: 38g Protein: 2g

Marsala Mushrooms in Slow Cooker

Try this mushroom receipt with Marsala sauce!

Prep time: 5 minutes Cooking time: 8 hours Servings: 3

INGREDIENTS:

1 small shallot

Cremini mushrooms

2 cloves garlic

1 tsp cornstarch

3 tbsp sweet Marsala

Half cup heavy whipping cream

3 tbsp chicken stock

2tbsp parsley

Salt pepper to taste

DIRECTIONS:

1. Lightly grease your slow cooker and cover its bottom with mushrooms. Sprinkle with minced parsley, shallot and garlic.
2. In separate bowl, combine chicken stock with Marsala. Pour over mushrooms with this mixture. Add some pepper and salt.
3. Cover the Slow Cooker lid and prepare mushrooms on LOW settings for 8 hours. In the end, dissolve cornstarch with heavy cream and add into Slow Cooker.
4. To serve, sprinkle with Parmesan and parsley.

Nutrition: Calories: 322 Fat: 16g Carbohydrates: 31g Protein: 12g

Hot Dogs with Chili and Cheese

Really spiced hotdogs!

Prep time: 11 minutes Cooking time: 3 hours Servings: 30

INGREDIENTS:

Worcestershire sauce

Tomato sauce

3medium onions

1tsp mustard

Half cup celery

Butter

Ground beef meat

Salt

Lemon juice

Brown sugar

Chili seasoning hot dog buns

1 pack sausages

Colby Jack cheese

DIRECTIONS:

1. In a medium skillet, melt butter and add chopped onion and celery. Cook for several minutes until tender.
2. In another pan, cook beef until lightly brown. Drain with paper towels. Grease your Slow Cooker and place the beef inti it.
3. Add the mixture from the first pan and all other ingredients. Cover with the lid and simmer on HIGH for 3-4 hours.
4. Place hot dogs into buns, along with chili and cheese.

Nutrition: Calories: 188 Fat: 18g Carbohydrates: 28g Protein: 41g

Beer chicken buns

Chicken with beer – why not?

Prep time: 5 minutes Cooking time: 8 hours Servings: 28

INGREDIENTS:

Chicken breasts

Salt and pepper to taste

2 tbsp flour

Beer

2tbsp chopped chives

2 tbsp butter

Half cup milk

Grated Cheddar

2 cloves garlic

DIRECTIONS:

1. Put chicken in the Slow Cooker, season with salt, garlic and pour in the beer. Turn on the Slow Cooker and choose the LOW mode. Cook for 8 hours.
2. When ready, shred the chicken with fork and knife or two forks.
3. Make a cheese sauce out of melted butter, milk and a little beer (just heat the ingredients in saucepan until thickened).
4. Turn heat to low and add chives and cheese. Serve on heated buns.

Nutrition: Calories: 276 Fat: 18g Carbohydrates: 21g Protein: 8g

Sandwiches with Pulled Beef

Satisfying sandwiches for you and your friends!

Prep time: 5 minutes Cooking time: 8 hours Servings: 25

INGREDIENTS:

3large bell peppers

1 cup beef broth

1beef chuck roast

Salt

American cheese

Black pepper

2medium onions

Half cup jalapenos

8 long sandwich buns

DIRECTIONS:

1. Slightly rub the beef with black pepper and salt.
2. Along with broth, add the beef chuck roast to Slow Cooker. Sprinkle with jalapenos and green peppers.
3. Place the lid and cook on LOW mode for 8 hours.
4. Shred the meat and divide it, along with vegetables, over the hot dog buns. Cover with the cheese and place into preheated oven until it melts.

Nutrition: Calories: 344 Fat: 27g Carbohydrates: 34g Protein: 12g

Buffalo Chicken Dip

Perfect and fast chicken dip!

Prep time: 5 minutes Cooking time: 3 hours Servings: 30

INGREDIENTS:

Cream cheese

Chicken meat

Half cup ranch dressing

Shredded Mozzarella cheese

Half cup hot wing sauce

Half cup crumbled blue cheese

2 tbsp unsalted butter

Half cup ranch dressing

DIRECTIONS:

1. Spray the cooking dish with non-stick spray or grease with melted butter.
2. In a bowl, combine chopped chicken, Mozzarella, cream cheese blue cheese, wing sauce, ranch dressing, butter, Stir well to combine.
3. Transfer the chicken mixture to Slow Cooker.
4. Cook under the lid on HIGH temperature mode for around 2-3 hours. Do not forget to stir every 40 minutes.
5. To serve, turn on LOW mode.

Nutrition: Calories: 158 Fat: 8g Carbohydrates: 31g Protein: 23g

Meatballs with Bacon in Slow Cooker

Tasty meatballs, upgraded with bacon strips!

Prep time: 5 minutes Cooking time: 2 hours Servings: 22

INGREDIENTS:

3 tbsp maple syrup

1 pack frozen meatballs

Cooked bacon

Pinch dried chili peppers

2 tbsp bourbon

1cup barbeque sauce

DIRECTIONS:

1. In a separate bowl, mix maple syrup, barbeque sauce, chili peppers and bourbon. Line your Slow Cooker with parchment and place frozen meatball over it.
2. Pour the bourbon sauce over it and set Slow Cooker on HIGH. Cook for 2 hours and stir time after time.
3. To serve, place the meatballs on long toothpick along with bacon strips.

Nutrition: Calories: 237 Fat: 16g Carbohydrates: 36g Protein: 28g

Chutney and Spiced Chips

Another delicious chutney for your evening!

Prep time: 5 minutes Cooking time: 2 hours Servings: 20

INGREDIENTS:

2large apples

1 sweet onion

4 tbsp balsamic vinegar

2 large pears

Ground cinnamon

1 cup cranberries

3 tbsp brown sugar

1 tsp fround ginger

Salt

Spiced chips

1tbsp cornstarch

Goat cheese

2tbsp cold water

DIRECTIONS:

1. Grease your Slow Cooker with plain butter or olive oil.
2. In the cooking dish, combine pears, onion, apples, brown sugar, cranberries, cinnamon, vinegar, salt and ginger.

3. Cover Slow Cooker with lid and cook for 1 hour on HIGH mode.
4. In a small plate combine water and cornstarch and pour into Slow Cooker. Cook for another hour. Serve warm with spicy chips.

Nutrition: Calories: 102 Fat: 2g Carbohydrates: 18g Protein: 11g

Broccoli Dip with Cheese

Just amazing for kids and grown-ups!

Prep time: 5 minutes Cooking time: 4 hours Servings: 22

INGREDIENTS:

Reduced-fat cream cheese

1 cup broccoli

Reduced-fat cheese product

Fat-free milk

3tbsp salsa

Potato dippers (to serve)

4tsp vegetable protein bits

DIRECTIONS:

1. Grease your Slow Cooker with anti-stick spray.
2. Right in a cooking dish, combine cheese product, cream cheese, salsa, broccoli and bacon-flavor bits.
3. Cover the Slow Cooker lid and set to LOW. Cook for 4 hours. Stir in the end, just before serving.
4. Serve along with Potato Dippers.

Nutrition: Calories: 147 Fat: 12g Carbohydrates: 22g Protein: 9g

Cocktail Sausages in Glaze

Just try this amazing glaze!

Prep time: 5 minutes Cooking time: 4 hours Servings: 34

INGREDIENTS:

3 tbsp maple syrup

Cocked and smoked Polish sausage

1 tbsp bourbon

Apricot preserves (low-sugar)

1 tsp quick-cooking tapioca

DIRECTIONS:

1. Cover the bottom and sides of your Slow Cooker with melted butter.
2. In a cooking dish, combine the sausage slices, maple syrup, apricot preserves. Sprinkle with bourbon and tapioca.

3. Cover the lid and leave for 4 hours on LOW-heat mode. Serve while hot with wooden toothpicks.

Nutrition: Calories: 211 Fat: 13g Carbohydrates: 31g Protein: 6g

Slow Cooker Snacks with Lemon Zest

The taste of lemon zest in it is everything!

Prep time: 5 minutes Cooking time: 2 hours Servings: 35

INGREDIENTS:

Half cup chopped walnuts

Multigrain cereal

3 tbsp pumpkin seeds

2 cups pita chips

1tsp dried rosemary

Ranch salad dressing mix (dry)

2 tbsp olive oil

2tbsp dried dill mix

1 tbsp lemon zest (finely shredded)

DIRECTIONS:

1. Grease Slow Cooker with cooking spray or line with the foil.
2. Right in Slow Cooker dish, mix pita chips, cereal, pumpkin seeds, walnuts. Add dill weed, salad dressing mix and dried rosemary.
3. Cook, covered, for 2 hours, using LOW temperature settings. Stir every 20 minutes. Sprinkle with lemon zest and slightly toss to combine.
4. Cool to serve.

Nutrition: Calories: 186 Fat: 22g Carbohydrates: 32g Protein: 7g

Pork Wraps in Slow Cooker

Amazing wraps for your dinner!

Prep time: 5 minutes Cooking time: 8-24 hours Servings: 10-20

INGREDIENTS:

5 tbsp water

Half cup lemon juice

1 cup sliced onion

1 tsp dried oregano

Half tsp ground cumin

3 cloves garlic

6 tbsp grapefruit juice

Ground black pepper

Boneless pork roast

Bottled salsa

Flour tortillas

DIRECTIONS:

1. To make marinade, mix lime juice, garlic, water, oregano, salt, grapefruit juice, cumin and pepper. Place the meat into marinade and leave in refrigerator for 8-24 hours.
2. Grease your Slow Cooker and arrange the minced onion over its bottom. Top with meat and marinade.
3. Cover and cook for 10-12 hours on LOW temperature mode. Shred meat and serve in tortillas with green onions.

Nutrition: Calories: 301 Fat: 23g Carbohydrates: 30g Protein: 9g

Italian Mix in Slow Cooker

Try this one for your family dinner!

Prep time: 5 minutes Cooking time: 6 hours Servings: 30

INGREDIENTS:

2 medium onions

2 tbsp red wine vinegar

1 cup sliced celery

Zucchini

Roma tomatoes

Eggplant

Half cup Italian parsley

3 tbsp tomato paste

Raisins

Salt to taste

1 tbsp sugar

DIRECTIONS:

1. Cut tomatoes, eggplant and zucchini into 2 inch-size slices. Chop onion and celery.
2. Grease your Slow Cooker with some melted butter or just with olive oil.
3. In Slow Cooker dish, mix tomatoes, celery, eggplant, zucchini, raisins, parsley, onion, vinegar, tomato paste pepper, sugar and salt.
4. Cover the lid and cook for 5-6 hours on LOW settings.

Nutrition: Calories: 224 Fat: 5g Carbohydrates: 14g Protein: 7g

Hoisin mushrooms with garlic

Another mushroom receipt for your kitchen!

Prep time: 5 minutes Cooking time: 6 hours Servings: 20

INGREDIENTS:

4 tbsp water

Half cup hoisin sauce (bottled)

1 tsp crushed red pepper

2tbsp minced garlic

Fresh button mushrooms

DIRECTIONS:

1. Wash and trim the mushrooms.
2. In a large bowl, combine water, hoisin sauce, red pepper and garlic.
3. Add trimmed mushrooms and stir well to coat them evenly with sauce mixture. Cover the lid of your Slow Cooker and set LOW temperature mode.
4. Cook for 5-6 hours.
5. To serve, discard the liquid and place the decorative toothpicks.

Nutrition: Calories: 228 Fat: 21g Carbohydrates: 34g Protein: 22g

Chicken with Peanut Sauce

Try this chicken in amazing sauce!

Prep time: 5 minutes Cooking time: 6 hours Servings: 20

INGREDIENTS:

3tbsp water

24 chicken wing drummettes

1 tbsp lime juice

Peanut sauce

Half tsp ground ginger

DIRECTIONS:

1. Place chicken wings into your Slow Cooker. Add lime juice and ginger, pour in a little water.
2. Cover your Slow Cooker with a lid and set LOW heat regime. Cook for 5-6 hours. Remove the liquid from chicken and toss the meat with ½ peanut sauce.
3. Serve warm with peanut sauce.

Nutrition: Calories: 312 Fat: 17g Carbohydrates: 15g Protein: 7g

Asian Tacos with Cabbage

Everything Asian is definitely tasty!

Prep time: 5 minutes Cooking time: 8 hours Servings: 25

INGREDIENTS:

2 cloves garlic

1 large orange

1 pork shoulder

1 pork shoulder

2 tbsp soy sauce

Balsamic vinegar

Dark sugar

Salt\pepper to taste

Red pepper flakes

1 medium carrot

1 small onion

8 small tortillas

Fresh ginger

Olive oil

DIRECTIONS:

1. Right in the Slow Cooker, mix vinegar, soy sauce, sugar, ginger, red pepper, garlic and orange zest.
2. Place the pork into Slow Cooker and toss to cover evenly. Cover the lid and cook on LOW for 7-8 hours.
3. In 30 minutes before serving, make the slaw and sprinkle it with orange juice, oil, pepper and salt. Warm tortillas in oven or microwave.
4. To serve, shred the meat and place it over tortillas, along with cabbage mix.

Nutrition: Calories: 198 Fat: 17g Carbohydrates: 33g Protein: 6g

Crab Dip in Slow Cooker

Seafood dip for crabmeat lovers!

Prep time: 5 minutes Cooking time: 2 hours Servings: 20

INGREDIENTS:

Cream cheese

Juice of 1 lemon

Half cup parmesan

2 cloves garlic

1 tbsp Worcestershire sauce

1 tsp Old Bay seasoning

Half cup mayonnaise

Green onions

Canned crab meat

Cracker for serving

DIRECTIONS:

116

1. In a wide dish, mix cream cheese, mayonnaise, garlic, minced green onions. Season with old Bay and Worcestershire sauce. Sprinkle with lemon juice.
2. Finely grate the Parmesan cheese and carefully stir in to other ingredients. Add canned crabmeat and stir it well to combine.
3. Cook on LOW temperature mode for 2 hours.
4. Serve with crackers and green onions and Parmesan garnish.

Nutrition: Calories: 177 Fat: 8g Carbohydrates: 25g Protein: 15g

Greek Meatballs with Cheese Stuffing

Amazing cheese stuffing makes this dish creamy!

Prep time: 5 minutes Cooking time: 3 hours Servings: 20

INGREDIENTS:

4 cloves garlic

2 chicken eggs

Ground lamb

Chopped green olives

1 cup bread crumbs (seasoned)

1 tsp salt

Chopped black olives

Lean ground beef

Greek Tomato Sauce

3 tbsp chopped parsley

Cubed feta cheese

DIRECTIONS:

1. In separate bowl, beat chicken eggs with fork and mix in green olives, breadcrumbs, garlic, parsley, black olives. Add salt/pepper.
2. Chop the cheese into small cubes and, using a meat mixture, form a ball around each one. Place the meatball into wide saucepan and bake in preheated oven for 35 minutes.
3. Transfer ball into Slow Cooker and pour over with Greek Tomato sauce, Toss. Cook, covered, for 3-4 hours on HIGH mode.

Nutrition: Calories: 341 Fat: 12g Carbohydrates: 41g Protein: 22g

Crabmeat Dip Recipe

You can cook this for white wine serving!

Prep time: 5 minutes Cooking time: 2 hours Servings: 15

INGREDIENTS:

Juice 1 lemon

2 medium onions

Cream cheese

2 cloves garlic

Half cup mayonnaise

1 tsp Old Bay seasoning

Crackers to serve

Canned crab meat

1tbsp Worcestershire sauce

DIRECTIONS:

1. Finely mince green onions and garlic cloves.
2. In separate bowl, combine Parmesan cheese, garlic, Old Bay seasoning, mayonnaise, lemon juice, green onions, Worcestershire and stir to combine.
3. Transfer this mixture into greased Slow Cooker. Fold the crabmeat into the mixture.
4. Cover the lid and cook for around 2 hours, use a LOW temperature mode. To serve, add crackers and garnish with green onions and Parmesan.

Nutrition: Calories: 201 Fat: 14g Carbohydrates: 33g Protein: 9g

Queso Dip for Slow Cooker

Enjoy this dip with your family!

Prep time: 5 minutes Cooking time: 2 hours Servings: 20

INGREDIENTS:

2tsp paprika

1cup milk

Velveeta

2cloves garlic

1 tsp cayenne pepper

2 jalapeno peppers

Kosher salt

Half cup cotija

Cilantro as a garnish

Tortilla chips (to serve)

DIRECTIONS:

1. Take a medium bowl and combine Cotija, minced jalapenos, Velveeta in it. Season with garlic, cayenne pepper, salt and paprika.

2. Grease your Slow Cooker with olive oil or simply spray with cooking spray. Transfer the Cotija mixture into Slow Cooker and cover its lid.

3. Turn on Slow Cooker and set on HIGH. Cook for 1-2 hours until bubbly.

4. To serve, garnish with remaining jalapenos, cilantro and Cotija. Serve with tortillas.

Nutrition: Calories: 211 Fat: 21g Carbohydrates: 44g Protein: 7g

Tamale Dish with Chips

Hot dip for chili-lovers!

Prep time: 5 minutes Cooking time: 2 hours Servings: 3

INGREDIENTS:

Cubed cream cheese

Monterey Jack

1 tbsp chili powder

1 jalapeno

Salt

Cheddar cheese

2 cloves garlic

1 can enchilada sauce

Ground black pepper

1 cup rotisserie chicken

Canned corn

Tortilla chips for garnish.

DIRECTIONS:

1. Finely mince jalapeno and garlic, shred Monterey Jack and Cheddar cheese.

2. In a deep bowl, mix cheeses, jalapeno, shredded rotisserie chicken, garlic, enchilada sauce, chili powder. Add black pepper and salt to taste.

3. Grease your Slow Cooker and start preheating it.

4. Transfer the cheese mixture into Slow Cooker and set to LOW mode. Cook for 2 hours. Serve along with tortilla chips and cilantro garnishing.

Nutrition: Calories: 136 Fat: 12g Carbohydrates: 2g Protein: 9g

Asian Spicy Wings

Asian-style wings for family dinner!

Prep time: 5 minutes Cooking time: 4 hours Servings: 3

INGREDIENTS:

3 tbsp honey

32 chicken wings

Half tsp chicken wings

2tbsp grated fresh ginger

1 cup teriyaki sauce

3tbsp lime juice

3 cloves garlic

DIRECTIONS:

1. Grate the fresh ginger (about 2 tablespoons). Cut the garlic cloves into small slices. Place the chicken wings onto slightly greased broiler pan.

2. Cook until it just browned, then transfer to Slow Cooker.

3. In separate bowl, stir together the remaining ingredients. Pour this mixture into your Slow Cooker. Cook under the lid for 4 hours on LOW settings.

Nutrition: Calories: 159 Fat: 8g Carbohydrates: 12g Protein: 22g

Lettuce Cups with Chicken

Healthy and interesting to make!

Prep time: 5 minutes Cooking time: 6 hours Servings: 15

INGREDIENTS:

Half tbsp. apple cider vinegar

1 yellow onion

Mayonnaise

Salt/pepper

4bacon slices

1 whole chicken

Ground red pepper

Green onion slices

6 garlic cloves

1 apple

Lettuce leaves

DIRECTIONS:

1. Combine wedged onion and apple with garlic and bacon in your Slow Cooker. Add half vinegar and half-cup water. Place the whole chicken into mixture.

2. Season with pepper and salt and cook for six hours on LOW mode. Remove the skin and bones from chicken, shred it and let to cool.

3. To make sauce, whisk the remaining chicken liquid with mayonnaise, vinegar and red pepper. Place chicken in lettuce leaves and serve while hot.

Nutrition: Calories: 147 Fat: 33g Carbohydrates: 14g Protein: 7g

FISH AND SEAFOOD RECIPES

Tilapia and Asparagus with Lemon Slices

The delicate fish is mild and exotic with lemon!

Prep time: 16 minutes Cooking time: 2 hours Servings: 11

INGREDIENTS:

Asparagus

Lemon pepper seasoning

9 tablespoons lemon juice

5 Tilapia fillets

4 tablespoon butter

DIRECTIONS:

15. Take a cooking foil and cut it to pieces - you need to have one piece for each fillet. Divide asparagus between your fillets evenly.
16. Lay each fillet onto the foil and sprinkle it with one teaspoon of lemon pepper seasoning and the lemon juice. Add some butter.
17. Top with asparagus.
18. Fold the fish with the foil evenly, and then fold the ends together tightly.
19. Repeat for all of the fish fillets. Then, put in the Slow Cooker on HIGH regime for 2 hours for fresh meat (or 3 for frozen).
20. To serve, arrange fish on a plate with fresh lemon slices.

Nutrition: Calories: 269 Fat: 13g Carbohydrates: 3g Protein: 52g

Chowder Soup with Seafood

You and your friends will appreciate the mild and creamy taste!

Prep time: 5 minutes Cooking time: 8 hours Servings: 11

INGREDIENTS:

Half bulb fennel

2 yellow potatoes

Salt

Diced celery

3 tbsp cornstarch

Dried thyme

1 onion

1/4 teaspoon pepper

Fresh parsley

Cayenne pepper

Clam juice (one bottle)

Cup whipping cream

bay leaves

Skinless salmon fillets

Peeled shrimp

5 sea scallops

DIRECTIONS:

1. Right in your Slow Cooker, mix fennel, onion, thyme, celery, potatoes, bay leaves, clam juice, salt/pepper, cayenne pepper and water. Stir to combine the ingredients.
2. Set to low and cook for about 8 hours (until the potatoes and fennel are tender). Remove bay leaves.
3. In a bowl, mix together cornstarch and cream until smooth. Stir the mixture with other ingredients. Add shrimp, scallops and salmon to Slow Cooker.
4. Prepare on HIGH for 30 minutes, until flaky and the soup is slightly thickened.

Nutrition: Calories:326 Fat: 9g Carbohydrates: 25g Protein: 9g

Salmon for Slow Cooker

Easy and tasty recipe for any occasion!

Prep time: 5 minutes

Cooking time: 2 hours Servings: 1

INGREDIENTS:

4 mushrooms

1 small onion

Plain rice

1 garlic clove

1 tbsp soy sauce

Margarine or butter

Half red pepper

1 tsp chili powder

1 tbsp lime juice

One salmon fillet

half cup vegetable stock

DIRECTIONS:

1. Finely chop mushrooms, red pepper and onion. Crush the garlic.

2. Add some butter to pan and sweat red pepper, mushrooms and onion in it.

3. Mix these ingredients with chili powder and vegetable stock and transfer to Slow Cooker. Prepare on HIGH regime for 30 minutes.

4. Add the rice and cook for another 15 minutes.

5. In a separate bowl, mix lime juice, soy sauce and garlic. Place the salmon in this sauce for 15 minutes.

6. Place the salmon along with sauce into Slow Cooker for another hour.

Nutrition: Calories: 224 Fat: 8g Carbohydrates: 11g Protein: 22g

Crabmeat with Asparagus

Healthy and flavored dish for the whole family!

Prep time: 13 minutes Cooking time: 1 hour Servings: 5

INGREDIENTS:

One cup tofu

1 tbsp oyster sauce

2 tbsp dried oregano

Fresh spinach

2 tbsp fish sauce

One can asparagus tips

Canned crabmeat

Clove garlic

DIRECTIONS:

1. Drain asparagus tips and crabmeat.

2. Crush the garlic and finely chop spinach. Dice tofu into small cubes.

3. In a separate bowl. Combine such ingredients as spinach, asparagus, fish sauce, crabmeat, oregano, tofu and crushed garlic.

4. Grease your Slow Cooker with a little amount of unsalted butter.

5. Transfer the asparagus mixture to Slow Cooker, cover and prepare for 1 hour on LOW (you will smell the spinach aroma).

Nutrition: Calories: 101 Fat: 4g Carbohydrates: 4g Protein: 17g

Fish and Shrimp Stew in Slow Cooker

This hearty and delicious soup will definitely warm you up!

Prep time: 24 minutes Cooking time: 5 hours Servings: 11

INGREDIENTS:

Minced garlic

1 tbsp olive oil

Canned tomato paste

Dried Italian seasoning

White fish (1-inch size)

Half cup white wine

2medium stalks celery

1 bay leaf

Canned crabmeat

Canned clams with juice

Sugar

Red pepper flakes

Chopped fresh parsley

Wine vinegar

Uncooked medium shrimp

DIRECTIONS:

1. Cover Slow Cooker with a small amount of olive or vegetable oil. Remove the tail from uncooked medium shrimp.

2. Place celery, tomatoes, onions, clam juice, garlic, tomato paste, Italian seasoning, sugar and pepper flakes.

3. Add wine and oil and stir the ingredients well. Cook, covered, for 4 hours on HIGH mode.

4. Stir in seafood and turn your Slow Cooker to low mode. Prepare for another 35 minutes. Use fresh parsley to serve.

Nutrition: Calories: 324 Fat: 8g Carbohydrates: 10g Protein: 36g

Slow Cooker Fish Soup with Halibut

This is delicious and low-fat, so brings not just taste, but health!

Prep time: 29 minutes Cooking time: 4 hours Servings: 9

INGREDIENTS:

2 cloves garlic

Sliced bacon

Two large potatoes

One chopped onion

One cup scallops

Red pepper flakes

Cup corn kernels

Canned evaporated milk

Bite-sized halibut

One cup shrimp

6 cups chicken stock

DIRECTIONS:

1. Before the start, peel and devein shrimp.
2. Using a large skillet, brown the bacon strips (from 6 to 8 minutes). Drain.
3. Add minced garlic and onion to bacon and cook for another five minutes, just to get translucent. Place bacon to Slow Cooker.
4. Add potatoes, corn and carrots. Pour the ingredients over with chicken stock. Add red pepper flakes and black pepper.
5. Cook for 3 hours on HIGH regime.
6. In the end, add scallops, halibut and shrimp. To serve, stir in evaporated milk

Nutrition: Calories: 235 Fat: 7g Carbohydrates: 28g Protein: 19g

Casserole with Salmon and Rice

Quick, easy and healthy dish for your delicious dinner!

Prep time: 9 minutes Cooking time: 3 hours Servings: 6

INGREDIENTS:

1 tsp lemon pepper

2 cups white rice

Frozen peas

1 tbsp dill weed

Cream of broccoli soup

3 cans salmon

Cream of chicken soup

DIRECTIONS:

1. Grease your Slow Cooker and set aside.
2. Take a deep bowl and whisk together chicken soup, water and broccoli soup. Place white rice and sliced salmon into Slow Cooker.

3. Pour over the salmon and rice with soup mixture. Season with lemon pepper and dill.
4. Set your Slow Cooker to HIGH mode and prepare for 2 hours. Add peas and cook for an additional hour.

Nutrition: Calories: 155 Fat: 8g Carbohydrates: 1g Protein: 7g

Brazil-styled Fish Chowder

Flavored and super easy meal!

Prep time: 11 minutes Cooking time: 1 hour Servings: 9

INGREDIENTS:

Tipalia fillets

Salt

fresh cilantro

Canned tomatoes

Canned coconut milk

Black pepper

3 tbsp limejuice

Paprika

Minced garlic

4 bell peppers

2 onions

Olive oil

DIRECTIONS:

1. In a separate bowl mix paprika, pepper, lime juice and pepper.
2. Place the tilapia fillets into species and toss to coat evenly. Hide fillets to the refrigerator, leave overnight.
3. Fry the onions in a large pot with a little of olive oil for 2 minutes. Add diced tomatoes, bell peppers and tilapia to Slow Cooker.
4. Add onions, cilantro and pour in the coconut milk.
5. Stir well and cover the lid. Cook for 2 hours on LOW mode.

Nutrition: Calories: 359 Fat: 21g Carbohydrates: 15g Protein: 28g

Seafood Hot Soup

Savory and hot, this is perfect for the winter season!

Prep time: 16 minutes Cooking time: 8 hours Servings: 4

INGREDIENTS:

One jar clam juice

1 tsp salt

2 medium onions

Canned peeled and mashed tomatoes

3 medium carrots

3 tbsp flour

4 tbsp light cream

Melted butter

Celery

Fresh parsley

Dried rosemary

DIRECTIONS:

1. Prepare the vegetables: chop celery, onions and carrots, In addition, finely chop fresh parsley. Grease your Slow Cooker with melted butter.

2. Right in a cooking dish, whisk clam juice, wine, rosemary and salt. Add fresh vegetables, parsley and canned tomatoes.

3. Cook under the lid for 8 hours on LOW temperature mode.

4. In the end, add remaining butter, flour, and light cream. Mix until thickened.

Nutrition: Calories: 344 Fat: 15g Carbohydrates: 15g Protein: 34g

Smoked Coley in Slow Cooker

Awesome main dish or a pair for pasta and rice.

Prep time: 11 minutes Cooking time: 2 hours Servings: 4

INGREDIENTS:

Olive oil

6 mushrooms

Canned chopped tomatoes

6 large potatoes

2 coley fillets (smoked)

Parsley to taste

Three cloves garlic

Half cup white wine

One onion

DIRECTIONS:

1. Finely chop onion and garlic. Slice mushrooms and cube potatoes. Grease your Slow Cooker as you like and start preheating on high mode.

2. Cover the bottom of your Slow Cooker with olive oil, place onion with garlic.

3. Add one can of chopped tomatoes, the rest of Slow Cooker space fill with water. Add some parsley and white wine.

4. Place the coley, potatoes and sliced mushrooms. Stir the ingredients well. Turn Slow Cooker on HIGH mode and cook for 3 hours.

Nutrition: Calories: 411 Fat: 8g Carbohydrates: 11g Protein: 9g

Classical Clam Soup in Slow Cooker

Quick and easy, perfect for cold weather!

Prep time: 13 minutes Cooking time: 16 hours Servings: 6

INGREDIENTS:

2 cups whipping cream

Canned clam chowder

Instant mash

Cream of chicken soup

Tinned baby clams

Cream of celery soup

5 cups single cream

DIRECTIONS:

1. In a separate bowl, combine claims, single cream, instant mash and cream. Stir well to combine. Slightly grease Slow Cooker with melted and unsalted butter.

2. Transfer the clam mixture to Slow Cooker.

3. Pour in the cream of chicken and celery soup and clam chowder. Stir one more time. Cover the lid tightly. Cook on LOW temperature mode for around 6 or 8 hours.

Nutrition: Calories: 211 Fat: 9g Carbohydrates: 13g Protein: 27g

Maple Syrup Salmon in Slow Cooker

Try this classic fish for Slow Cooker!

Prep time: 22minutes Cooking time: 1 hour Servings: 12

INGREDIENTS:

lime juice

3 cloves garlic

Ginger root

5 tbsp soy sauce

maple syrup

6 salmon fillets

DIRECTIONS:

1. Cover the bottom and sides of your Slow Cooker with a small amount of melted butter. Put the salmon fillets into Slow Cooker. You can use fresh or frozen if you like.

2. In a bowl, mix lime juice, maple syrup, soy sauce.

3. Add crushed garlic and grated ginger root and mix well. Pour in the sauce over the salmon pieces. Turn on your Slow Cooker. Set to HIGH temperature mode. Cover the lid. Cook for 1 hour.

4. To serve, transfer the fish to serving plate. Garnish with lime slices.

Nutrition: Calories: 356 Fat: 13g Carbohydrates: 28g Protein: 30g

Tilapia seasoned with Citrus

Tasty fish dinner will be ready just in few hours!

Prep time: 8 minutes Cooking time: 2 hours Servings: 6

INGREDIENTS:

4 tilapia fillets

Salt

2 tbsp garlic butter

Canned mandarin oranges

Black pepper to taste

Aluminum foil

DIRECTIONS:

1. Cut the aluminum foil into pieces big enough to wrap tilapia fillets. Spray the bottom of your Slow Cooker with cooking spray.

2. Place the fish on the foil and drizzle with butter evenly.

3. Put a handful of oranges over each fish piece and season with remaining species. Wrap the foil. Place fish wraps into your Slow Cooker and cover the lid. Cook on HIGH mode for 2 hours.

4. To serve, arrange tilapia pieces over the large serving plate. You can garnish it with orange or tangerine slices.

Nutrition: Calories: 238 Fat: 8g Carbohydrates: 11g Protein: 9g

Seafood with rice soup

Classical Asian meal is now available for your Slow Cooker

Prep time:12 minutes Cooking time: 5 hours Servings: 6

INGREDIENTS:

One medium onion

1 tbsp olive oil

Canned chopped tomatoes

Thawed seafood mix

Half tsp paprika

2 cloves garlic

One bay leaf

1 cup short grain rice

3 cups fish stock

Water

3 tbsp white wine

DIRECTIONS:

1. Using a deep pan, sauté onion and crushed garlic. Add some paprika and cook a little to get the flavor.

2. Add chopped tomatoes to the pan. Leave to simmer for about 10 minutes. When it is almost ready, add white wine and prepare for 1 minute.

3. Transfer the pan mixture to your Slow Cooker. Add bay leaf and pour in with stock.

4. Turn on the Slow Cooker and cook for 5 hours on LOW mode. Add rice and cook for an half hour.

Nutrition: Calories: 312 Fat: 7g Carbohydrates: 34g Protein: 26g

Classical Asian Miso Soup

Try this one in an unusual way – into your Slow Cooker

Prep time: 14 minutes Cooking time: 2 hours Servings: 4

INGREDIENTS:

3 cloves garlic

Spring onion

2 tbsp Miso paste

fish stock powder

Dried wakame seaweed

leafy greens

DIRECTIONS:

1. Slightly coat your Slow Cooker with anti-stick-cooking spray. Finely mince garlic and dice spring onion.

2. In a separate bowl, combine garlic and onion with leafy greens, fish stock powder, dried wakame seaweed and miso paste.

3. Spray your Slow Cooker with cooking spray.

4. Transfer the ingredients to Slow Cooker and pour in one cup water. Blend everything and cook for 2 hours using HIGH temperature mode.

5. To serve, pour the soup over small serving bowls. Serve while hot, garnish with sesame seeds and fresh herbs.

Nutrition: Calories: 157 Fat: 4g Carbohydrates: 16g Protein: 10g

Summer Soup with Lemon Salmon

Perfectly tastes both hot and cold!

Prep time: 5 minutes Cooking time: 5 hours Servings: 5

INGREDIENTS:

2 cups milk

Salmon fillets

2 tbsp butter

Potatoes

Salt

One pinch basil

Dried oregano

Black pepper

1 tbsp lemon zest

Dried thyme

Additional water (to cover)

DIRECTIONS:

1. Grease your Slow Cooker well (you can use olive oil or simple butter).
2. Cut potatoes into medium cubes and layer them over your Slow Cooker's bottom. Pour in water to cover the potatoes.
3. Add lemon zest, remaining butter basil, salt, thyme, pepper and oregano. Turn your Slow Cooker to LOW and cook for 5 hours, loosely covered.
4. Stir in milk and prepare for 2 more hours.
5. To serve, pour soup into small serving bowls. Use lemon wedges as a garnish.

Nutrition: Calories: 324 Fat: 8g Carbohydrates: 12g Protein: 17g

Easy Seafood Pie

Try this tasty and easy to cook one!

Prep time: 5 minutes Cooking time: 2 hours Servings: 8

INGREDIENTS:

Half tsp salt

1 pack crabmeat

1 pack cream cheese

1 cup Bisquick mix

Ground nutmeg

1 cup milk

2 chicken eggs

1 cup Mozzarella

1 can diced pimientos

DIRECTIONS:

1. Grease your Slow Cooker and start preheating it. Dice onions and finely shred Mozzarella cheese.
2. Carefully combine crabmeat, onions and pimientos in a big bowl.
3. Add all the remaining ingredients into Mozzarella mixture and blend well. Pour the fish pie dough into your Slow Cooker.
4. Prepare for 2 hours using HIGH temperature mode. Check the readiness of your pie with a long wooden toothpick.
5. Serve seafood pie while it is hot, with your favorite sauce or fresh vegetables.

Nutrition: Calories: 311 Fat: 4g Carbohydrates: 27g Protein: 25g

Jambalaya in Slow Cooker

The French and Spanish inspiration!

Prep time: 17 minutes Cooking time: 8 hours Servings: 8

INGREDIENTS:

Large onion

1 tsp parsley flakes

2 cups rice

Canned diced tomatoes

¼ tsp red pepper sauce

3 garlic cloves

green bell pepper

2 celery stalks

Cooked smoked sausage

Pepper/salt

Uncooked medium shrimp

DIRECTIONS:

1. Cover the bottom and sides of your Slow Cooker with melted butter or anti-stick spray.
2. Mix all ingredients (except shrimp and rice) in a separate bowl. Blend well and transfer to Slow Cooker.
3. Turn to LOW mode and cook for 7 or 8 hours.
4. In the end of time, stir in shrimp and cook for one more hour. Cook rice according to package directions.
5. Serve jambalaya meal over a large serving plate with cooked rice.

Nutrition: Calories: 356 Fat: 12g Carbohydrates: 30g Protein: 21g

Summer Seafood Casserole

Pasta and seafood due with Alfredo sauce

Prep time: 5 minutes Cooking time: 2 hours Servings: 12

INGREDIENTS:

Half cup milk

4 cups uncooked pasta

One can Alfredo sauce

Parmesan cheese

Pepper to taste

Canned crabmeat

Cooked medium shrimp

¼ cup breadcrumbs

DIRECTIONS:

1. Cook pasta separated, following the package directions. When it is 2 minutes of cooking pasta is remaining, add some broccoli. Drain and set aside.
2. In a large bowl, whisk together milk, pepper and Alfredo sauce.
3. Add shrimp, parsley, crabmeat and 2 tablespoons of shredded Parmesan cheese. Place all ingredients into Slow Cooker, toss to combine.
4. Cover the lid, and cook for 2 hours on HIGH mode.
5. To serve, transfer the casserole to a large plate and garnish with fresh herbs and lime wedges.

Nutrition: Calories: 355 Fat: 15g Carbohydrates: 21g Protein: 36g

Hearty fish soup with corn

Perfect for a busy daytime!

Prep time: 21 minutes Cooking time: 6 hours Servings: 7

INGREDIENTS:

2 cloves garlic

Half cup chicken broth

Medium onion

Nonfat milk powder

Whitefish fillets

Cream of celery soup

Kernel corn

Pack lima beans

Canned stewed tomatoes

Lemon-pepper seasoning

DIRECTIONS:

1. Cover your Slow Cooker's bottom with thick parchment paper. You need to cover the bottom and sides of the cooking dish.
2. Cut and combine potatoes, garlic and onion. Add cream of celery soup and lima beans, along with corn and lemon-pepper seasoning. Pour in the broth. Add white wine.
3. Transfer the mixture to Slow Cooker, cook for 7 hours using a LOW-heat settings. Meanwhile, wash and rinse fish.
4. Place it into Slow Cooker. Cook for an additional hour.

Nutrition: Calories: 315 Fat: 7g Carbohydrates: 46g Protein: 23g

Asian Seafood mix

Incredible soup with homemade broth!

Prep time: 21 minutes Cooking time: 2 hours Servings: 12

INGREDIENTS:

1 can diced abalone

Barley

2 tbsp dried scallops

3 Oyster sauce

Fish maw

6 Chinese mushrooms

One dried cuttlefish

Chicken bones

DIRECTIONS:

1. To make the broth, boil cleaned chicken bones and dried cuttlefish in enough amount of water. Soak mushrooms in cold water and fish maw in hot water, both for 30 minutes.
2. When the fish and mushrooms are ready, remove them from water and cut into small pieces. Add all the other ingredients to chicken soup. Add oyster sauce just to your taste.
3. Stir everything and cook in your Slow Cooker for 2 hours (HIGH temperature mode). If you want a thicker broth, add some corn flour before serving.

Nutrition: Calories: 289 Fat: 10g Carbohydrates: 29g Protein: 33g

Coconut Rice with Mango Shrimp

Perfect for lunchtime on busy days!

Prep time: 317 minutes Cooking time: 1 hour Servings: 9

INGREDIENTS:

One cup rice

Half tsp Caribbean jerk seasoning

One cup coconut milk

One cup shrimp

diced mango (with juice)

DIRECTIONS:

1. Peel the shrimp. Remove tails. Cook shrimp in slightly salted water. Grease your Slow Cooker with a cooking spray.
2. Combine rice, Caribbean jerk seasoning, mango along with its' juice and cooked shrimp to the Slow Cooker pot.
3. Pour in one cup of coconut milk and stir well.
4. Cover your Slow Cooker with the lid and cook on HIGH for 1 hour. Try if the rice is tender, cook for 1 hour more.
5. Serve immediately as soon as ready with French bread slices or cubed bread crisps.

Nutrition: Calories: 251 Fat: 5g Carbohydrates: 12g Protein: 18g

Jamaican Spicy Salmon

Spicy, but tasty and healthy receipt for your family!

Prep time: 18 minutes Cooking time: 2 hours Servings: 2

INGREDIENTS:

1 tsp salt

1 tsp mixed cloves, ginger, cayenne pepper, nutmeg and thyme

Chipotle chili powder

Half tsp cinnamon

Black pepper

Fresh salmon fillets

1 tsp onion powder

2 tsps white sugar

DIRECTIONS:

1. In a separate small bowl, combine all the spice ingredients and mix well.
2. Spread the spicy mixture all over the foil length and put the fish slices over it. Fold the foil. Slightly spray your Slow Cooker with cooking spray to avoid sticking of foil.
3. Place the foil wraps over the bottom of your Slow Cooker. Cover the lid and leave for 2 hours on LOW regime.
4. You can also cook some rice or pasta as a garnish or just serve with fresh vegetables.

Nutrition: Calories: 301 Fat: 10g Carbohydrates: 12g Protein: 27g

Sweet and Sour Slow Cooker Shrimp

The amazing taste for any party!

Prep time: 5 minutes Cooking time:

Servings:

INGREDIENTS:

2 tsp soy sauce

Fluffy rice

2 tbsp cornstarch

1 chicken bouillon cube

3 tbsp sugar

1 can pineapples

2 cans shrimp

1 pack Chinese pea pods

1 cup water

Ground ginger

2 tbsps cider vinegar

DIRECTIONS:

1. Spray your Slow Cooker with cooking spray.
2. Combine drained pineapple and pea pods into your Slow Cooker. In a separated saucepan, mix granulated sugar with cornstarch.
3. Bring the water to boil and dissolve one bouillon cube. Add juice, ginger and soy sauce, bring to boil, and then blend with pods and pineapples.
4. Cover the Slow Cooker's lid and cook on LOW mode for 5 hours. When it is almost time, add shrimp and vinegar.
5. Serve hot over the rice.

Nutrition: Calories: 134 Fat: 12g Carbohydrates: 9g Protein: 16g

Crawfish and Shrimp Duo

Amazing choice for any occasion!

Prep time: 5 minutes Cooking time: 4 hours Servings: 8

INGREDIENTS:

Simple butter

Fresh shrimp

2 celery stalks

4 green onions

Minced garlic

Canned and diced tomatoes

Minced garlic

Water

Tomato paste

Crawfish tails

Ground black pepper

Hot cooked rice

Spices: basil, oregano, thyme, red pepper

Salt

Fresh parsley

DIRECTIONS:

1. Peel shrimp and devein well. Then set aside.
2. Finely chop red pepper, green onions, simple onion and two celery stalks.
3. In a deep saucepan, melt butter and add chopped garlic and other vegetables. Stir in flour and cook for 1 minute till smooth.
4. Add tomatoes, tomato paste and water. Season with thyme, basil and oregano and stir to combine.
5. Transfer the mixture to preheated Slow Cooker and prepare on LOW for 4 hours. Add seafood and cook for another hour.

Nutrition: Calories: 187 Fat: 12g Carbohydrates: 37g Protein: 23g

Shrimp Marinara for Slow Cooker

Unusual taste of Spicy Shrimp

Prep time: 11 minutes Cooking time: 7 hours Servings: 14

INGREDIENTS:

Canned peeled tomatoes

Dried oregano

2 tsp minced parsley

Grated Parmesan cheese

Canned tomato paste

Cooked shrimp

Cooked spaghetti or pasta

Dried basal

2 clove garlic

DIRECTIONS:

1. Cook the shrimp and remove the shells and tails. Finely grate Parmesan cheese.
2. Grease your Slow Cooker with melted and unsalted butter or simply with olive oil.
3. Right in your Slow Cooker pot, combine tomatoes, salt, oregano, basil, parsley. Add tomato paste. Cover the lid and cook on LOW regime for 7 hours.

4. Then stir in shrimp and turn to high for 13-15 minutes. Serve with pasta and shredded parmesan.

Nutrition: Calories: 210 Fat: 14g Carbohydrates: 31g Protein: 33g

Asian-styled salmon with diced vegetables

Healthy and delicious fish in Asian sauce

Prep time: 16 minutes Cooking time: 3 hours Servings: 2

INGREDIENTS:

Fresh salmon fillets

Salt

soy sauce

Pepper

1 pack Asian vegetable blend

2 tbsp lemon juice

1 tbsp honey

1sesame seeds

DIRECTIONS:

1. Coat your Slow Cooker with vegetable or olive oil. Place the vegetable mix into Slow Cooker.
2. Rub salmon meat with salt and pepper to your taste and place on vegetables.
3. In a small bowl, whisk together lemon juice, honey and soy sauce. Sprinkle the salmon with this sauce.
4. Drizzle with sesame seeds.
5. Cook with the lid on for 3 hours (use LOW temperature mode).
6. Serve on a large serving dish along with fresh vegetables or preferred side dish.

Nutrition: Calories: 235 Fat: 6g Carbohydrates:26g Protein: 53g

Creamy spaghetti with shrimp and cheese

An unusual mix of corn, shrimp, and cheese – the perfect choice for a cold day!

Prep time: 5 minutes Cooking time: 7 hours Servings: 4

INGREDIENTS:

One spaghetti squash

1 tbsp butter

Salt

Half cup Parmesan cheese

Pepper to taste

1 tsp Italian seasoning

Jarred minced garlic

Fresh medium shrimp

One cup pasta sauce

Olive oil

DIRECTIONS:

1. Cut the squash to remove the seeds.
2. Slightly drizzle the squash halves with oil and sprinkle with enough of seasoning.
3. Place the halves into Slow Cooker and ass 2 cups of water. Cook for 6 hours on LOW mode until it is easy to shred.
4. Mix in sauce and top with shredded cheese and cook for 30 minutes.
5. Using a skillet with oil, cook shrimp and garlic just for 4 minutes. Salt and pepper. Serve right in halves.

Nutrition: Calories: 121 Fat: 21g Carbohydrates: 39g Protein: 32g

Poached Salmon in Slow Cooker

The amazing choice for a family!

Prep time: 5 minutes Cooking time: 5 hours Servings: 6

INGREDIENTS:

2 cups water

1 bay leaf

1 cup dry wine

6 salmon fillets (with skin)

Ground black pepper

One shallot

6 sprigs fresh herbs

Salt

Black peppercorns

Lemon wedges to serve

DIRECTIONS:

1. Slightly coat your Slow Cooker with a melted unsalted butter.
2. Take a wide bowl and combine lemon, herbs, shallots, peppercorns. Mix and transfer to Slow Cooker.
3. Pour over with wine and water. Add one bay leaf.
4. Place the salmon fillets into Slow Cooker (skin side down). Season with pepper and salt. Cover the lid and do not open often until the dish is not ready.

5. Cook under cover on LOW mode until salmon is easy to flake with a fork. To serve, drizzle with olive oil and decorate with thin lemon wedges.

Nutrition: Calories: 155 Fat: 8g Carbohydrates: 1g Protein: 7g

Clam Casserole with Green Peppers

Delicious and super-easy to cook!

Prep time: 5 minutes Cooking time: 6 hours Servings: 4

INGREDIENTS:

4 chicken eggs

Canned minced clams

4 tbsp milk

Butter

3 medium onions

Crackers

Green pepper

Salt to taste

DIRECTIONS:

1. Prepare the vegetables: peel and mince the onions and green peppers. Also, mince the clams. Melt butter and whisk it with milk and chicken eggs. Beat until the ingredients just combined, about for 2 minutes.
2. Crush the crackers and add to the milk mixture.
3. Mix everything in one bowl and transfer to Slow Cooker.
4. Cover the lid and prepare the casserole for 6 hours on LOW temperature mode. Do not open the lid until it is the time.
5. Serve with freshly diced green peppers and sesame seed sprinkles.

Nutrition: Calories: 123 Fat: 4g Carbohydrates: 18g Protein: 54g

Tuna and Celery Meat Casserole

Fresh and hot dish for your breakfast!

Prep time: 19 minutes Cooking time: 8 hours Servings: 7

INGREDIENTS:

Tuna meat (can be tinned)

1 cup potato chips

3 chicken eggs

Celery

Cream of celery soup

Half cup salad dressing

Black pepper

DIRECTIONS:

1. Put chicken eggs into saucepan and boil until hard-cooked. Finely chop. Grease your Slow Cooker with melted butter or vegetable oil.

2. In a deep bowl, combine tuna, black pepper, diced celery, chopped eggs. Mix well until the mixture is smooth enough.

3. Add salad dressing and condensed cream of tuna soup. Transfer the mixture into Slow Cooker and top with potato chips. Cook, covered, for 8 hours on LOW temperature mode.

4. To serve, garnish pie with sesame seeds or leaves of fresh salad leaves.

Nutrition: Calories: 125 Fat: 7g Carbohydrates: 1g Protein: 23g

Halibut with Lemon and Dill

This meal will make a holiday out of any occasion!

Prep time: 29 minutes Cooking time: 1 hour Servings: 2

INGREDIENTS:

Halibut fillet (fresh or frozen)

1 tbsp fresh lemon juice

Salt to taste

1 tsp dried or 1 tbsp fresh dill

1 tbsp olive oil

Black pepper

DIRECTIONS:

1. Take a large piece of aluminum non-stick foil and place your halibut fillet in the middle of it. Pepper and salt.

2. Grease your Slow Cooker or simply coat with cooking spray. In a bowl, whisk lemon juice, dill and olive oil.

3. Crimp the foil edges together, but leave some space inside so fish can steam. Place the foil into Slow Cooker and set on HIGH for 2 hours.

4. When it is the time – carefully open the foil and check if the fish is flaky. Serve with the spinach and fresh dill.

Nutrition: Calories: 143 Fat: 32g Carbohydrates: 4g Protein: 43g

Slow Cooker Chowder with Shrimp and Bacon

This will be a big heat for your dinner!

Prep time: 5 minutes Cooking time: 4 hours Servings: 6

INGREDIENTS:

4 medium onions

Half tsp paprika

2 cups water

4 slices bacon

Chives

Red potatoes

Black pepper

Small shrimp

Evaporated milk

2 packs frozen corn

1 tsp Worcestershire sauce

DIRECTIONS:

1. Finely chop the onion and chives.

2. Dice the red potatoes (if you want, you can replace them with frozen hash-browns).

3. Fry the bacon to get crispy. Add chopped onion and cook until soften. Transfer onions with bacon to Slow Cooker.

4. One by one, ass Potatoes, Worcestershire sauce, corn, salt, water and pepper. Cook under the lid for 4 hours on LOW just until the potatoes are softened.

5. Add evaporated milk and shrimp and cook for 30 minutes. When it is time to serve, add chives.

Nutrition: Calories: 362 Fat: 23g Carbohydrates: 73g Protein: 45g

Crabmeat dip in Slow Cooker

Super tasty and easy appetizer with crabmeat!

Prep time: 5 minutes Cooking time: 2 hours Servings: 5

INGREDIENTS:

Half cup mayonnaise

2 cans crab meat

1 tsp hot sauce

1 tsp parsley

Red bell pepper

lemon juice

Worcestershire sauce

Green bell pepper

Half tsp mustard powder

2 tbsp horseradish sauce

1 tsp dry parsley

Cream cheese

DIRECTIONS:

1. Dice red bell pepper and green bell pepper. Grease your Slow Cooker with extra virgin olive oil.

2. Start preheating your Slow Cooker while combining all the ingredients in a separated bowl. Transfer the bowl mixture to Slow Cooker and cook on LOW mode for 2 hours. Stir occasionally every 20 or 35 minutes.

3. To serve, stir well and serve with bread slices or crackers.

Nutrition: Calories: 245 Fat: 32g Carbohydrates: 13g Protein: 53g

Salmon with Lemon and Dijon sauce

Lovely meal for your dinner!

Prep time: 7 minutes Cooking time: 2 hours Servings: 9

INGREDIENTS:

Salt

Fresh salmon fillets

2 cups water

Minced garlic

1 cup barley

Dried dill weed

2 tsp oil

Black pepper

Water

1 tsp chicken bouillon

Half cup diced onion

Half cup Dijon mustard

Sour cream

2 tbsp olive oil

Lemon juice

DIRECTIONS:

1. Chop the onion and garlic and transfer to a bowl. Place into the microwave for 5 minutes, then transfer to Slow Cooker.

2. Add bouillon, barley, dill weed and pour in with water. Finely stir everything.

3. Rub salt and pepper into salmon meat and arrange in over the mixture in Slow Cooker. Cover the lid and prepare, using a LOW temperature mode, for 2 hours.

4. In a small bowl, make a sauce: combine Dijon mustard, lemon juice, olive oil. Sour cream and minced garlic.

5. Serve as a main dish with bread or vegetables.

Nutrition: Calories: 412 Fat: 23g Carbohydrates: 20g Protein:55g

New England Clam Dip in Slow Cooker

The perfect choice for cold winter days!

Prep time: 5 minutes Cooking time: 1 hour Servings: 14

INGREDIENTS:

3 cans chopped clams

5 tbsp beer

1/3 cup cooked bacon

2 medium onions

3 packs cream cheese

1 tbsp Worcestershire sauce

Crushed oyster crackers

Melted butter

DIRECTIONS:

1. Slice green onions.

2. In a bowl, mix cream cheese, clams, bacon slices, green onions (reserve small part for topping), Worcestershire sauce and beer.

3. Transfer the clam mixture to your greased Slow Cooker.

4. In a small bowl, mix butter, remaining green onions and crushed crackers. Spread the topping over the clam mix.

5. Cover the lid and cook for 1 hour on HIGH setting. To serve, use crackers or chips.

Nutrition: Calories: 354 Fat: 32g Carbohydrates: 34g Protein: 62g

Tuna and Noodle casserole

Easy and tasty, just like in the childhood!

Prep time: 5 minutes Cooking time: 4 hours Servings: 6

INGREDIENTS:

Dried pasta

2 cups soy milk

Cup frozen peas

1 can of tuna

Shredded parmesan

Cream of mushroom soup

Half cup crushed tortilla

DIRECTIONS:

1. Spray the inside of your Slow Cooker with cooking spray. If you do not have one, use a melted butter for greasing.

2. Right in Slow Cooker pot, mix soup, noodles, cheese, milk and drained tuna. Stir with a spoon until smooth mass.

3. Cook under the lid on LOW temperature mode for 4 hours.

4. Forty minutes before serving, add frozen peas and stir everything one more time. Cook for 30 minutes or more, just until the peas are ready.

5. Serve while the casserole is hot, along with chips, fresh vegetables or salted cookies.

Nutrition: Calories: 235 Fat: 9g Carbohydrates: 19g Protein: 34g

Shrimp casserole with white

Satisfying and delicious family dish!

Prep time: 14 minutes Cooking time: 8 hours Servings: 7

INGREDIENTS:

red bell pepper

dried parsley

1 yellow onion

ground pepper

Cream of celery soup

Fresh garlic powder

salt

yellow bell pepper

cup chicken broth

Cream of chicken soup

white rice

Frozen shrimp

DIRECTIONS:

1. Grease your Slow Cooker with some olive oil and start preheating it on low temperature. Devein and peel shrimp, remove the tails.

2. Chop yellow onion, red and yellow bell peppers. Combine into one mixture. Combine all the ingredients in the Slow Cooker, finely stir to combine.

3. Cook on LOW temperature during 8 hours.

4. Serve while hot, maybe with your favorite vegetables or even bread slices.

Nutrition: Calories: 218 Fat: 12g Carbohydrates: 12g Protein: 38g

Pineapple Milkfish in Slow Cooker

The sweet and delicious fish meal!

Prep time: 11 minutes Cooking time: 4 hours Servings: 4

INGREDIENTS:

Canned pineapple (with juice)

Milkfish fillet

3 tbsp white vinegar

3 jalapeno peppers

Ginger root

6 cloves garlic

Half tbsp. black peppercorns

DIRECTIONS:

1. Grease your Slow Cooker dish with olive or even vegetable oil. Carefully peel and thinly slice the ginger.

2. Cut jalapeno peppers into a medium (can be 1-inch sized) pieces. Season milkfish with salt, rub well.

3. Combine fish with the other ingredients and transfer to Slow Cooker.

4. Turn on your Slow Cooker and cover the lid. Cook for 4 hours on LOW mode. When the fish is ready, carefully transfer it from Slow Cooker to large serving plate. Serve along with lime or small lemon wedges.

Nutrition: Calories: 125 Fat: 2g Carbohydrates: 7g Protein: 45g

Lobster Bisque in Slow Cooked

Quick and easy way to get your dinner to the new level!

Prep time: 5 minutes Cooking time: 8 hours Servings: 12

INGREDIENTS:

3 cups chicken broth

1 onion

Sliced mushrooms

1 tsp dried parsley

1 large leek

2 lobster tails

2 tsp Old Bay

Lemon wedges (to garnish)

1 tsp dill

1 cup heavy cream

DIRECTIONS:

1. In a large Slow Cooker, combine tomatoes, clam juice, onions, leek, mushrooms, parsley, Old Bay seasoning and dill.

2. Pour in 3 cups of chicken broth.

3. Set your Slow Cooker to LOW mode and cook for 8 hours.

4. With an immersible blender, make a chowdery soup out of ingredients. Add lobster tails and stir in heavy cream.

5. Cook until the bisque is slightly thick.

6. Serve with bread slices and freshly diced vegetables.

Nutrition: Calories: 324 Fat: 18g Carbohydrates: 53g Protein: 36g

Clam and Vegetable Soup

Satisfying and healthy, this dish is perfect for any season!

Prep time: 5 minutes Cooking time: 3 hours Servings: 6

INGREDIENTS:

2 large potatoes

6 slices bacon

Salt

3 small carrots

2 cans minced clams

1 onion

3 tsp flour

2 cans evaporated milk

1 tsp Worcestershire sauce

Clam juice

Water

DIRECTIONS:

1. In a medium dish, combine clam liquid and add enough water so you can get half cup in total. Add the mixture to Slow Cooker.

2. Place minced onion, diced potatoes and carrots and bacon into Slow Cooker. Add salt and pour in one more cup of water.

3. Cook covered for 3 hours on LOW temperature mode. In a separate bowl, whisk flour with evaporated milk. Add to Slow Cooker, along with clams and milk.

4. Cook, stirring, for another 30 minutes.

Nutrition: Calories: 213 Fat: 6g Carbohydrates: 1g Protein: 44g

Quick and easy Tuna Casserole

Super fast, delicious and easy!

Prep time: 5 minutes Cooking time: 3 hours Servings: 12

INGREDIENTS:

1 can cream of mushroom

3 cans tuna

Canned evaporated milk

2 cups water

Fresh mushrooms

1 can cheese soup

Noodles

Frozen peas and carrots

Shredded cheese

Salt/pepper

DIRECTIONS:

1. Slightly spray the dish of your Slow Cooker with a cooking spray. Place tuna and reserved tuna juice from 2 cans into your Slow Cooker.

2. Add noodles, water, cream of mushroom and cheese soup. Stir together. Mix in vegetables and milk.

3. Salt and pepper. You can also add another species to your taste. Cook under the lid for 3 hours on HIGH temperature.

4. To serve, transfer tuna casserole to a wide serving dish and sprinkle with shredded cheese.

Nutrition: Calories: 138 Fat: 42g Carbohydrates: 32g Protein: 9g

Crab Soup with Dry Sherry

Try this spicy and tasty one!

Prep time: 5 minutes Cooking time: 3 hours Servings: 11

INGREDIENTS:

Crab meat

6 tbsp butter

2 cans mushroom soup

Half tsp Worcestershire sauce

3 tbsp dry sherry

3 green onions

Half cup light cream

2 chicken eggs

Salt/pepper

DIRECTIONS:

1. To start, pick over and carefully flake crabmeat. Finely chop green onions.

2. Combine all the ingredients from the list (except chicken eggs) and mix them into Slow Cooker. Cover with the lid and cook for 1 hour, using a high temperature mode.

3. Reduce heat to LOW and prepare for 2-3 hours. When it is the last hour, stir in eggs.

4. To serve, let crab soup stand for 5 minutes. Then, serve in small deep bowls. You can also garnish it with fresh herbs if you want.

Nutrition: Calories: 124 Fat: 32g Carbohydrates: 10g Protein: 23g

Crabmeat and Cream Corn Soup

An unusual combination, but delicious meal!

Prep time: 7 minutes Cooking time: 8 hours Servings: 6

INGREDIENTS:

4 cups chicken broth

1 sliced avocado

Half tsp cayenne pepper

1 tsp salt

1 tbsp butter

2 garlic cloves

Frozen corn

1 can lump crabmeat

Heavy cream

DIRECTIONS:

1. To start, pour in the broth into your Slow Cooker, add butter and diced onion. Stir in garlic, frozen corn, cayenne pepper, crabmeat and butter.
2. Cover with the lid and cook on LOW mode for 8 hours.
3. If you want to get a thicker broth, you can also pulse the mixture with immersible blender for several times.
4. In the end, add cream.
5. Serve in small bowls while hot and serve with French bread slices and cream.

Nutrition: Calories: 323 Fat: 23g Carbohydrates: 15g Protein: 43g

Spice Chowder with Seafood

Delicious and easy to prepare!

Prep time: 9 minutes Cooking time: 6 hours Servings: 7

INGREDIENTS:

One cup onion

Red bell pepper

Chicken broth

Chopped celery

Sweet white corn

2 tsp cajun seasoning

2 cups small shrimp

Half cup potato flakes

White fish fillets

DIRECTIONS:

1. Right in your Slow Cooker, combine chopped celery, onions, corn and chopped red bell pepper. Add Cajun seasoning.

2. Pour in 4 cups of chicken broth. Stir everything well.
3. Cover and cook on LOW for around 6 hours, or until the vegetables are tender. When it is ready, make a puree with immersion blender. Mix for 5 minutes.
4. Add and stir in instant potato flakes, milk, fish, and shrimp. Prepare for another 30 minutes. Serve hot in small bowls with cubed bread or fresh vegetables.

Nutrition: Calories: 199 Fat: 12g Carbohydrates: 5g Protein: 44g

Seafood Spicy Soup

Simple to cook and very fast to eat – perfect for cold days!

Prep time: 5 minutes Cooking time: 3 hours Servings: 11

INGREDIENTS:

1 cup garlic clove

Onion salt

2 packs stevia

2 large Roma tomatoes

Creole seasoning

Onion salt

1 pack any seafood mix

DIRECTIONS:

1. Grease your Slow Cooker with olive oil (or you can use a special cooking spray if you like). Preheat the large skillet and pour in some olive oil. Cook seafood mix with chopped onion. Add all the remaining ingredients and let to simmer for 15 minutes.
2. Transfer your skillet mixture into Slow Cooker.
3. Cover the lid and cook for 2 or 3 hours on LOW temperature mode.
4. To serve, pour soup into small bowls and eat with white or French bread.

Nutrition: Calories: 143 Fat: 44g Carbohydrates: 12g Protein: 35g

Salmon Fillets in Asian Style

This Asian dish will amaze you with its taste

Prep time: 5 minutes Cooking time: 3 hours. Servings: 15

INGREDIENTS:

Medium salmon fillets

Salt

2 tbsp honey

Black pepper

1 tsp sesame seeds

Lemon juice

Asian vegetable blend

DIRECTIONS:

1. Grease your Slow Cooker with olive oil or cover with a special cooking spray. Add packed frozen vegetables as a base.
2. Season fish with salt and pepper just to your taste. Place the fish over the vegetables.
3. In a bowl, whisk the soy sauce with some honey and lemon juice. Add to Slow Cooker and top with sesame seeds.
4. Cover Slow Cooker with a lid. Prepare salmon fillets for 3 hours on LOW mode, tasting during the process.
5. To serve, cook some brown rice and to each portion with one salmon fillet. Serve while hot as soon as it ready.

Nutrition: Calories: 358 Fat: 9g Carbohydrates: 18g Protein: 46g

Hot Stew with Seafood

This meal is perfect for cold weather!

Prep time: 5 minutes Cooking time: 4 hours Servings: 8

INGREDIENTS:

4 cups broth

Canned tomatoes

3 cloves garlic

Half cup white wine

Dried thyme

Dutch baby potatoes

Half onion

Seafood mix

Pepper

Cilantro

Cayenne pepper

Red pepper flakes

Pepper/salt to your taste

DIRECTIONS:

1. Slightly grease your slow cooker dish. Dice the potatoes and finely chop onion.
2. Place the vegetables along with all the other ingredients into prepared slow cooker. Mix everything well.
3. Cover the lid of your slow cooker.

4. Leave to cook for 3 hours, using a HIGH temperature mode. When it is ready, add seafood mix and cook for 1 hour more. Serve with freshly sliced bread and sesame seeds sprinkles.

Nutrition: Calories: 235 Fat: 2g Carbohydrates: 19g Protein: 24g

Scampi with fresh Shrimp

The popular stove-cooked meal is available for your Slow Cooker now!

Prep time: 5 minutes Cooking time: 2 hours Servings: 6

INGREDIENTS:

Chicken broth

2 tsp garlic (finely chopped)

Half cup white wine

Large shrimp

Olive oil

Minced parsley

DIRECTIONS:

1. Grease your Slow Cooker with some olive oil. If you want, you can also use cooking spray. Right in your Slow Cooker, combine chopped garlic, lemon juice, white wine, olive oil and fresh minced parsley.
2. Pour the mixture into your Slow Cooker and add half cup chicken broth. Add thawed shrimp to the dish.
3. Place the lid on. Turn on Slow Cooker and cook on LOW mode for two hours.
4. Serve in the small bowls. Firstly, place the shrimp in a bowl, and secondly, cover it with remaining liquid.

Nutrition: Calories: 114 Fat: 12g Carbohydrates: 4g Protein: 22g

Fresh tilapia seasoned with citrus

The exotic taste of this meal – that is what your family will like!

Prep time: 5 minutes Cooking time: 2 hours Servings: 4

INGREDIENTS:

Four tilapia fillets

Pepper and salt to taste

2 tbsp garlic butter

Canned mandarin oranges

DIRECTIONS:

1. Chop the garlic butter into small cubes. Set aside for a little while.

2. Place the fish fillets over the foil pieces and sprinkle over with minced garlic.

3. Place a handful of oranges over each fish slice. Drizzle with some pepper and salt. Fold the foil over each fish piece and carefully place the fillets in your Slow Cooker. Place the lid on. Set your slow cooker to HIGH and cook for 2 hours.

4. To serve, transfer fish from Slow Cooker to large serving plate. Garnish with orange wedges.

Nutrition: Calories: 158 Fat: 13g Carbohydrates: 36g Protein: 28g

Juicy Salmon from Slow Cooker

Use maple syrup and lime juice to give this an excellent taste!

Prep time: 5 minutes Cooking time:

Servings:

INGREDIENTS:

6 salmon fillets (better take fresh)

6 tbsp lime juice

Half cup maple syrup

Crushed garlic

4 tbsp soy sauce

1tsp minced ginger

DIRECTIONS:

1. Take a medium mixing bowl and gather maple syrup, garlic, soy sauce and minced ginger root in it.

2. Cover the bottom of your Slow Cooker with special cooking spray. Place the fish fillets in your Slow Cooker dish.

3. Pour the garlic sauce over the fillets. Cover the lid of your Slow Cooker.

4. Cook salmon fillets for 1 hour on a HIGH temperature mode.

5. To serve, transfer salmon a large plate and garnish with lime wedges and sesame seeds.

Nutrition: Calories: 125 Fat: 1g Carbohydrates: 28g Protein: 42g

Pompano with soy sauce and ginger

Hot and Asian-spiced dish for any family dinner!

Prep time: 5 minutes Cooking time: 5 hours Servings: 6

INGREDIENTS:

Whole pompano fish

Chinese cooking wine

2 tsp soy sauce

Sliced ginger

2 tbsp honey

Garlic

Leeks

cilantro

DIRECTIONS:

1. Cut and scale the fish. Make small diagonal slits on the both sides of it.

2. In a small bowl, combine Chinese cooking wine, honey, sesame oil and honey. Grease the bottom of your slow cooker with melted butter or fresh olive oil.

3. Cover the bottom of your Slow Cooker with sliced leeks. Place the fish over the leeks pillow.

4. Pour in the soy-wine mixture to cover the fish evenly. Cover the lid and cook for around 5 hours on LOW mode.

5. To serve, transfer pompano over large serving dish and garnish with lime wedges.

Nutrition: Calories: 264 Fat: 23g Carbohydrates: 21g Protein: 52g

Clams with black bean sauce

Try this one you will never regret!

Prep time: 5 minutes Cooking time: 1 hour Servings: 8

INGREDIENTS:

Razor clams

Shallots

Ginger

Minced garlic

Red chili

3 tbsp oyster sauce

2 tbsp black beans

4 tbsp water

Cilantro

Sugar

cornstarch

DIRECTIONS:

1. Grease your slow cooker with olive oil or preheated butter.

2. Right in the Slow Cooker dish, mix the minced shallots, ginger and minced garlic. Add red chili, oyster sauce, minced black beans and cilantro.

3. Add razor clams and stir everything well. Season with cilantro and sugar.

4. In a small bowl, dissolve cornstarch with water. Pour the liquid into Slow Cooker. Cover and cook for 1 hour on LOW temperature regime or until the clams open. To serve, separate over small bowls and garnish with lime and sesame seeds.

Nutrition: Calories: 167 Fat: 10g Carbohydrates: 8g Protein: 21g

Asian milkfish with pineapple and oranges

Unusual taste of the fish with tropical fruits!

Prep time: 5 minutes Cooking time: 4 hour Servings: 8

INGREDIENTS:

1 cup milkfish

Thinly sliced ginger

Minced garlic

One cup pineapple chunks

1 jalapeno pepper

1 tsp white vinegar

1 cup pineapple juice

Black peppercorns

DIRECTIONS:

1. Season milkfish with some salt and rub well. Peel and slice ginger into small pieces.
2. Mix the vegetables with canned pineapple chunks (along with juice) add white vinegar and black peppercorns.
3. Stir all the ingredients well and pour into greased and preheated Slow Cooker. Cover with the lid and prepare on LOW temperature regime for 4 hours.
4. To serve, place the milkfish over a large bowl and garnish with vegetables or lemon wedges.

Nutrition: Calories: 324 Fat: 21g Carbohydrates: 32g Protein: 72g

Hot mussel with potato rice

True Italian taste in one pot!

Prep time: 17 minutes Cooking time: 2 hours Servings: 14

INGREDIENTS:

Three cups mussels

1 cup white wine

Salt

7 medium potatoes

Finely chopped shallots

DIRECTIONS:

1. Coat the bottom of your Slow Cooker unsalted melted butter or use a cooking spray with anti-stick effect.
2. In a saucepan, mix chopped shallots with mussels. Add water to cover. Bring to boil and cook for 5 minutes (set aside when the mussels open).
3. Remove the shells.
4. Chop the potatoes and layer them over the bottom of crockpot. Add rice layer and mussel layer. Pour in the remaining mussel stock.
5. Set your Slow Cooker to HIGH mode. Prepare for 2 hours.
6. To serve, transfer mussel with rice into small bowls. Serve hot. Garnish with sesame seeds or small lime wedges.

Nutrition: Calories: 411 Fat: 33g Carbohydrates: 23g Protein: 53g

Vietnamese catfish in Slow Cooker

Amazing taste with Asian flavors!

Prep time: 5 minutes Cooking time: 6 hours Servings: 12

INGREDIENTS:

One piece catfish

3 red chili peppers

Ginger strips

Fish sauce

Coconut sugar

One piece shallot

Vietnamese coriander leaves

DIRECTIONS:

1. In a small saucepan, preheat sugar until caramel condition. Stir in coconut water, ginger, fish sauce and shallots. Stir well.
2. Grease your Slow Cooker with melted and unsalted butter. If you prefer, you can use for greasing anti-stick cooking spray.
3. Transfer all ingredients into prepared Slow Cooker. Carefully place catfish into Slow Cooker mixture.
4. Turn your slow cooker on LOW temperature mode and cook for 6 hours. To serve, garnish with fresh leaves of coriander.

Nutrition: Calories: 413 Fat: 12g Carbohydrates: 41g Protein: 34g

Soy squid with ginger

This is really worth cooking!

Prep time: 5 minutes Cooking time: 8 hours Servings: 6

INGREDIENTS:

Squid

2 bay leaves

Half cup brown sugar

2 tbsp soy sauce

One bulb garlic

Ginger

2 stalks leeks

DIRECTIONS:

1. Cut the squid into thin rings.
2. Peel and crush garlic, finely chop ginger, thinly slice leeks.
3. Cover the bottom and sides of your Slow Cooker with melted butter to avoid sticking. If you want, you can use special cooking spray or olive oil.
4. Place the squid, leeks and ginger into Slow Cooker. Add bay leaves. Mix sugar with soy sauce. Sprinkle this mixture over the ingredients. Mix and cook on LOW temperature mode for 8 hours.
5. To serve, spoon squid into small plates or serve in a large bowl or right from Slow Cooker.

Nutrition: Calories: 177 Fat: 3g Carbohydrates: 19g Protein: 31g

Miso spiced salmon in Slow Cooker

Hot broth for especially cold days!

Prep time: 5 minutes Cooking time: 4 hours Servings: 12

INGREDIENTS:

3 cups fish stock

Ginger

2 tsp salt

Half cup miso paste

One cup mushrooms

Half cup scallions

DIRECTIONS:

1. Thinly slice scallions and fresh ginger root.
2. In a bowl, combine scallions, ginger and miso paste. Mix well until the mass is smooth. Pour in the fish stock and transfer to Slow Cooker.
3. Prepare, covered, for 4 hours using a LOW temperature mode.
4. When it is time, turn temperature to high and place the salmon fillets along with mushrooms into Slow Cooker. Cook for another 10 minutes.

5. To serve, pour into small and deep bowls and season with fish sauce or simply salt to taste.

Nutrition: Calories: 119 Fat: 2g Carbohydrates: 51g Protein: 12g

Hot prawns with chili in Slow Cooker

This beautiful Malay dish will be awesome in your Slow Cooker!

Prep time: 5 minutes Cooking time: 2 hours Servings: 8

INGREDIENTS:

Shell-on prawns

Minced shallot

2 tbsp cider vinegar

2 tbsp Sambal Oelek

Half cup catsup

One chicken egg

1 tbsp fish sauce

Sugar

Sesame oil

Half cup scallions

1 bulb garlic

DIRECTIONS:

1. Finely mince ginger, shallot, and garlic. Finely slice scallions.
2. In a bowl, mix shallots, Sambal Oelek, cider vinegar, garlic, sugar, scallions and catsup. Stir well and transfer this mixture to Slow Cooker.
3. On a HIGH heat, cook for 1 hour. Then, add prawns and cook for 10 minutes.
4. Beat in one chicken egg and add sesame oil. Cook for another 10 minutes under the lid. To serve, season with fish sauce.

Nutrition: Calories: 212 Fat: 14g Carbohydrates: 21g Protein: 37g

Seabass with cream coconut sauce

Rich flavor and amazing taste will make you enjoy this dish!

Prep time: 5 minutes Cooking time: 2 hours Servings: 8

INGREDIENTS:

One seabass

Salt to taste

4 stalks Bok Choy

2 cups coconut cream

Fresh ginger

1 tbsp fish sauce

2 stalks scallions

DIRECTIONS:

1. Thinly slice scallions and cut ginger into small strips.
2. Grease your Slow Cooker with melted butter or fresh olive oil.
3. Right in the cooking dish, combine ginger, coconut cream, peppers, scallions and fish sauce. Top the mixture with fish.
4. Place the Bok Choy stalks over the fish.
5. Cover with lid and cook for 2 hours on HIGH temperature regime.¬¬
6. Serve seabass over a large plate. Top with the sauce from Slow Cooker and garnish with sesame seeds. Serve hot.

Nutrition: Calories: 212 Fat: 19g Carbohydrates: 29g Protein: 12g

POULTRY RECIPES

Turkey breast with herbs

Try this one as a main dish for a family meeting!

Prep time: 11 minutes Cooking time: 4 hours Servings: 6

INGREDIENTS:

2 tbsp softened butter

1 turkey breast half

Fresh parsley

Ground black pepper

Dried basil

Dried thyme

Garlic powder

1 tbsp soy sauce

Dried sage

Whipped cream cheese

DIRECTIONS:

1. Grease your Slow Cooker, using simple unsalted butter.
2. Do not remove the bone from turkey and place it into Slow Cooker.
3. In a small bowl, combine parsley, whipped cream cheese, garlic powder, soy sauce, black pepper, sage, melted butter, basil and thyme.
4. Mix well and pour the herb mixture over turkey. Rub the meat with your hands. Cover the lid of your Slow Cooker. Cook on LOW mode to 8 or 10 hours.

Nutrition: Calories: 324 Fat: 8g Carbohydrates: 1g Protein: 60g

Spicy Buffalo Wings in Slow Cooker

Serve this with your favorite dressing!

Prep time: 26 minutes Cooking time: 4 hours Servings: 8

INGREDIENTS:

Half cup butter

1 bottle hot sauce

2 tsp dried oregano

Chicken wing sections

2 tsp garlic powder

2 tsp onion powder

Worcestershire sauce

DIRECTIONS:

1. In a saucepan, whisk butter, hot pepper sauce, oregano, Worcestershire sauce, onion, garlic. Place saucepan over medium heat and bring to boil. Reduce to low and simmer for 6 minutes. Put chicken wings in greased and preheated Slow Cooker. Pour over with sauce.
2. Cook for 4 hours: first 2 hours on HIGH and the second 2 – on LOW.
3. Before serving, spread the wings over the baking sheet and cook for 30 minutes.

Nutrition: Calories: 385 Fat: 34g Carbohydrates: 3g Protein: 16g

Slow Cooker Jambalaya

Hot and flavored homemade meal!

Prep time: 21 minutes Cooking time: 8 hours Servings: 12

INGREDIENTS:

Andouille sausage

2 tsp parsley

Dried oregano

1 large onion

1 tsp cayenne pepper

Dried thyme

Celery

2 tsp Cajun seasoning

1 green bell pepper

Cooked shrimp without tails

Canned tomatoes

One cup chicken broth

DIRECTIONS:

1. Cut chicken breast and sausage into small cubes. Finely chop onion, celery and green bell pepper.

2. Right in your Slow Cooker dish, mix sausage, chicken, onion, tomatoes (along with the juice), celery, and pepper.

3. Pour in chicken broth and stir everything finely.

4. Season with Cajun seasoning, oregano, cayenne pepper, parsley and thyme. Cook under cover for 4 hours on HIGH mode.

5. Add shrimp during last 30 minutes of cooking.

Nutrition: Calories: 235 Fat: 14g Carbohydrates: 6g Protein: 21g

Italian-styled creamy chicken

This is amazing to serve with hot rice or pasta!

Prep time: 9 minutes Cooking time: 4 hours Servings: 4

INGREDIENTS:

Unsalted butter

Half cup white wine

Onion cream cheese

Italian salad dressing mix

Golden mushroom soup

4 chicken breast halves

DIRECTIONS:

1. Remove the skin from chicken breasts. If needed, remove the bones too. In a saucepan, melt unsalted butter and turn medium heat.

2. Add cream cheese, the salad dressing mix, wine and mushroom soup. Stir until smooth. Grease your Slow Cooker and place chicken meat over its' bottom.

3. Pour the saucepan sauce over the chicken meat.

4. Cover and cook about 4 hours on LOW, until the chicken is tender.

Nutrition: Calories: 456 Fat: 28g Carbohydrates: 13g Protein: 27g

Tortilla Soup with Duck

It tastes better than in a restaurant!

Prep time: 31 minutes Cooking time: 5 hours Servings: 8

INGREDIENTS:

Cooked and shredded duck

Vegetable oil

Canned and peeled tomatoes

7 corn tortillas

Canned enchilada sauce

Chopped cilantro

1 medium onion

Bay leaf

Green chili peppers

1 pack frozen corn

2 cloves garlic

Black pepper

1 cups water

Salt

Canned chicken broth

1 tsp chili powder

1 tsp cumin

DIRECTIONS:

1. Combine duck meat, enchilada sauce, peeled tomatoes, garlic, chiles and green onions in your Slow Cooker.

2. Pour in mixed water and broth.

3. Add seasoning of mixed cumin, salt, chili powder, black pepper. Add bay leaf. In the end, add corn and cilantro.

4. Turn on your Slow Cooker on LOW setting and prepare for 8 hours. Using an oven, slightly fry the tortillas and cut them into strips.

5. Serve soup with tortillas.

Nutrition: Calories: 262 Fat: 11g Carbohydrates: 25g Protein: 18g

Chicken Fajitas in Slow Cooker

Perfect on cold days!

Prep time: 5 minutes Cooking time: 7 hours Servings: 16

INGREDIENTS:

2 chicken breasts

3 tbsp chunky salsa

1 medium onion

Chopped tomatoes

1 large green bell pepper

Guacamole

Shredded cheese

Sour cream

16 inch flour tortillas

Fajita seasoning mix

139

Cayenne pepper

DIRECTIONS:

1. Grease your Slow Cooker with melted butter and place the chicken into it.
2. Dice green bell pepper and onion and place the vegetables onto chicken in Slow Cooker.
3. In separate bowl, mix sauce: combine fajita seasoning, salsa and cayenne pepper. Pour over the chicken.
4. Place the lid on Slow Cooker and set to LOW mode. Cook for 7 hours.
5. To serve, spoon the chicken mixture over each tortilla with a slotted spoon. Serve while hot.

Nutrition: Calories: 332 Fat: 9g Carbohydrates: 43g Protein: 19g

Spice Chicken legs

This is so tasty and simple!

Prep time: 6 minutes Cooking time: 3 hours Servings: 6

INGREDIENTS:

12 chicken drumsticks

Salt to taste

Half tsp onion powder

Black pepper

3 tbsp butter

Hot red pepper sauce

1-2 cups blue cheese salad dressing

Half tsp garlic powder

DIRECTIONS:

1. Grease your Slow Cooker with some olive oil or melted unsalted butter.
2. Put the chicken drumsticks into Slow Cooker and sprinkle with cubed unsalted butter. Pour in the red hot pepper sauce.
3. Mix onion and garlic powders and salt/pepper. Season the chicken with spicy mixture. Cover the lid and cook for 3 hours on HIGH mode.
4. Serve with blue cheese salad dressing.

Nutrition: Calories: 685 Fat: 55g Carbohydrates: 6g Protein: 41g

Latin Chicken in Slow Cooker

The spicy mix gives this amazing taste and flavor!

Prep time: 27 minutes Cooking time: 4 hours Servings: 6

INGREDIENTS:

Lime wedges

Olive oil

3 cloves garlic

Skinless chicken thighs

Ground cumin

Cilantro leaves

2 sweet potatoes

Hot salsa

Red bell pepper

Half cup chicken broth

2 cans black beans

Half tsp allspice

DIRECTIONS:

1. Preheat the olive oil in the large skillet over the medium heat.
2. Rub the chicken thighs with salt and pepper. Additionally, sprinkle with cilantro. Brown the chicken for 5 minutes on each side.
3. Transfer the thighs to the Slow Cooker and arrange them all over its' bottom. Cover with chopped potatoes, black beans and red bell peppers.
4. In a separate bowl, mix together cilantro leaves, chicken broth, cumin, salsa, garlic and allspice. Add to Slow Cooker.
5. Cook on LOW mode for 4 hours. Serve with lime wedges.

Nutrition: Calories: 591 Fat: 18g Carbohydrates: 57g Protein: 50g

Turkey for Thanksgiving

You can place ingredients into Slow Cooker in the morning, so the night will smell like Thanksgiving!

Prep time: 16 minutes Cooking time: 8 hours Servings: 12

INGREDIENTS:

1 tsp dried sage

5 slices bacon

1 tbsp Worcestershire sauce

Canned turkey gravy

1 bone-in turkey breast

2 tbsp all-purpose flour

Half tsp garlic pepper

DIRECTIONS:

1. Cook the bacon on medium heat until it is evenly brown. Cool, then drain and crumble. Spray your Slow Cooker with enough cooking spray.
2. Transfer turkey to Slow Cooker.
3. Mix garlic with pepper and season the turkey.
4. In a small bowl, mix gravy, bacon, Worcestershire sauce, flour, sage. Pour over the meat in Slow Cooker.
5. Cover the lid. Cook for 8 hours using LOW temperature mode.

Nutrition: Calories: 382 Fat: 15g Carbohydrates: 3g Protein: 54g

Whole Baked Chicken

Amazing the people, who owned a large Slow Cooker!

Prep time: 22 minutes Cooking time: 10 hours Servings: 11

INGREDIENTS:

Whole chicken

1 tsp paprika

Salt

Aluminum foil

Black pepper

DIRECTIONS:

1. Make three balls out of foil. Place the balls into Slow Cooker.
2. Rinse the chicken under cold running water. Drain and dry chicken, use the paper towels. Sprinkle the chicken with salt, paprika and freshly ground black pepper.
3. Carefully arrange the chicken over the aluminum balls in Slow Cooker.
4. Set your Slow Cooker to HIGH mode and cook the first hour, then turn on low temperature for 10 hours.

Nutrition: Calories: 411 Fat: 29g Carbohydrates: 1g Protein: 35g

Boneless Turkey with Garlic and Herbs

Amazing for both Thanksgiving and simple family dinner!

Prep time: 12 minutes Cooking time: 8 hours Servings: 11

INGREDIENTS:

1 tbsp dried oregano

garlic powder

Boneless turkey breast

Water

1 tbsp dried basil

Dry onion soup mix

Seasoned salt

Onion powder

DIRECTIONS:

1. Grease your Slow Cooker and transfer the turkey into it. Whisk water with onion soup and pour carefully over turkey.
2. In a bowl, stir onion powder and garlic powder, basil, seasoned salt, parsley, oregano. Sprinkle over the meat.
3. Set your Slow Cooker to LOW regime and cook for 9 hours. You can serve it with mashed potatoes, pasta or rice.

Nutrition: Calories: 468 Fat: 3g Carbohydrates: 6g Protein: 99g

Chicken Corn with Chili

These Great for a cold winter dinners!

Prep time: 16 minutes Cooking time: 12 hours Servings: 6

INGREDIENTS:

2 chicken breasts

Canned pinto beans

Canned salsa

Mexican-style corn

2 tsp garlic powder

1 tsp ground cumin

Salt

1 tsp chili powder

Black pepper

DIRECTIONS:

1. Remove skin and bones out of the chicken breasts. Grease your Slow Cooker with enough amount of olive oil. Rub the chicken with salsa and transfer to Slow Cooker.
2. Season to your taste with chili powder, black pepper, cumin, salt, garlic powder. Turn on Slow Cooker and set to LOW. Cook for 7 hours.
3. In 4 hours, shred the meat with two forks and add pinto beans and corn. Cook the remaining time.

Nutrition: Calories: 188 Fat: 3g Carbohydrates: 23g Protein: 21g

Barbeque Goose for Sandwich

Easy and fast goose receipt!

Prep time: 7 minutes Cooking time: 6 hours Servings: 3

INGREDIENTS:

2 tbsp butter

1 goose breast

2 cups chicken broth

1 clove garlic

2 tbsp Worcestershire sauce

1 yellow onion

DIRECTIONS:

1. Finely mince 1 clove garlic. Slice one small yellow onion.

2. In a large saucepan, melt unsalted butter (use medium heat). Cook onion and garlic just for 5 minutes.

3. Place goose breast into saucepan and cook until evenly browned. Transfer goose to Slow Cooker and sprinkle with Worcestershire sauce. Pour in chicken broth (just to cover).

4. Cook on HIGH temperature setting for 7 hours. Shred to serve.

Nutrition: Calories: 200 Fat: 16g Carbohydrates: 5g Protein: 10g

Turkey Soup with Split Peas

Smoked turkey for those who do not like pork!

Prep time: 21 minutes Cooking time: 4 hours Servings: 8

INGREDIENTS:

One onion

Dried split peas

3 small carrots

Dried oregano

Celery

Half tsp garlic powder

3 cups chicken broth

Smoked turkey legs

2 bay leaves

Water

2 potatoes

DIRECTIONS:

1. Finely chop onion, celery and carrot. Place smoked turkey legs to Slow Cooker.

2. In a large bowl, combine peas, carrots, potatoes, celery and onion. Top the turkey with vegetable mix.

3. Pour in water and chicken broth.

4. Season with oregano and garlic powder. Add bay leaves. Cook on HIGH mode for 5 hours.

Nutrition: Calories: 613 Fat: 18g Carbohydrates: 50g Protein: 63g

Classic Pheasants for Slow Cooker

Very simple and fast receipt for tender meat!

Prep time: 21 minutes Cooking time: 5 hours Servings: 16

INGREDIENTS:

One small onion

4 small pheasants

Canned sliced mushrooms

Sliced bacon

Salt

One cup water

Black pepper

Dry onion soup mix

One cup sour cream

Cream of mushroom soup

DIRECTIONS:

1. Slice bacon and finely chop small onion.

2. Grease your Slow Cooker with melted and unsalted butter. Clean and rinse peasants. Place birds into Slow Cooker.

3. Cover the pheasants with sliced bacon. Try to cover the birds as much as you can.

4. In a bowl, whisk sour cream, condensed soup, water, finely chopped onion, mushrooms and onion soup mix. Add some salt and pepper and pour over pheasants.

5. Cook for 9 hours on LOW temperature mode.

Nutrition: Calories: 256 Fat: 18g Carbohydrates: 4g Protein: 20g

Cornish Hens in Plum Glazing

Try this as a holiday meal!

Prep time: 11 minutes Cooking time: 8 hours Servings: 6

INGREDIENTS:

Half tsp crushed red pepper flakes

3 Cornish game hens

Dry onion soup mix

Plum jam

2 kiwi fruits

DIRECTIONS:

1. Slightly grease your Slow Cooker.

2. Place the game hens into cooking dish and sprinkle over with red pepper flakes. In a bowl, mix onion soup mix and plum jam. Brush the mixture over the hens.

3. Turn on Slow Cooker and set to LOW temperature regime. Cook for 8 hours. Serve the hens garnished with kiwi slices.

Nutrition: Calories: 437 Fat: 22g Carbohydrates: 35g Protein: 26g

Shredded Chicken in Barbeque Sauce

You can eat this as a main dish or as a sandwich ingredient!

Prep time: 11 minutes Cooking time: 8 hours Servings: 5

INGREDIENTS:

Cup barbeque sauce

1 chicken breast

1 sweet onion

DIRECTIONS:

1. Wash the chicken under cold running water. Remove skin and bones. Finely chop sweet onion.

2. Grease your Slow Cooker with unsalted butter.

3. Place chicken into Slow Cooker and set on HIGH. Prepare for 4 hours. Shred your chicken with two forks. Continue to cook for 2 more hours.

Nutrition: Calories: 203 Fat: 2g Carbohydrates: 21g Protein: 22g

Whole Lemon Chicken in Slow Cooker

Simple dish for the lazy weekends!

Prep time: 17 minutes Cooking time: 8 hours Servings: 6

INGREDIENTS:

1 tsp Worcestershire sauce

olive oil

Whole chicken

1 tsp sesame oil

lemon juice

4 tbsp honey

2 cloves garlic

5 tbsp soy sauce

DIRECTIONS:

1. First of all, wash the chicken and remove the skin. If needed, empty inner cavity. Remove excess liquid with paper towel.

2. Grease Slow Cooker with olive oil. Place the chicken into Slow Cooker.

3. In a bowl, whisk together soy sauce, chicken broth, honey, Soy sauce, Worcestershire sauce, lemon juice, balsamic vinegar, garlic and sesame oil.

4. Pour the sauce mixture over chicken.

5. Cover the lid and cook for 8 hours on LOW mode.

Nutrition: Calories: 393 Fat: 28g Carbohydrates: 15g Protein: 22g

Buffalo Soup with Chicken Wings

A true Buffalo dish just matching for Slow Cooker!

Prep time: 19 minutes Cooking time: 7 hours Servings: 9

INGREDIENTS:

6 cups sour cream

4 carrots

3 cans cream of chicken soup

3 celery stalks

2 chicken breast halves

3 potatoes

Blue cheese

Hot pepper sauce

DIRECTIONS:

1. In a saucepan filled with water, cook chicken breasts. Shred and drain. Dice carrots and celery stalks. Peel and cube the potatoes.

2. In a bowl, combine sour cream, cream of chicken soup, hot pepper sauce, chicken meat, celery, carrots and potatoes.

3. Stir well and transfer to Slow Cooker.

4. Cover and set to LOW. Cook for 6 hours. Stir time after time. When it is one hour left, stir in blue cheese.

Nutrition: Calories: 634 Fat: 42g Carbohydrates: 36g Protein: 28g

Young Goose for Slow Cooker

The mild taste of wild goose!

Prep time: 21 minutes Cooking time: 6 hours Servings: 6

INGREDIENTS:

3 tbsp fresh rosemary

Chopped celery

Cream of mushroom soup

Fresh sage

2 goose

Cream of celery soup

Fresh thyme

Cream of chicken soup

1 cup mushrooms

1 pack baby carrots

DIRECTIONS:

1. Finely mince fresh thyme, rosemary, and sage leaves. Chop celery and baby carrots.
2. In a wide bowl, mix cream of celery, carrots, cream of chicken soup. Celery, cream of mushroom soup, sage, thyme, mushrooms and rosemary.
3. Cut goose into pieces and place into Slow Cooker. Pour the cream mixture over the meat.
4. Set to HIGH and cook for 8 hours until tender.

Nutrition: Calories: 998 Fat: 56g Carbohydrates: 17g Protein: 91g

Homemade Chicken with Dumplings

Try this freshly cooked chicken with your family!

Prep time: 21 minutes Cooking time: 6 hours Servings: 6

INGREDIENTS:

1 cup water

4 cans chicken broth

4 carrots

Salt

2 tbsp flour

4 baking potatoes

2 cups baking mix

2 cups chopped broccoli

Black pepper

4 tbsp milk

DIRECTIONS:

1. Right in Slow Cooker, mix potatoes, chicken meat, broccoli and carrots.
2. In a separate bowl, mix water and flour until it appears to be paste-like. Season with pepper and salt to taste.
3. Pour in over the Slow Cooker ingredients and stir well. Cover and cook for 5 hours on LOW mode.
4. In small bowl, combine baking mix and milk. Carefully add to Slow Cooker, using a teaspoon. Cook for another hour.

Nutrition: Calories: 649 Fat: 22g Carbohydrates: 62g Protein: 47g

Mexican-styled Slow Cooker Chicken

Add this to your tacos and salads, or just serve with pasta or rice!

Prep time: 11 minutes Cooking time: 4 hours Servings: 4

INGREDIENTS:

Half cup tomato salsa

Half cup tomato preserves

Half cup chipotle salsa

One chicken

DIRECTIONS:

1. In a bowl, mix pineapple preserves, chipotle salsa and tomato salsa. If needed, remove skin and bones from the chicken meat.
2. Place chicken into Slow Cooker and pour over with the sauce. Toss meat to cover evenly. Cook for 3 hours on LOW mode.
3. Remove chicken meat from Slow Cooker and finely shred with two forks. Return to Slow Cooker and prepare for 1 more hour.

Nutrition: Calories: 238 Fat: 2g Carbohydrates: 31g Protein: 23g

Yellow Rice with Turkey wings

Quick and easy for working days!

Prep time: 21 minutes Cooking time: 6 hours Servings: 6

INGREDIENTS:

1 tsp seasoned salt

3 turkey wings

1 tsp garlic powder

Ground black pepper

Water to cover

Cream of mushroom soup

1 pack saffron rice

DIRECTIONS:

1. Clean the turkey wings and transfer to Slow Cooker.
2. In a bowl, mix garlic powder, salt, cream of mushroom soup, black pepper. Season the wings with this mixture.
3. Pour in water into Slow Cooker – just enough to cover the wings. Stir everything well and cover. Cook for 8 hours on LOW mode.
4. When it is time, stir the rice into Slow Cooker and prepare for 20 minutes more.

Nutrition: Calories: 272 Fat: 5g Carbohydrates: 39g Protein: 17g

Slow Cooker Turkey Wings

You can try it with your favorite sauce and side dishes!

Prep time: 11 minutes Cooking time: 7 hours Servings: 12

INGREDIENTS:

Salt

Ground black pepper

6 turkey legs

3 tsp poultry seasoning

DIRECTIONS:

1. Wash the turkey legs with running water and remove excess liquid.
2. Rub each turkey leg with one teaspoon of poultry seasoning. Add salt and black pepper. Cut aluminum foil into leg-fitting parts and wrap each turkey leg with a foil.
3. Place the wrapped legs into Slow Cooker. Add no water or other liquids. Cook on LOW for 8 hours. Check the tenderness before serving.

Nutrition: Calories: 217 Fat: 7g Carbohydrates: 1g Protein: 36g

Chicken Alfredo in Slow Cooker

Easy with Alfredo sauce and Swiss cheese!

Prep time: 16 minutes Cooking time: 4 hours Servings: 6

INGREDIENTS:

Black pepper

3 tbsp grated Parmesan cheese

4 chicken breast halves

Salt

4 slices Swiss cheese

Garlic powder

DIRECTIONS:

1. Wash your chicken breasts with running water. Remove the bones and skin. Cut chicken meat into small cubes.
2. Right in Slow Cooker, combine chicken cubes and Alfredo sauce. Toss to cover. Cook under lid on LOW mode, approximately for two hours.
3. Add both cheeses and cook for another 30 minutes.
4. Just before serving, season with salt, garlic powder and black pepper to taste.

Nutrition: Calories: 610 Fat: 50g Carbohydrates: 9g Protein: 31g

Quick-to-Cook Chicken

It will wait for you to come home!

Prep time: 16 minutes Cooking time: 8 hours Servings: 6

INGREDIENTS:

Half cup sour cream

4 chicken breast halves

Cream of celery

Cream of chicken soup

DIRECTIONS:

1. Discard the skin and bones from the chicken. Wash and drain.
2. Grease your Slow Cooker with melted butter or olive oil. If you prefer cooking spray, use it. Transfer cleared chicken into Slow Cooker.
3. In a bowl, whisk both creams. Mix well until smooth. Pour the chicken meat with cream mixture.
4. Cover with the lid and prepare for 8 hours on LOW mode. Just before serving, add the sour cream.
5. To serve, transfer cooked chicken onto a large bowl. Garnish with chopped green onion or other vegetables or berries. Serve hot.

Nutrition: Calories: 304 Fat: 16g Carbohydrates: 12g Protein: 27g

Slow Cooker Turkey with Dumplings

Creamy and hot, perfect choice for a cold day!

Prep time: 9 minutes Cooking time: 4 hours Servings: 4

INGREDIENTS:

3 medium carrots

1 cans cream of chicken soup

Garlic powder

1 can chicken broth

Half onion

Buttermilk biscuit dough

5 large potatoes

2 tbsp butter

Cooked turkey

Poultry seasoning

DIRECTIONS:

1. Cook the turkey before start.
2. Chop the potatoes, onion and carrots.
3. In a bowl, mix butter, onion, potatoes, turkey, chicken broth and cream of chicken soup. Season with garlic powder.
4. Transfer into Slow Cooker and pour in water to cover. Cook on HIGH mode for 3 hours, stirring occasionally. Place the biscuits over turkey and cook for 1 more hour

Nutrition: Calories: 449 Fat: 22g Carbohydrates: 38g Protein: 23g

Flavored Chicken in Rustic Italian Style

Perfect with veggies and Italian seasoning!

Prep time: 22 minutes Cooking time: 5 hours Servings: 6

INGREDIENTS:

3 cups penne pasta

Red bell pepper

Chicken thighs

Canned tomatoes

Salt

Canned crushed tomatoes

Black pepper

Fresh mushrooms

2 carrots

4 garlic cloves

DIRECTIONS:

1. Grease Slow Cooker with oil or spray with anti-stick cooking spray. Transfer chicken to Slow Cooker.
2. Chop carrots into 1-inch slices, slice bell peppers and mushrooms. Mice garlic.
3. Add the vegetables and add canned tomatoes, salt/pepper and season with two tablespoons of Italian seasoning.
4. Cover and cook on LOW for 8 hours.
5. To serve, use 3 cups penne pasta or fresh parsley.

Nutrition: Calories: 441 Fat: 16g Carbohydrates: 41g Protein: 31g

Hot Turkey Meatballs

Perfectly to serve with vegetables!

Prep time: 17 minutes Cooking time: 3 hours Servings: 4

INGREDIENTS:

Water

Dry onion soup mix (2 envelopes)

2 Chicken eggs

Beef flavored rice

Fresh turkey meat

DIRECTIONS:

1. Fill your Slow Cooker with water and onion soup mix (there should be enough liquid to fill crockpot halfway).
2. Turn on Slow Cooker to high and leave until the liquid boils.
3. Meanwhile, make meatballs. In a bowl, combine rice with turkey and flavoring mix. Add beaten chicken eggs and mix together.

4. Form 2-inch meatballs and fry them to brown on large skillet with oil.
5. When soup is boiling. Transfer meatballs to Slow Cooker and prepare 9 hours on LOW temperature mode.

Nutrition: Calories: 567 Fat: 22g Carbohydrates: 42g Protein: 47g

Shredded Turkey in Barbeque Sauce

Full of protein and healthy meal!

Prep time: 13 minutes Cooking time: 10 hours Servings: 8

INGREDIENTS:

1 tsp ground cumin

8 potato rolls

2 cans baked beans

1 medium onion

1 tbsp yellow mustard

2 bone-in turkey thighs

salt

DIRECTIONS:

1. Finely chop onion.
2. Grease your Slow Cooker with melted plain butter.
3. Right in Slow Cooker pot, combine onion, baked beans, barbeque sauce, cumin, yellow mustard and salt.
4. Carefully place the turkey thighs into the mixture.
5. Set Slow Cooker to LOW temperature and cook for 11 hours.
6. Remove turkey and discard bones. Shred and place back to Slow Cooker. Serve the turkey placed over potato rolls.

Nutrition: Calories: 385 Fat: 6g Carbohydrates: 59g Protein: 26g

Lemon-Fragrant Chicken

Easy and great to taste!

Prep time: 22 minutes Cooking time: 9 hours Servings: 6

INGREDIENTS:

1 medium onion

1 cup hot water

Salt

One stalk celery

One whole chicken

One big apple

Half tsp dried rosemary

zest and juice of 1 lemon

ground black pepper

146

DIRECTIONS:

1. Peel and core apple. Cut into quarters.
2. Wash the chicken and dry with a paper towel.
3. Rub the salt and pepper mix into chickens' skin and place apple and chopped celery into chicken. Place chicken into Slow Cooker and sprinkle with chopped onion, lemon zest and juice, rosemary. Pour in one cup water.
4. Cover and cook on HIGH for 1 hour. Then, turn to LOW and cook for 7 hours.

Nutrition: Calories: 309 Fat: 17g Carbohydrates: 7g Protein: 31g

Turkey with Indian Spice

Perfect with rice and fresh herbs!

Prep time: 17 minutes Cooking time: 6 hours Servings: 4

INGREDIENTS:

Turkey thigh meat

Canned stewed tomatoes

3 tbsp dried onion flakes

Dried thyme leaves

4 tbsp white wine

Half tsp Italian seasoning

6 cubes chicken bouillon

Garlic powder

Lemon pepper seasoning

DIRECTIONS:

1. In a bowl, whisk together wine and canned tomatoes.
2. Pour in the tomato mixture into your Slow Cooker and add onion flakes, bouillon cubes and thyme. Season with garlic powder and Italian seasoning.
3. Carefully place the turkey into Slow Cooker.
4. Cover the lid and cook for 10 hours on LOW temperature mode.

Nutrition: Calories: 317 Fat: 7g Carbohydrates: 9g Protein: 51g

Gluten-free Chicken Soup

Easy to cook on a busy day!

Prep time: 13 minutes Cooking time: 8 hours Servings: 9

INGREDIENTS:

Medium onion

1/2 cup water

2 carrots

Gluten-free chicken broth

Salt

Frozen vegetables

4 tbsp. long-grain rice

2 celery stalks

Garlic

Black pepper

Dried basil

tomatoes

Red pepper flakes

DIRECTIONS:

1. In a bowl, combine diced tomatoes, diced carrots, garlic, celery and onions.
2. Transfer the vegetable mix into Slow Cooker and season with dried basil, red pepper flakes, salt and pepper.
3. Carefully place chicken into the mixture. Stir everything well to cover the meat. Cook on LOW temperature mode for 7 hours.
4. Add rice and frozen vegetable mix. Cook for 1 more hour on HIGH.

Nutrition: Calories: 198 Fat: 6g Carbohydrates: 20g Protein: 16g

Hawaiian Spice Slow Cooker Chicken

Amazingly tastes with rice!

Prep time: 5 minutes Cooking time: 4 hours Servings: 9

INGREDIENTS:

Chicken breasts

Canned sliced pineapples

1 tsp soy sauce

1 bottle honey bbq sauce

DIRECTIONS:

1. Carefully grease the bottom and sides of your Slow Cooker with melted butter or spray with anti- stick spray.
2. Wash and drain chicken breasts, place into Slow Cooker.
3. In a bowl, mix pineapple slices and barbeque sauce, add soy sauce. Pour in this mixture over chicken breasts into Slow Cooker.
4. Cover the lid and turn Slow Cooker to HIGH temperature mode. Cook for 5 hours. To serve, garnish chicken with chopped parsley and green onion. Serve while hot.

Nutrition: Calories: 274 Fat: 3g Carbohydrates: 29g Protein: 30g

Chicken Soup with Rice

Your whole family will like this soup!

Prep time: 5 minutes Cooking time: 8 hours Servings: 6

INGREDIENTS:

3 celery sticks

4 tbsp long-grain rice

2 cups frozen mixed vegetables

Half cup water

1 tbsp dried parsley

Lemon seasoning

3 cans chicken broth

Herb seasoning

DIRECTIONS:

1. Remove bones from chicken breast halves. Cook and dice the meat. In a bowl, combine chopped celery, rice, mixed vegetables.

2. Season the mixture with lemon and herbal seasoning. Add some salt to taste and transfer to Slow Cooker.

3. Whisk water and chicken broth; pour over the vegetable and chicken mixture in Slow Cooker. Cover and cook for 8 hours, using LOW temperature mode.

Nutrition: Calories: 277 Fat: 7g Carbohydrates: 27g Protein: 25g

Creamy Chicken with Pasta

Make your chicken absolutely tender with sour cream and mushrooms!

Prep time: 12 minutes Cooking time: 6 hours Servings: 4

INGREDIENTS:

1 tsp Italian seasoning

Sour cream

1 pack cream cheese

2 chicken breast halves

DIRECTIONS:

1. 2 hours before cooking take cream cheese out of refrigerator – it should be at room temperature. Wash the chicken breast under cold running water. Discard bones and skin, cut into 1-inch cubes. Grease your Slow Cooker and right in it mix cream of mushroom soup, cream cheese, Italian seasoning and sour cream.

2. Carefully stir in chicken cubes until smooth. Cook for 6 hours, using LOW temperature mode.

Nutrition: Calories: 357 Fat: 28g Carbohydrates: 7g Protein: 19g

Summer Burrito with Turkey

You can use Thanksgiving leftovers for these burritos!

Prep time: 13 minutes Cooking time: 1 hour Servings: 10

INGREDIENTS:

1 cup prepared stuffing

Salt to taste

3 cups cooked turkey

3 tbsp self-rising flour

3 tbsp jalapeno juice

1 tbsp dried parsley

Shredded Cheddar

1 large onion

Turkey broth

3 jalapeno peppers

1 cup mashed potatoes

1 cup gravy

Black pepper

10 flour tortillas

DIRECTIONS:

21. Grease your Slow Cooker with olive oil or anti-stick spray.

22. Right in a cooking pot, mix turkey, broth, stuffing, gravy, mashed potatoes, onion. Cook for 1 hour on HIGH temperature mode.

23. Meanwhile, warm tortillas, using a dry frying pan or baking sheet.

24. Spoon the Slow Cooker mixture over each tortilla, add cheese and roll into burrito. Garnish with chopped parsley and jalapeno slices.

Nutrition: Calories: 516 Fat: 15g Carbohydrates: 54g Protein: 28g

Bloody Mary Chicken

Incredibly easy and tasty chicken receipt!

Prep time: 18 minutes Cooking time: 4 hours Servings: 4

INGREDIENTS:

2 chicken breasts

Blue cheese dressing

Brown sugar

Vegetable juice cocktail

Small lemon

Celery salt

Hot pepper sauce

1 tsp horseradish

Worcestershire sauce

4 stalks celery

Steak sauce

DIRECTIONS:

1. Remove skin off chicken breasts, place them into Slow Cooker.

2. Combine celery salt, lemon juice, sugar, Worcestershire sauce, hot pepper sauce and horseradish.

3. Pour in the vegetable juice cocktail, stir until sugar is fully dissolved. Pour the mixture into Slow Cooker.

4. Add blue cheese dressing into Slow Cooker and combine well. Set Slow Cooker to LOW and cook for 8 hours.

Nutrition: Calories: 530 Fat: 34g Carbohydrates: 23g Protein: 27g

Super Easy Cornish Hens

Juicy hens with awesome flavor!

Prep time: 18 minutes Cooking time: 4 hours Servings: 6

INGREDIENTS:

Lemon juice

Salt

3 tbsp margarine

1\4 cup cubed margarine

Garlic powder

Red pepper flakes

Thyme

Ground cumin

Chicken broth

2 Cornish hens

DIRECTIONS:

1. In a bowl, mix melted margarine, garlic powder, lemon juice, red pepper flakes and cumin. Rub the lemon mixture into two Cornish game hens.

2. In a bowl, mix thyme, black pepper and salt and sprinkle the hens. Start preheating your Slow Cooker and fill in to half with chicken broth.

3. Place one tablespoon of margarine onto each chick and carefully transfer hens into Slow Cooker. Cook on LOW for 8 hours.

Nutrition: Calories: 516 Fat: 43g Carbohydrates: 4g Protein: 26g

Balsamic Chicken in Slow Cooker

You can cook this even with frozen chicken!

Prep time: 17 minutes Cooking time: 4 hours Servings: 6

INGREDIENTS:

Half cup vinegar

Olive oil

Dried rosemary

1 tsp oregano

4 chicken breast halves

Garlic

2 cans crushed tomatoes

Dried basil

Dried thyme

Dried oregano

One large onion

Black pepper/salt to taste

DIRECTIONS:

1. Remove skin from chicken breasts.

2. Drizzle some olive oil over the bottom of your Slow Cooker.

3. Place the breasts into Slow Cooker, rub each one with pepper/salt to your taste. Dice onion and garlic, place atop the chicken breasts.

4. Season with basil, oregano, thyme and rosemary. Pour tomatoes and balsamic vinegar.

5. Cook for 4 hours using HIGH temperature mode.

Nutrition: Calories: 200 Fat: 7g Carbohydrates: 18g Protein: 19g

Hot Turkey in Italian Style

Serve this with veggies or sandwiches!

Prep time: 27 minutes Cooking time: 8 hours Servings: 6

INGREDIENTS:

Worcestershire sauce

4 ouillon cubes

Dried oregano

1 medium onion

1 turkey breast half

Half cup water

White vinegar

Green bell pepper

Brown gravy mix

2 cloves garlic

DIRECTIONS:

1. Pour one quart water into your Slow Cooker. Dissolve bouillon cubes in it. Remove skin from turkey and place meat into Slow Cooker.

2. Cover and cook for 8 hours on LOW temperature regime.

3. Two hours before the end, stir in Worcestershire sauce, vinegar, green bell pepper, oregano, onion and garlic.

4. In the end, combine some water and gravy mix in a small bowl and add into Slow Cooker. Cook for additional 20 minutes.

Nutrition: Calories: 117 Fat: 1g Carbohydrates: 6g Protein: 20g

Slow Cooker Baked Chicken with Paprika

Perfectly fits for busy days!

Prep time: 21 minutes Cooking time: 10 hours Servings: 6

INGREDIENTS:

Salt

1 tsp paprika

One whole chicken

Black pepper to taste

DIRECTIONS:

1. Roll small balls out of aluminum foil and place them into your Slow Cooker.

2. Rinse the chicken all over (inside and out), better under cold running water. Dry with paper towels. Mix black pepper, paprika and salt and rub the chicken with this mixture.

3. Place seasoned chicken onto aluminum balls in Slow Cooker.

4. Set HIGH mode and cook firstly for an hour, then turn to LOW and cook for approximately 9 hours.

Nutrition: Calories: 408 Fat: 28g Carbohydrates: 1g Protein: 35g

Sour and Sweet Chicken

Quick and tasty weekend meal!

Prep time: 19 minutes Cooking time: 8 hours Servings: 4

INGREDIENTS:

2 chicken breast halves

Half tsp thyme leaves

3 tbsp lemon juice

Black pepper

Chicken broth

2 tbsp butter

Garlic

2 cups rice

DIRECTIONS:

1. Remove skin and bones from your chicken breast halves. Transfer chicken breast to Slow Cooker.

2. In separate dish, whisk chicken stock and lime juice. Pour into Slow Cooker. Add minced garlic, chopped pepper, butter and thyme.

3. Cover with the lid. Cook until tender (on LOW mode for 10 hours). In the end, stir in rice and continue to prepare for 15 more minutes.

4. To serve, take the chicken out of Slow Cooker and serve on a large dish.

Nutrition: Calories: 395 Fat: 9g Carbohydrates: 40g Protein: 37g

Tunisian-Styled Turkey

Satisfying and tasty dish for any holiday!

Prep time: 11 minutes Cooking time: 4 hours Servings: 6

INGREDIENTS:

2 tbsp flour

1 turkey breast half

Chipotle chili powder

1 tbsp olive oil

Half tsp garlic powder

1 acorn squash

Ground cinnamon

3 large carrots

Coriander

2 red onions

Salt

6 garlic cloves

Ground black pepper

DIRECTIONS:

1. Mix chipotle and garlic powder, black pepper, cinnamon and salt.

2. Rub turkey meat with spicy mix and brown in a large skillet (use medium heat). Grease your Slow Cooker with olive oil.

3. Cover the bottom of Slow Cooker with diced carrots, acorn squash quarters, garlic cloves and red onions.

4. Place the turkey atop the vegetables. Cook on HIGH mode for 8 hours.

Nutrition: Calories: 455 Fat: 5g Carbohydrates: 19g Protein: 81g

Hot Buffalo Chicken Lettuce Envelopes

So much healthier than traditional Buffalo wings!

Prep time: 11 minutes Cooking time: 6 hours Servings: 10

INGREDIENTS:

2 chicken breasts

1 pack ranch dressing mix

One head Boston lettuce leaves

Cayenne pepper sauce

DIRECTIONS:

1. Remove skin and bones from the chicken and put the breasts into Slow Cooker.
2. In a bowl, stir to smooth ranch dressing mix and cayenne pepper. Stir the mixture until it is smooth.
3. Pour the chicken breasts with the sauce. Make sure that all the chicken surface is covered with the sayce.
4. Cover and cook during 7 hours (use LOW temperature mode).
5. Using spotted spoon, place chicken meat over the lettuce leaves and roll.

Nutrition: Calories: 105 Fat: 2g Carbohydrates: 2g Protein: 18g

Chicken with Pear and Asparagus

Unusual seasoning for incredibly tasty dish!

Prep time: 21 minutes Cooking time: 4 hours Servings: 4

INGREDIENTS:

4 cloves garlic

1 tbsp vegetable oil

2 tbsp balsamic vinegar

4 chicken breast halves

3 tbsp apple juice

One onion

Dried rosemary

Black pepper, salt

Grated fresh ginger

Two Bartlett pears

2 tbsp brown sugar

Fresh asparagus

DIRECTIONS:

1. Core and slice Bartlett pears.
2. Warm the olive on preheated skillet. Cook chicken meat until it is completely browned. Transfer to Slow Cooker.
3. Dice the onion and spread it over the chicken. Season with salt and pepper.
4. Place asparagus and pears into Slow Cooker.
5. Separately mix balsamic vinegar, sugar, apple juice, sugar, ginger and garlic. Add to Slow Cooker. Cover and cook for 5 hours on LOW mode.

Nutrition: Calories: 309 Fat: 7g Carbohydrates: 33g Protein: 29g

Sweet Chicken with Parmesan

This one will be your favorite!

Prep time: 11 minutes Cooking time: 5 hours Servings: 6

INGREDIENTS:

Black pepper

6 tbsp butter

Salt to taste

Onion soup mix

Cream of mushroom soup

Grated Parmesan

1 cup milk

1 cup rice

6 chicken breasts

DIRECTIONS:

1. Remove skin and bones off the chicken.
2. Separately mix milk, onion soup mix, rice and cream of mushroom soup. Slightly grease Slow Cooker, lay chicken meat over the bottom.
3. Pour the sauce mixture all over it.
4. In addition, season with pepper/salt.
5. Finally, cover with grated Parmesan cheese.
6. Set Slow Cooker to LOW and prepare for 10 hours.

Nutrition: Calories: 493 Fat: 21g Carbohydrates: 37g Protein: 35g

Cornish Hens with Olives

Perfect with wild rice or vegetables!

Prep time: 21 minutes Cooking time: 4 hours Servings: 2

INGREDIENTS:

1 tsp garlic salt

151

2 Cornish game hens

One large zucchini

Golden mushroom soup

Pimento-stuffed green olives

Baby Portobello mushrooms

DIRECTIONS:

1. To start, prepare the vegetables: chop zucchini, mushrooms and green olives. Slightly coat the hens with 3 tablespoons of golden mushroom soup.

2. In a bowl, mix olives, remaining mushroom soup, garlic salt and zucchini. Stuff the hens with this mixture.

3. Transfer hens into Slow Cooker and pour over with some more mushroom soup (all that remained).

4. Set your Slow Cooker to HIGH mode and cook for 4 hours.

Nutrition: Calories: 851 Fat: 57g Carbohydrates: 24g Protein: 59g

Slow Cooker Chicken in Thai Sauce

Slightly spiced, this is an awesome dish for any occasion!

Prep time: 23 minutes Cooking time: 5 hours Servings: 6

INGREDIENTS:

Half cup roasted peanuts

6 chicken breast halves

Fresh cilantro

1 large bell pepper

3 green onions

Large onion

Chicken broth

Soy sauce

3 cloves garlic

2 tbsp cornstarch

Salt/pepper

6 tbsp creamy butter cream

1 tbsp ground cumin

Red pepper flakes

DIRECTIONS:

1. Grease your Slow Cooker with melted butter.

2. Right in a cooking pot, combine chopped bell pepper, onion and chopped to trips chicken. In a bowl, whisk together red pepper flakes, minced garlic, cumin, pepper/salt. Stir to blend. Cover Slow Cooker with the lid and cook for 5 hours on low mode.

3. Drain 1 cup liquid from Slow Cooker to whisk lime juice, soy sauce, peanut butter and cornstarch in it. Pour in back to Slow Coker.

4. Cook on HIGH for 30 minutes more.

5. To serve, garnish with cilantro, green onions and chopped peanuts.

Nutrition: Calories: 410 Fat: 26g Carbohydrates: 18g Protein: 35g

Leftovers Soup with Turkey Meat

A hearty soup with noodles and turkey for your family!

Prep time: 23 minutes Cooking time: 10 hours Servings: 8

INGREDIENTS:

2 cups penne pasts

Chicken broth

Small onion

Cream of mushroom soup

One turkey carcass

2 bay leaves

3 cup cooked turkey

Chopped celery

3 celery steaks

One quartered onion

2 medium carrots

DIRECTIONS:

1. Place the turkey carcass into your Slow Cooker.

2. Place quartered onion, halved celery and carrots and bay leaves into Slow Cooker too. Cover and cook for approximately 4 hours. Carefully remove solids from Slow Cooker. Add chopped vegetables and cook for 3 hours on LOW regime.

3. Add penne paste and leave to prepare for additional 2 hours.

4. In the end of time, mix in mushroom cream and turkey meat. Cook for 30 minutes.

Nutrition: Calories: 1876 Fat: 140g Carbohydrates: 54g Protein: 87g

Chicken Livers Mix

Perfect with noodles and rice!

Prep time: 34 minutes Cooking time: 6-7 hours Servings: 4

INGREDIENTS:

3 green onions

1 tsp salt

Dry white wine

3 slices bacon

Black pepper

One cup chicken stock

Canned sliced mushrooms

1 pound chicken livers

Golden mushroom soup

DIRECTIONS:

1. In a medium bowl, mix salt, flour and pepper. Place livers into this mixture and toss to cover. Cook bacon on a skillet, over the medium heat). Remove and drain with paper towels.

2. Place the livers into the same skillet and cook until lightly browned. Place the livers and bacon into Slow Cooker. Pour in the chicken stock. Add golden mushroom soup and wine.

3. Cook under the lid for 6 hours. Use LOW temperature mode.

Nutrition: Calories: 352 Fat: 16g Carbohydrates: 21g Protein: 24g

Slow Cooker Chicken with Italian dressing

This melts in the mouth!

Prep time: 19 minutes Cooking time: 6 hours Servings: 7

INGREDIENTS:

Sea salt

1 pack angel hair pasta

Pepper

Malt vinegar

1 tsp garlic powder

Ground cumin

Plain flour

Italian seasoning

Sour cream

Italian salad dressing

Parmesan cheese

DIRECTIONS:

1. In a bowl, whisk pepper, garlic powder, paprika, salt, cumin, cumin and Italian seasoning. Add Italian dressing, Parmesan, cream of mushroom soup, vinegar, flour, sour cream.

2. Set Slow Cooker to low. Cook for 6 hours using LOW temperature mode. Shred the chicken, continue cooking.

3. Separately, cook angel hair.

4. Serve chicken over the cooked pasta.

Nutrition: Calories: 483 Fat: 25g Carbohydrates: 40g Protein: 24g

Barbeque Chicken Sliders

Creamy and delicious taste for your family!

Prep time: 23 minutes Cooking time: 3 hours Servings: 7

INGREDIENTS:

16 mini rolls

4 breast halves

Sugar

1 tbsp olive oil

Red wine vinegar

1 pack coleslaw mix

3 tbsp mayonnaise

1 cup barbeque sauce

Half cup water

Salt/Black pepper

DIRECTIONS:

1. Place skinless, boneless chicken breast on aluminum foil. Season with salt and pepper. Place wraps over dry skillet or grill for 3 minutes.

2. Transfer chicken breasts into Slow Cooker and pour over with mixed bbq sauce and water. Cover and cook for 5 hours on LOW mode.

3. Take out the chicken and shred it using two forks.

4. Mix chicken meat with mayonnaise, coleslaw, sugar, vinegar and pepper/salt. Serve over sweet rolls.

Nutrition: Calories: 396 Fat: 12g Carbohydrates: 340g Protein: 13g

Slow Cooker Turkey in Beer Marinade

Feel the traditional flavors of turkey with ranch seasoning!

Prep time: 14 minutes Cooking time: 8 hours Servings: 7

INGREDIENTS:

6 slices bacon

Cooking spray

Light beer

Ranch dressing mix

Bone-in turkey breast

Butter

DIRECTIONS:

1. Spray the inside of your Slow Cooker with cooking spray. In a bowl, combine half pack of ranch dressing with butter.

2. Carefully place butter mixture under the turkey's skin. Transfer to Slow Cooker.

3. Sprinkle turkey with remaining ranch dressing mix. Arrange the bacon pieces over turkey. Pour in lager beer.

4. Cook on HIGH 1 hour. Then, turning to LOW, continue cooking for 8 hours.

Nutrition: Calories: 194 Fat: 15g Carbohydrates: 3g Protein: 8g

French Onion and Chicken Soup

Super easy and delicious meal!

Prep time: 16 minutes Cooking time: 5 hours Servings: 9

INGREDIENTS:

White sugar

6 tbsp. butter

Shredded Mozzarella

1 bay leaf

Shredded Parmesan

4 yellow onions

Emmental cheese

Gruyere cheese

Garlic

7 cups broth

Cooking sherry

Sea salt

Chicken breast half

Dried thyme

French bread slices

DIRECTIONS:

1. Heat butter on a skillet and cook onions until translucent. Add sugar and cook for 30 minutes over medium heat. Add garlic and cook until fragrant.

2. Pour in sherry into onion mixture, transfer to Slow Cooker. Add beef broth and cubed chicken meat.

3. Season with species and place a bay leaf.

4. Cook on HIGH for 6 hours or on LOW for 10 hours.

5. Mix four shredded cheeses and top each bowl of soup with cheese. Warm bread slices. Serve with soup.

Nutrition: Calories: 258 Fat: 14g Carbohydrates: 17g Protein: 11g

Turkey Bacon Cassoulet

Simple and delicious French receipt!

Prep time: 32 minutes Cooking time: 4 hours Servings: 6

INGREDIENTS:

2 bay leaves

Fresh parsley

Olive oil

Dried thyme

Canned diced tomatoes

Ground black pepper

6 slices turkey bacon

3 cans Northern beans

One large onion

3 cloves garlic

Smoked sausage

3 tbsp. tomato paste

Black pepper

DIRECTIONS:

1. Cook the turkey bacon on a greased skillet until crispy. Dry with paper towel. Set aside. In the same skillet, fry onion until translucent.

2. Add chicken meat, bay leaves, thyme, sausage, black pepper and garlic. Cook for around 7 minutes.

3. Stir in tomato paste and transfer the mixture to Slow Cooker. Add northern beans, turkey bacon and diced tomatoes.

4. Cook for 5 hours on LOW temperature setting.

Nutrition: Calories: 522 Fat: 19g Carbohydrates: 53g Protein: 35g

Tagine Chicken in Slow Cooker

Moroccan chicken meal for your Slow Cooker

Prep time: 24 minutes Cooking time: 5 hours Servings: 12

INGREDIENTS:

Olive oil

1 cup couscous

8 chicken thighs

1 cup water

1 eggplant

Black pepper

2 onions

Cinnamon

2 cups chicken broth

4 carrots

1 tsp ground ginger

Half cup dried cranberries

Cumin

2 tbsp lemon juice

2 tbsp tomato paste

Half cup dried apricots

Flour

Garlic salt

DIRECTIONS:

1. Cut chicken and eggplant. Cook both on large greased skillet until the chicken is slightly browned. Place the skillet ingredients into Slow Cooker, cover with diced carrots, onion, garlic, apricots and cranberries.

2. In a bowl, whisk tomato paste, chicken broth, flour, lemon juice and species. Pour the spicy mixture over the chicken.

3. Cook under the lid for 8 hours on LOW mode. Serve with couscous.

Nutrition: Calories: 380 Fat: 15g Carbohydrates: 38g Protein: 22g

Slow Cooker Turkey with Potatoes

Hearty and healthy for you and your friends!

Prep time: 21 minutes Cooking time: 6 hours Servings: 6

INGREDIENTS:

Black pepper

6 cups water

Cream of chicken soup

2 cups rice

Cream of mushroom soup

Garlic powder

3 turkey legs

3 medium onions

Seasoned meat tenderizer

Green bell pepper

Salt

Red bell pepper

DIRECTIONS:

1. Right in Slow Cooker, combine creams of chicken and mushroom soup. Add chopped onion and red and green bell peppers.

2. Place the turkey legs over the bottom of your Slow Cooker and pour over with the sauce. Set your Cooker HIGH temp mode and cook for 3 hours, stirring time after time.

3. Stir in garlic powder, salt/pepper, tenderizer and diced potatoes.

4. Take out turkey and cut off meat off the bones. Return and cook for one more hour. Serve with separately cooked rice.

Nutrition: Calories: 655 Fat: 17g Carbohydrates: 74g Protein: 45g

Chicken Breast with Bacon and Feta

Just five ingredients for tasty receipt!

Prep time: 17 minutes Cooking time: 3 hours Servings: 8

INGREDIENTS:

Half cup crumbled feta

2 tbsp fresh basil

8 slices bacon

Diced tomatoes

8 chicken breast halves

DIRECTIONS:

1. Preheat a large skillet over medium heat. Place the bacon into it. Cook about 10 minutes. Drain and dry with paper towels.

2. Using a small bowl, mix feta cheese and crumbled bacon.

3. Cut split lengthwise chicken meat to create some kind of pocket. Fill it with the sauce mixture. To secure, use toothpicks. Transfer chicken to Slow Cooker. Top with tomatoes and chopped basil. Cook on HIGH regime for about three hours.

Nutrition: Calories: 246 Fat: 7g Carbohydrates: 7g Protein: 33g

Chicken with Quinoa and Mustard

Quickly and easy receipt for your weekend or holiday!

Prep time: 15 minutes Cooking time: 3 hours Servings: 4

INGREDIENTS:

1 tbsp honey

1 cup quinoa

4 chicken breasts

Dill weed

Hot water

3 tbsp spicy brown mustard

1 tsp onion powder

1 tbsp chopped chives

1 tsp red wine vinegar

Sea salt

3 tbsp nutritional yeast flakes

1 tbsp butter

Ground turmeric

DIRECTIONS:

1. In a small bowl, soak quinoa just for several minutes and drain.

2. In a bowl, combine dill, yeast flakes, turmeric, sea salt, chives and onion powder. Stir in quinoa, one cup water, vinegar and butter.

3. Add yeast flake mixture. Stir everything well and pour into Slow Cooker. Place chicken meat atop the mixture and season with salt or species you like. Spoon mixed honey and mustard over.

4. Cook for 3 hour on HIGH mode.

Nutrition: Calories: 344 Fat: 8g Carbohydrates: 34g Protein: 31g

MEAT RECIPES

Barbeque Ribs with Hot Sauce

Now you do not need a barbeque!

Prep time: 7 minutes Cooking time: 8 hours Servings: 26

INGREDIENTS:

Hot sauce

Salt

Pork ribs

Black pepper

Worcestershire sauce

Chili sauce

4 tbsp vinegar

Baked brown sugar

Oregano

2 cups ketchup

DIRECTIONS:

1. Preheat your oven for 200 degrees.

2. Place baby pork ribs onto baking sheet, season with black pepper/salt. Cook until brown. In a bowl, combine chili sauce, ketchup, oregano, Worcestershire sauce, sugar, hot sauce, vinegar.

3. Transfer ribs into Slow Cooker and cover with sauce.

4. To cook, turn your Slow Cooker to LOW and prepare for 8 hours.

Nutrition: Calories: 497 Fat: 29g Carbohydrates: 39g Protein: 25g

Beef Tacos in Korean style

So full of taste and flavor!

Prep time: 17 minutes Cooking time: 8 hours Servings: 8

INGREDIENTS:

Beef chuck roast

16 corn tortillas

Half onion

Salt

Soy sauce

Half cup brown sugar

Black pepper

Sesame oil

10 cloves garlic

1 fresh ginger

Jalapeno pepper

Rice vinegar

DIRECTIONS:

1. Wash chuck roast and place it on the bottom of your Slow Cooker.

2. Mix minced garlic, brown sugar, jalapeno pepper, soy sauce, rice vinegar, ginger root and sesame oil. Season with pepper and salt.

3. Pour the mixture over chuck roast.

4. Cover the lid and cook for around 10 hours on LOW mode. When it is time, shred meat with the help of two forks.

5. Serve with tortillas and your favorite topping.

Nutrition: Calories: 456 Fat: 22g Carbohydrates: 40g Protein: 23g

Pepperoni Roast in Pots

Perfectly fits with pasts or mashed potatoes!

Prep time: 11 minutes Cooking time: 5 hours Servings: 6

INGREDIENTS:

1 pack au jus mix

5 pepperonchini peppers

1 pack ranch dressing mix

Unsalted butter

1 beef chuck roast

DIRECTIONS:

1. Carefully wash and drain chuck roast under running water. Remove all the excess parts like skin and small bones.

2. Grease your Slow Cooker with melted butter or just spray with cooking spray. Transfer beef roast into Slow Cooker.

3. With a knife, form a pocket atop of the roast.

4. Fill the pocket with pepperoncini, butter, au jus and ranch mixes. Use LOW temperature mode to cook. Prepare for 8 hours.

5. To serve, arrange beef meat over the salad leaves and serve along with fresh vegetables.

Nutrition: Calories: 537 Fat: 39g Carbohydrates: 5g Protein: 36g

Juicy Ham from Slow Cooker

Delicious and good sensation with only two ingredients!

Prep time: 13 minutes Cooking time: 8 hours Servings: 24

INGREDIENTS:

8 pound ham

2 cups brown sugar (packed)

DIRECTIONS:

1. If needed, remove the bones from ham. The meat should be clear when you cooking, so avoid any excesses.

2. Grease your Slow Cooker with cooking spray and let dry.

3. Spread one cup of sugar all over the bottom of your Slow Cooker.

4. Place ham into Slow Cooker (so it lays flat side down). The ham slices could slightly overlap each other.

5. Rub the remaining sugar into ham.

6. Cook for around 8 hours using LOW temperature mode.

7. Serve with sandwiches or simply atop the cooked rice, mashed potatoes or any other side dish you like.

Nutrition: Calories: 360 Fat: 20g Carbohydrates: 18g Protein: 25g

Corned beef with juicy cabbage

Serve warm, so you will get juicy and flavored meal!

Prep time: 15 minutes Cooking time: 9 hours Servings: 8

INGREDIENTS:

Half head cabbage

4 large carrots

Beer

10 baby red potatoes

1 corned beef brisket

4 cups water

1 onion

DIRECTIONS:

1. Prepare the vegetables: finely chop half onion, quarter potatoes and cup carrots into matchsticks. Place the vegetables all over the bottom of your Slow Cooker and pour in with water.

2. Arrange beef brisket atop the vegetables in Slow Cooker. Pour in the beer and add species from packet.

3. Set your Slow Cooker to HIGH and cook for about 8 hours.

4. When it is one hour left before serving, add the cabbage for 1 hour more.

Nutrition: Calories: 472 Fat: 19g Carbohydrates: 49g Protein: 23g

Spice Baby Back Ribs

It is an awesome meal for busy days!

Prep time: 16 minutes Cooking time: 4 hours Servings: 8

INGREDIENTS:

1 clove garlic

baby back ribs

Half onion

Salt to taste

bottled barbeque sauce

Half cup water

clove garlic

Black pepper

DIRECTIONS:

1. To start, season and rub the ribs with salt and black pepper to your taste. Place the ribs into Slow Cooker. Pour over with water.

2. Slice onion, finely mince garlic, place the veggies all over the ribs.

3. Cook on HIGH temperature mode during 4 hours. If you have time, cook for 8 hours on low regime.

4. When it is time, transfer ribs to a baking sheet and coat with hot barbeque sauce. Bake for additional 15 minutes.

Nutrition: Calories: 501 Fat: 29g Carbohydrates: 32g Protein: 24g

Pulled Pork with Mango and Bourbon

Spicy and smoky meal!

Prep time: 21 minutes Cooking time: 6 hours Servings: 10

INGREDIENTS:

1 bottles barbeque sauce

2 mangos

Bourbon whiskey

1 pork shoulder roast

2 tsp honey

Black pepper

2 cups water

1 tsp salt

1 tsp chipotle powder

Balsamic vinegar

DIRECTIONS:

1. Peel and remove pits from mangos. Arrange pits over the bottom of your Slow Cooker, then chop the mangos and set aside.
2. Place pork shoulder into Slow Cooker and finely rub with species. Sprinkle with water and balsamic vinegar.
3. Cook covered for 8 hours on LOW mode.
4. When ready, remove mango pits and shred the roast.
5. Meanwhile, make puree out of mango, chipotle powder, honey and whiskey. Return the meat and sauce to Slow Cooker for an additional hour.

Nutrition: Calories: 319 Fat: 8g Carbohydrates: 34g Protein: 23g

Slow Cooker Spiced Barbeque

This will just melt while you eating!

Prep time: 12 minutes Cooking time: 9 hours Servings: 8

INGREDIENTS:

1 bottle barbeque sauce

1 chuck roast

Salt to taste

Garlic powder

Fresh black pepper

1 tsp onion powder

DIRECTIONS:

1. If needed, discard the bones from chuck roast. Wash the meat under the running water. Drain it with paper towels.

2. Grease your Slow Cooker with olive oil. You can also take a special cooking spray with anti- sticking effect.
3. Place clear meat into Slow Cooker. Do not forget to season with onion and garlic powders, add salt and pepper to your taste.
4. Pour over with barbeque sauce.
5. Cover and cook for 6 or 8 hours on LOW temperature mode. Shred meat and cook for one more hour.
6. To serve, arrange the meat along with vegetables or any side dish you like.

Nutrition: Calories: 347 Fat: 16g Carbohydrates: 23g Protein: 20g

Chili beef with species and veggies

Satisfying and super tasty!

Prep time: 28 minutes Cooking time: 4 hours Servings: 10

INGREDIENTS:

Half cup shredded Cheddar

Ground beef

2 cloves garlic

1 tsp black pepper

2 tbsp chili powder

2 cans diced tomatoes

2 onions

2 cans kidney beans

Salt

1 can tomato sauce

1 green bell pepper

DIRECTIONS:

1. In a previously preheated skillet, cook ground beef. Cook until crumbly, about 6 minutes. Drain and dry with a paper towels.
2. In a bowl, combine kidney beans, ground beef, tomato sauce, diced tomatoes, bell pepper, onion, and species.
3. Transfer bowl mixture to Slow Cooker.
4. Cook on LOW temperature regime for 10 hours.
5. To serve, place into serving plates, garnished with large salad leaves (optional) and shredded Cheddar cheese.

Nutrition: Calories: 308 Fat: 13g Carbohydrates: 22g Protein: 23g

Meat Loaf in Sweet Sauce

Extra taste and flavor!

Prep time: 14 minutes Cooking time: 7 hours Servings: 8

INGREDIENTS:

Half cup sliced mushrooms

2 chicken eggs

Half tsp Worcestershire sauce

ground mustard

Dried onion

2 tbsp. brown sugar

3 tbsp. bread crumbs

salt

Ketchup

Half tsp rubbed sage

Ground beef

DIRECTIONS:

1. In a large bowl, whisk chicken eggs, diced mushrooms, milk and bread crumbs. Season the mixture with sage and salt.

2. Crumble the ground beef all over the mixture and stir everything to combine. Form a round loaf out of the dough mixture and transfer it to Slow Cooker.

3. Cook on LOW for 5-6 hours.

4. In a bowl, whisk mustard, ketchup, brown sugar and Worcestershire sauce. Cook for additional 15 minutes and let stand a little before serving.

Nutrition: Calories: 328 Fat: 17g Carbohydrates: 18g Protein: 24g

Pepper Steak in Slow Cooker

Delicious and flavorful recipe for your friends!

Prep time: 29 minutes Cooking time: 4 hours Servings: 6

INGREDIENTS:

1 tsp salt

1 tbsp. cornstarch

Beef sirloin

Cubed beef bouillon

3 tbsp. soy sauce

Canned stewed tomatoes

White sugar

Hot water

Vegetable oil

Garlic powder

2 green bell peppers

Small chopped onion

DIRECTIONS:

1. Cut sirloin to strips. Then, sprinkle with garlic powder to your taste.

2. Transfer meat strips to preheated skillet and cook until slightly brown. Place into Slow Cooker. Dissolve cornstarch and bouillon cube in a hot water.

3. Pour the bouillon mixture all over the meat in Slow Cooker.

4. Add chopped onion, stewed tomatoes, green peppers and soy sauce, Add sugar and salt, Cook for 8 hours on LOW temperature mode.

Nutrition: Calories: 301 Fat: 15g Carbohydrates: 11g Protein: 28g

Apple-Cider Marinated Pork

You will get not only pork, but flavored sauce for it!

Prep time: 5 minutes Cooking time: 7 hours Servings: 8

INGREDIENTS:

1 bay leaf

2 cups apple cider

2 tbsp cold butter

Salt

2 shallots

4 cloves garlic

1 tbsp chopped herbs

Half cup apple cider vinegar

1 tbsp vegetable oil

Cayenne pepper

1 tsp Dijon mustard

1 rib celery

Ground black pepper

DIRECTIONS:

1. Season pork with salt and pepper and bring to brown on a large skillet. Transfer to Slow Cooker. In the same skillet, cook celery, shallots and cider vinegar. Pour into Slow Cooker.

2. Add garlic cloves, apple cider and bay leaf.

3. Cook on LOW for 6 hours. Turn pork time after time.

4. When ready, preheat the Slow Cooker mixture in a saucepan; add cayenne pepper and Dijon mustard. Set aside and mix in cold butter and fresh herbs.

5. Serve the meat along with the sauce.

Nutrition: Calories: 388 Fat: 25g Carbohydrates: 13g Protein: 23g

Pepperoncini Beef in Slow Cooker

Super easy filling for any sandwiches!

Prep time: 22 minutes Cooking time: 8 hours Servings: 8

INGREDIENTS:

16 slices provolone cheese

1 beef chuck roast

8 hoagie rolls

1 jar pepperoncini

4 cloves garlic

DIRECTIONS:

1. First of all, grease your Slow Cooker as you like, using plain unsalted butter or preferred olive oil. Cut the beef into small cuts.
2. Finely chop garlic and place each slice into cuts in chuck roast.
3. Place your chuck roast into Slow Cooker and cover with canned pepperoncini along with its liquid. Cover the lid and cook on LOW mode for 8 hours. Do not forger to open the lid time after time and stir the contents of Slow Cooker.
4. Serve as a stuffing for sandwiches along with cheese, fresh salad leaves, and vegetables.

Nutrition: Calories: 998 Fat: 52g Carbohydrates: 71g Protein: 55g

Chili Beef Soup

Easy and very quick receipt!

Prep time: 22 minutes Cooking time: 6 hours Servings: 6

INGREDIENTS:

Lean ground beef

Half cup red wine

Salt

Dash Worcestershire sauce

3 cans dark kidney beans

Dried parsley

3 cans stewed tomatoes

2 tbsp chili powder

Cumin

Red wine vinegar

2 stalks celery

1 red bell pepper

DIRECTIONS:

1. Take a large skillet and fry beef until it is evenly browned. Drain and season with pepper and salt just a little.
2. Right in Slow Cooker, combine kidney beans, chopped celery and red bell pepper, tomatoes and red wine vinegar. Stir all the ingredients until smooth consistency.
3. Place the cooked beef into Slow Cooker. Stir one more time. Cook on LOW mode for 8 hours.
4. During the last 2 hours of cooking, pour in red wine.

Nutrition: Calories: 414 Fat: 11g Carbohydrates: 49g Protein: 28g

Juicy Kalua Pig in Slow Cooker

Try this traditional Hawaiian meal right in your Slow Cooker!

Prep time: 11 minutes Cooking time: 20 hours Servings: 11

INGREDIENTS:

1-2 tbsp Hawaiian sea salt

1 pork butt roast

1 tbsp liquid smoke flavoring

DIRECTIONS:

1. To start, wash pork meat with running water and pierce it with carving fork.
2. Grease your Slow Cooker with melted butter or spray with anti-stick spray for cooking. Season meat with sea salt and liquid smoke. Rub species into the meat.
3. Transfer pork to Slow Cooker and cook on LOW mode from 16 to 20 hours. Remember to stir kalua pig for several times during cooking.
4. Remove meat from cooking pot and finely shred.
5. Serve along with mashed potatoes, pasta or simply on sandwiches with fresh salad leaves.

Nutrition: Calories: 243 Fat: 14g Carbohydrates: 1g Protein: 25g

Slow Cooker Braciole in Slow Cooker

Cook classical Italian dish in your Slow Cooker!

Prep time: 28 minutes Cooking time: 6 hours Servings: 6

INGREDIENTS:

2 tbsp vegetable oil

2 jars marinara sauce

5 slices bacon

2 chicken eggs

1 cup Italian cheese blend

Half cup bread crumbs

Black pepper

1 flank steak

1 tsp salt

DIRECTIONS:

1. Preheat the marinara sauce into Slow Cooker on high mode.
2. Meanwhile, combine breadcrumbs and chicken eggs in a separated bowl. Sprinkle meat with salt and pepper from all sides.
3. Place breadcrumbs, bacon slices and shredded cheese mix over one side of meat. Carefully roll and secure with toothpicks or string.
4. Brown stuffed flank over preheated skillet and transfer to Slow Cooker. Cook in Slow Cooker for 8 hours using LOW temperature mode.

Nutrition: Calories: 614 Fat: 36g Carbohydrates: 41g Protein: 28g

Greek Pulled Pork in Slow Cooker

You can serve it with pasta or simply with chips and dip.

Prep time: 12 minutes Cooking time: 4 hours Servings: 8

INGREDIENTS:

1 pork tenderloin

Canned pepperoncini peppers

Tbsp. Greek seasoning

DIRECTIONS:

1. Wash pork tenderloin and carefully place it into Slow Cooker. Drain and dry with paper towels. Sprinkle the meat with Greek seasoning to cover evenly.
2. Pour over with canned pepperoncini peppers (sliced ones) along with the liquids. Cover Slow Cooker with the lid and cook for 4 hours on HIGH temperature mode.
3. In 15 minutes before serving shred the meat and cook for 10-15 minutes. When it is ready, set aside and let to cool just for several minutes.
4. Serve hot with your favorite side dish or simply fresh vegetables.

Nutrition: Calories: 146 Fat: 4g Carbohydrates: 3g Protein: 21g

Pork with Sauerkraut in Slow Cooker

Easy and delicious dish for your Slow Cooker!

Prep time: 11 minutes Cooking time: 8 hours Servings: 4

INGREDIENTS:

One cup water

Whole pork tenderloin

4 tbsp butter

1 bag baby potatoes

Salt

Canned sauerkraut

Black pepper to taste

DIRECTIONS:

1. Grease your Slow Cooker with plain unsalted butter. You can also spray the crockpot with cooking spray, if you like this method more.
2. Wash whole pork tenderloin and place it into your Slow Cooker.
3. Place unpeeled baby potatoes all around the pork. Arrange the ingredients evenly in layers.
4. Cut cooled butter into small cubes and arrange them, along with black pepper and salt, into Slow Cooker.
5. Cook until the pork is tender, on LOW mode for 9 hours. Add more water if needed.

Nutrition: Calories: 358 Fat: 14g Carbohydrates: 35g Protein: 22g

Texas-styled pulled pork

Serve this over buttered or toasted roll!

Prep time: 14 minutes Cooking time: 5 hours Servings: 8

INGREDIENTS:

1 tsp vegetable oil

2 tbsp butter

1 pork shoulder

8 hamburger buns

1 cup barbeque sauce

Dried thyme

Half cup cider vinegar

2 cloves garlic

Half cup chicken broth

1 large onion

3 tbsp light brown sugar

1 tbsp chili powder

1 tbsp yellow mustard

1 tbsp Worcestershire sauce

DIRECTIONS:

1. Pour one tablespoon over the bottom of Slow Cooker and place pork roast into it. Combine barbeque sauce, chicken broth and apple cider vinegar over the pork.
2. Add yellow mustard, sugar, chili powder, Worcestershire sauce, garlic, thyme and onion. Cook under the lid for 6 hours on HIGH.
3. To serve, shred the meat and arrange over the buns.

Nutrition: Calories: 527 Fat: 23g Carbohydrates: 45g Protein: 31g

London Broil in Slow Cooker

Easy and creamy taste for any occasion!

Prep time: 11 minutes Cooking time: 10 hours Servings: 8

INGREDIENTS:

1 pack dry onion soup

2 pounds flank steak

Condensed tomato soup

Condensed mushroom soup

DIRECTIONS:

1. Grease your Slow Cooker with olive oil or melted unsalted butter.
2. Place the meat into Slow Cooker and arrange evenly over the bottom. If needed, cut it into smaller pieces to fit.
3. In a separate bowl, combine tomato and mushroom soups. Mix until smooth and pour over the meat.
4. Add the dry onion soup mixture sprinkles.
5. Cook under the cover for 10 hours, use LOW temperature mode.
6. To serve, arrange the Slow Cooker meal over a nice serving plate. You can also serve it with favorite side dish.

Nutrition: Calories: 198 Fat: 11g Carbohydrates: 9g Protein: 15g

Three Packs roast mix

Just three spice mixes for amazing taste!

Prep time: 12 minutes Cooking time: 6 hours Servings: 6

INGREDIENTS:

Beef chuck roast

1 pack ranch dressing mix

2 pack dry Italian salad dressing

One cup water

Dry brown gravy mix

DIRECTIONS:

1. If needed, discard the bones from chuck roast. Remove the skin and fat, and all the other excess parts.
2. In a bowl, mix ranch dressing mix, Italian dressing mix and brown gravy mix. Combine until smooth.
3. Pour one cup water into a bowl and whisk well.
4. Transfer the beef roast into Slow Cooker and pour over with the spicy sauce. Turn on Slow Cooker and cook on LOW mode for 6 to 8 hours.
5. To serve, prepare fresh leaves of salad or tortillas and place the hot roast mix on them.

Nutrition: Calories: 610 Fat: 46g Carbohydrates: 6g Protein: 39g

Mongolian Beef in Slow Cooker

Your kids and friends will love this!

Prep time: 28 minutes Cooking time: 4 hours Servings: 4

INGREDIENTS:

1 flank steak

Half cup hoisin sauce

Cornstarch

Half tsp minced ginger

2 tsp olive oil

Half cup brown sugar

1 onion

3 green onions

Half cup soy sauce

1 tbsp minced garlic

DIRECTIONS:

1. Coat the flank steak with a cornstarch. Rub to coat evenly. Preheat the large skillet with olive oil over medium heat.
2. Place the steak over the skillet and brown until it is evenly brown – just for 4 minutes. Set aside to cool a little bit.
3. Add sliced diagonally green onions, water, garlic, steak, onion, ginger, sugar and hoisin sauce to Slow Cooker.
4. Carefully place cooled pork into Slow Cooker mixture.
5. Set Slow Cooker to LOW temperature setting and cook for 4 hours.

Nutrition: Calories: 450 Fat: 13g Carbohydrates: 55g Protein: 28g

Sweet Pork in Slow Cooker

Serve this with vegetables and make a healthy dinner for your family!

Prep time: 12 minutes Cooking time: 8 hours Servings: 6

INGREDIENTS:

Dry spaghetti

Soy sauce

Canned water chestnuts

3 cloves garlic

1 cup snow peas

2 tbsp brown sugar

2 stalks celery

Pork shoulder

1 tsp sesame oil

2 carrots

1 tbsp oyster sauce

3 cups broccoli florets

1 tbsp chile paste

DIRECTIONS:

1. Grease your Slow Cooker or line it with parchment paper.
2. In a separate bowl, whisk chili paste, soy sauce, brown sugar, minced ginger and garlic, oil. Place the pork shoulder into Slow Cooker and pour it over with whisked sauce.
3. Cover the lid and cook on a LOW temperature for 8 hours. Separately cook spaghetti according to package instructions. Serve immediately, meat atop the pasta.

Nutrition: Calories: 506 Fat: 8g Carbohydrates: 72g Protein: 32g

Shoyu Pork Recipe for Slow Cooker

Cook it to infuse the delicate taste and flavors!

Prep time: 11 minutes Cooking time: 8 hours Servings: 9

INGREDIENTS:

One cup sake

1 pork butt roast

3 cloves garlic

1 cup white sugar

Canned tomato sauce

Soy sauce

DIRECTIONS:

1. Grease your Slow Cooker using some olive oil or spray with anti-sticking-effect cooking spray. Transfer pork roast into Slow Cooker.
2. In a bowl, mix sugar, tomato paste, sake, minced garlic and soy sauce. Whisk everything until smooth.

3. Pour the sauce mixture into Slow Cooker. Cover your Slow Cooker with the lid. Set Slow Cooker to LOW temperature regime and prepare for 10 hours.
4. In an hour before the pork is ready, prepare your favorite side dish or just serve the meat with vegetables.
5. Serve the meal while it is still hot.

Nutrition: Calories: 427 Fat: 17g Carbohydrates: 30g Protein: 27g

Ham and Pineapple in Slow Cooker

Amazing holiday dish for all your family!

Prep time: 11 minutes Cooking time: 7 hours Servings: 14

INGREDIENTS:

Cola-flavored carbonated beverage

1 picnic ham

Canned pineapple rings

Water (additional)

DIRECTIONS:

1. Start with preheating your Slow Cooker. Cut ham into thick slices.
2. Drain the pineapple rings and attach the ham slice to each ring (you can use toothpicks). Place pineapples with ham into Slow Cooker and pour in remaining pineapple juice.
3. Pour cola into Slow Cooker. If needed, add water to cover the ingredients.
4. Cook on LOW mode for 8 or 10 hours. Check occasionally the readiness of the meal. Stir time after time.
5. To serve, use a large cooking plate garnished with vegetables.

Nutrition: Calories: 382 Fat: 23g Carbohydrates: 9g Protein: 30g

Pork Spare Ribs in Slow Cooker

Tender and delicious for your friends or family!

Prep time: 14 minutes Cooking time: 8 hours Servings: 5

INGREDIENTS:

2 tbsp soy sauce

Cold water (optional)

Condensed tomato soup

Worcestershire sauce

1 tsp cornstarch

Medium onion

Brown sugar

163

Pork spareribs

3 cloves garlic

DIRECTIONS:

1. In a large pot, bring the ribs to boil and simmer for 13 minutes.
2. In a bowl, combine onion, brown sugar, Worcestershire sauce, onion, soy sauce and soup. Drain ribs and place them in Slow Cooker. Carefully arrange the ribs on the bottom of the crockpot, so they will be cooked through.
3. Pour the ribs over with the sauce mixture.
4. Cook under the lid for 8 hours, using a LOW temperature mode.
5. To cook sauce, drain some liquid from Slow Cooker and combine with cornstarch.

Nutrition: Calories: 483 Fat: 31g Carbohydrates: 18g Protein: 31g

Puerto Rican styled Pork

So much tender and flavors!

Prep time: 19 minutes Cooking time: 6 hours Servings: 6

INGREDIENTS:

One lime

4 cloves garlic

Pork loin roast

Large onion

White wine vinegar

Chopped fresh oregano

Olive oil

Ground cumin

Black pepper

Ground ancho chili pepper

Salt to taste

DIRECTIONS:

1. Combine quartered onion, cumin, garlic, chili pepper, black pepper, oregano and salt.
2. To grease your Slow Cooker, use slightly melted and unsalted butter, or just coat with cooking spray.
3. Pour in vinegar and olive oil. Blend until smooth.
4. Carefully place pork loin into Slow Cooker and cover it with blended mixture. Set your Slow Cooker to LOW mode and cook for 8 hours.

5. To serve, cut the meat into chunks and garnish with lime wedges or preferred vegetables.

Nutrition: Calories: 367 Fat: 21g Carbohydrates: 5g Protein: 37g

Juicy Turkey Breast in Slow Cooker

Quick and delicious dish!

Prep time: 17 minutes Cooking time: 8 hours Servings: 12

INGREDIENTS:

Dry onion soup mix

Salt

Olive oil

Black pepper

1 turkey breast with bone in

DIRECTIONS:

1. Wash turkey breast under running water. Discard the excess skin, if needed, except breast skin. Leave the bones in the breast.
2. Grease your Slow Cooker with butter or oil. If you like, you may also use a cooking spray. Mix species and rub the turkey with the mix, along with the breast parts under the skin.
3. Transfer turkey to Slow Cooker. Stir the mixture and spread it evenly over the bottom. Cook on HIGH for 1 hour. Then, cook for 7 hours on LOW mode.
4. When the meal is ready, serve it on a beautiful plate. Garnish with chopped vegetables and salad leaves.

Nutrition: Calories: 273 Fat: 1g Carbohydrates: 1g Protein: 58g

Black Beans with Pork Tenderloin

Healthy and satisfying recipe!

Prep time: 18 minutes Cooking time: 10 hours Servings: 12

INGREDIENTS:

Pork tenderloin

pinch chili powder

small onion

ground cumin

1 can salsa

oregano

Half cup chicken broth

Small red bell pepper

3 cans black beans

DIRECTIONS:

1. In a bowl, combine salsa, black beans, red pepper, onion, cumin, chili powder and oregano. Rub pork tenderloin with pork mixture and place into Slow Cooker.
2. Carefully, trying not to wash species off, pour in chicken broth.
3. Set Slow Cooker to LOW temperature mode and cook for 9 to 10 hours. Break up pork pieces before serving, so you can get a thickened chili.
4. Serve over cooked rice or any other side dish you prefer.

Nutrition: Calories: 248 Fat: 31g Carbohydrates: 31g Protein: 24g

Slow Cooker Chuck and Potato Roast

Juicy and delicious pork with vegetables!

Prep time: 15 minutes Cooking time: 9 hours Servings: 8

INGREDIENTS:

Chuck roast

1 stalk celery

Salt

3 carrots

Black pepper

Onion soup mix

1 onion

water

3 great potatoes

DIRECTIONS:

1. Peel and cube potatoes. Dice potatoes into quarters. Chop the other vegetables. Season the meat with salt and pepper to your taste.
2. Use a large skillet with olive oil to brown meat from all sides (approximately 4 minutes per one size).
3. Put the roast into Slow Cooker.
4. Arrange chopped vegetables around it and season with soup mix. Pour in one cup water. Stir all ingredients to combine well.
5. Set slow cooker to LOW and cover the lid. Cook for 9 hours or more, if needed.

Nutrition: Calories: 540 Fat: 30g Carbohydrates: 18g Protein: 45g

Beef Barbacoa with Tomato Sauce

It could be served over tortillas or simply with vegetables!

Prep time: 17minutes Cooking time: 6 hours Servings: 7

INGREDIENTS:

1 onion

Salt

Beef chuck roast

Garlic powder

Chili powder

Black pepper

3 tbsp white vinegar

Canned tomato sauce

DIRECTIONS:

1. Grease your Slow Cooker and place the roast in it.
2. Cover with chopped onion, black pepper, bay leaves, vinegar, garlic powder. Toss the cooking dish just to be sure that everything is well combined.
3. Pour in the water to cover completely. Set Slow Cooker to HIGH temperature.
4. Remove meat from Slow Cooker and drain any excess liquids.
5. To serve, shred meat and mix in tomato sauce, salt and chili powder. Place back to Slow Cooker for another 2 hours.

Nutrition: Calories: 292 Fat: 19g Carbohydrates: 9g Protein: 22g

Cranberry Pork in Slow Cooker

Tangy and sweet recipe for your family!

Prep time: 11 minutes Cooking time: 4 hours Servings: 6

INGREDIENTS:

Pork loin roast

Canned cranberry sauce

Large onion

5 tbsp French salad dressing

DIRECTIONS:

1. Wash pork meat under running water and drain with paper towels.
2. In a separate bowl, combine cranberry sauce, chopped onion and French salad dressing. Stir well. Grease your Slow Cooker with plain unsalted butter before you start using it.
3. Transfer pork to Slow Cooker and cover with the sauce.
4. Cover the lid and leave to cook for 8 hours (use a LOW temperature mode). Serve with chopped vegetables or simply make sandwiches.

Nutrition: Calories: 374 Fat: 15g Carbohydrates: 32g Protein: 26g

Slow Cooker Beef Lasagna

Easy and delicious meal for the weekend!

Prep time: 24 minutes Cooking time: 4 hours Servings: 10

INGREDIENTS:

Shredded Mozzarella cheese

Lean ground beef

Parmesan cheese

Salt

One onion

Cottage cheese

Canned tomato paste

One pack lasagna noodles

Canned tomato sauce

Dried oregano

4 cloves garlic

DIRECTIONS:

1. Take a large skillet and preheat it with olive oil. Fry ground beef with onion and garlic until brown.
2. Add tomato paste and sauce, season with oregano and salt. When heated through, set aside. In a bowl, combine shredded cheeses and toss well.
3. Pour one spoon of meat mixture into Slow Cooker, top with noodles and cheese. Repeat layers until the end.
4. Cook under the lid for 6 hours on LOW mode.

Nutrition: Calories: 446 Fat: 20g Carbohydrates: 35g Protein: 31g

Pork Chops for Slow Cooker

Easy and delicious creamy recipe!

Prep time: 32 minutes Cooking time: 2 hours Servings: 12

INGREDIENTS:

Large onion

Salt

Water

Dry onion soup

Pepper

Canned mushroom soup

Trimmed pork chops

Ranch dressing mix

DIRECTIONS:

1. Grease your Slow Cooker with melted butter and start to preheat it on low temperature mode. Meanwhile, cut the onion and spread a half of it over the bottom of Slow Cooker.
2. Place the chops over onion and cover with remaining onion. If needed, arrange pork chops in layers.
3. Mix cream of onion soup and cream of mushroom soup over pork chops. Season with onion soup mix, salt, ranch dressing and black pepper.
4. Cover. Cook on HIGH for 3 hours.
5. Serve the chops while hot, with mashes or vegetable dishes.

Nutrition: Calories: 273 Fat: 10g Carbohydrates: 9g Protein: 25g

Slow Cooker Beef Chops

Perfect and tender for all members of your family!

Prep time: 14 minutes Cooking time: 8 hours Servings: 6

INGREDIENTS:

1 tbsp butter

1 beef tongue

Water

2 cloves garlic

Ground pepper and salt

1 bay leaf

Small onion

DIRECTIONS:

1. Gather chopped onion, beef tongue, bay leaf and garlic in your Slow Cooker. Combine the ingredients well.
2. Season with salt and black pepper to your taste. Pour in enough water to cover the ingredients.
3. Turn on your Slow Cooker and set to LOW temperature. Cook during 8 hours.
4. Take out the tongue and remove all excess skin and rough end. Cut into small bite-sized slices. Preheat butter in a large skillet and cook chopped tongue for 10 minutes.
5. Serve the beef chops along with mashed potatoes or fresh vegetables.

Nutrition: Calories: 492 Fat: 38g Carbohydrates: 1g Protein: 32g

Leg of Lamb with Herbs

Super easy and delicious for any taste!

Prep time: 23 minutes Cooking time: 7 hours Servings: 6

INGREDIENTS:

Fresh cracked pepper

1 lamb leg

Dried thyme

Sea salt

1 juiced lemon

Half cup red wine

Dried rosemary

3 cloves garlic

2 tbsp Dijon mustard

1 tbsp apple cider vinegar

2 tbsp raw honey

DIRECTIONS:

1. Grease your Slow Cooker with melted butter or oil.
2. Take a lamb leg of room temperature, if using frozen – leave it on the table for several hours. Pour the wine into your Slow Cooker.
3. In a bowl, combine sea salt, thyme, black pepper, rosemary, garlic, mustard, honey and lemon juice.
4. When the sauce is thick, massage it into lamb leg. Cook for 5 hours on LOW temperature level.
5. You can serve lamb as a main dish along with mashers or hot rice.

Nutrition: Calories: 285 Fat: 14g Carbohydrates: 10g Protein: 25g

Whole Meat Loaf in Slow Cooker

Slow Cooker will make it mild and flavored!

Prep time: 32 minutes Cooking time: 5 hours Servings: 6

INGREDIENTS:

2 chicken eggs

2 tbsp ketchup

Salt

5 tbsp milk

Ground mustard

Half tsp Worcestershire sauce

Ground beef

Dried minced onion

2 tbsp brown sugar

Half cup seasoned breadcrumbs

Half cup mushrooms

Half tsp sage

DIRECTIONS:

1. In a bowl, combine eggs, onion, breadcrumbs, salt, mushrooms and sage. Place ground beef into mixture and crumble well to combine.
2. Shape a large meat loaf of this mixture.
3. Grease your Slow Cooker with simple or olive oil.
4. Transfer loaf into Slow Cooker. Cook for 6 hours on LOW mode.
5. In a bowl, combine brown sugar, ketchup, Worcestershire sauce and mustard. Spoon over loaf and cook for 10 minutes.

Nutrition: Calories: 328 Fat: 17g Carbohydrates: 18g Protein: 24g

Bulgari Beef in Slow Cooker

Could be a lazy main dish for your dinner!

Prep time: 28 minutes Cooking time: 6 hours Servings: 4

INGREDIENTS:

1 green onion

Half cup soy sauce

Beef

4 tbsp sesame oil

White sugar

1 tsp ground pepper

2 cloves garlic

Half tsp sesame seeds

DIRECTIONS:

1. To start, cut the beef into slices and marinate overnight. To make the meat marinated well, hide it to the refrigerator.
2. To make the marinade, whish 1 tablespoon soy sauce, sesame oil and sugar. Add minced garlic and black pepper.
3. Leave the beef slices in the refrigerator until the next day.
4. In the morning, toast sesame seeds in a skillet. When they become light brown, set aside. Transfer marinated beef along with liquid into Slow Cooker.
5. Add green onions and sesame seeds. Cook on LOW mode during 8 hours.

Nutrition: Calories: 365 Fat: 19g Carbohydrates: 16g Protein: 30g

Squirrel and Liver Dish

The perfect meal for the winter season!

Prep time: 23 minutes Cooking time: 6 hours Servings: 8

INGREDIENTS:

Olive oil

Bay leaf

2 cups tomato juice

2 squirrels

Black pepper

1 green bell pepper

6 cloves garlic

Salt

4 carrots

2 sweet onions

Dried thyme

Beef liver

Dried oregano

DIRECTIONS:

1. Skin and gut squirrels, slice beef liver into thin strips. Preheat a skillet with olive oil over medium heat.

2. Cook liver and squirrels until they are evenly brown on all sides. Place into Slow Cooker. Add chopped vegetables: bell pepper, carrots, garlic and onion.

3. Pour in tomato juice. Stir the contents of your Slow Cooker well to combine the ingredients. Season with species, add bay leaf.

4. Cook for 6 hours on HIGH temperature mode.

Nutrition: Calories: 267 Fat: 7g Carbohydrates: 15g Protein: 33g

Slow Cooker Burrito Beef Pie

This will fit for any kind of side dishes!

Prep time: 14 minutes Cooking time: 5 hours Servings: 16

INGREDIENTS:

Colby cheese

Ground beef

Canned taco sauce

1 onion

12 flour tortillas

Minced garlic

2 cans refried beans

Canned green chili peppers

Canned tomatoes

DIRECTIONS:

1. Start with greasing with olive oil and preheating your Slow Cooker.

2. Place ground beef in the large skillet with olive oil. Sauté meat for 5 minutes. Add chopped onion and garlic, cook for another 5 minutes.

3. Add olives, tomatoes, peppers, refried beans and taco sauce. Simmer for 15 minutes.

4. Grease your Slow Cooker and place several tortillas. Top with a little meat and shredded cheese. Continue layers until it is no ingredients.

5. Cook on LOW for 4 to 5 hours.

Nutrition: Calories: 432 Fat: 23g Carbohydrates: 33g Protein: 20g

Small Meatloaves in Slow Cooker

Easy to make and fast to eat!

Prep time: 5 minutes Cooking time: 6 hours Servings: 8

INGREDIENTS:

1 tsp prepared mustard

One chicken egg

5 tbsp ketchup

3 tbsp ground beef

3 tbsp brown sugar

1 cup shredded Cheddar

1 tsp salt

Half cup quick cooking oats

DIRECTIONS:

1. Grease and start to preheat your Slow Cooker on high mode. In a bowl, combine milk, chicken egg, oats and cheese.

2. Stir in ground beef and combine well until smooth.

3. Form eight small meatloaves and carefully place them into Slow Cooker, one by one.

4. In a separate bowl, whisk brown sugar, mustard and ketchup. Pour the sauce mixture into Slow Cooker.

5. Set to LOW mode and cook for 6 hours.

6. To serve, slice meatloaves into portion slices and serve with any of your favorite side dishes.

Nutrition: Calories: 255 Fat: 14g Carbohydrates: 16g Protein: 15g

Island Spiced Kielbasa

Easy and fast meal for lazy days!

Prep time: 9 minutes Cooking time: 5 hours Servings: 6

INGREDIENTS:

Canned pineapple chunks

168

Kielbasa sausage

2 cups brown sugar

2 cups ketchup

Olive oil to grease

DIRECTIONS:

1. Grease your Slow Cooker with enough olive oil to cover bottom and sides. Set aside for a little while.
2. Slice kielbasa sausage into small pieces – half-inch-sized will be enough.
3. Combine kielbasa slices and pineapple chunks and transfer the mix into Slow Cooker.
4. In a bowl, mix ketchup and sugar. Pour into Slow Cooker. Make sure that the sauce covered all other ingredients well. Toss to be sure/
5. Cover the lid and set your Slow Cooker to LOW mode. Cook for 6 hours. Serve with your favorite side dish or with slices of fresh bread.

Nutrition: Calories: 866 Fat: 41g Carbohydrates: 98g Protein: 20g

Stout Stew for your Slow Cooker

Flavored and hot – the perfect choice for wintertime!

Prep time: 23 minutes Cooking time: 8 hours Servings: 8

INGREDIENTS:

Chopped fresh parsley

3 tbsp flour

2 tbsp vegetable oil

Salt

2 cups Irish beer

Beef stew meat

2 yellow onions

2 large potatoes

1 sprig thyme

2 carrots

DIRECTIONS:

1. Sprinkle the beef with flour. Toss and rub evenly, just to coat all sides.
2. In a large skillet, preheat olive oil and cook beef until even brown color. Drain with paper towels. In Slow Cooker dish, combine diced potatoes, carrots, onions and thyme.
3. Add beef and combine.
4. Pour the beer all over ingredients.

5. Cook on LOW temperature mode for 8 hours.

Nutrition: Calories: 463 Fat: 22g Carbohydrates: 32g Protein: 27g

Philippine Sandwich Meat

Fast, easy and delicious for all your family!

Prep time: 21 minutes Cooking time: 8 hours Servings: 4

INGREDIENTS:

2 cubes beef bouillon

Dried thyme

1 can beer

Large onion

Half tsp sauce

3 cloves garlic

1 tsp mustard

Beef sirloin

1 tsp Worcestershire sauce

2 tbsp bourbon whiskey

Ground cumin

Soy sauce

Paprika

Dried basil

Half tsp garlic powder

Black pepper

DIRECTIONS:

1. Wash beef sirloin and cut in into two or more strips. Grease your Slow Cooker or just spray with cooking spray.
2. Cover the bottom of your Slow Cooker with diced onion and garlic. Layer beef strips atop the vegetables.
3. Season with onion powder, black pepper, paprika, cumin and other species. Pour in mixed bourbon, mustard, hot sauce, beer and Worcestershire sauce. Cook on LOW for around 8 hours.

Nutrition: Calories: 251 Fat: 10g Carbohydrates: 7g Protein: 20g

Stuffed Peppers in Slow Cooker

Prepare in the morning – you'll have an awesome dish by the dinner!

Prep time: 16 minutes Cooking time: 5 hours Servings: 6

INGREDIENTS:

White rice

Velveeta cheese

Half cup or more water

4 green bell peppers

Half cup barbeque sauce

Frozen peas

Ground pork

DIRECTIONS:

1. Remove pepper tops and discard seeds.
2. In a bowl, combine peas, ground meat, rice, barbeque sauce and water. Stir well before the mixture is smooth.
3. Spoon the pea mixture into hollow pepper shells.
4. Pour some water (you can also blend it with some barbeque sauce) into your Slow Cooker. Place the peppers over the Slow Cooker's bottom.
5. Cook on LOW for around 7 hours, covered with the lid.

Nutrition: Calories: 383 Fat: 14g Carbohydrates: 42g Protein: 19g

Slow Cooker Brats in Wisconsin Style

Easy and delicious!

Prep time: 17 minutes Cooking time: 4 hours Servings: 8

INGREDIENTS:

Half cup ketchup

8 bratwurst

One large onion

1 bottles beer

DIRECTIONS:

1. Finely slice the onion.
2. Cover the bottom and sides of your Slow Cooker with an olive oil, just in case that nothing is going to stick.
3. Place sliced onion, ketchup, bratwurst and beer into Slow Cooker. Pour in some water until everything is evenly covered.
4. Cook on HIGH temperature for 4 hours.

Nutrition: Calories: 377 Fat: 27g Carbohydrates: 12g Protein: 13g

Shepherd's Homemade Pie

A tasty casserole that even your kids will love!

Prep time: 12 minutes Cooking time: 2 hours Servings: 7

INGREDIENTS:

One onion

4 large potatoes

Butter

2 tbsp flour

Half cup beef broth

5 carrots

Shredded Cheddar

Ketchup

Ground beef

Vegetable oil

DIRECTIONS:

1. In a pot, cook the potatoes until soft. Darin and mash with butter. Mix in chopped onion and three tablespoons shredded cheese.
2. In a pot, boil carrots for just 4 minutes, then add to mashed potatoes.
3. On a large skillet, cook ground beef with remaining onion until it is slightly brown. Stir in ketchup and simmer for 5 minutes.
4. Grease Slow Cooker and spread mashed potatoes over its bottom. Add beef and mashed carrots. Top with cheese.
5. Cook on HIGH mode for 2 hours.

Nutrition: Calories: 452 Fat: 17g Carbohydrates: 52g Protein: 23g

Texas Beef and Squash

A satisfying meal for the whole family!

Prep time: 12 minutes Cooking time: 10 hours Servings: 10

INGREDIENTS:

beef chuck roast

4 cups cubed butternut squash

2 cans roasted diced tomatoes

1 cup beef broth (or just water)

1 large onion

canned diced green chiles

ancho chile powder

unsweetened cocoa powder

ground cumin

dried oregano

3 cloves garlic

fresh cilantro

polenta or rice

DIRECTIONS:

1. Trim beef roast well and cut beef into 2-inch pieces.

2. In your Slow Cooker mix together beef, tomatoes, squash, beef broth, chiles, chile powder, onion, cocoa powder, oregano, cumin and garlic.

3. Cover with the lid and cook on LOW setting for 10 hours. To serve, sprinkle each portion with cilantro.

4. Serve as the main dish or with polenta or rice.

Nutrition: Calories: 379 Fat: 23g Carbohydrates: 29g Protein: 28g

Minestrone with Beef

Delicious Summer Dish!

Prep time: 17 minutes Cooking time: 9 hours Servings: 8

INGREDIENTS:

Beef chuck

Diced tomatoes with species

Canned beef broth

Canned cannellini beans

Red kidney beans

2 carrots

Salt to taste

Black pepper

Bow tie pasta

Medium yellow squash

Grated parmesan (optional)

DIRECTIONS:

1. Grease Slow Cooker with your favorite olive oil.

2. Right in your Slow Cooker; combine meat, salt, undrained tomatoes, cannellini beans, beef broth, kidney beans, carrots and pepper.

3. Cover and cook on LOW mode for 8 hours Stir in pasta and squash.

4. Cover again and prepare for 45 minutes more until pasta gets tender. Season with salt and pepper.

5. To serve, top with shredded Parmesan.

Nutrition: Calories: 411 Fat: 29g Carbohydrates: 41g Protein: 48g

Spicy Sluppy Joes in Slow Cooker

Perfect for a cold day!

Prep time: 22 minutes Cooking time: 8 hours Servings: 6

INGREDIENTS:

Canned salsa

4 cloves garlic

Dried basil

Lean ground beef

Fresh mushrooms

Cayenne pepper

6 kaiser rolls

Salt

Tomato paste

3 carrots

DIRECTIONS:

1. Take a large skillet and preheat some olive oil in it. Place beef and cook over medium heat until evenly brown from all sides.

2. Grease your Slow Cooker with softened and unsalted butter. If you have one, spray the inside of your Slow Cooker with cooking spray.

3. Drain beef off fat and transfer it into Slow Cooker.

4. Crush 4 cloves garlic, slice mushrooms, cayenne pepper and carrots. Add to Slow Cooker. Cook on HIGH mode with the lid on. In 6 hours, turn your Slow Cooker off.

5. Serve while hot, on toasted Kaiser Rolls. Could be garnished with sour cream and salad leaves.

Nutrition: Calories: 386 Fat: 22g Carbohydrates: 29g Protein: 39g

Roast Beef in Dakota Style

Perfect for summer picnics and meet-ups with friends!

Prep time: 5 minutes Cooking time: 7 hours Servings: 12

INGREDIENTS:

Beef top round

1 yellow onion

3 tbsp flour

Half cup dry red wine

Kosher salt

1 tsp Worcestershire sauce

Chicken stock

3 tbsp unsalted butter

5 cloves garlic

Ground black pepper

Thick cut bacon

DIRECTIONS:

1. Pat the beef with paper towels until dry. Generously season with salt and pepper. Cook sliced bacon in the skillet until golden brown.
2. Add the beef to skillet and cook until it becomes golden brown. Transfer skillet mixture to Slow Cooker.
3. On the same skillet, cook onions until translucent.
4. Pour in wine and simmer for 5 minutes. Transfer to Slow Cooker. Cook on LOW for 7 hours.
5. Serve with chopped green onion.

Nutrition: Calories: 582 Fat: 24g Carbohydrates: 82g Protein: 43g

Meatballs Sandwiches in Slow Cooker

Especially needed for lazy days!

Prep time: 18 minutes Cooking time: 4 hours Servings: 8

INGREDIENTS:

1 chicken egg

Breadcrumbs

Salt

1 large onion

Dried oregano

8 hoagie buns

Ground black pepper

Lean ground beef

Canned tomato sauce

Green sweet pepper

2 tbsp brown sugar

1 tbsp yellow mustard

Chili powder

Pinch garlic salt

Hot pepper sauce

Shredded mozzarella

DIRECTIONS:

1. In a large bowl, whisk chicken egg, breadcrumbs, chopped onion, salt, oregano, and black pepper. Add ground beef and mix well. Shape 32 small balls out of meat mixture.
2. Place meatballs into a layer in baking pan. Bake for 25 minutes. When ready, drain off fat. Right in Slow Cooker, make sauce: stir together mustard, tomato sauce, onion, sweet pepper, sugar, garlic salt, chili powder, black pepper, pepper sauce. Pour in meatballs.
3. Cook, covered on LOW for 4 hours.

4. To serve, place four meatballs on the buns with sauce or Mozzarella.

Nutrition: Calories: 403 Fat: 19g Carbohydrates: 41g Protein: 23g

Beef Brisket Ragu

Tender and flavored with pasta and Parmesan!

Prep time: 5 minutes Cooking time: 4 hours Servings: 6

INGREDIENTS:

Olive oil

Beef brisket

1 brown onion

2 carrots

Celery stalk

Baby mushrooms

1 bay leaf

Thyme

3 garlic cloves

Massel beef stock

Tomato paste

2 tbsp red wine

DIRECTIONS:

1. In a large skillet, heat two tablespoons of olive oil (use high heat).
2. Place half beef on a skillet and cook for around 3 minutes just until brown. Grease your Slow Cooker with slightly melted butter or vegetable oil.
3. On the same skillet, cook the second batch of beef and transfer all meat to Slow Cooker.
4. Fry chopped carrots, mushrooms, celery on onion in the same skillet. Cook for 6 minutes, then add garlic and wait until fragrant. Season with species and add a bay leaf.
5. Transfer to Slow Cooker. Add tomato paste, Massel Liquid Stock and wine. Cook for 4 hours on HIGH temperature.

Nutrition: Calories: 378 Fat: 27g Carbohydrates: 41g Protein: 55g

Slow Cooker Chicken and Sausage Gumbo

Quick and simple Slow Cooker meal!

Prep time: 31 minutes Cooking time: 6 hours Servings: 6

INGREDIENTS:

Vegetable oil

All-purpose flour

Smoked sausage

3 cups water

cubed chicken

Sliced okra

Chopped onion

Green bell pepper

Celery

Cloves garlic

Salt

Ground black pepper

Cayenne pepper

DIRECTIONS:

1. Place a large saucepan on a medium heat. Pour in vegetable oil.
2. Sift in the flour so you can mix a thick paste. Continue cooking and stirring until smooth (for 3 minutes).
3. Reduce heat to low and continue to cook. Continue stirring, until the flour turns to a dark reddish- brown color. Set aside to cool a little bit.
4. Place the saucepan into greased Slow Cooker. Add sausage, okra, onion, chicken, bell pepper, garlic, salt/pepper and cayenne pepper.
5. Pour in enough water to cover.
6. Cook with the lid on with LOW temperature setting for 7 hours.

Nutrition: Calories: 447 Fat: 33g Carbohydrates: 13g Protein: 24g

Braised Short Ribs with Sauce

Satisfying and fitting for any party!

Prep time: 9 minutes Cooking time: 8 hours Servings: 12

INGREDIENTS:

Short ribs

vegetable oil

Salt

Black pepper

1 large onion

4 cloves garlic

3 cups beer

Fresh thyme

DIRECTIONS:

1. Season the meat with salt/pepper to your taste. Rub each rib with vegetable oil.
2. Place the ribs in one layer. Leave space between, place into the oven. Cook for 5 minutes for each side.
3. Turn the heat to medium. Add chopped onion and finely minced garlic. Cooke for another 5 minutes.
4. Then, pour in beer and bring to simmer. Place the herbs over the meat. Transfer to Slow Cooker. Prepare for 8 hours using a LOW mode.

Nutrition: Calories: 434 Fat: 32g Carbohydrates: 19g Protein: 41g

Beef Shank with Wine and Pepper

Awesome and delicious meal for any occasion!

Prep time: 13 minutes Cooking time: 8 hours Servings: 12

INGREDIENTS:

Beef crosscut shank

Bay leaf

4 cups beef broth

Stalk celery

Peanut oil

Salt

Bottled red wine

Rosemary sprig

Balsamic vinegar

Black pepper

2 yellow onions

DIRECTIONS:

1. Preheat unsalted butter into the deep skillet over medium heat. Dry the beef with paper towels and rub with pepper and salt.
2. Drizzle the bottom of Slow Cooker with peanut oil and transfer beef into it. Dice onion, celery and garlic. Add to Slow Cooker.
3. In the saucepan, mix red wine, rosemary sprig, bay leaf. Pour in beef broth. Simmer for 20 minutes.
4. Pour the wine sauce into Slow Cooker and prepare for 8 hours on LOW mode. Serve over polenta or pasta.

Nutrition: Calories: 511 Fat: 12g Carbohydrates: 72g Protein: 30g

Barbacoa Beef in Slow Cooker

Flavored and delicious meat meal from Slow Cooker!

Prep time: 5 minutes Cooking time: 8 hours Servings: 11

INGREDIENTS:

4 canned chipotle peppers

1 head garlic

Half cup apple cider vinegar

Kosher salt

5 bay leaves

4 cups beef stock

4 limes (juiced)

Beef brisket

Ground cloves

Medium red onion

Fresh cilantro

DIRECTIONS:

1. Grease your Slow Cooker with melted butter or just coat with cooking spray.
2. Right in Slow Cooker dish, combine chipotle peppers, red onion, cilantro, clove, garlic, salt, lime juice and cider vinegar.
3. Transfer beef brisket to Slow Cooker and place atop the vegetables. Place the lid on and cook on LOW temperature node for 8 hours.
4. To serve, shred beef with two forks and arrange over warmed tortillas, chopped onion or salsa.

Nutrition: Calories: 452 Fat: 21g Carbohydrates: 62g Protein: 36g

Brisket with Yellow Onions

Try this one at a family meeting!

Prep time: 17 minutes Cooking time: 8 hours Servings: 12

INGREDIENTS:

3 yellow onions

Coarse salt

Beef brisket

Worcestershire sauce

2 cups beef broth

Soy sauce

Black pepper

DIRECTIONS:

1. On a large and preheated skillet, warm oil and caramelize chopped onions (cook for 20 minutes). Pat beef with paper towels and rub it with salt and pepper. Place beef in skillet and cook until brown.

2. Sprinkle minced garlic over beef brisket.
3. Add Worcestershire sauce, beef broth and soy sauce.
4. Grease your Slow Cooker with melted butter or spray with nonstick cooking spray. Transfer beef to Slow Cooker.
5. Cook on LOW temperature mode for 8 hours.
6. To serve, arrange beef over the large serving plate and garnish with chopped parsley.

Nutrition: Calories: 535 Fat: 17g Carbohydrates: 85g Protein: 44g

Slow-Cooker Shredded Orange Pork

Awesome dish for family dinner!

Prep time: 9 minutes Cooking time: 8 hours Servings: 16

INGREDIENTS:

Pork butt

Ground cumin

Garlic, smashed

4 chipotle peppers

Cayenne pepper, or to taste

Dried oregano

Orange juice

Ground black pepper

DIRECTIONS:

1. Trim all the excess fat from the pork and discard the bones and skin. Transfer all ingredients from the list to Slow Cooker.
2. Set your Slow Cooker to LOW temperature mode and leave to cook for 8 hours. You can also leave your dish cooking overnight. When the meat is ready, it will fall off the bone.
3. Cool for 25 minutes so you can remove the meat from Slow Cooker. Transfer pork to a large wide bowl and shred with two fork or knives.
4. To serve, add the meat into tacos or serve with warm tortillas. You can also serve this with radishes, salad leaves, chopped onions or even lime wedges.

Nutrition: Calories: 391 Fat: 23g Carbohydrates: 29g Protein: 44g

Tater Tot and Beef Casserole

Easy, but tasty and satisfying dish!

Prep time: 5 minutes Cooking time: 7 hours Servings: 12

INGREDIENTS:

2 cans cream soup

1 bag Tater Tots

Browned hamburger

1 bag frozen vegetables

Melted butter

DIRECTIONS:

1. Cook the beef in a large skillet. Use medium heat and cook for several minutes until there is no more pink.
2. Grease the dish of your Slow Cooker with melted butter. If desired, use special cooking spray. Transfer half bag of Tater Tots into Slow Cooker. Add cream soup and cooked vegetables.
3. Top with remaining Tater Tots. Cover the lid.
4. Turn on your Slow Cooker and set to LOW temperature mode for 7 hours.
5. To serve, arrange meal over a large and wide serving dish. Garnish with fresh herbs and vegetables.

Nutrition: Calories: 531 Fat: 19g Carbohydrates: 42g Protein: 51g

VEGETABLE RECIPES

Slow Cooker Vegetable Soup

Amazing dish with leftover vegetables!

Prep time: 31 minutes Cooking time: 6 hours Servings: 8

INGREDIENTS:

6 cups vegetable broth

Pack frozen vegetables

Can diced tomatoes

2 potatoes,

1 large onion

Barley

3 cloves garlic

Dried parsley

Dried oregano

Dried basil

1 bay leaf

Salt

2 cups flour

Black pepper

Vegetable shortening

Vegetable broth

DIRECTIONS:

1. In a large bowl, combine frozen vegetables, diced potatoes, tomatoes along with their juice, barley, onion, parsley and minced garlic. Season with salt, basil, oregano and black pepper. Add bay leaf.
2. Pour in six cups of vegetable broth. If you do not have one, you can use chicken broth. Transfer to Slow Cooker and choose LOW temperature. Cook for 6 hours.
3. In a bowl, place shortening and flour. Combine until coarse crumbs and form into a long log. Cut into small pieces so you can make dumplings. Transfer to Slow Cooker.
4. Serve while hot, in small bowls. Add coarse bread cubes.

Nutrition: Calories: 333 Fat: 9g Carbohydrates: 57g Protein: 9g

Slow Cooker Hot Tomato Sauce

This will be your favorite!

Prep time: 5 minutes Cooking time: 15 hours Servings: 25

INGREDIENTS:

10 plum tomatoes

Small onion

Black pepper

3 tbsp olive oil

Minced garlic

Dried oregano

Dried basil

Salt

Cayenne pepper

DIRECTIONS:

1. Grease your Slow Cooker with a melted butter or any oil. Crush tomatoes and remove the peel.
2. Right in Slow Cooker dish, combine tomatoes with minced garlic and finely chopped onion. Pour in olive oil.
3. In a bowl, combine basil, dried oregano, cayenne pepper, black pepper and some salt. You can also add cinnamon.
4. Mix the mixture in Slow Cooker and cover with the lid. Prepare for 15 hours on LOW temperature mode.
5. Tastes good while hot, but this also can be served cold. Serve with meat, sandwiches or as taco ingredient.

Black Bean Soup

Easy and fast for the weekend!

Prep time: 5 minutes Cooking time: 6 Servings: 10

INGREDIENTS:

Dry black beans

Water

One carrot

Chopped celery stalk

Large red onion

2 green bell peppers

Crushed garlic

2 jalapeno peppers

2 tbsp dry lentils

1 can diced tomatoes

Ground cumin

Chili powder

Oregano

3 tbsp wine vinegar

Salt

2 cups rice

DIRECTIONS:

1. Place a large pot over high heat. Pour in water and place the beans into the pot. Slightly bring to boil and simmer for 10 minutes.
2. When the beans are cooked, remove the pot from heat and let stand for an hour.
3. Grease your Slow Cooker and place drained and rinsed beans into it. Cover with water and cook for 3 hours on HIGH temperature mode.
4. Add chopped carrots, minced garlic, sliced onion, jalapeno and red bell peppers, lentils and tomatoes (along with liquid). Stir well.
5. Add cumin, chili powder, black pepper, oregano, salt and red wine vinegar. Switch your Slow Cooker to LOW mode and cook for another 3 hours.
6. In the last 30 minutes of cooking, add rice and stir well.
7. To serve, slightly puree the soup with an immiscible blender, then serve into nice soup bowls.

Nutrition: Calories: 231 Fat: 1g Carbohydrates: 43g Protein: 12g

Eggplant Parmesan For the Slow Cooker

Beautiful with marinara and cheese!

Prep time: 5 minutes Cooking time: 5 Servings: 8

INGREDIENTS:

Eggplant

1 tbspn salt

One cup olive oil

Seasoned breadcrumbs

2 chicken eggs

4 tbsp water

3 tbsp flour

Half cup parmesan

Can marinara sauce

Mozzarella cheese

DIRECTIONS:

1. Cut eggplant into thin rings and arrange in a large bowl in layers. Slightly sprinkle with kosher salt and leave it for 30 minutes. When eggplant drains, rinse it and dry with paper towels.
2. In a large skillet, preheat olive oil.
3. Meanwhile, whisk flour with water until smooth.
4. Dig each eggplant piece in a flour mixture and cook in a skillet till slightly brown. In a separate bowl, combine grated Parmesan with seasoned breadcrumbs.
5. Layer eggplants, breadcrumb mixture, marinara and mozzarella in Slow Cooker. Arrange all ingredients in several layers.
6. Cover the lid of your Slow Cooker.
7. Cook for 5 hours on LOW temperature mode.

Nutrition: Calories: 401 Fat: 18g Carbohydrates: 38g Protein: 23g

Wild Rice Casserole

Easy and fast for busy days!

Prep time: 5 minutes Cooking time: 9 hours Servings: 8

INGREDIENTS:

3 celery

2 chopped onions

2 packs long grain rice

Half cups water

Cream of mushroom soup

American cheese

Half cup butter

Half cup fresh mushrooms

DIRECTIONS:

1. To start, finely chop onions and celery. Transfer to a large bowl. Add rice mix and fresh chopped mushrooms.
2. Pour in water and condensed cream of mushroom soup. Top with American cheese. Combine all the ingredients to make a smooth mass.
3. Spray your Slow Cooker with nonstick cooking spray and transfer the bowl mixture into the crockpot.
4. Cook under the lid. Set your Slow Cooker to LOW temperature mode and prepare for 9 hours. To serve, transfer the casserole to a beautiful dish and garnish with fresh herbs.

Nutrition: Calories: 408 Fat: 23g Carbohydrates: 39g Protein: 11g

Refried Beans Without the Really Refry

Healthy and delicious right from Slow Cooker!

Prep time: 19 minutes Cooking time: 8 hours Servings: 9

INGREDIENTS:

3 cups pinto beans

Large onion

Small jalapeno pepper

Salt

Minced garlic

Cumin

Black pepper

Cold water

DIRECTIONS:

1. Grease your Slow Cooker with some melted butter. If want, you can use vegetable oil.
2. In a dish, combine chopped jalapeno pepper, onion, garlic and rinsed pinto beans. Finely season with salt. Add freshly ground black pepper.
3. Mix the ingredients and transfer to Slow Cooker.
4. Pour the water into Slow Cooker - just to cover the vegetables. Stir to combine. Cover with the lid. Turn on the Slow Cooker and set to HIGH mode. Cook for 8 hours, pouring in additional water.

5. To serve, finely mash the beans with a potato masher and serve hot.

Nutrition: Calories: 367 Fat: 17g Carbohydrates: 83g Protein: 74g

Vegetable Cheese Soup

A hearty, healthy and zesty vegetarian soup!

Prep time: 5 minutes Cooking time: 9 hours Servings: 12

INGREDIENTS:

3 large potatoes

1 tsp celery seed

2 chopped carrots

Creamed corn

Ground black pepper

Small onion

2 cans vegetable broth

Can cheese sauce

DIRECTIONS:

1. Take a large bowl and combine can corn and celery seeds in it. Season with black pepper to your taste and mix well.
2. Chop the carrots and onion; dice the potatoes into small cubes.
3. Add the vegetables to a bowl and combine with seasoned corn. Toss to mix well. Transfer the vegetable mixture to your Slow Cooker.
4. Pour in two jars of vegetable broth and cover with the lid.
5. Choose the LOW temperature regime and turn your Slow Cooker on. Prepare for 9 hours.
6. In the end, stir cheese sauce and wait until it is melted. Serve right from Slow Cooker.

Nutrition: Calories: 316 Fat: 16g Carbohydrates: 32g Protein: 11g

Meatballs with Absolutely No Meat

Perfect dish for your Vegetarian friends!

Prep time: 12 minutes Cooking time: 2 hours Servings: 26

INGREDIENTS:

8 chicken eggs

4 cups shredded Mozzarella

Vegetable oil

Milk

2 cups crumbs of cracker

1 cup ground pecans

Dry onion soup mix

Cream of mushroom soup

2 tsp celery salt

DIRECTIONS:

1. Take a large bowl and whisk chicken eggs, pecans, cracker crumbs, and Mozzarella cheese in it. Season with celery salt and onion soup mix. Stir well to combine.

2. Form small "meatballs" out of the mixture and set aside for a little while.

3. In a large and wide skillet, fry the meatballs until golden brown. Use paper towels to drain excess fat.

4. Grease your Slow Cooker with vegetable oil or simply coat with cooking spray. Transfer meatballs to Slow Cooker and pour over with cream of mushroom soup. Cook on LOW temperature mode for 2 hours.

Nutrition: Calories: 246 Fat: 16g Carbohydrates: 14g Protein: 11g

Monterey Hot Cream Spaghetti

Awesome dish for cold winter days!

Prep time: 5 minutes Cooking time: 4 hours Servings: 13

INGREDIENTS:

One chicken egg

Spaghetti

3 cups shredded Monterey cheese

1 pack frozen spinach

1 cup sour cream

Crushed garlic

Grated Parmesan

French fried onions

DIRECTIONS:

1. Take a large pot and boil salted water in it. Place spaghetti into a bowl and cook until al dente and drain.

2. In a bowl, blend together minced garlic, grated Parmesan and sour cream. Beat in chicken egg and stir to integrate it into the mixture.

3. Grease your Slow Cooker with melted butter and transfer the bowl mixture into it.

4. Add drained spaghetti, thawed spinach, two cups of grated Monterey Lack cheese and half of chopped French onion. Stir just to blend.

5. Cook on LOW temperature mode for 8 hours.

6. To serve, sprinkle with shredded cheese and cubed French bread.

Nutrition: Calories: 396 Fat: 25g Carbohydrates: 18g Protein: 16g

Slow Cooker Vegan Jambalaya

A perfect combination of products to freeze and put in the slow cooker when busy!

Prep time: 5 minutes Cooking time: 4 hours Servings: 14

INGREDIENTS:

Olive oil

Smoked vegan sausage

Canned diced tomatoes

Cubed seitan

Small green bell pepper

Cup vegetable broth

3 stalks celery

2 cloves garlic

Dried thyme

Fresh parsley

Dried oregano

Miso paste

DIRECTIONS:

1. Sprinkle the bottom of your Slow Cooker with olive oil.

2. Into a deep bowl, combine stirred tomatoes, chopped sausage, miso paste, minced garlic, onion, celery and green bell pepper.

3. Season with thyme and oregano. If preferred, add Cajun seasoning. Pour in the vegetable broth and stir until the mixture is smooth enough. Transfer the soup mixture from a bowl to prepared Slow Cooker.

4. Cook under the lid for 4 hours. Use a LOW temperature regime.

5. When it is almost time, stir in rice and continue cooking for another 30 minutes. To serve, garnish jambalaya with freshly chopped parsley.

Nutrition: Calories: 334 Fat: 10g Carbohydrates: 40g Protein: 20g

Veggie and Chili Slow Cooker Soup

You can serve it right from your Slow Cooker!

Prep time: 5 minutes Cooking time: 2 hours Servings: 12

INGREDIENTS:

Canned bean soup

Canned kidney beans

Canned vegetarian beans

Dried basil

Dried parsley

1 tbsp chili powder

1 green bell pepper

Canned garbanzo beans

Canned tomatoes in puree

Dried oregano

Can whole kernel corn

2 cloves garlic

DIRECTIONS:

1. Take a large bowl and combine garbanzo beans, baked beans, kidney beans and tomatoes in puree in it.
2. Add chopped onion, celery and bell pepper. Pour over with black bean soup.
3. Grease your Slow Cooker with unsalted melted butter or just coat slightly with a cooking spray. Transfer the bean mixture to Slow Cooker and carefully place the corn kernels into it as well.
4. Add garlic and season with chili powder, basil and oregano.
5. Cover the lid and cook for two hours over HIGH temperature setting.

Nutrition: Calories: 260 Fat: 2g Carbohydrates: 52g Protein: 12g

Mushroom Lentil Barley Stew

Satisfying and delicious, especially in wintertime!

Prep time: 5 minutes Cooking time: 10 hours Servings: 8

INGREDIENTS:

Vegetable broth

2 cups fresh mushrooms

2 tbsp pearl barley

Dry onion flakes

2 tsp minced garlic

Ground black pepper

Summer savory

Dried lentils

Dried summer savory

Dry lentils

DIRECTIONS:

1. Grease your Slow Cooker with a thin layer of olive oil or just coat with cooking spray.
2. In a bowl, combine fresh chopped mushrooms, garlic savory, lentils, barley, minced garlic, onion flakes.
3. Finely season with grounded black pepper and salt. Transfer the mixture into your Slow Cooker.
4. Pour in the vegetable broth and add bay leaves. Cover the lid. Prepare during 10 hours on LOW temperature level.
5. To serve, remove bay leaves and place stew into small serving bowls.

Nutrition: Calories: 213 Fat: 1g Carbohydrates: 43g Protein: 8g

Easy Apple Cider

You can mix it with rum or fresh orange juice!

Prep time: 23 minutes Cooking time: 1 hour Servings: 12

INGREDIENTS:

One bottle apple cider

1 tsp allspice

3 large cinnamon sticks

Brown sugar

1 tsp cloves

DIRECTIONS:

1. Start with preheating your Slow Cooker.
2. In a bowl, pour the apple cider and place cinnamon sticks into it. Blend slightly to drown the sticks. Let cider stand for several minutes and pour into Slow Cooker.
3. Add brown sugar and stir until it dissolves.
4. Cut a small piece of cheesecloth and place cloves and allspice over it. Wrap species tightly and add to Slow Cooker.
5. Set your Slow Cooker to HIGH temperature mode and cover with the lid. Prepare during one hour. Keep warm to serve. Pour cider into high glass cups and garnish with orange wedges.

Nutrition: Calories: 171 Fat: 1g Carbohydrates: 43g Protein: 1g

Slow Cooker Mediterranean Stew

Cook this with your kids!

Prep time: 27 minutes Cooking time: 10 hours Servings: 6

INGREDIENTS:

One butternut squash

1 eggplant

1 zucchini

Medium onion

Tomato

Ground cumin

1 pack okra

Ground turmeric

Half cup vegetable broth

Ground cinnamon

Paprika

Garlic

2 tbsp raisins

DIRECTIONS:

1. Chop the tomato, butternut squash, eggplant, zucchini, carrots and onion. Gather the vegetables in a large bowl.

2. Stir in tomato sauce and raisins. Mix well to combine.

3. Transfer the mixture into Slow Cooker and pour half cup vegetable broth over the ingredients. Season with cinnamon, red pepper, paprika, turmeric and cumin.

4. Close the lid and cook for 10 hours over LOW heat. Serve hot, when all vegetables are tender.

Nutrition: Calories: 122 Fat: 1g Carbohydrates: 30g Protein: 3g

Slow Cooker Spicy Vegetarian Minestrone

Cook it for your family or guests!

Prep time: 5 minutes Cooking time: 8 hours Servings: 12

INGREDIENTS:

Vegetable broth

Canned crushed tomatoes

Canned kidney beans

1 small zucchini

2 large carrots

2 ribs celery

Fresh parsley

Black pepper

Grated Parmesan

Dried oregano

Salt

Chopped fresh spinach

Dried thyme

DIRECTIONS:

1. In a bowl, combine tomatoes, onion kidney beans, celery, green beans, carrots, and zucchini. Season with minced garlic, oregano, salt, thyme, parsley, and black pepper.

2. Grease your Slow Cooker with melted butter or simply coat with cooking spray. Transfer the vegetables to Slow Cooker and pour them over with a vegetable broth. Set your Slow Cooker to LOW temperature mode and prepare for 8 hours.

3. Stir in chopped spinach.

4. Meanwhile, cook a pasta until al dente. Serve minestrone over the pasts.

Nutrition: Calories: 138 Fat: 2g Carbohydrates: 25g Protein: 7g

Slow Cooker Squash and Sweet Apple Dish

This perfectly fits both Thanksgiving and Christmas!

Prep time: 5 minutes Cooking time: 4 hours Servings: 12

INGREDIENTS:

Small butternut squash

4 apples

Cup dried cranberries

Half white onion

Ground nutmeg

Cinnamon

DIRECTIONS:

1. Peel and core squash and apples. Slice apples into small half moons and squash to small cubes. In a large bowl, combine chopped apples and squash, add cranberries and finely chopped onion. Season with nutmeg and cinnamon. Stir well to combine.

2. Transfer the mixture to your Slow Cooker and cover with the lid.

3. Cook on HIGH temperature for 4 hours. Stir occasionally. When the vegetables are tender, set aside.

4. To serve, transfer to a large serving bowl. Serve hot, garnish with cheese or fresh cranberries.

Nutrition: Calories: 123 Fat: 1g Carbohydrates: 32g Protein: 2g

Slow Cooker Amazing Spaghetti Sauce

This is fat-free so you can eat this even on a diet!

Prep time: 5 minutes Cooking time: 4 hours Servings: 14

INGREDIENTS:

Dried rosemary

5 cans tomato sauce

Dried oregano

3 cloves garlic

Tomato Paste

Dried thyme

1 bay leaf

Red pepper flakes

DIRECTIONS:

25. Take a large cooking bowl and gather tomato paste, onion and tomato sauce. Stir well until smooth.

26. Season with minced garlic, rosemary, thyme, oregano, parsley. Add bay leaf. Sprinkle with red pepper flakes. Stir one more time.

27. Grease your Slow Cooker with a thin layer of melted butter or coat with cooking spray. Transfer the mixture to Slow Cooker. Cover the lid.

28. Cook the meal for 4 for hours (choose HIGH temperature mode). Stir time after time. Serve spaghetti sauce over separately cooked pasta or macaroni.

Nutrition: Calories: 157 Fat: 2g Carbohydrates: 35g Protein: 8g

Vegan-Styled Pumpkin Chili

Easy and delicious meal for the autumn season!

Prep time: 9 minutes Cooking time: 8 hours Servings: 13

INGREDIENTS:

2 cups vegan broth

Canned pumpkin puree

Canned black beans

Medium onion

Canned garbanzo beans

Tomato sauce

Baby spinach

Ground coriander

3 red bell peppers

Sliced black olives

Species to taste

1 tbsp cocoa powder

brown sugar

1 tbsp tomato paste

Orange juice

5 cloves garlic

DIRECTIONS:

1. In a large bowl, combine kidney beans, diced tomatoes, onion, red bell peppers, baby spinach, green chili peppers, olives and garlic.

2. Stir in tomato sauce and tomato paste.

3. Season with your favorite spices: cumin, salt, coriander, cocoa powder. Add brown sugar. Transfer the mixture to greased Slow Cooker.

4. Pour in vegetable broth, orange juice and vegetable oil.

5. Cover the lid of your Slow Cooker and cook on LOW for 8 hours. Stir occasionally to get flavors fully combined.

Nutrition: Calories: 260 Fat: 9g Carbohydrates: 31g Protein: 11g

Indian Coconut and Veggie Curry

Delicious and easy to cook!

Prep time: 27 minutes Cooking time: 4 hours Servings: 11

INGREDIENTS:

Chili powder

5 large potatoes

3 carrots

Curry powder

Coconut cream water

Red bell pepper

2 tbsp flour

Red pepper flakes

Onion soup mix

Green bell pepper

Green peas

Cilantro

DIRECTIONS:

1. Generously grease the bottom of your Slow Cooker with melted butter. Chop the potatoes and arrange them over the bottom of your Slow Cooker.

2. In a bowl, mix chili powder, flour, red pepper flakes, curry powder, cayenne pepper. Sprinkle the pepper mixture all over the potatoes.

3. Add chopped red bell pepper, onion soup mix, green bell pepper along with coconut cream. Stir to combine.

4. Cover Slow Cooker with the lid. Start cooking on LOW temperature mode. Cook for 4 hours. Stir in peas, carrots. Prepare until veggies are tender.

5. Serve in a bowl with cilantro garnishing.

Vegetarian Style Bacon Chili

This tastes great with sour cream and shredded cheese!

Prep time: 5 minutes Cooking time: 8 hours Servings: 12

INGREDIENTS:

2 cans kidney beans

Canned tomatoes

1 pack vegetarian beef crumbs

Vegetarian bacon bits

Medium onion

Peeled lime

Curry

Cayenne pepper

Cinnamon

Chili powder

Serrano pepper

salt

DIRECTIONS:

1. Grease your Slow Cooker with olive oil or cooking spray with nonstick effect.
2. Transfer canned tomatoes, kidney beans, minced garlic and vegetarian beef crumbs into your Slow Cooker.
3. Pour over with kidney beans liquid. Add some water, if needed, to cover vegetables. In a small bowl, grind vegetarian bacon bits with a kitchen processor.
4. In a blender, combine onion, serrano pepper and lime until the smooth paste. Combine pepper paste with bacon and add to kidney mixture.
5. Set your Slow Cooker to LOW and leave the dish cooking for one hour.
6. Mix in chili powder, cinnamon, cayenne pepper, curry powder, oregano and salt. Cook for 4 hours more.

Nutrition: Calories: 263 Fat: 4g Carbohydrates: 47g Protein: 11g

Mashed potatoes in Slow Cooker

Flavored and mild mashed potatoes!

Prep time: 6 minutes Cooking time: 3 hours Servings: 7

INGREDIENTS:

8 red potatoes

bouillon cubes

Minced garlic

Salt

Half cup butter

Sour cream

grounded pepper

DIRECTIONS:

1. Pour some water into a large pot. Add salt to your taste.
2. Add diced potatoes, minced garlic. Add bouillon cubes. Cook until tender, around 15 minutes. Drain and reserve the water.
3. In a large bowl, mash potatoes with cream cheese and sour cream. Add some water to get needed consistency.
4. Grease your Slow Cooker with simple cooking spray. Transfer mashed potatoes to Slow Cooker. Cover the lid. Prepare on LOW temperature mode for two or three hours.

Nutrition: Calories: 408 Fat: 10g Carbohydrates: 17g Protein: 24g

Baked Potatoes in your Slow Cooker

Fast and easy baking potatoes recipe!

Prep time: 5 minutes Cooking time: 7 hours Servings: 10

INGREDIENTS:

4 baking potatoes

Kosher salt

Cooking spray

1 tbsp extra virgin olive oil

Aluminum foil

DIRECTIONS:

1. Grease your Slow Cooker with a small amount of olive oil or coat with cooking spray. Peel and prick the potatoes with knife or fork.
2. Sprinkle the potatoes with salt and rub with olive oil.
3. Cut the foil into small pieces, big enough to wrap each potato. Transfer the potato wraps to Slow Cooker and cover with the lid. Cook for 7 hours using LOW temperature mode.
4. Serve the potatoes right in the wraps with any salad or herbal garnishing.

Nutrition: Calories: 254 Fat: 3g Carbohydrates: 51g Protein: 6g

Roasted Pasilla with Chili pepper

Hot and spiced Mexican meal for your kitchen!

Prep time: 5 minutes Cooking time: 10 hours Servings: 8

INGREDIENTS:

Ground beef

Frozen corn

Mexican chili cooking sauce

1 red bell pepper

Canned and diced tomatoes

Canned kidney beans

Minced garlic

Chopped cilantro

Small sweet onion

Sour cream

DIRECTIONS:

1. Grease your Slow Cooker with a simple butter and start to preheat.
2. On a large skillet, heat the oil and cook the meat over medium high heat. Transfer beef to Slow Cooker.
3. Add frozen corn, diced tomatoes, chopped onion, red bell pepper, cilantro and kidney beans. Top with shredded cheddar cheese and sour cream. Stir until smooth.
4. Cook covered on LOW temperature mode for 10 hours.
5. To garnish, use chopped cilantro, sour cream or shredded cheese.

Nutrition: Calories: 326 Fat: 13g Carbohydrates: 73g Protein: 23g

African Shrimp with Peanuts

Amazing combination of ingredients for autumn!

Prep time: 17 minutes Cooking time: 6 hours Servings: 10

INGREDIENTS:

2 tbsp olive oil

4 cloves garlic

chopped onion

2 chicken breasts

2 medium carrots

sweet potatoes

4 cups chicken broth

Chili powder

Ground cumin

4 cloves garlic

Red pepper flakes

Crunchy peanut butter

1 cup brown rice

DIRECTIONS:

1. Cook the chicken on a skillet. Prepare until golden brown from both sides. Grease Slow Cooker and place chicken into it.
2. On the same skillet, cook red bell peppers, onion, and minced garlic until translucent. Add sweet potatoes, chicken broth and species to the large dish.
3. Mix spicy mixture well and transfer to Slow Cooker.
4. Cook on HIGH temperature mode for 6 hours. If needed, add more chicken broth during cooking.

Nutrition: Calories: 205 Fat: 8g Carbohydrates: 22g Protein: 10g

Corn and Cream Vegetable Soup

Delicious and low-fat recipe!

Prep time: 5 minutes Cooking time: 3 hours Servings: 4

INGREDIENTS:

3 cans corn

3 hot cherry peppers

One large onion

3 tbsp butter

3 bell peppers

1 pack hash browns

4 cups sour cream

2 poblano peppers

3 stalks celery

3 large carrots

DIRECTIONS:

1. Grease your Slow Cooker with unsalted melted butter.
2. Pour whole kernel corn with cream style corn into Slow Cooker and start preheating on low mode. Add hash browns to your Slow Cooker and stir well to combine.
3. Cook red and white onion over the buttered skillet.
4. Add celery, bell peppers, carrots, jalapenos, cherry and poblano peppers. Cook until translucent, for around 10 minutes.
5. Transfer the vegetables to Slow Cooker and stir in the sour cream. Cook for 3 hours on HIGH temp, frequently stirring.

Nutrition: Calories: 267 Fat: 9g Carbohydrates: 44g Protein: 6g

Grilled Green Beans, Potatoes and Sausage

Awesome grill in your Slow Cooker!

Prep time: 5 minutes Cooking time: 4 hours Servings: 6

INGREDIENTS:

1 tsp salt

Fresh green beans

1 tsp butter

Ground black pepper

Smoked sausage

Large onion

3 tbsp water

1 tsp vegetable oil

Red potatoes

DIRECTIONS:

1. Grease your Slow Cooker with melted butter and start to preheat on low temperature. Take a large sheet of foil and cut it into small pieces.
2. Chop the vegetables and separate to portions: place each vegetable portion onto foil piece. Arrange chopped sausage between portions.
3. Wrap foils and place them into Slow Cooker. Pour in some water.
4. Cook for 4 hours on LOW mode. If needed, continue cooking for another 2 hours.

Nutrition: Calories: 544 Fat: 38g Carbohydrates: 21g Protein: 28g

Scalloped Potatoes in Slow Cooker

Creamy recipe for the whole family!

Prep time: 5 minutes Cooking time: 4 hours Servings: 8

INGREDIENTS:

4 large potatoes

Chopped ham

Black pepper

Half tsp garlic powder

Cream of mushroom soup

Salt

Half cup water

Black pepper

DIRECTIONS:

1. Grease your Slow Cooker with melted butter or cooking spray.

2. Slice potatoes and arrange them over the bottom of your Slow Cooker. In a bowl, whisk together water and cream of mushroom soup.
3. Season to your taste with salt, garlic powder, and freshly ground black pepper. Pour the mixture over potato slices in Slow Cooker.
4. Cook covered on HIGH mode for approximately 4 hours.

Nutrition: Calories: 256 Fat: 10g Carbohydrates: 33g Protein: 10g

Cabbage Tamales in Slow Cooker

The mix of German and Mexican cuisines!

Prep time: 5 minutes Cooking time: 4 hours Servings: 8

INGREDIENTS:

8 cabbage leaves

Half cup chopped onions

Uncooked white rice

Mexican chile powder

Ground beef

2 cans tomato sauce

1 cup rice

2 cloves garlic

Chopped onion

2 cans diced tomatoes

Salt/pepper

DIRECTIONS:

1. Blanch cabbage leaves, for approximately 3 minutes.
2. In a bowl, mix ground beef, tomato sauce, garlic, uncooked rice, salt, onion, black pepper and chili powder.
3. Mix with your hands. When combined, divide the mixture to 8 parts. Place each part on a cabbage leave.
4. Roll leaves and transfer tamales into greased Slow Cooker. Cook covered for 4 hours, on HIGH temperature mode.

Nutrition: Calories: 341 Fat: 15g Carbohydrates: 36g Protein: 13g

Green Village Chili

The perfect meal for a large family!

Prep time: 5 minutes Cooking time: 6 hours Servings: 12

INGREDIENTS:

4 tomatillos

3 chile peppers

1 medium onion

3 jalapenos

1 green bell pepper

Olive oil

4 cloves garlic

2 tomatoes

1 bouillon cube

Fresh oregano

Chili powder

Cream cheese

Canned lager beer

Fresh parsley

Ground cumin

DIRECTIONS:

1. Firstly, preheat your oven and arrange tomatillos, chiles, bell peppers onion and tomatoes over a baking sheet. Add salt.

2. Cool the vegetables and chop them into bite-sized pieces. Transfer the vegetables into greased Slow Cooker.

3. Mix well. Stir in garlic, beef bouillon cube, oregano, beer, cumin, parsley and chili powder. Set your Slow Cooker to LOW mode and cook for 6 hours.

4. Stir cream cheese just before serving.

Nutrition: Calories: 174 Fat: 12g Carbohydrates: 8g Protein: 7g

Sweet Potato Casserole

Easy goes with any poultry or meat!

Prep time: 5 minutes Cooking time: 4 hours Servings: 6

INGREDIENTS:

Melted butter

2 cans sweet potatoes

2 tbsp white sugar

Chopped pecans

Half cup milk

2 chicken eggs

2 tbsp flour

DIRECTIONS:

1. Lightly grease your Slow Cooker with melted butter. If you want, you can replace butter with special cooking spray.

2. Take a large bowl and combine sweet potatoes, butter, white and brown sugar. Whisk in chicken eggs, orange juice and milk.

3. Mix the mixture well and transfer to Slow Cooker.

4. In a smaller bowl, combine brown sugar, pecans, butter and flour. Spread pecan mixture over the potatoes.

5. Cover Slow Cooker with a lid and cook for 4 hours on HIGH temperature mode.

Nutrition: Calories: 406 Fat: 13g Carbohydrates: 66g Protein: 6g

Hash Brown Casserole for the Slow Cooker

Make it ahead of time and just start cooking!

Prep time: 5 minutes Cooking time: 5 hours Servings: 12

INGREDIENTS:

2 cups sour cream

Half cup chopped onion

cream of mushroom soup

Salt

2 cups shredded cheese

teaspoon pepper

1 pack frozen hash browns

DIRECTIONS:

1. In a large bowl, combine together the cream of mushroom soup, sour cream, cheese, salt, onion and pepper.

2. Carefully mix in chopped hash browns until they are evenly coated.

3. Grease the inside of your Slow Cooker with cooking spray or simple melted and unsalted butter. Spoon the potato mixture into previously prepared Slow Cooker.

4. Cover it with the lid. Prepare the dish on High temperature mode for around 1 hour. When it is time, reduce the heat to LOW temperature. Prepare for two more hours.

Nutrition: Calories: 198 Fat: 16g Carbohydrates: 14g Protein: 6g

Slow Cooker Hot Vegetable Chili

This is a very delicious and hearty chili recipe!

Prep time: 19 minutes Cooking time: 4 hours Servings: 14

INGREDIENTS:

green bell pepper

canned tomatoes

can garbanzo beans

2 zucchini

2 stalks celery

1 onion

2 carrots

red bell pepper

chili powder

chile peppers

2 cloves garlic

1 tbsp dried oregano

2 tsp cumin

1 tsp salt

DIRECTIONS:

1. Take a large bowl and gather garbanzo beans, canned tomatoes, green chile peppers.
2. Finely chop the vegetables: tomatoes, onion, zucchini, celery, red bell peppers and carrots. Add minced garlic.
3. Season with dried cumin, oregano and salt to your taste. Mix all the ingredients.
4. Grease your Slow Cooker with preferred oil or plain melted butter. Cover the lid and cook for 8 hours on LOW temperature mode.

Nutrition: Calories: 150 Fat: 2g Carbohydrates: 30g Protein: 6g

Vegan Chili in your Slow Cooker

Tasty vegetarian meal!

Prep time: 17 minutes Cooking time: 8 hours Servings: 8

INGREDIENTS:

Half cup olive oil

4 cloves garlic

2 green bell peppers

Liquid hot pepper sauce

Ground cumin

4 onions

Chili powder

Can crashed tomatoes

4 cans black beans

White vinegar

1 pack firm tofu

Oregano

Salt/pepper

DIRECTIONS:

1. Take a large skillet and heat it with olive oil over medium heat. Add chopped onions and cook until soft.

2. Stir in chopped green peppers, tofu, garlic and red peppers. Cook for 10 minutes. Grease your Slow Cooker with melted butter. Add beans.
3. Transfer the skillet mixture to Slow Cooker and combine well with beans. Add tomatoes. Season with pepper, cumin, salt, oregano, chili powder and hot pepper sauce.
4. Cook on LOW mode for 8 hours.

Nutrition: Calories: 455 Fat: 18g Carbohydrates: 58g Protein: 21g

Spiced Applesauce in Slow Cooker

Great even with meat dishes!

Prep time: 5 minutes Cooking time: 8 hours Servings: 20

INGREDIENTS:

Half tsp pumpkin pie spice

8 large apples

Half cup water

3 tbsp brown sugar

DIRECTIONS:

1. Sprinkle your Slow Cooker with olive oil, if you prefer.
2. Wash the apples. Remove the peel and core. Slice to small half-moons. Place the apples into Slow Cooker and pour in enough water to cover slightly.
3. Cover the lid of your Slow Cooker and prepare during 8 hours on LOW temperature setting. Open the lid and stir in brown sugar carefully.
4. Season with pumpkin pie spice and slightly stir to combine. Cover the lid again and continue cooking for another 30 minutes. Serve with sandwiches or simply with meat dishes.

Nutrition: Calories: 150 Fat: 1g Carbohydrates: 39g Protein: 0g

Sweet creamy Corn in Slow Cooker

Easy and simple to cook!

Prep time: 5 minutes Cooking time: 6 hours Servings: 11

INGREDIENTS:

1 pack cream cheese

Pepper to taste

1 tbsp white sugar

1 pack frozen corn kernels

Half cup butter

Half cup milk

DIRECTIONS:

1. To start, slightly coat the bottom and sides of your Slow Cooker with melted butter. If you want, you can also use cooking spray.
2. Start to preheat your Slow Cooker.
3. In a bowl, combine cream cheese, sugar, butter. Pour in milk.
4. Season with salt and pepper according to your taste. Whisk well to combine. Pour the mixture into prepared Slow Cooker and close the lid.
5. Cook for 6 hours on LOW temperature mode.
6. To serve, separate corn between small dishes. Serve with white bread.

Nutrition: Calories: 192 Fat: 15g Carbohydrates: 13g Protein: 3g

Whole Kernel Slow Cooker Soup

Unusual, but tasty and satisfying!

Prep time: 5 minutes Cooking time: 7 hours Servings: 12

INGREDIENTS:

Fresh whole corn kernels

One clove garlic

3 cups vegetable broth

1 tbsp parsley flakes

Chili powder

One large onion

3 potatoes

Black pepper flakes

3 tbsp margarine

Soy sauce

Salt

2 red chile peppers

DIRECTIONS:

1. Generously grease your Slow Cooker dish with olive oil or unsalted melted butter.
2. Right in Slow Cooker, combine corn kernels, chopped potatoes, red chili peppers, garlic and onion.
3. Season with black pepper, parsley and salt.
4. Pour in vegetable broth. Mix vegetables to smooth.
5. Set your Slow Cooker to LOW temperature mode and cook for 7 hours. Stir in margarine and soy milk.
6. To serve, add lime juice.

Nutrition: Calories: 320 Fat: 10g Carbohydrates: 53g Protein: 9g

Cajun peanuts Boiled in Slow Cooker

Try this bean recipe on a nearest party!

Prep time: 5 minutes Cooking time: 8 hours Servings: 9

INGREDIENTS:

Raw peanuts (in shells)

Water

1 can jalapenos

1 pack dry crab boil

salt

DIRECTIONS:

1. Do not peel peanuts and place them whole into Slow Cooker. Arrange over the bottom evenly. Open the package with dry crab boil and sprinkle over the peanuts.
2. Pour as much cold water as it required to cover peanuts completely.
3. Open the jalapeno jar. If using whole jalapenos, cut them into small slices and also transfer to Slow Cooker.
4. Cover the lid of Slow Cooker and cook peanuts on LOW temperature mode from 8 hours to overnight.
5. When peanuts float to the surface, remove from Slow Cooker, drain and serve. Serve with fresh vegetables and green onion sprinkles.

Nutrition: Calories: 403 Fat: 35g Carbohydrates: 11g Protein: 18g

Southwest Vegetable Dinner

Even vegetarians will love this!

Prep time: 12 minutes Cooking time: 2 hours Servings: 9

INGREDIENTS:

Dried black-eyed peas

Green bell pepper

Can sweet corn

3 garlic cloves

Chopped onion

Ground cumin

Half cup shredded cheddar

Chili powder

DIRECTIONS:

1. In a large pot with cold water, soak black-eyed peas overnight.
2. In the morning, drain the peas. Rinse and set aside for a little while.

3. In a bowl, combine peas, green pepper, minced garlic, onion and tomatoes. Sprinkle with cumin and chili powder. Combine the ingredients until smooth. Transfer to Slow Cooker and cover with the lid.

4. Cook for 2 hours on HIGH mode.

5. Stir in cheese and rinsed rice. Cook for another 30 minutes. Serve in bowls. You can also serve it with fresh vegetables.

Nutrition: Calories: 344 Fat: 6g Carbohydrates: 59g Protein: 17g

Squash in Cheesy Cream

Mild taste from your Slow Cooker!

Prep time: 15 minutes Cooking time: 1 hour Servings: 10

INGREDIENTS:

Small onion

3 tbsp butter

Large yellow summer squash

Processed cheese food

DIRECTIONS:

1. Finely grease Slow Cooker with melted butter or coat with nonstick spray.

2. Peel and seed the squash. Place into a large pot. Pour over with water to cover.

3. Add onion and bring to boil. Simmer the vegetables for about 10 minutes to get tender. Do not stir. Drain both onion and squash. Transfer to Slow Cooker.

4. Add processed cheese food and butter to Slow Cooker.

5. Set your Slow Cooker to LOW temperature setting and cook just until the squash gets really tender (approximately for 1 hour).

6. Serve in small serving bowls with white or French crispy bread.

Nutrition: Calories: 189 Fat: 12g Carbohydrates: 12g Protein: 7g

Veggie Cassoulet with navy beans

Easy vegetarian meal!

Prep time: 5 minutes Cooking time: 9 hours Servings: 7

INGREDIENTS:

One onion

2 tbsp olive oil

4 cups mushroom broth

1 sprig lemon thyme

1 bay leaf

1 sprig rosemary

Navy beans

1 large potato

1 cube vegetable bouillon

1 sprig fresh savory

DIRECTIONS:

1. Soak navy beans in cold water overnight.

2. Preheat a skillet with a small amount of oil. Add chopped carrots and onion. Stir until tender. Grease Slow Cooker and transfer the skillet mixture into it.

3. Add beans, bouillon, potato and bay leaf. Add water to cover the ingredients.

4. Tie together herbal sprigs and place inside the cooking dish. Cook for 9 hours over LOW temperature mode.

5. To serve, transfer to a large dish and garnish with lime wedges.

Nutrition: Calories: 279 Fat: 5g Carbohydrates: 47g Protein: 15g

Marinated Mushrooms in Slow Cooker

Fast and delicious with vegetables!

Prep time: 5 minutes Cooking time: 10 hours Servings: 20

INGREDIENTS:

2 cups water

2 cups white sugar

4 packs fresh mushrooms

2 cups soy sauce

1 cup butter

DIRECTIONS:

1. Take a medium saucepan and place it over medium heat. Pour in water. Add soy sauce and butter.

2. Cook, stirring, just until butter has melted.

3. Mix in sugar and continue to stir until the crystals are completely dissolved. Remove stems from the mushrooms. Place mushrooms to Slow Cooker.

4. Pour in the saucepan mixture.

5. Cook on LOW temperature setting for 10 hours.

6. When ready, drain mushrooms and let to cool. You can even place it in the refrigerator for a couple of hours.

7. Serve in a bowl along with chopped green onions and olive oil.

Nutrition: Calories: 228 Fat: 11g Carbohydrates: 29g Protein: 4g

Vegan Corn Chowder in Slow Cooker

Wonderfully easy and tasty!

Prep time: 9 minutes Cooking time: 1 hour Servings: 7

INGREDIENTS:

3 cans kernel corns

3 diced potatoes

Clove garlic

Salt

Large onion

3 cups vegetable broth

1 tbsp. Chili powder

2 red chili peppers

Parsley flakes

Soy sauce

Black pepper

Juiced lime

Margarine

DIRECTIONS:

1. Grease your Slow Cooker with cooking spray or simple butter at room temperature.
2. Fill a large bowl with chopped potatoes, red chile peppers, minced garlic, chili powder and salt/pepper.
3. Pour in vegetable broth.
4. Place the mixture into kitchen blender and mix well until puree consistency. Transfer puree mixture to your Slow Cooker.
5. Pour in soy milk with slightly melted margarine.
6. Set Slow Cooker to LOW mode and cook for one hour.

Nutrition: Calories: 320 Fat: 10g Carbohydrates: 53g Protein: 9g

Green Collard Beans in Slow Cooker

Tender beans for any occasion!

Prep time: 12 minutes Cooking time: 8 hours Servings: 8

INGREDIENTS:

3 slices bacon

Bunch collard greens

2 sliced jalapenos

Chicken stock

Salt

Black pepper

DIRECTIONS:

1. Generously grease your Slow Cooker with some melted butter or coat with special cooking spray. In a large pot, combine collard beans and salted water. Slowly bring to boil and simmer for 10 minutes.
2. In a large skillet, cook bacon until it is evenly browned on all sides (for around 10 minutes). Drain the beans and transfer to prepared Slow Cooker.
3. Add bacon and jalapenos. Pour in chicken stock. Season with salt and black pepper.
4. Set to LOW temperature, cook for 8 hours or even overnight.

Nutrition: Calories: 124 Fat: 10g Carbohydrates: 4g Protein: 4g

Loaded Potato Soup in Slow Cooker

Everyone will love this creamy taste and amazing flavors!

Prep time: 5 minutes Cooking time: 4 hours Servings: 6

INGREDIENTS:

4 cups milk

1 pack hash browns

4 green onions

Ground black pepper

Sour cream

1 pack cream cheese

8 slices cooked bacon

1 pack Cheddar cheese

DIRECTIONS:

1. Spray the dish of your Slow Cooker with a cooking spray or grease with melted butter. Right in Slow Cooker dish, combine cream cheese, pepper and sour cream.
2. Pour in milk and stir. Mix well until you are sure the mixture is smooth.
3. Add diced potatoes, bacon slices and shredded Cheddar cheese. Combine and close the lid. Cook on LOW temperature mode for 4 hours.
4. To serve, sprinkle with chopped green onions.

Nutrition: Calories: 240 Fat: 14g Carbohydrates: 19g Protein: 10g

Hot Smashed Potato Soup

This will be your favorite recipe!

Prep time: 5 minutes Cooking time: 10 hours Servings: 6

INGREDIENTS:

3 large potatoes

Ground black pepper

Small sweet yellow pepper

4 cups chicken broth

Roasted garlic

Cheddar cheese

Half cup whipping cream

Green onions

DIRECTIONS:

1. Slightly grease your Slow Cooker with melted butter.
2. Right in the cooking dish, combine chopped potatoes, sweet peppers, black pepper and garlic. Pour the broth over vegetables. Mix everything well until the consistency is smooth.
3. Cook covered for 10 hours using LOW setting. When ready, mash potatoes with potato masher.
4. Add shredded Cheddar, whipping cream and sliced green onions.
5. Serve in small bowls, garnished with green onions and white bread cubes.

Nutrition: Calories: 289 Fat: 11g Carbohydrates: 37g Protein: 10g

Onion, Pepper and Sausage Mix

This is fast and Easy for busy days!

Prep time: 5 minutes Cooking time: 8 hours Servings: 12

INGREDIENTS:

Sweet Italian sausage

1 pack elbow macaroni

2 green bell peppers

1 jar pasta sauce

Hot Italian sausages

1 red bell pepper

1 large sweet pepper

DIRECTIONS:

1. Grease your Slow Cooker with melted butter.
2. Chop onions, sweet sausage, green bell peppers, hot sausage, red bell pepper. Combine the ingredients along with pasta sauce in prepared Slow Cooker.
3. Add one cup water.
4. Set your Slow Cooker to LOW mode and cook for 8 hours.

5. When It is 30 minutes left before serving, cook elbow macaroni according to package directions. Serve Slow Cooker dish over cooked macaroni. Garnish with shredded cheese or chopped green onions.

Nutrition: Calories: 573 Fat: 24g Carbohydrates: 61g Protein: 25g

Taco Chili in Slow Cooker

A flavored meal with low fat!

Prep time: 5 minutes Cooking time: 8 hours Servings: 6

INGREDIENTS:

Two cans tomatoes

Ground beef

Enchilada sauce

Canned chili beans

Can corn with peppers

1 pack seasoning mix

1 can homily

1 can kidney beans

One pack taco seasoning

DIRECTIONS:

1. Preheat an oiled skillet over medium heat.
2. Cook beef for around 5-7 minutes until golden brown. Add one packet taco seasoning to skillet. Set aside.
3. Generously grease your Slow Cooker with olive oil or cooking spray.
4. Place corn and peppers, tomatoes, hominy, kidney beans, enchilada sauce and chili beans into Slow Cooker.
5. Add cooked beef. Stir to combine and close the lid. Cook for 8 hours on LOW temperature mode.
6. Serve hot in small bowls.

Nutrition: Calories: 504 Fat: 19g Carbohydrates: 56g Protein: 29g

Black-Eyed Peas with Greens and Rice

Perfect for New Year's Day!

Prep time: 5 minutes Cooking time: 5 hours Servings: 7

INGREDIENTS:

Hot water

Cup black-eyed peas

clove garlic

2 bunches collard greens

chopped onion

cube vegetable bouillon

smoked ham hock

Water

1 cup rice

Species to taste

DIRECTIONS:

1. In a large soup pot, combine the peas and pour in enough water to cover.

2. Bring to boil and cook for several minutes. Reduce heat and simmer for an hour. In a hot water, dissolve one bouillon cube. Pour this mixture to Slow Cooker.

3. Transfer the beans to Slow Cooker.

4. Add red pepper flakes, collard greens, garlic, vegetable broth, ham hock and onion to Slow Cooker.

5. Add some more water as needed to cover. Set to HIGH and cook for 5 hours.

6. Season with salt/pepper.

Nutrition: Calories: 342 Fat: 8g Carbohydrates: 51g Protein: 16g

Pinto Beans in Slow Cooker

Easy and perfect to serve with enchiladas!

Prep time: 5 minutes Cooking time: 4 hours Servings: 10

INGREDIENTS:

1 chopped onion

Bacon

5 cloves garlic

Dry pinto beans

2 fresh tomatoes

1 can beer

Canned jalapeno peppers

Fresh cilantro

DIRECTIONS:

1. Place dry pinto beans in your Slow Cooker. Cover with cold water. Add salt and garlic. Cook for 1 hour, using HIGH temperature mode.

2. In a skillet with olive oil, cook sliced bacon until it is evenly browned. Drain the excess fat. Add chopped onion and cook until mild.

3. Add tomatoes and jalapenos. Prepare just until heated through. Transfer the skillet ingredients to Slow Cooker and stir well.

4. Cook covered for 4 hours using LOW temperature mode. Serve in a large bowl or just from Slow Cooker!

Nutrition: Calories: 353 Fat: 13g Carbohydrates: 39g Protein: 16g

Easy Pumpkin Soup

Make this one day before serving to make a better taste!

Prep time: 5 minutes Cooking time: 10 hours Servings: 8

INGREDIENTS:

1 cup chopped onion

1 tbsp butter

3 cans pumpkin puree

1 can chicken broth

Cream

Cooked ham

1 tsp minced garlic

DIRECTIONS:

1. Melt butter in a large skillet over medium heat.

2. Chop garlic and onion and transfer them to skillet. Cook until completely soft.

3. In a large bowl, combine pumpkin puree, thyme, cream, rosemary, ham and pepper/ Add the skillet mixture and combine well.

4. Transfer all ingredients to prepared Slow Cooker. Set your Slow Cooker to LOW mode for 10 hours.

5. When the pumpkin is very soft and falls apart, turn off and serve. Serve in small bowls and crispy bread cubes.

Nutrition: Calories: 241 Fat: 15g Carbohydrates: 14g Protein: 12g

Potato Soup in Slow Cooker

Perfect with bacon and shredded cheese!

Prep time: 5 minutes Cooking time: 6 hours Servings: 7

INGREDIENTS:

1 diced onion

Grated carrot

2 stalks celery

2 tbsp olive oil

6 large potatoes

8 cups water

2 bay leaves

2 tbsp vegetable stock powder

Dry sage leaves

Ground black pepper

DIRECTIONS:

1. Drizzle oil over the bottom and sides of your Slow Cooker. Chop the potatoes, carrot and celery. Mince garlic.

2. Gather the vegetables in prepared Slow Cooker. Pour in enough water to cover the vegetables.

3. Add vegetable stock powder and stir well until dissolved. Season with sage, salt, bay leaves, thyme and ground pepper. Cook for around 6 hours using HIGH mode.

4. Serve in small deep bowls along with fresh bread.

Nutrition: Calories: 220 Fat: 4g Carbohydrates: 40g Protein: 4g

Green cabbage Soup

Plain and light meal for busy days!

Prep time: 5 minutes Cooking time: 5 hours Servings: 8

INGREDIENTS:

Small head cabbage

4 green onions

Chopped celery

Sliced carrot

3 leaves kale

4 leaves Swiss chard

3 cubes chicken bouillon

1 tsp dried marjoram

Dried sage

Parsley

Water to cover

DIRECTIONS:

1. Generously grease your Slow Cooker with melted butter or simply coat with cooking spray.

2. In a large bowl, combine processed cabbage, chopped green onions, celery and carrots. Mix well. Add kale and chard. Mix one more time and transfer to Slow Cooker.

3. Add marjoram, sage, parsley and pour over with chicken bouillon. Cover with cold water and close the lid.

4. Cook on HIGH for 5 hours.

5. Serve with crispy white or French bread and green onion sprinkles.

Nutrition: Calories: 158 Fat: 10g Carbohydrates: 11g Protein: 5g

German Potato Salad in Slow Cooker

Try it with your friends or during family dinner!

Prep time: 5 minutes Cooking time: 6 hours Servings: 12

INGREDIENTS:

3 large potatoes

Cup sliced celery

Half cup vinegar

Ground black pepper

One cup onion

Half cup chopped red bell pepper

Half cup cooking oil

Salt

6 slices bacon

Fresh parsley

DIRECTIONS:

1. Coat the bottom of your Slow Cooker with cooking spray or melted unsalted butter. Dice potatoes, green bell pepper and chop onion. Mix vegetables in a large bowl. Add vinegar, salt, cooking oil and black pepper to taste.

2. Mix well and transfer the mixture from bowl to Slow Cooker. Set your Slow Cooker to LOW and cook for 6 hours.

3. To garnish, use chopped parsley, green salad leaves and bacon slices.

Nutrition: Calories: 243 Fat: 12g Carbohydrates: 45g Protein: 24g

Hot Potato Soup with Cauliflower

Cook this when the weather is cold!

Prep time: 12 minutes Cooking time: 3 hours Servings: 5

INGREDIENTS:

Water

1 head cauliflower

5 baby carrots

2 large red potatoes

cube chicken bouillon

Half cup milk

Cream of chicken soup

Dried onion flakes

shredded Cheddar

Fresh parsley

DIRECTIONS:

1. In a pot, combine cauliflower, onion flakes and carrots. Cover with the water. Add bouillon cubes and cook for 10 minutes.
2. Sprinkle your Slow Cooker with olive or vegetable oil.
3. Transfer the pot mixture into Slow Cooker and pour in one cup of cooking liquid. Add milk, cream of chicken soup, bacon bits and cream cheese.
4. Set your Slow Cooker to LOW and cook for 2 hours. Serve with white French bread.

Nutrition: Calories: 329 Fat: 26g Carbohydrates: 54g Protein: 35g

Moist Slow Cooker Stuffing

Amazing for a big crowd!

Prep time: 5 minutes Cooking time: 8 hours Servings: 6

INGREDIENTS:

1 cup butter

1 tsp poultry seasoning

12 cups bread cubes

Dried sage

2 cups chopped celery

Chopped onion

Fresh parsley

Sliced mushrooms

2 chicken eggs

Salt

Dried marjoram

4 cups chicken broth

Black pepper

DIRECTIONS:

1. Take a large skillet. Melt the butter over medium heat.
2. Add chopped celery, onion and mushrooms. Stir in parsley and cook for several minutes, stirring frequently.
3. In a mixing bowl, combine skillet mixture with dry bread cubes. Season with sage, poultry seasoning, marjoram, thyme, pepper/salt. Add water and beat in chicken eggs. Transfer to Slow Cooker.
4. Cook on high for the first 45 minutes. Then, switch to LOW and continue cooking for 8 hours.

Nutrition: Calories: 325 Fat: 5g Carbohydrates: 52g Protein: 23g

Homemade Vegetable Soup

Good for vegetarians!

Prep time: 5 minutes Cooking time: 7 hours Servings: 5

INGREDIENTS:

1 pack frozen vegetables

Large onion

6 cups broth

Half cup barley

3 cloves garlic

2 potatoes

Canned dried tomatoes

1 bay leaf

Black pepper

Dried basil

Vegetable shortening

DIRECTIONS:

1. Sprinkle your Slow Cooker with olive oil.
2. In a bowl, combine diced vegetables with parsley, frozen vegetables, salt, basil, bay leaf, black pepper and oregano.
3. Transfer to Slow Cooker and cook covered for 6 hours. Use LOW mode. In a bowl, combine flour with shortening. Blend with a kitchen mixer.
4. Add vegetable broth and mix dough. Cut into small slices and transfer to Slow Cooker. Cook for 1 more hour.
5. Serve while hot along with crispy bread.

Nutrition: Calories: 333 Fat: 7g Carbohydrates: 57g Protein: 9g

Green Stew with Chiles in Mexican Style

Amazing dish for lazy days!

Prep time: 5 minutes Cooking time: 8 hours Servings: 9

INGREDIENTS:

Cubed beef tenderloin

Mosa harina

1 tbsp olive oil

Fresh tomatoes

1 red onion

Ground cumin

2 cups beef broth

Diced green chiles

3 cloves garlic

Dash cayenne pepper

salt

DIRECTIONS:

1. Rub beef tenderloin cubes with mosa harina.
2. On a large oiled skillet, prepare beef until it is evenly browned.
3. Chop red onion, green chile peppers, potato, tomatoes and meat into greased Slow Cooker. Season with cumin, oregano, black pepper, garlic, cayenne pepper, salt, white pepper and cilantro.
4. Cook on LOW mode for 8 hours.
5. Garnish with jalapeno slices and chopped green onion.

Nutrition: Calories: 295 Fat: 14g Carbohydrates: 19g Protein: 22g

Vegetable Afritad in Slow Cooker

Pilipino receipt right from your Slow Cooker!

Prep time: 5 minutes Cooking time: 4 hours Servings: 8

INGREDIENTS:

Juiced lemon

Boneless chicken breast

Half cup olive oil

Soy sauce

3 cloves garlic

Sliced onion

2 tomatoes

Black pepper

2 chopped carrots

3 red potatoes

Yellow bell pepper

Cup green peas

Green bell pepper

DIRECTIONS:

1. Generously grease your Slow Cooker with melted butter or coat with olive oil. Rub chicken with minced garlic and bell pepper. Transfer to Slow Cooker.
2. Season with lemon juice, soy sauce and olive oil.
3. Add chopped tomatoes, bell peppers, onion, red potatoes and peas into Slow Cooker. Set your Slow Cooker to HIGH and cook for 4 hours.
4. Serve over a large serving plate with lemon wedges.

Nutrition: Calories: 332 Fat: 20g Carbohydrates: 19g Protein: 19g

Sweet Potato Curry With Coconut

Amazing flavors and sweet taste of simple dish!

Prep time: 17 minutes Cooking time: 8 hours Servings: 10

INGREDIENTS:

2 large onions

Passata

1 tsp papriks

Ginger root

2 red chili peppers

peanut butter

Red cabbage

Sweet potatoes

Cayenne

3 garlic cloves

Coconut milk

DIRECTIONS:

1. In a large nonstick skillet, preheat olive oil and add chopped onion. Cook for 10 minutes. Add garlic, cayenne and paprika. Cook for one minute. Transfer to Slow Cooker.
2. In the same skillet, cook shredded cabbage and red pepper. In 5 minutes, place to Slow Cooker too.
3. Fry sweet potatoes for 5 minutes. Transfer to Slow Cooker.
4. In a bowl, mix coconut milk and passata. Pour to Slow Cooker. Stir the ingredients well. Cover the lid and cook for 8 hours on LOW mode.

Nutrition: Calories: 434 Fat: 22g Carbohydrates: 47g Protein: 6g

Vegetable Bake in Italian Style

Irresistible for both meat and vegetarian menu!

Prep time: 5 minutes Cooking time: 6 hours Servings: 8

INGREDIENTS:

Oregano leaves

Canned tomatoes

3 beef tomatoes

Mozzarella cheese

Green salad leaves

Canned red peppers

Chili flakes

Small baguette

Baby auberlines

Bunch basil

DIRECTIONS:

1. Start with preheating of your Slow Cooker on high mode.

2. Add canned tomatoes, chopped garlic, chili, oregano leaves. Cook under the lid.
3. Chop auberlines, tomatoes, red peppers. Cover with sauce, chopped basil and oregano. Chop baguette into thin slices.
4. Open Slow Cooker and carefully place sliced vegetables and baguette slices into layers. Add chopped onion, shredded Mozzarella and tomato sauce.
5. Cook on HIGH mode for 6 hours.
6. To serve, garnish with leftover basil and green salad leaves.

Nutrition: Calories: 274 Fat: 10g Carbohydrates: 31g Protein: 14g

DESSERTS RECIPES

Chocolate and Peanut Butter Cake

This perfectly matches with chocolate syrup!

Prep time: 18 minutes Cooking time: 2 hours Servings: 12

INGREDIENTS:

Cooking spray

Brown sugar

Almond pure extract

Plain flour

Baking powder

Creamy peanut butter

Baking soda

Sour cream

3 tablespoons butter

Cocoa powder

White sugar

Boiling water

Chocolate syrup

DIRECTIONS:

1. Coat the inside parts and bottom of Slow Cooker with a special cooking spray. In a bowl, whisk flour, add baking powder, brown sugar and baking soda.
2. In a separate bowl, add peanut butter, melted butter, sour cream, almond extract, and 2 tablespoons boiling water. Mix until smooth.
3. Combine the mixtures to make a thick batter. Transfer butter to Slow Cooker.
4. In another bowl, whisk sugar, water and cocoa powder. Pour chocolate mix over batter. Cook on HIGH temperature, about 1 hour.
5. To serve, cool and sprinkle with chocolate syrup.

Nutrition: Calories: 329 Fat: 17g Carbohydrates: 38g Protein: 8g

Triple-Berry Cobbler

You can cook this both with fresh or frozen berries!

Prep time: 23 minutes Cooking time: 2 hours Servings: 6

INGREDIENTS:

One cup flour

2 chicken eggs

2 tbsp milk

Cup water

Half-and-half

6 cups frozen berries

Cinnamon

Ground nutmeg

Sugar

Quick-cooking tapioca

Baking powder

DIRECTIONS:

1. Take a medium bowl. Combine sugar, salt, baking powder, sifted flour, nutmeg and cinnamon. In a smaller bowl, whisk eggs with milk and oil.
2. Pour the egg mixture into the flour and combine until moistened.
3. In a large skillet, bring to boil frozen berries with tapioca, sugar and water. Meanwhile, grease your Slow Cooker with melted butter.
4. Once the berry mixture boils, spoon it into Slow Cooker.
5. Top berries with batter and cover the lid of your Slow Cooker. Cook on HIGH mode of temperature for 2 hours.
6. Serve in dessert dishes with half-and-half or ice cream.

Nutrition: Calories: 285 Fat: 12g Carbohydrates: 7g Protein: 23g

Chocolate Pudding Cake

Simple and fast enough for Slow Cooker!

Prep time: 9 minutes Cooking time: 1 hour Servings: 16

INGREDIENTS:

Chocolate pudding mix

Sour cream

4 chicken eggs

Water

1 pack chocolate cake mix

Vegetable oil

Chocolate chips

DIRECTIONS:

1. In a bowl, combine cake mix with pudding mix.
2. Pour in some sour cream, beaten chicken eggs, water, oil. Whisk until all ingredients are smoothly blended.
3. Stir in fresh semisweet chocolate chips. Blend to stir chips into the mixture. Coat Slow Cooker with cooking spray, pour batter into it.
4. Cover and prepare on LOW temp for around 6 hours.

Nutrition: Calories: 384 Fat: 25g Carbohydrates: 37g Protein: 5g

Vanilla Tapioca Pudding

You can serve this warm or cool!

Prep time: 5 minutes Cooking time: 6 hours Servings: 14

INGREDIENTS:

Half cup whole milk

1cup white sugar

small pearl tapioca

4 chicken eggs

vanilla extract

DIRECTIONS:

1. Grease your Slow Cooker with olive oil or simply cover with cooking spray to avoid sticking. In a bowl, combine half cup milk, tapioca, white sugar and eggs.
2. Mix everything until perfectly smooth and transfer to Slow Cooker crock.
3. Set your Slow Cooker to LOW temperature mode and cook, stirring once per hour. Prepare for 6 hours.
4. Just before the serving. Stir the vanilla extract into the pudding.

5. To serve, pour in cooked pudding into a small bowl and garnish with fresh mint, lime wedges or fresh berries to your taste.

Nutrition: Calories: 218 Fat: 6g Carbohydrates: 35g Protein: 6g

Apples with Cinnamon and Dark Brown Sugar

Easy preparations and minimal cleanup!

Prep time: 26 minutes Cooking time: 3 hours Servings: 4

INGREDIENTS:

4 tart baking apples

Raisins

Half cup regular oats

2 tbsp brown sugar

Cinnamon

1 tbsp butter

Apple juice

DIRECTIONS:

1. To start, cover the bottom of Slow Cooker with parchment paper or grease with butter. Pell and carefully core the apples. Layer them over the bottom of Slow Cooker.
2. In a small bowl, combine one by one cinnamon, oats, brown sugar, raisins and butter. Stir everything well, spoon the mixture into cored apples just to fill them.
3. Transfer stuffed apples into Slow Cooker and sprinkle with the remaining oat mixture. Cover the lid and cook for 3 hours. Use LOW temperature mode for cooking.
4. To serve, place the apples in a small portion bowls and pour over with the cooking mixture.

Nutrition: Calories: 211 Fat: 8g Carbohydrates: 1g Protein: 2g

Bananas Foster in Slow Cooker

Perfect with tea and ice-cream!

Prep time: 11 minutes Cooking time: 2 hours Servings: 5

INGREDIENTS:

4 bananas

4 tablespoons butter

1 cup brown sugar

4 tbsp rum

Vanilla extract

5 tbsp walnuts

Cinnamon

Shredded coconut

DIRECTIONS:

1. To start the cooking process, peel the bananas and slice them into 1-inch pieces.

2. Cover the bottom and sides of your Slow Cooker with melted butter or anti-stick cooking spray. Comfortably layer banana slices over the bottom of your Slow Cooker.

3. In a separate bowl, combine rum, butter, vanilla, sugar and cinnamon and stir well to combine. Pour the rum mixture into Slow Cooker. Toss to cover all the banana slices evenly.

4. Cover the lid. Using a LOW temperature mode, prepare for 2 hours.

5. When it is about thirty minutes before the end of cooking time, add walnuts with coconut atop the bananas.

Nutrition: Calories: 539 Fat: 20g Carbohydrates: 83g Protein: 3g

Slow Cooker Reindeer Poop

Little sweet candies for any occasion!

Prep time: 15 minutes Cooking time: 2 hours Servings: 50

INGREDIENTS:

White candy coating

German sweet chocolate

Semi-sweet chocolate chips

2 cans roasted peanuts

DIRECTIONS:

1. Slightly grease your Slow Cooker with vegetable or olive oil.

2. In a bowl, whisk together white candy coating, chocolate chips, German sweet chocolate and peanuts. Stir well to make a smooth batter-like mixture.

3. Transfer the chocolate batter into Slow Cooker.

4. Set your Slow Cooker to LOW temperature mode and cover the lid. Cook for 2 hours, and then gently stir the mixture.

5. Leave to cook for another 45 to 60 minutes.

6. When the time is over, line the baking sheet with the parchment and place small drops of the mixture over it. Wait for sweets to cook and became thick. Serve.

Nutrition: Calories: 174 Fat: 12g Carbohydrates: 13g Protein: 4g

Warm Berry Slow Cooker Compote

Serve as a dessert or with ice cream!

Prep time: 19 minutes Cooking time: 2 hours Servings: 7

INGREDIENTS:

6 cups mixed berries

Half cup sugar

Orange zest (grated)

4 tbsp orange juice

Cornstarch

2 tbsp water

DIRECTIONS:

1. In a bowl, combine together frozen berries, grated zest of the orange and white sugar. Pour in the juice from one orange. Mix all ingredients to combine well.

2. Transfer to Slow Cooker and prepare on HIGH mode for about 1 or 2 hours. In a cup (or bowl), dissolve 2 tablespoons cornstarch in water.

3. Pour your cornstarch mixture into Slow Cooker and combine with other ingredients. Cook covered with the lid for additional ten minutes (or until the mixture become thick). Serve while the dessert is still warm or at least at room temperature.

Nutrition: Calories: 149 Fat: 1g Carbohydrates: 37g Protein: 1g

Triple Coconut Cake

Super delicious and unusual for your table!

Prep time: 7 minutes Cooking time: 3 hours Servings: 10

INGREDIENTS:

Coconut oil

Cup sugar

3 chicken eggs

Baking powder

Unsalted butter

Half cup coconut milk

Cream cheese

Vanilla

Coconut flakes

2 cups flour

Salt

DIRECTIONS:

1. In a bowl, beat with a mixer sugar, butter and coconut oil. One by one, add chicken eggs and beat for one more time. In a bowl, whisk flour, salt and baking powder.

2. Carefully stir flour mixture into the butter mixture. Add coconut milk. Stir well until everything is combined.

3. Cover the inside of your Slow Cooker with a cooking spray. Transfer the batter into crockpot and spread evenly.

4. Use HIGH temperature for cooking. Cook for 2 hours.

5. To serve, cool and make a frosting out of cream cheese with butter.

Nutrition: Calories: 761 Fat: 47g Carbohydrates: 73g Protein: 8g

Slow Cooker Black Forest Cake

Amazing berry mix!

Prep time: 5 minutes Cooking time: 3 hours Servings: 12

INGREDIENTS:

Butter

Canned pineapples

Chocolate cake mix

Cooking spray

Canned cherry pie filling

DIRECTIONS:

1. Take a large saucepan and melt the butter in it.

2. Pour in the pineapple liquid and chocolate mix. Simmer for several minutes and remove from fire. Coat the inside surface of your Slow Cooker with a cooking spray.

3. Layer the bottom with pineapple chunks.

4. Top the chunks with cherry pie filling. Arrange the filling into the even layer. Stir the saucepan-butter mixture and pour it into your Slow Cooker.

5. Prepare on LOW mode for about 3 hours. Cool before serving. Serve with milk or tea.

Nutrition: Calories: 385 Fat: 17g Carbohydrates: 57g Protein: 3g

Apple Bread Pudding with Cinnamon

Perfect for cold autumn and winter nights!

Prep time: 17 minutes Cooking time: 4 hours Servings: 9

INGREDIENTS:

4 large apples

1- inch bread cubes

4 chicken eggs

2 cans milk

Brown sugar

Cinnamon to taste

DIRECTIONS:

1. Prepare the apples: peel them and remove the core. Cut apples into small cubes. Gather chopped apples in a bowl.

2. Grease crock-pot of your Slow Cooker with butter or oil to your choice. You need to do this to avoid sticking of batter during the cooking process.

3. Transfer chopped apples into Slow Cooker. Add cubed bread and mix the ingredients. In a bowl, beat chicken eggs with milk.

4. Stir in white sugar. Add nutmeg and cinnamon.

5. Pour in the egg and cinnamon mixture over bread and apples.

6. Turn your Slow Cooker on and set to HIGH. Prepare on HIGH regime for 4 hours.

Nutrition: Calories: 266 Fat: 7g Carbohydrates: 48g Protein: 11g

Peanut Butter Cake in Slow Cooker

Amuse your friends with this happy recipe!

Prep time: 12 minutes Cooking time: 2 hours Servings: 11

INGREDIENTS:

Cup peanut butter

Baking soda

1 cup flour

Vanilla extract

4 tbsp warm milk

Baking powder

Salt

Cocoa powder

Sour cream

White sugar

DIRECTIONS:

1. In a bowl, carefully combine flour, salt, baking soda, brown sugar and baking powder. In another bowl, combine sour cream, peanut butter, boiling water and simple butter.

2. Generously spray the inside of your Slow Cooker with a cooking spray. Carefully check there is no missed space without spray bits.

3. Spread the batter mixture all over the bottom of Slow Cooker. Set Slow Cooker to HIGH and cook for approximately 2 hours.

4. To serve, let the cake to cool and place each portion in a bowl, or arrange it with tea or preferred ice-cream.

Nutrition: Calories: 610 Fat: 32g Carbohydrates: 74g Protein: 13g

Bread Pudding in the Slow Cooker

Simple ingredients and healthy recipe!

Prep time: 12 minutes Cooking time: 3 hours Servings: 12

INGREDIENTS:

One cup raisins

8 cups cubed bread

4 chicken eggs

3 tbsp white sugar

2 cups milk

Melted butter

2 tsp nutmeg

Vanilla

DIRECTIONS:

1. Slightly grease your Slow Cooker with melted butter.
2. Combine cubed bread with raisins and transfer to Slow Cooker. Arrange evenly over the bottom. In a bowl, beat chicken eggs and whisk them with butter, milk, nutmeg and vanilla extract.
3. Pour the egg mixture into Slow Cooker and toss to cover the bread with the mixture.
4. Set Sow Cooker to LOW mode and cook for 3 hours. Check the readiness with a knife or wooden toothpick.
5. When ready, serve bread pudding with tea or coffee to your taste.

Nutrition: Calories: 396 Fat: 14g Carbohydrates: 57g Protein: 11g

Peach Upside Down Cake

Amazing choice for a summer dessert!

Prep time: 5 minutes Cooking time: 3 hours Servings: 8

INGREDIENTS:

Three cans peaches

2 cups flour

Salt

5 tbsp melted butter

Baking powder

Almond extract

5 tbsp brown sugar

Cinnamon

Nutmeg

1 cup whole milk

DIRECTIONS:

1. Drain the peaches, but reserve liquid from the cans.
2. Melt the butter, pour it into Slow Cooker. Spread evenly over its surface to coat.
3. Combine brown sugar, ground nutmeg and cinnamon. Sprinkle the sweet mixture over butter in Slow Cooker.
4. Place peaches in one layer over the butter and sugar mix.
5. Using an electric mixer, combine white sugar with softened butter. Add eggs and almond extract. Separately, mix flour, salt and baking powder. Working in batches, combine all the ingredients and make a batter.
6. Place into Slow Cooker and fit the batter over the bottom. Cook for 2 hours using HIGH temperature mode.

Nutrition: Calories: 654 Fat: 27g Carbohydrates: 97g Protein: 6g

Apple-Cherry Cobbler

Warm and Autumn-Spiced Dessert!

Prep time: 5 minutes Cooking time: 3 hours Servings: 6

INGREDIENTS:

Half cup sugar

Quick-cooking tapioca

Light cream

Cooking apples

Half cup dried cherries

Apple pie spice

Ice cream,

Refrigerated crescent rolls

Melted butter

Pitted tart cherries

DIRECTIONS:

1. Line the bottom of your Slow Cooker with a parchment paper.
2. Right in a cooking dish, combine sugar, apple pie spice, tapioca. Slightly stir to combine. Chop apples into small slices and place into Slow Cooker.
3. Add canned cherries (along with liquids), and dried cherries. Stir for one more time. Cover the lid of your Cooker. Turn it on LOW temp and prepare for 7 hours.

4. Serve cherry-and-apple mixture over your favorite buns or with apple chips.

Nutrition: Calories: 414 Fat: 12g Carbohydrates: 71g Protein: 5g

Chocolate Cherry Slow Cooker Cake

The great dessert for any holiday!

Prep time: 5 minutes Cooking time: 4 hours Servings: 8

INGREDIENTS:

Half cup water

Chocolate chips

Red velvet cake mix

Half cup sour cream

2 chicken eggs

Chocolate fudge mix

Canned cherry filling

DIRECTIONS:

1. Grease your Slow Cooker with preferred oil or simply with unsalted melted butter.
2. In a bowl, combine beaten chicken eggs, chocolate pudding mix, sour cream and water. You can also do in with a kitchen mixer.
3. Add cake mix and mix for one more time.
4. In a bowl, combine chocolate chips with canned cherry filling. When it is all smooth, stir into the main batter.
5. Transfer the mixture into Slow Cooker and stir for one more time. Cover the lid. Cook, using a LOW temperature regime, for at least 4 hours.

Nutrition: Calories: 558 Fat: 17g Carbohydrates: 97g Protein: 7g

Slow Cooker Apple Crisp

It tastes delicious with ice cream!

Prep time: 38 minutes Cooking time: 3 hours Servings: 6

INGREDIENTS:

Light brown sugar

Ground cinnamon

Cup flour

Nutmeg

Salt

Half cup butter

Cornstarch

Chopped walnuts

Ground ginger

Lemon juice

3 apples

DIRECTIONS:

1. In a large bowl, combine brown and white sugars with cinnamon, salt and grounded nutmeg. Stir together until smooth.
2. Stir the butter into flour mixture until it is crumbled. You can use a fork for it or simply combine the ingredients with your fingers.
3. In another bowl, combine cornstarch, sugar, cinnamon and ginger.
4. Arrange chopped apples over the Slow Cookers' bottom add lemon juice and cornstarch mixture. Stir everything well.
5. Sprinkle with walnut sprinkles.
6. Cook under the lid for 2 hours using HIGH temperature mode.

Nutrition: Calories: 593 Fat: 29g Carbohydrates: 83g Protein: 5g

Rice Pudding in a Slow Cooker

Perfect with baked apples!

Prep time: 14 minutes Cooking time: 2 hours Servings: 19

INGREDIENTS:

White sugar

Vanilla extract

Ground nutmeg

2 cans evaporated milk

1 cup white rice

Cinnamon stick

DIRECTIONS:

1. In a bowl, combine uncooked rice, vanilla, sugar, nutmeg.
2. Pour the rice mixture over with evaporated milk. Whisk the ingredients to distribute evenly with milk.
3. Grease Slow Cooker with melted butter, just in case. Start preheating it. Pour the rice mixture into prepared Slow Cooker.
4. Place the cinnamon stick into the mixture.
5. Cover the lid of your Slow Cooker. Start to cook on LOW mode for around 2 hours. Remember to stir the content time after time.

6. To serve, remove cinnamon stick. Stick while the pie is still warm.

Nutrition: Calories: 321 Fat: 7g Carbohydrates: 56g Protein: 8g

Caramel Apples in Sweet Dip

Amazing Autumn Flavors in Your House

Prep time: 5 minutes Cooking time: 2 hours Servings: 18

INGREDIENTS:

3 medium onions

Salt

One cup milk

Cinnamon

2 tbsp sugar

Pinch nutmeg

1 can caramel sauce

Refrigerated pie dough

DIRECTIONS:

1. Grease your Slow Cooker or simply cover it with cooking spray.
2. Right in your Slow Cooker, bring together cored and chopped apples, nutmeg and cinnamon. Stir in caramel and add one pinch of salt. Stir well to combine all ingredients well.
3. Cook for 2 hours on HIGH temperature regime. When ready, transfer pie crust onto baking sheet.
4. In a separate bowl mix cinnamon with sugar and sprinkle the pie. Cook in oven for several minutes. Serve.

Nutrition: Calories: 341 Fat: 16g Carbohydrates: 66g Protein: 34g

Autumn Pumpkin Sweet Pie

Crusty and flavored for the season!

Prep time: 5 minutes Cooking time: 4

Servings: 20

INGREDIENTS:

2 cans evaporated milk

Half tsp baking powder

4 tbsp brown sugar

2 tbsp melted butter

Half cup flour

2 tsp pumpkin spice

Salt

2 chicken eggs

1 large pumpkin

DIRECTIONS:

1. Grease your Slow Cooker with olive oil or melted butter, just what you like better. Peel pumpkin and remove all the seeds. Cut into small bite-sized pieces.
2. In a bowl, whisk chicken eggs, evaporated milk, remaining melted butter, brown sugar, salt, pumpkin spice and baking powder.
3. When all the other ingredients are well combined, stir in sliced pumpkin. Cover the lid of your Slow Cooker and turn it on.
4. Cook the pie for 4 hours, use LOW temperature mode.

Nutrition: Calories: 380 Fat: 12g Carbohydrates: 32g Protein: 9g

Sweet Scones with Chocolate Drops

Hot and delicious for tea and coffee!

Prep time: 5 minutes Cooking time: 2 hours Servings: 14

INGREDIENTS:

Pinch salt

Self-raising flour

Half cup chocolate chips

Half cup milk

Cubed butter

1 tbsp sugar

DIRECTIONS:

1. In a bowl, combine the flour with sugar and some salt to your taste. Slightly melt the butter cubes and carefully stir them into the flour mixture. Add milk and whisk until the mixture transforms into a soft dough.
2. Add chocolate chips or any other filling you may like.
3. Form into long and cut into small bite-sized pieces. You may also form small triangles out of this dough if you like.
4. Place into greased Slow Cooker for approximately 2 hours. Cook on HIGH temperature mode.

Nutrition: Calories: 235 Fat: 7g Carbohydrates: 21g Protein: 3g

Pumpkin and Coffee Sweet Cake

Amazing duo of two tastes!

Prep time: 8 minutes Cooking time: 2 hours Servings: 10

INGREDIENTS:

Baking soda

Salt

2 cups pastry flour

Chicken egg

Vanilla extract

Unsalted butter

Maple syrup

1 cup pumpkin puree

Ginger

Lemon juice

Nutmeg

Baking powder

Cinnamon

DIRECTIONS:

1. Cover the bottom of Slow Cooker with a foil and spray with anti-sticking cooking spray. In a bowl, whisk flour and oats. Add cinnamon, as you usually like.
2. Pour in melted and unsalted butter and maple syrup. Stir well to make a homogenous mass without any dry bits.
3. In a bowl, combine flour along with the other cake ingredients. In a third bowl, mix egg white with vanilla and melted butter.
4. Add maple syrup along with lemon juice. Mix in pumpkin.
5. Place the batter all over the Slow Cooker bottom. Prepare on LOW for 2 hours.

Nutrition: Calories: 385 Fat: 4g Carbohydrates: 33g Protein: 12g

Peach Cobbler in Slow Cooker

Try this with ice cream in summer!

Prep time: 17 minutes Cooking time: 4 hours Servings: 11

INGREDIENTS:

Cinnamon

Three peaches

3 tbsp sugar

Bisquick mix

Half cup milk

Nutmeg

Vanilla extract

DIRECTIONS:

1. Cover the bottom and sides of Slow Cooker with your favorite cooking spray. You can also line the bottom with a parchment.
2. In a bowl of medium size, combine peaches with sugar and ground cinnamon. Place the spiced peaches all over the bottom of your cooking pot.
3. Take a bowl one more time and place the Bisquick mix, cinnamon, brown or white sugar, nutmeg and extract of vanilla in it. Pour in milk and stir to get a smooth mass.
4. Pour and spread the milk mixture all over the peaches in your Slow Cooker. Set your Slow Cooker to LOW temperature setting and leave for 4 hours.
5. Serve with vanilla ice cream and mint leaves.

Nutrition: Calories: 229 Fat: 1g Carbohydrates: 33g Protein: 9g

Cinnamon Roll for Slow Cooker

Easy and fast sweet dessert!

Prep time: 8 minutes Cooking time: 2 hours Servings: 12

INGREDIENTS:

1 tsp cinnamon

Half cup unsalted butter

Granulated sugar

Canned cinnamon rolls

Half cup brown sugar

DIRECTIONS:

1. Open the cans of cinnamon rolls and cut each roll into six slices. Sprinkle sliced rolls with granulated sugar and set aside.
2. In a medium bowl, combine brown sugar with previously melted plain butter.
3. Spray the sides and bottom of your Slow Cooker with cooking spray or simply coat with a thin layer of melted butter.
4. Place cinnamon slices into Cooker and evenly arrange all over the bottom. Pour in with the butter mixture.
5. Cover the lid tightly. Prepare the dessert for 2 hours on HIGH temperature regime.

Nutrition: Calories: 311 Fat: 9g Carbohydrates: 14g Protein: 24g

Pineapple and Coconut Cake

Exotic conclusion for any dinner!

Prep time: 14 minutes Cooking time: 2 hours Servings: 11

INGREDIENTS:

Yellow cake mix

Melted butter

Cup crashed pineapples

3 chicken eggs

Cup water

Coconut

Chopped pecans

DIRECTIONS:

1. Spray your Slow Cooker with special cooking spray or simply grease with olive oil.
2. Slice coconut into small pieces and mix it with melted butter, one cup water and three beaten eggs.
3. Carefully stir in crashed pineapples and chopped pecans. Season with yellow cake mix. Transfer the batter into Slow Cooker and make it spread evenly, use the spatula or large spoon. Cover the lid and do not remove it until the cake is ready. Cook for 2 hours using a HIGH temperature mode.
4. To serve, add some whipped cream on the serving plate.

Nutrition: Calories: 288 Fat: 6g Carbohydrates: 24g Protein: 55g

Chocolate Chip Slow Cooker Cookie

Amazing with chocolate ice cream!

Prep time: 5 minutes Cooking time: 3 hours Servings: 24

INGREDIENTS:

Room temperature butter

Half cup sugar

Baking powder

2 cups flour

Half cup dark chocolate

Raisins

Muscovado sugar

Half cup choco-chips

Vanilla extract

Salt to taste

DIRECTIONS:

1. In a bowl, beat to fluffy chicken eggs, slightly melted butter, vanilla extract and both sugars. In a large bowl, finely combine the flour with salt to your taste and baking powder.

2. Working in small batches, combine the flour with butter mixture.
3. Add the chocolate chips and mix to smooth mass. The chips should be completely distributed in the dough.
4. Grease your Slow Cooker and start preheating it.
5. Pour the dough into Slow Cooker and cook for 3 hours with the lid on. Use a LOW temperature regime.

Nutrition: Calories: 299 Fat: 12g Carbohydrates: 14g Protein: 61g

Pumpkin and Bread Pecan Pudding

Healthy and delicious choice!

Prep time: 5 minutes Cooking time: 4 hours Servings: 8

INGREDIENTS:

2- day-old bread loaf

Ground ginger

Cinnamon

Ground cloves

Half cup toasted pecans

1 cup cream

Canned pumpkin

Half cup sugar

Caramel topping

Ice cream

DIRECTIONS:

1. Cut the yesterday bread into small cubes. Slice enough cubes to fill eight full cups. Grease your Slow Cooker with melted and unsalted butter.
2. Place bread cubes into Slow Cooker and spread evenly. Slightly sprinkle with cinnamon and chopped pecans.
3. In a bowl, whisk chicken eggs with cream and melted butter.
4. Add nutmeg, vanilla, pumpkin, melted butter cloves and ground ginger. Mix and pour the liquid mixture over the bread in Slow Cooker.
5. Cover with the lid and cook for 4 hours on LOW mode.

Nutrition: Calories: 431 Fat: 23g Carbohydrates: 4g Protein: 24g

Carrot Cake with Creamy Topping

Sweet root vegetables for your tea!

Prep time: 5 minutes Cooking time: 3 hours Servings: 18

INGREDIENTS:

Unsweetened applesauce

3 chicken eggs

Baking powder

Soda

2 cups sugar

Shredded coconut

Vanilla extract

2 cups flour

3 grated carrots

1 cup nuts

Canned pineapple

DIRECTIONS:

1. Cover the bottom of your Slow Cooker with foil or parchment paper.

2. In a bowl, beat chicken eggs and whisk them with sugar and applesauce. Add baking soda, flour, salt, baking soda and cinnamon.

3. Mix well and combine with chopped carrots, vanilla extract, chopped nuts, pineapple and coconut. Make sure that all ingredients are combined and smooth. Pour the batter mixture into Slow Cooker.

4. Cook on LOW temperature mode for 3 hours. Check the readiness with a wooden toothpick. If needed, cook for one more hour.

Nutrition: Calories: 412 Fat: 8g Carbohydrates: 33g Protein: 8g

Dump Cake with Chocolate

This is amazing for all chocolate fans!

Prep time: 5 minutes Cooking time: 4 hours Servings: 12

INGREDIENTS:

One cup Nutella

Devils cake mix

Chocolate pudding mix

One stick butter

One cup milk

DIRECTIONS:

1. Cover the bottom of your Slow Cooker with parchment paper or special cooking spray. Arrange dry cake mix all over the bottom of your Slow Cooker.

2. Place the second layer with chocolate pudding mix and pour it over with melted butter. Pour in milk and slightly stir.

3. Finally, top everything with the content of one Nutella can. Press the mixture with a spoon or just your hands so all dry ingredients can be wet.

4. Set your Slow Cooker to LOW temperature mode and leave to cook for 4 hours. You may serve it right from Slow Cooker or transfer into small bowls.

Nutrition: Calories: 155 Fat: 8g Carbohydrates: 1g Protein: 7g

Fudged Brownies in Slow Cooker

Full of chocolate and flavors!

Prep time: 15 minutes Cooking time: 3 hours Servings: 12

INGREDIENTS:

2 chicken eggs

1 box brownie mix

Water

Mini chocolate chips

Packed caramel bits

Hot fudge sauce

3 tbsp applesauce

Heavy cream

3 tbsp chopped pecans

DIRECTIONS:

1. Generously spray your Slow Cooker with cooking spray.

2. In a separate bowl, bring together chocolate chips, brownie mix, water, applesauce (or oil), chicken eggs and hot water. Mix to combine all ingredients well.

3. Carefully transfer your brownie batter in prepared Slow Cooker.

4. Separately, cook the caramel and heavy cream. Combine ingredients into a bowl and place into microwave. Cook for several minutes, stopping each 30 seconds and stirring, until caramel is completely dissolved.

5. Stir in pecans and pour the caramel sauce over the brownie mixture. With a knife, swirl the caramel in.

6. Whisk hot fudge sauce with water until smooth and add to Slow Cooker. Cook on HIGH temperature mode for 3 hours.

Nutrition: Calories: 386 Fat: 32g Carbohydrates: 32g Protein: 19g

Dump Cherry Cake

Sweet and melt-in-your-mouth!

Prep time: 5 minutes Cooking time: 4 hours Servings: 8

INGREDIENTS:

Boxed yellow cake mix

Canned cherry pie filling (you need 2 cans)

Half cup melted butter

DIRECTIONS:

1. In a separated bowl. Combine cake mix with melted butter. Stir until the mix is well distributed with melted butter.

2. Reserve some melted butter and spend it to grease your Slow Cooker. You can also use special spray with anti-stick effect.

3. Open the cans with cherry filling and pour the filling inside the Slow Cooker. Spread evenly. Carefully transfer the butter mixture over the cherries. Arrange it over cherry filling so you do not mix them.

4. Cover the lid of your Slow Cooker. Leave the dish cooking for 4 hours on LOW temperature mode.

Nutrition: Calories: 324 Fat: 21g Carbohydrates: 44g Protein: 36g

Fudgy Brownies with Strawberries

A perfect dessert for a breakfast!

Prep time: 17 minutes Cooking time: 3 hours Servings: 10

INGREDIENTS:

Butter

1 tsp vanilla

1 cup strawberry jam

3 tbsp flour

Whipped dessert topping

Raspberries or strawberries

Salt

Refrigerated egg product

Unsweetened chocolate

DIRECTIONS:

1. Slightly coat the bottom and sides of your Slow Cooker with cooking spray.

2. Take a medium saucepan and slowly melt the butter in it. Add chocolate and continue melting over low heat.

3. When the chocolate is liquid, remove saucepan from heat and beat in eggs. Stirring, add vanilla, jam and sugar.

4. Stir in flour, salt and baking powder.

5. Pour the batter into Slow Cooker and leave under the lid on HIGH mode for 3 hours. To serve, use chocolate topping and fresh berries.

Nutrition: Calories: 198 Fat: 12g Carbohydrates: 5g Protein: 3g

Butterscotch Fondue

The next level of fondue!

Prep time: 5 minutes Cooking time: 5 hours Servings: 12

INGREDIENTS:

Sweetened condensed milk

Melted butter

Vanilla

Apples

Cubed sponge cake

Rum or milk

Whole strawberries

Cubed brownies

Light corn syrup

DIRECTIONS:

1. Grease your Slow Cooker with olive oil or use remaining butter.

2. In a large cooing bowl, combine brown sugar, corn syrup and melted butter. Pour in the milk and stir to the dough mixture.

3. Pour the dough into preheated Slow Cooker and spread evenly over the bottom with a spoon or kitchen spatula.

4. Set Slow Cooker for 3 hours and cook on low heat setting. Time after time, open the lid to stir pie slightly.

5. Add rum and turn Slow Cooker to LOW. Cook for another 2 hours. Serve with brownie slices and fresh slices of your favorite fruits.

Nutrition: Calories: 279 Fat: 17g Carbohydrates: 33g Protein: 38g

Stuffed Apples

You can choose the stuffing by yourself!

Prep time: 17 minutes Cooking time: 5 hours Servings: 4

INGREDIENTS:

4 medium apples

1 tbsp butter

Apple juice

Raisins

4 figs

Half tsp apple spice

Cinnamon

2 tbsp brown sugar

DIRECTIONS:

1. Wash and carefully core the apples: you need to remove the core without slicing fruits. Cut a strip of peel from the top of each fruit.
2. Coat the bottom of your Slow Cooker with a cooking spray or just a little bit of slightly melted butter.
3. In a bowl, whisk apple pie spice, cinnamon and brown sugar. Add figs and raisins. Using a spoon, fill the apples with fig mixture.
4. Pour the apple juice into Slow Cooker. Place a small piece of butter atop each apple. Cook for 5 hours on LOW heat. Cover the lid to get better flavors.
5. Serve, while warm, in small dessert bowls.

Nutrition: Calories: 311 Fat: 9g Carbohydrates: 18g Protein: 7g

Hazelnut Pudding Cake

A sweet dessert that all your guests will love!

Prep time: 16 minutes Cooking time: 3 hours Servings: 11

INGREDIENTS:

Half cup butter

Water

Fudge brownie mix

1 cup water

Chocolate-hazelnut spread

Cocoa powder

Sugar

Hazelnut liqueur (optional)

Half cup hazelnuts

2 chicken eggs

DIRECTIONS:

1. Before you start cooking, coat the bottom and sides of your Slow Cooker with melted butter or cooking spray.
2. In a bowl, make a base dough: mix water, melted butter, eggs and sugar. Add hazelnuts and combine until smooth.
3. Pour the mixture into greased Slow Cooker and spread the batter evenly over the bottom.
4. Using a spoon, drop chocolate-hazelnut spread over the batter and make a little swirl with a knife. In a bowl, mix

liquor with water and add to Slow Cooker. Mix in cocoa powder with sugar/ Pour into Slow Cooker.

5. Cook covered for 2 hours. Use HIGH temperature mode.

Nutrition: Calories: 299 Fat: 10g Carbohydrates: 7g Protein: 20g

Cherry-Chocolate Cluster Bits with Salted Almonds

Small and tasty, this is very simple to cook!

Prep time: 23 minutes Cooking time: 32

Servings: 2 hours

INGREDIENTS:

Sweet baking chocolate

Sea salt

Three cups almonds

Semisweet chocolate pieces

Half pack vanilla coating

Dried sweet cherries

DIRECTIONS:

1. Slightly coat your Slow Cooker with melted unsalted butter.
2. Finely chop the almonds and sprinkle them around the bottom of your Slow Cooker. Top the almonds with baking chocolate and semisweet chocolate pieces.
3. Add dry cherries and, finally, top with candy coating.
4. Place with the lid. Turn your Slow Cooker to LOW temperature setting and cook for around 2 hours (wait until the chocolate is melted).
5. To serve, spoon the chocolate mixture into small paper bowls. Sprinkle with sea salt. Serve.

Nutrition: Calories: 335 Fat: 6g Carbohydrates: 15g Protein: 28g

Nutty Pumpkin-Pie Pudding

The perfect one for the autumn season!

Prep time: 5 minutes Cooking time: 2 hour Servings: 6

INGREDIENTS:

Canned pumpkin

Evaporated milk

Cup sugar

Pumpkin pie spice

Yellow cake mix

Cup walnuts

Butter, melted

Dessert topping

DIRECTIONS:

1. Lightly cover the inside of your Slow Cooker with cooking spray or simply line with parchment paper.

2. Right in greased Slow Cooker, stir evaporated milk, pumpkin, sugar, and pumpkin pie spice. Spread the batter evenly in the cooking dish of Slow Cooker.

3. Separately, combine cake mix, pumpkin spice, preferred nuts, Sprinkle over pumpkin in Slow Cooker. Carefully sprinkle with melted butter.

4. Cover the lid. Cook on HIGH setting. Turn Slow Cooker off in around 2 hours. Remove the lid. Let cool for 30 minutes.

5. Serve in dessert dishes with your favorite dessert topping.

Nutrition: Calories: 324 Fat: 7g Carbohydrates: 32g Protein: 45g

Crispy and Sweet Holiday Treats

Small sweets for your weekend or party!

Prep time: 30 minutes Cooking time: 3 hours Servings: 36

INGREDIENTS:

Tiny marshmallows

Pistachios

Cup dried cranberries

Butter

Crisp rice cereal

DIRECTIONS:

1. Cover the inside of your Slow Cooker with melted butter.

2. In a large bowl, combine butter and several cups of tiny marshmallows. Set your Slow Cooker on LOW heat regime.

3. Cover the lid and cook for next 2 hours. Open lid every 30 minutes to check the dish and stir it. Add dried cranberries, cereal, and pistachios. Stir to coat evenly.

4. Turn off and let stand to cool.

5. Form 36 small balls out of Slow Cooker mixture. Arrange bowls over a large plate and leave them until thick and non-sticky.

6. Serve along with hot tea or other drinks.

Nutrition: Calories: 328 Fat: 9g Carbohydrates: 5g Protein: 20g

Caramel-Pear Pudding Cake

You should definitely try this!

Prep time: 32 minutes Cooking time: 3 hours Servings: 19

INGREDIENTS:

Greek yogurt

Flour

Flax seed

Sugar

Butter

Canola oil

Fat-free milk

Dried apples

Hot water

Baking powder

Pure pear nectar

Brown sugar

DIRECTIONS:

1. Coat your Slow Cooker with a cooking spray.

2. In a medium bowl, combine flour, flax seed meal, baking powder, grounded cinnamon, granulated sugar.

3. Stir in milk and add some olive oil. Stir until the mixture is evenly smooth. Add dried pears. Mix for again.

4. Pour the batter into Slow Cooker. Using a large spoon, arrange evenly over the bottom.

5. In a saucepan, whisk the water, brown sugar, pear nectar. Stir in the butter. Simmer until the sugar dissolves. Pour into Slow Cooker.

6. Cook on LOW setting for 3 hours.

Nutrition: Calories: 132 Fat: 4g Carbohydrates: 51g Protein: 33g

Double-Berry Cobbler

Fresh berries and delicious topping!

Prep time: 29 minutes Cooking time: 3 hours Servings: 7

INGREDIENTS:

Fresh blueberries

Fresh blackberries

Sugar

Water

Tapioca

Cup flour

Cornmeal

Sugar

Baking powder

Salt

1 chicken egg

Cup milk

Butter, melted

Lemon zest

Vanilla ice cream

DIRECTIONS:

1. Grease your Slow Cooker with a small amount of melted butter.

2. Right in your Slow Cooker, combine one egg, tapioca, sugar, milk, water, half cup flour and baking powder.

3. Combine all the ingredients well and cover the lid of your Slow Cooker. Cook on HIGH temperature mode for 1 hour.

4. Meanwhile, make a topping out of fresh berries, lemon zest, melted butter. When the cobbler is ready, serve it with berry topping.

Nutrition: Calories: 354 Fat: 12g Carbohydrates: 24g Protein: 23g

Dark Chocolate Fondue with Fruit Kabobs

Unusual recipe with sweet ingredients!

Prep time: 23 minutes Cooking time: 1 hour Servings: 16

INGREDIENTS:

Whipped dessert topping

Dark chocolate pieces

Hot strong coffee

Strawberry halves

Pineapple

Apple

Kiwifruit chunks

Raspberries

DIRECTIONS:

1. Grease your Slow Cooker with butter or cooking spray.

2. In a bowl, combine fresh whipped topping with chocolate pieces. Stir the mixture until smooth, the transfer to Slow Cooker.]

3. Cover the lid. Set you Slow Cooker to LOW temperature mode and cook for 45 minutes (just until the chocolate melts).

4. Whisk in coffee - use the spoon and continue adding coffee until pourable.

5. Make fruit kabobs - dice fruits and place it on large and long toothpicks along with berries. Serve warm with fruit kabobs.

Nutrition: Calories: 198 Fat: 2g Carbohydrates: 5g Protein: 7g

Raspberry Fudge Brownies

So delicious with fresh berries and gooey chocolate!

Prep time: 32 minutes Cooking time: 2 hours Servings: 18

INGREDIENTS:

Half cup margarine

Unsweetened chocolate

Two chicken eggs

3 tbsp sugar

Red raspberry jam

Vanilla

Flour

Baking powder

Vanilla ice cream (optional)

DIRECTIONS:

1. Generously grease two cooking jars and sprinkle them with the flour. In a large saucepan, melt margarine with chocolate (set low heat).

2. When ready, remove from heat and stir in jam, eggs, vanilla and sugar. Slightly beat and combine with flour mixture.

3. Pour the mixture into jars, and place the jars into Slow Cooker. Cook on HIGH temperature mode for 2 hours.

4. Serve with fresh berries or vanilla jam. You can add your favorite topping – chocolate or fruit.

Nutrition: Calories: 263 Fat: 23g Carbohydrates: 32g Protein: 53g

Walnut Apple Crisp

Amazing and fast one for busy days!

Prep time: 11 minutes Cooking time: 4 hours Servings: 8

INGREDIENTS:

Granulated sugar

2 tsps lemon juice

Teaspoons cornstarch

Ground ginger

Ground cinnamon

6 tart apples

Half cup flour

Light brown sugar

Ground nutmeg

Salt

Unsalted butter

Chopped walnuts

Vanilla ice cream (optional)

DIRECTIONS:

1. Coat the inside surface of your Slow Cooker with cooking spray.
2. In a large bowl mix three tablespoons of granulated sugar, add lemon juice, cornstarch and cinnamon.
3. Carefully stir in the spice mixture chopped apples. Transfer apple butter to your Slow Cooker.
4. Meanwhile, make the topping. In a small bowl whisk flour with granulated sugar, light brown sugar, and mixed cinnamon, salt and nutmeg. Stir in walnuts.
5. Add the topping over the main butter in Slow Cooker.
6. Cover the lid tightly. Leave the meal preparing for 4 hours. Use LOW heat mode. Serve with preferred ice cream.

Nutrition: Calories: 128 Fat: 3g Carbohydrates: 8g Protein: 2g

Peppermint Pretzel Candies

Unusual recipe with white chocolate and nuts!

Prep time: 25 minutes Cooking time: 2 hours Servings: 24

INGREDIENTS:

Vanilla-flavor candy coating

White baking chocolate

Butter-flavor shortening

Peppermint extract

1 pack pretzel twists

Round peppermint candies

Dark chocolate

DIRECTIONS:

1. Grease your Slow Cooker with olive oil or butter. You can also use the cooking spray if you want. Right in Slow Cooker, gather white chocolate, candy coating, shortening. Carefully stir until smooth.
2. Cover your Slow Cooker with a lid. Cook on LOW temperature setting for 1 hour. When the mixture is melted and became smooth, start to stir every 30 minutes.
3. Add peppermint extract, pretzels. Stir in peppermint candies.
4. When ready, transfer the mixture to two baking sheets and drizzle with melted dark chocolate. Cook for 5 or 7 minutes.

5. To serve, sprinkle with peppermint candies.

Nutrition: Calories: 311 Fat: 8g Carbohydrates: 17g Protein: 20g

Pumpkin Spiced and Pomegranate Cheesecake

The perfect duo of two different kinds of fruits!

Prep time: 23 minutes Cooking time: 3 hours Servings: 11

INGREDIENTS:

Cream cheese

Granulated sugar

All-purpose flour

Pumpkin pie spice

Vanilla

Canned pumpkin

Frozen egg product

Shredded orange peel

Warm water

Pomegranate juice

Sugar

Cornstarch

Pomegranate seeds

DIRECTIONS:

1. Lightly coat your Slow Cooker with a cooking spray or melted butter. In a large bowl beat cream cheese (use an electric mixer).
2. Add sugar, sifted flour, pumpkin pie spice and vanilla. Beat until combined. Add pumpkin and egg product until smooth.
3. Sprinkle with orange peel.
4. Pour the dough into Slow Cooker.
5. Cover with the lid. Prepare on HIGH mode for 2 hours.

Nutrition: Calories: 342 Fat: 23g Carbohydrates: 47g Protein: 33g

Coconut-Mocha Poached Pears

Tropical taste from your Slow Cooker!

Prep time: 23 minutes Cooking time: 4 hours Servings: 8

INGREDIENTS:

6 ripe pears

Sugar

Cocoa powder

Light coconut milk

Strong coffee

2 tbsp coffee liqueur

Whipped dessert topping

Toasted coconut

Grated chocolate

DIRECTIONS:

1. Wash and eel pears. Quarter the pears lengthwise, carefully remove the cores. Put pears into greased with melted butter Slow Cooker.

2. In a bowl, combine sugar with cocoa powder. Add coconut milk, coffee, liqueur.

3. Pour the coffee mixture over the pears in your Slow Cooker. Cover under cover during 4 hours. Use LOW temperature setting

4. With a slotted spoon, place the pears in dessert dishes. Add cooking liquid. To serve, use dessert topping, coconut or chocolate.

Nutrition: Calories: 523 Fat: 34g Carbohydrates: 35g Protein: 32g

Ginger-Orange Cheesecake

You can forget about baking with this one!

Prep time: 24 minutes Cooking time: 3 hours Servings: 11

INGREDIENTS:

Cream cheese

Half cup sugar

1 tsp orange peel

Orange juice

1tbsp flour

Vanilla

Half cup sour cream

Frozen egg product

Water

2 blood oranges

DIRECTIONS:

1. Cover your Slow Cooker dish with thin layer of melted butter. In a bowl, mix sugar, cream cheese and vanilla.

2. Pour in orange juice and beat everything with a kitchen mixer. Add sour cream and beat again until it is all smooth.

3. Add orange peel and pour the batter with some water into greased Slow Cooker. Cook on HIGH temperature mode for around 3 hours.

4. To serve, garnish pie with sliced orange or crystallized ginger.

Nutrition: Calories: 243 Fat: 23g Carbohydrates: 21g Protein: 45g

Candy Bar Fondue

The easy and delicious dessert you will not forget!

Prep time: 12 minutes Cooking time: 3 hours Servings: 12

INGREDIENTS:

4 bar nougat with almonds

Milk chocolate

Jar marshmallow crème

Whipping cream

Finely chopped almonds

Raspberry liqueur (optional)

Assorted dippers

DIRECTIONS:

1. In a large bowl, combine chopped nougat bars, milk chocolate bars and cream. Grease your Slow Cooker. You can use plain melted butter or olive oil.

2. Mix well and transfer nougat mixture into Slow Cooker. Cover the lid tightly.

3. Set your Slow Cooker to LOW temperature mode and prepare for 2 hours. When ready, add almonds and your favorite liquor (if desired).

4. Once it is ready, serve with fruit dippers or cookies.

Nutrition: Calories: 182 Fat: 2g Carbohydrates: 1g Protein: 12g

Dutch Apple Sweet Pudding Cake

Homespun and healthy recipe!

Prep time: 23 minutes Cooking time: 3 hours Servings: 6

INGREDIENTS:

Apple pie filling

Dried cherries

Flour

Sugar

Baking powder

Salt

Half milk

Butter

Chopped walnuts

Apple juice

Brown sugar

Melted butter

Whipped cream

Walnuts

DIRECTIONS:

1. Slightly grease your Slow Cooker with cooking spray or melted butter.
2. In a small saucepan, bring apple pie filling to boil. Stir in cherries and simmer for several minutes. Transfer the cherry-apple mixture greased Slow Cooker.
3. In a medium bowl, mix flour with baking powder and granulated sugar. Add a pinch of salt. Pour in milk and add melted butter. Stir well just to combine the ingredients.
4. Transfer the mixture to your Slow Cooker and spread evenly over the bottom. Cook for 2 hours. Use a HIGH temp setting.

Nutrition: Calories: 242 Fat: 21g Carbohydrates: 65g Protein: 72g

Chocolate Fondue

Just three ingredients for the delicious recipe!

Prep time: 11 minutes Cooking time: 2 hours Servings: 16

INGREDIENTS:

Milk chocolate bar

Large marshmallows

Half-and-half

Assorted dippers

DIRECTIONS:

1. Grease your Slow Cooker with unsalted and melted butter.
2. In a large bowl, gather chocolate, half-and-half and large marshmallows. Stir well. Cover your Slow Cooker with a lid.
3. Set LOW temperature setting and cook for two hours. Once during the cooking process, open the lid and stir the ingredients.
4. Serve just after it is ready.

Nutrition: Calories: 352 Fat: 32g Carbohydrates: 24g Protein: 61g

Crustless Lemony Cheesecake

Try this one with your friends!

Prep time: 21 minutes Cooking time: 3 hours Servings: 8

INGREDIENTS:

Cream cheese

Sugar

Lemon juice

Flour

Vanilla

Sour cream

3 chicken eggs

Shredded lemon peel

Warm water

Fresh raspberries

Mint

DIRECTIONS:

1. Cover the bottom of your Slow Cooker with a layer of melted butter or just a spray.
2. In a bowl, whisk cream cheese, lemon juice, plain sugar, vanilla and flour. Beat with a kitchen mixer.
3. Add eggs and stir in lemon peel. Beat until smooth.
4. Transfer the mixture into prepared Slow Cooker. Cover with the lid.
5. Start cooking on HIGH temperature. Turn your Slow Cooker off in 2 hours. To serve, you can garnish the dish with mint leaves or fresh raspberries.

Nutrition: Calories: 352 Fat: 32g Carbohydrates: 62g Protein: 26g

Gingerbread Pudding Cake

An awesome taste for the cold autumn season!

Prep time: 14 minutes Cooking time: 2 hours Servings: 8

INGREDIENTS:

Pack gingerbread mix

Milk

Cup raisins

Water

Brown sugar

Butter

Ice cream (optional)

DIRECTIONS:

1. Grease your Slow Cooker with a cooking spray. If you do not have one, simply use melted butter. In a bowl, combine milk and gingerbread mix. Stir until it is evenly wet.
2. Add raisins and mix again until the batter is thick.
3. Transfer the mixture into Slow Cooker and spread evenly all over its' bottom.
4. In a saucepan, mix brown sugar, butter, water. Stir until sugar dissolves. Pour into Slow Cooker. Cook under the lid for 2 hours. Apply HIGH temperature mode.

5. Serve in small dessert bowls with your favorite ice cream.

Nutrition: Calories: 132 Fat: 32g Carbohydrates: 44g Protein: 21g

Chocolate Bread Pudding with Mocha

Amazing for those who are fans of chocolate!

Prep time: 21 minutes Cooking time: 3 hours Servings: 8

INGREDIENTS:

Fat-free milk

Semisweet chocolate pieces

Cocoa powder

Frozen egg substitute

Chia seeds

Bread cubes

Mocha sauce

DIRECTIONS:

1. Grease your Slow Cooker - use melted butter or cooking spray. Heat the milk in a saucepan until warm, but not boiling.
2. Add cocoa powder and chocolate pieces. Don't stir! Let stand for several minutes, then slightly whisk.
3. In a bowl, combine chia seeds, egg substitute. Pour in the chocolate mixture. Add bread cubes. Transfer the mixture to Slow Cooker and cover the lid.
4. Choose a LOW temperature mode and cook for 2 hours. Serve with Mocha sauce.

Nutrition: Calories: 264 Fat: 13g Carbohydrates: 41g Protein: 21g

Orange-Caramel Pudding Cake

Sweet and a little spicy dessert for your family!

Prep time: 23 minutes Cooking time: 5 hours Servings: 6

INGREDIENTS:

1cup flour

Granulated sugar

Baking powder

Ground cinnamon

Salt

Half cup milk

2tbsp butter

Half cup pecans

Raisins

Cup water

Finely shredded orange peel

Orange juice

Brown sugar

Tablespoon butter

Caramel ice cream topping

Pecans

Whipped cream

DIRECTIONS:

1. Lightly grease the inside of your Slow Cooker with melted butter or cooking spray. Set crockpot aside.
2. In a bowl, combine and whisk flour, baking powder, sugar, cinnamon. Add a little salt Add milk and some melte butter. Slightly mix just until combined.
3. Add pecans and fresh currants.
4. Spread the mixture in the prepared cooker and spread it evenly.
5. In a preheated saucepan, mix the water with orange peel, juice, dark brown sugar, and melted butter. Bring to boil.
6. Carefully pour the saucepan mixture in cooker. Cover the lid. Prepare with LOW mode on for 5 hours.
7. Let stand, without the lid, for 45 minutes.

Nutrition: Calories: 186 Fat: 1g Carbohydrates: 8g Protein: 5g

Fruit Compote with Spicy Ginger

Use as many fruits as you like!

Prep time: 16 minutes Cooking time: 8 hours Servings: 11

INGREDIENTS:

3 medium pears

Can pineapple chunks

Dried apricots, quartered

Frozen orange juice

Brown sugar

Tapioca

Grated fresh ginger

Frozen unsweetened cherries

Flaked coconut

Macadamia nuts

DIRECTIONS:

1. In a large bowl, combine undrained pineapple, pear and dried apricots. Add brown sugar, ginger and tapioca.

2. Pour in the orange juice. Stir everything well to dissolve sugar.

3. Grease your Slow Cooker with melted butter or olive oil. If can, use special cooking spray. Transfer the mixture to Slow Cooker and cover tightly with the lid.

4. Prepare during 8 hours on LOW mode.

5. Cool a little to serve. Serve warm in a little dessert dishes.

Nutrition: Calories: 218 Fat: 9g Carbohydrates: 2g Protein: 10g

Old-Fashioned Rice Pudding

This is awesome and easy to prepare!

Prep time: 16 minutes Cooking time: 3 hours Servings: 11

INGREDIENTS:

4 cups rice

Evaporated milk

Cup milk

Cup sugar

Cold water

Raisins

Dried cherries

Softened butter

Tablespoon vanilla

Teaspoon ground cinnamon

DIRECTIONS:

1. Cover the bottom and sides of your Slow Cooker with melted butter or cooking spray with anti-stick effect.

2. Take a large bowl and gather cooked rice and sugar. Combine until mixed well. Add butter, raisins, cinnamon and vanilla. Transfer to Slow Cooker.

3. Pour over with plain milk, water and evaporated milk. Mix until sugar dissolved. Cover the lid of your Slow Cooker. Prepare during 3 hours on LOW setting.

4. To serve, stir for one more time.

Nutrition: Calories: 342 Fat: 14g Carbohydrates: 21g Protein: 34g

White Chocolate with Apricot Bread Pudding

Delicious and simple summertime dessert!

Prep time: 32 minutes Cooking time: 4 hours Servings: 8

INGREDIENTS:

1 cup half-and-half

White chocolate squares Snipped dried apricots

2 chicken eggs

Cup sugar

Ground cardamom

Dried bread cubes

Sliced almonds

Cup warm water

Fresh raspberries

DIRECTIONS:

1. In a small saucepan preheat half-and-half using a medium heat. When it is warm enough, but not boiling yet, set aside.

2. Add finely chopped white baking squares along with apricots. Blend until chocolate squares are completely melted.

3. In another bowl, beat chicken eggs with a fork. Add and whisk cardamon and sugar. Blend egg mixture with a hot chocolate mixture. Stir in almonds.

4. Transfer the mixture into Slow Cooker. Leave to prepare hours on LOW temperature setting. Serve warm in small dessert dishes. Garnish with chocolate or fresh berries.

Nutrition: Calories: 422 Fat: 24g Carbohydrates: 23g Protein: 56g

Strawberry Mojito Shortcakes

Sweet and easy receipt for summer!

Prep time: 34 minutes Cooking time: 2 hours Servings: 6

INGREDIENTS:

Sugar

1 cup flour

Butter

Baking powder

2 tbsp rum

1 chicken egg

Half cup whipping cream

Lime zest

Fresh mint

2 cup strawberries

1 cup sour milk

DIRECTIONS:

1. In a wide bowl, combine baking soda, flour, butter, and sour milk. In addition, blend everything with a blender.

2. In a separate bowl, beat one egg and whisk it with buttermilk. Combine two mixtures and stir, until the smooth consistency.

3. Prepare small cake cooking jars and cover each jar with a small piece of foil. Place into Slow Cooker and leave for 2 covers under HIGH heat mode.

4. Make a topping out of crushed strawberries, zest, mint, sugar and rum.

5. Cool the topping for several hours. To serve, top cakes with strawberry mixture and garnish with whole strawberries and mint leaves.

Nutrition: Calories: 159 Fat: 3g Carbohydrates: 10g Protein: 22g

Peach Graham Cracker Summer Cake

This will make your life so much simpler!

Prep time: 23 minutes Cooking time: 3 hours Servings: 8

INGREDIENTS:

Butter

White sugar

3 peaches

Baking soda

Cup milk

Ginger

Salt

Graham cracker

Grated nutmeg

2 cups flour

Vanilla ice cream

DIRECTIONS:

1. Grease your Slow Cooker with olive oil or just spread cooking over its bottom and sides. Slice the peaches and add them to Slow Cooker.

2. In a saucepan, sugar, softened butter and one cup sugar. Cook on high heat until the sugar is dissolved.

3. Pour the peaches into sugar mixture from the saucepan.

4. In a bowl, combine graham crackers (previously crashed) and milk.

5. Add chicken eggs, ginger, nutmeg, baking soda, sifted flour. Mix the ingredients and add to Slow Cooker.

6. Cook on HIGH mode for approximately 2 hours. Serve with white vanilla ice cream or fruit topping.

Nutrition: Calories: 371 Fat: 22g Carbohydrates: 31g Protein: 32g

Slow Cooker Berry Crisp

Fast and delicious dessert for summertime!

Prep time: 5 minutes Cooking time: 3 hours Servings: 8

INGREDIENTS:

2 cups blueberries

1 cup blackberries

Old fashioned oats

Flour

1 cup raspberries

Brown sugar

2 cups strawberries

Cinnamon

1/2 cup butter

DIRECTIONS:

1. Before you start cooking, chop the berries into halves and set aside for a little while.

2. Finely grease your Slow Cooker with melted butter. If you prefer, use for greasing special anti-stick spray.

3. In a bowl, combine brown sugar, oats and flour. Add room temperature butter and stir until crumbly.

4. Place the berries into prepared Slow Cooker. Sprinkle fruits with sugar and oats mixture.

5. Put the lid on and start cooking on HIGH temperature mode for 2 hours.

Nutrition: Calories: 211 Fat: 1g Carbohydrates: 2g Protein: 7g

Ginger Chicken in Lettuce Cups

The spicy chicken will light your day!

Prep time: 16 minutes Cooking time: 7 hours Servings: 4

INGREDIENTS:

2clove garlic

3tbsp. brown sugar

1 tbsp. soy sauce

Half teaspoon red pepper (crushed)

1 tbsp. fresh ginger (grated)

2-4chicken thighs (boneless)

¾ cup white rice (long grain)

2 scallions

1 large orange

1 small Boston lettuce)

Balsamic vinegar

DIRECTIONS:

1. Butter your Slow Cooker and mix in it the sugar, soy sauce, balsamic vinegar, garlic, ginger and red pepper.

2. Add chicken and toss to coat with balsamic mixture.

3. Cook under the lid for 6-7 hours on LOW temperature mode or for 3-4 hour on HIGH. When it is about thirty minutes left before serving, cook the rice according to the package instruction.

4. Meanwhile, cut and peel the orange, remove the peel and white parts. Fold in the scallions. When the chicken is ready, shared it with two forks and mix with the cooking liquid.

5. To serve, fill the lettuce with the rice, chicken and orange slices.

Nutrition: Calories: 746 Fat: 55g Carbohydrates: 76g Protein: 88g

Printed in Great Britain
by Amazon